A LIFETIME WITH LOCOMOTIVES

A LIFETIME WITH LOCOMOTIVES

Roland C. Bond

C.Eng., F.I.C.E., F.I.Mech.E.

GOOSE & SON
PUBLISHERS

Goose and Son Publishers Limited
Salisbury House, Station Road,
Cambridge, CB1 2LA, England

Trade Distribution:
Goose and Son Publishers Limited
Warner House, Folkestone, Kent

First Published 1975

ISBN 0 900404 30 2

Text set in 12 pt. Photon Imprint, printed by photolithography,
and bound in Great Britain at The Pitman Press, Bath

Contents

For my son and daughter,
in memory of their mother, Jean,
and of Frances.

Foreword

by E. S. Cox, C.Eng.F.I.Mech.E.

THE RAILWAY LOCOMOTIVE HAS, since its first appearance in the earliest years of the nineteenth century, cast a spell of interest and indeed of fascination, equally upon those who worked with it, and those who only travelled behind it. It is still with us, although greatly diminished in numbers and variety, and the band of faithful devotees is much reduced by those who have turned aside to worship those other gods of movement, the automobile, the aeroplane and the space rocket. On the other hand, railways were the sinews of the industrial revolution and today still have an important part to play in our overcrowded environment. As a form of mechanical engineering, the development of the locomotive through 170 years is a matter of considerable historic interest, much enhanced if it is possible at the same time to learn something of the organisational, human and even personal problems which accompanied its progress.

Roland Bond, the author of the present book is one who has lived for, and worked with, locomotives through the period of their greatest development. From the time of the relatively unsophisticated machines of the individual railway companies of pre-1923, he occupied positions of increasing responsibility as steam traction was brought to its final flowering just before and just after the last war, and he can indeed be named as one of the very last of the Chief Mechanical Engineers who practised in steam. He worked upon the first stages of electric traction in India as early as 1929 and was one of the those who, in association with H. G. Ivatt saw the first main line diesel locomotive in this country onto the rails in 1947. It fell to his lot to be in the very centre of the total changeover in the forms of traction on British Railways, from the first large scale orders for further main line diesels in 1954, to the final disappearance of steam in 1968.

It is clear that such a man must have an interesting story to tell, but all too few of similar background have been either willing or able to put pen to paper and share their thoughts and experiences, their successes and their failures, with a wider public. The thanks of posterity are due to those who have so dared. In the story which this book unfolds, the reader will not only be given a ring side seat to watch engineering development through the years, but will also learn something of the problems of the technical organisation which accompanied the passing of some twenty-one principal individual railways into the four grouped companies of the inter-war years, and of the much greater problems which followed their expansion into a single monolithic state concern, which in turn has shrunk into an entity having today less locomotives to maintain than did more than one of the old grouped companies.

Recent publications have provided considerable insight into the design and motive power sides of the locomotive world. While not ignoring these aspects in which he took an intense interest, Bond has, by the nature of the positions which he held, concentrated mainly on the rather less well known maintenance and workshop sides, which, if less immediately spectacular, are of just as great an interest in rounding off the whole corpus of locomotive work.

It is fortunate that the author, besides presenting the technical side in an eminently readable form, has felt able to dwell upon a wealth of personal experiences with which to illuminate his story, to comment in a forthright but kindly manner upon some of the many 'characters' of both high and low degree with whom he has come in contact and even to dare to question some of the decisions of 'High Authority' under which he was made to suffer.

It was one evening in 1926, in the old Drawing Office under the clock tower at the entrance to Derby Locomotive Works that Roland and I met for the first time. He was completing a drawing as part of his thesis for entry to the Institution of Civil Engineers, and I as an ordinary draughtsman was working on overtime to finish the drawings for the forthcoming Fowler 2-6-4 Tank Engines. From that day onwards, as we both climbed the ladder of promotion, we have been closely associated in the vast kaleidoscope which comprises locomotive engineering, and I have found his account of the years so well known to both of us to be fascinating indeed. I hope that readers of this book will be able to pass the same judgment.

E. S. Cox
Sidmouth, Devon.

Preface

ALTHOUGH DURING MY LIFETIME with locomotives I had written technical papers for presentation to the Institutions of which I am a member, countless reports and memoranda, and two Presidential Addresses, it had never entered my head to write a book on any technical subject, still less an autobiography. For one thing, there would not have been time available while still in active service. For another, I would have felt it presumptuous to suppose that anyone outside my immediate family, and perhaps a very few close friends, would be remotely interested in anything I might write about my career as a railway Mechanical Engineer. However, a talk with John Moore, my publisher, following an introduction by a mutual friend at a meeting of the Newcomen Society, set me thinking.

Surely, Moore said, I must have a great deal of material from which to distill an interesting story of events, with which I had been personally concerned during a period of development and change in locomotive engineering without precedent in railway history – a period in which steam locomotives reached their peak of performance and efficiency, thereafter giving place to diesel and electric traction. Certainly I had no lack of material. From my earliest days at Derby I have been a compulsive collector of copies of reports and papers on all manner of technical and managerial matters with which the Chief Mechanical Engineers Department of a railway is concerned. I have copies of most of my own reports and memoranda.

After further thought, and encouraged by my wife, I decided that John Moore had given me a challenge which had to be accepted. This book is the result. Lest there should be any doubt on the matter, let me say at once that this book is not a comprehensive history of the engineering works and railway departments in which I spent my working life. It is no more than a strictly personal account and commentary on a continuing pattern of everyday affairs, on events which stand out vividly in my memory, and on people, some in positions of power and authority – some not – but all of whom, in one way and another, influenced or decided the course of events which I recall.

What I have written about my daily life and contemporary locomotive engineering history, which necessarily forms a background to my story, will I hope convey some impression of the intense interest and variety of a career in locomotive engineering extending over a span of forty-eight years, all but three of which were spent in the service of British Railways and two – no – three! – of the great railway companies before the days of nationalisation.

I have not sought to espouse any particular cause, except in a general way that of railway engineers being given direct and unequivocal authority over the men and machines for whose activities they are held responsible. I have attempted to draw some conclusions, and express opinions, which are entirely my own, on some matters which I regard as important to the future well-being of British Railways. If this book revives for others, as the writing of it has for me, many agreeable memories of a full and rewarding life in the service of our railways, I shall be well content. It may provide my son and daughter with a ready-made answer to the question 'What did Grandpa do?'

My thanks are due to the British Railways Board, and to the Institution of Mechanical Engineers for permitting me to use, and quote extracts from, official papers to supplement my own records and memoranda. I am most grateful to my old chief and friend R. A. Riddles, to Eric Merrill, Controller of Public Relations and Publicity, British Railways Board, and to Kenneth Platt, Secretary of the Institution of Mechanical Engineers for comments and wise advice; and to the last named for allowing his secretary Sybil Mealing to provide me with copies of my manuscript pages. I owe a particular debt of gratitude to Stewart Cox for his early encouragement of this venture, for patiently reading through the script, and for comments, corrections as to facts, and many most valuable and salutary suggestions. To all those who have provided photographs from which the illustrations have been prepared I am most grateful.

Finally, my special thanks to Margaret Gunn, my secretary for ten years up to my retirement, for typing at home in her own time, the manuscript which I delivered to her in instalments over a much longer period than I originally intended.

Roland Bond
Pinkney's Green,
Maidenhead, 1975.

List of Illustrations

19. Midland design at its best – heavy freight locomotive built for the Somerset & Dorset Joint Railway by Robert Stephenson & Co. at Darlington at the time of the Railway Centenary.

20. The most important inspection job. One of the *Royal Scots* as originally built. David Gibson, a celebrated Caledonian driver, with whom the author rode many hundred miles, is on the footplate.

21. The *Royal Scots* in their final form – as rebuilt by Sir William Stanier.

22. A Midland compound as developed for service throughout the L.M.S.

23. Midland *Class 3* 4-4-0 No. 777 on which the author carried out coal and water consumption tests.

24. Electric freight locomotive for the Great Indian Peninsula Railway – ready for shipment from the Vulcan Foundry.

25. Saturday afternoon relaxation in Bombay.

26. Operation over the Ghats between Bombay and Poona after the inauguration of electric service.

27. Our first home – 'Spring Cottage', Rivington. An oasis in the heart of industrial Lancashire.

28. Jean.

29. On leave – relaxing in the heather at Kyle of Lochalsh.

30. The second of Stanier's *Pacifics, Princess Elizabeth* – the locomotive which earned the author a rebuke – and a commendation – from Robert Riddles.

31. *Princess Elizabeth* on the record breaking non-stop run from Euston to Glasgow, 16th November, 1936.

32. One of the 'might have beens' – a Southern Region *Merchant Navy* brought to a stand without mishap after a broken driving axle.

33. Sir William Stanier's Turbine Locomotive – built at Crewe in 1935.

34. The Turbine Locomotive – rebuilt as a normal four-cylinder locomotive, No. 46202, *Princess Anne*.

35. Sir William Stanier's masterpiece. The first of five streamlined *Pacifics* for working the *Coronation Scot* trains.

36. Sir William A. Stanier, F.R.S.

37. The silver stripes on which much time was spent. The first three *Pacifics* outside the Paint Shop at Crewe.

38. General arrangement of the Locomotive Testing Plant at Rugby.

39. The Locomotive Testing Station – when work was suspended at the outbreak of war in September 1939.

40. The Locomotive Testing Plant completed and in use.

41. The dire result of shortage of water – the bulged fire box crown torn off the roof stays of L.M.S. 4-6-2 No. 6224.

42. Spitfire fuselages under repair at Barassie.

43. A *Covenanter* tank – of which 161 were built at Crewe.

44. *Matilda* tanks, the hull plates of which were machined at Crewe, being assembled at Horwich.

70. 25,000 volt flashover to a locomotive chimney.

71. English-Electric Gas Turbine locomotive *GT3* under construction at the Vulcan Foundry. The designer, J.O.P. Hughes and the author on the locomotive.

72. *GT3* on special test train passing Shap Summit.

73. Refuelling Denver and Rio Grande triple unit diesel hauling the *California Zephyr* en route to Oakland, California.

74. Going East on the Santa Fe *Super-Chief* from Los Angeles to Chicago.

75,} En route from Melbourne to Sydney. Steam and Diesel Motive
76.} Power, New South Wales Government Railways.

77. The Duke of Edinburgh, watched by Sir Brian Robertson, unveils the nameplate of *Warship* class diesel hydraulic locomotive *Magpie*.

78. Frances.

79. An off-duty social occasion – Frances and the author.

80. The President casts an anxious glance at his notes. The Annual Dinner of the Institution of Mechanical Engineers 1963.

81. The Royal visit to Wolverton Carriage Works.

82. Carriage and Wagon work at Crewe.

83. L.N.E.R. *A4 Pacific, Bittern* No. 60019 on which the author had his last trip on a steam locomotive in revenue earning service.

84. Large or small – the absorbing interest persists!

Acknowledgements for Illustrations

The author would like to thank the following for permission to reproduce illustrations.

Eric Ager, Northampton 79
Allwork, Tonbridge 10
G. A. Barlow 84
R. H. Bond 3
British Railways Board 2, 6, 7, 11, 12, 14, 16, 17, 19, 21, 30, 33, 34, 35, 36, 37, 38, 42, 43, 44, 45, 46, 49, 51, 52, 54, 58, 62, 63, 64, 65, 67, 68, 70, 77, 82
Ronald A. Chapman F.I.I.P., F.R.P.S., Enfield 81
E. S. Cox 55, 57, 69
Derek Cross 59, 60, 61, 72
Fox Photos Ltd 31
J. Hardman, Kendal 47
R. H. N. Hardie 5
Thomas Jaski Ltd 80
Leicester Evening Mail 48
Locomotive and General Railway Photographs 4, 8, 9
R. C. S. Low 73, 74
O. S. Nock Collection 1
North British Locomotive Co. Ltd 66
Henry Pooley & Son Ltd 53
Real Photograph Co. Ltd 13, 18, 22, 23, 83
W. S. Rendell, Yeovil 32
The Times 56
Topical Press Agency 40
The Vulcan Foundry 24, 71

Plates 25, 27, 28, 29, 50 and 78 are from the author's collection. The origin of any illustrations not included above is unknown. The author apologises if he has inadvertently omitted to credit, or has wrongly credited, any individual illustration.

List of Abbreviations

A.R.L.E.	Association of Railway Locomotive Engineers.
B.B. & C.I.	Bombay, Baroda & Central India Railway.
B.R.	British Railways.
B.T.C.	British Transport Commission.
C.E.G.B.	Central Electricity Generating Board.
C.E.I.	Council of Engineering Institutions.
C.M. & E.E.	Chief Mechanical & Electrical Engineer.
C.M.E.	Chief Mechanical Engineer.
E.C.A.F.E.	Economic Commission for Asia & the Far East.
E.I.J.C.	Engineering Institutions Joint Council.
G.I.P.R.	Great Indian Peninsular Railway.
G.W.R.	Great Western Railway.
I.Mech.E.	Institution of Mechanical Engineers.
I.R.C.A.	International Railway Congress Association.
L. & N.W.	London & North Western Railway.
L. & Y.	Lancashire & Yorkshire Railway.
L.M.S.	London, Midland & Scottish Railway.
L.N.E.R.	London & North Eastern Railway.
L.T. & S.	London, Tilbury & Southend section of the L.M.S.
M. & G.N.	Midland & Great Northern Joint Railway.
M.E.Ctte.	Mechanical Engineering Committee.
N.B.Loco.Co.	North British Locomotive Company.
N.C.C.	Northern Counties Committee Railway – Northern Ireland.
O.R.E.	Office for Research & Experiments of the International Union of Railways.
R.E.	Railway Executive.
P.R.R.	Pennsylvania Railroad, United States of America.
S.N.C.F.	French National Railways.
T.D. & R.Ctte.	Technical Development & Research Committee.
W.D.	War Department.

CHAPTER ONE

Introduction:
The Early Years

ONE OF THE MORE DIFFICULT problems which seems to face many of my friends is in giving advice to their sons on the choice of a career. My father was never confronted with this difficulty. From my earliest years, and for no discernible reason, I developed a deep and abiding interest for railway locomotives. And in those days, that meant steam locomotives and nothing else. It was an interest which grew and developed with the years; and long before the age at which the vital decision of the choice of career has usually to be taken, I was quite clear in my mind that I intended to become a locomotive engineer.

With increasing knowledge gained from regular reading of *Railway Magazine*, given to me by our next door neighbour, who must, I think, have been a shareholder of the Great Eastern Railway, I saw no reason why, in the fullness of time, I should not be able to design and build steam locomotives myself. And thus was born my ambition to become Chief Mechanical Engineer, or as the position was then more often known, Locomotive Superintendent, of one of the British railway companies. It was an ambition which has been the mainspring of my life – the attainment of which has been the driving force throughout my professional career.

There was no influence deriving from heredity or environment to account for the absorbing interest which locomotives had for me. My father was a wine merchant in Ipswich. My grandfather, with a background of farming in Suffolk, founded the firm of Robert Bond & Sons, Auctioneers and Land Agents; and he was for fifty years Secretary of the Suffolk Agricultural Association. Similarly, on my mother's side, the family interests were concerned with country pursuits. True, an uncle was for a short time in the traffic department of the Great Eastern Railway, but ill-health compelled his early retirement. We seldom saw him and this remote connection with the railway service, of which for many years I was quite unaware, could have played no part in guiding me towards railway mechanical engineering. There is probably nothing to be gained, at this distance in time, from trying to establish why a particular interest, for which there is no apparent cause, develops in a young mind. What matters is that the inevitable consequence, in terms of a career, was accepted without question by my parents.

My younger sister and I – there were just the two of us – had a very happy childhood. Both sides of our family had lived in or near Ipswich for many years, and we enjoyed a wide circle of friends. There was stability and order in all things – the pattern of life varied little. It included, on Sunday afternoons, a visit to the grandparents' home on the outskirts of the town, the main interest of which to me, was that the branch line to Felixstowe passed on a high viaduct in sight of my grandfather's property. The down distant signal for Derby Road Station was also in view – in the days when all distant signals carried red lights instead of yellow for the caution indication. The Great Eastern fitted their distant signals with a special lamp which showed a white >, in addition to the main light, which no doubt went some way towards making life easier for the men on the footplate.

As my father was one of a large family these gatherings on Sunday afternoons could become rather overpowering. Some of the uncles and aunts took less kindly than others to young children. But under the benign influence of my grandparents I do not remember ever being bored. All in all, life was very agreeable. Afternoon walks were, however, often a matter of acute controversy. The usual alternative destinations were London Road to watch the trains, or Christchurch Park. As my inclinations were totally different from my sister's the decision had frequently to be made by the toss of a coin. When we did get to London Road bridge – and it was very often – there was always much of absorbing interest to be seen.

Ipswich is an important junction on the Colchester main line from Liverpool Street to Norwich and Yarmouth. At East Suffolk Junction, a mile or so from the station where the engines of nearly all trains were changed, the line to Great Yarmouth diverged from the main route to Norwich. The junction was most conveniently situated just under London Road bridge spanning the main lines and the connections to the goods yards.

Express passenger trains were worked almost exclusively by the *Claud Hamilton* class 4-4-0s, in those days non-superheated engines, some with round-top fireboxes and some with Belpaire boilers. They were first rate locomotives, simple and sturdy in design.

For many years after the first of them won a gold medal at the Paris Exhibition in 1900, until the *1500* class 4-6-0s took over, they bore the brunt of working the Great Eastern express passenger services. They were later rebuilt with larger superheated boilers, and in their final form with $9\frac{1}{2}''$ diameter long travel piston valves they were as good as any 4-4-0 of generally similar size. With their large side window cabs and compressed air operation of the reversing gear and water pick-up scoop, they were clearly designed by James Holden's people at Stratford with the comfort and convenience of the enginemen well in mind. Painted dark blue, lined in red with brass capped chimneys, and in the spotless condition one took for granted in the days before the first World War, they were an imposing sight. Coupling rods painted bright vermilion red, added to the splendour of these engines, though in later years one learnt that to guarantee finding incipient fatigue flaws, to which highly stressed mechanical parts are always liable, coupling rods should not be painted. Alas, the *Claud Hamiltons* have long since disappeared — all that now remains so far as I am concerned, are memories, and one of the nameplates from the *D16/3* rebuild of the original locomotive — now suitably mounted outside my home.

Secondary passenger services were often worked by rebuilt *T19* class 4-4-0s or *Humpty-Dumpty* 2-4-0s. These, with the dome on the first ring of an overgrown boiler, their short wheelbase and single side window cabs, were odd looking engines — their nickname was well chosen. The Felixstowe branch trains were monopolised by the *F3* 2-4-2 engines — the tank engine version of the *E4 Intermediate* 2-4-0s, the last one of which restored to its original 1895 condition is now preserved.

There was also, of course, a varied assortment of 0-6-0 freight tender and tank engines to be seen shunting in the Upper Yard. But the three passenger classes, the *Claud Hamiltons*, the rebuilt *T19s* and the 2-4-2 tanks made most impression on my mind. For them, I devised a very simple classification — they were known as London Engines, Norwich Engines and Felixstowe Engines respectively.

During the second year of the Great War, my father's business affairs took him to Great Yarmouth and we had to move thence from Ipswich. The usual domestic upheaval was involved to which in later years, as one progressed from one appointment to the next in the railway service, I became quite hardened. But at the impressionable age of twelve, migration to a new home, though only fifty miles away and in the same county was no minor incident in my life.

The move to Gorleston-on-Sea on the outskirts of the town had important consequences for me, both immediate and in the longer term. Though Ipswich was only twelve miles from the sea, and we often sailed down the River Orwell to Harwich on one of the Great Eastern's paddle steamers, it was not the same thing as living on the coast, which quickly developed in me a love of the sea, which has persisted strongly to this day.

A change of school was perforce involved. I was left behind in Ipswich for some weeks to complete the summer term at Ipswich School, during which I lived with an uncle — William Bantoft, Town Clerk of the

Borough, an awe inspiring man of very strict principles. He must have had a softer side to his character, as he allowed me to ruin a part of his lawn by digging a tunnel under it as a feature of my 0-gauge model railway! I conceived a strong dislike for the school at Yarmouth which I attended for two years before going on to Tonbridge. In my judgment this school had nothing to commend it except its situation adjoining the Midland and Great Northern Joint Railway, a line of whose existence I was then only dimly aware, but which in later years I came to know very well in travelling to and from Derby. There was a level crossing immediately outside the school grounds, controlled from Salisbury Road signal box, which was also the block post at which the double line from Yarmouth Beach Station became single track onwards to Caister-on-Sea. It was not long before I struck up an acquaintance with signalmen on duty during the break between morning and afternoon school and received the desired invitation to visit the box. I soon became reasonably proficient in working the double line block, the single line tablet instrument and the tablet catchers. Thus was my interest in railway working still further stimulated.

The Midland and Great Northern Joint Line served parts of East Anglia and Lincolnshire, predominantly agricultural country. Although single track throughout most of its length, it was in every sense a main line, forming an important connecting link between East Anglia and the industrial Midlands and North. One route joined the Great Northern main line at Peterborough and the other connected with the Midland at Saxby Junction. During the summer months, particularly at week-ends, the line carried a very heavy traffic of holiday makers to and from the Norfolk Coast resorts, with through coaches from Leicester, Derby, Birmingham and even further afield. Punctuality was not always beyond reproach, which was scarcely surprising, bearing in mind the single line and the capacity of the locomotives in relation to the weight of the trains they worked.

In everything save their golden brown colour, the locomotives, with a few exceptions, proclaimed their Midland origin. Spring balance safety valves on the dome, and other details so characteristic of locomotives designed by Samuel Johnson, who before going to Derby as Locomotive Superintendent of the Midland had been in charge at Stratford, were no longer to be seen on the Great Eastern. On the Midland and Great Northern they were familiar to the end. While no doubt the Locomotive Works at Melton Constable enjoyed considerable freedom in what they did, policy was always dictated from Derby – and it was through the M. & G.N. that my interest in Midland locomotives was particularly aroused.

However, my interest in the Great Eastern Railway and its locomotives remained undiminished. During school holidays, and at weekends during term time, I haunted South Town station, the terminus of the East Suffolk main line, and the starting point for trains over the Norfolk and Suffolk Joint Line to Lowestoft. By staring hard enough and long enough at the drivers and firemen of engines standing in the station, invitations to the footplate were often forthcoming. I spent many profitable hours absorbing knowledge from the best of all possible teachers – those who actually did the job. Usually one jumped down reluctantly, on to the platform at the last moment before the locomotive left with its train, or backed out to the Shed. But one morning stands out in my memory above all others. A driver, whom I knew well, was given the right-away, and without a word, opened the regulator while I was still in the cab. I was actually riding on a living locomotive – one of the *F3* 2-4-2 tanks running bunker first on a passenger train to Lowestoft, which took me to Gorleston-on-Sea. This was the first, but by no means the last of my clandestine footplate trips, which culminated in a journey on a *Claud Hamilton* from Beccles to Yarmouth, South Town.

Returning home one day from a visit to London, I found a particular friend of mine – Ted Burgess – one of the South Town top-link drivers in charge of the 3.30 express to Yarmouth, stopping at Ipswich and Beccles only. 'Come along at Beccles' Ted said, 'and we'll see what we can do!' I remember I had some difficulty when we arrived at Beccles, persuading the aunt with whom I was travelling, that I should be perfectly safe on the front with Ted. There was no time to argue, and I won the day. *Claud Hamilton* cabs were large and comfortable and there was plenty of room for me tucked away in the corner on top of the splasher on the fireman's side. I remember this trip over the final twelve miles of the East Suffolk main line, now no longer in existence, as though it were yesterday. Many people, who have never been there, consider Suffolk is flat. And so it is compared, say, with Devon. But the Great Eastern was built over, rather than through, the country and the line is a series of sharp undulations, sometimes steeper than 1 in 100 and by no means free from curves. From Beccles onwards to the coast, with severe speed restrictions over two single-line swing bridges, was not an easy stretch. I expected the fireman would be kept busier than in fact he was; but I knew nothing then of the art of letting down the fire to just the right thickness at the end of a day to ensure plenty of steam – and the minimum amount of work dropping the fire on the ashpit. It was a good, fast run; and what better end to a day could be imagined?

One further consequence of our move to Yarmouth is perhaps worth recalling. The war made an impact, at once sharper and more continuous than before. There had been one desultory air raid on Ipswich, during which we passed an uncomfortable night downstairs. There were some bomb explosions, but they were comfortably far away. Certainly the whole episode frightened me very much less than had a severe thunderstorm some years earlier. Though enemy air activity was as nothing compared with twenty-five years later, nevertheless the war seemed very much nearer on the coast. There was a large Royal Naval Air Service aerodrome on the narrow strip of land between the river and the sea. Here there were stationed a variety of aircraft, all of them stick and string biplanes, which were always in the air flying along the coast or further afield over the North Sea, meeting and chasing the Zeppelin airships which made fairly frequent sorties to our shores.

There were no sirens in those days, and often the first one knew of an impending raid was the sound of airship engines coming in from the sea. We became reconciled and sometimes oblivious, to these airships passing overhead. But bombardment from the sea, though it happened only twice was quite a different matter! Shortly before dawn on 25th April, 1916, we were wakened by explosions much louder and sharper than anything we had previously heard. My father and I went out, a hundred yards up the road to where we had a clear view over the river and out to sea. The gas-works up the river towards the town had been hit. Flames were pouring out of a hole punctured in the side of a gasometer. No ships were visible out at sea — but we saw a gunflash on the horizon; and moments later the shell hit and burst in a warehouse near the aerodrome, half a mile from where we were standing. It was an astonishing sight, and clearly it was time for us to go. Bombardment from the sea was held to be a prelude to imminent invasion, and if it happened the civil population had been instructed to leave at once and make their way inland. Waiting long enough only to throw on some clothes and lock the front door, we set out on foot along the road to Beccles and Ipswich. Hundreds were already on the march, some pushing prams and some with overcoats over their night clothes, and all presumably wondering what was to happen next. A few shells were still passing overhead and bursting in open country behind the town. Soon, however, the firing ceased, and after we had trudged about three miles, the procession was overtaken by a local doctor sent out in his car by the Civil Defence people. He told us it was all over and we could now return home!

The second bombardment by enemy ships, early in 1918, took place in the middle of the night. We had become fairly blasé by then, and in spite of a good deal of noise, remained in bed. In the morning we discovered that a part of our garden wall had been knocked down by a 4″ shell, which fortunately did not explode, and ended up in the front room of a nearby cottage. These were outstanding incidents, in sharp contrast to the normally unexciting, though ever present, background of war conditions to which we had become accustomed, but which seemed to make remarkably little difference to the normal pattern of living.

It was during these war years that my firm intention to become a locomotive engineer had to be translated into plans for my future career. It was intended, as soon as circumstances permitted, that I should go away to boarding school. Thereafter at about eighteen years of age, I was clear in my own mind that the next step would be to serve an apprenticeship at the Locomotive Works of one of the Railway Companies. From extensive reading of railway books, I had by this time acquired a fairly complete knowledge of the career pattern which most of the Locomotive Superintendents of that day had followed. Membership of one or both of the two professional institutions, the 'Civils' and the 'Mechanicals' was clearly a distinction which had to be achieved. But equally clearly, a University degree was not in those days, an essential qualification for the appointment on which I had set my mind one day to hold.

There was no question of my going on to a University to read Mechanical Sciences. Even if professional advice had been forthcoming to the contrary, I feel sure I should have resisted any such proposal. I was far too impatient to get into the Shops, to work among locomotives as soon as the time came for me to leave school. I took it for granted that essential academic qualifications would have to be obtained by part-time study for the Institutions' examinations concurrently with practical training. Thus, as I viewed the matter, there was every advantage to be gained in the future from having, while still at school, the best possible grounding in basic scientific principles upon which the art and profession of engineering depends.

In 1918 few of the Public Schools paid very much attention to the needs of those with leanings to a scientific or engineering career. The classics, English, modern languages and history tended to dominate what went on in school hours. There were however, at least two exceptions to the general rule. Tonbridge and Oundle both had comprehensive science and engineering sides, supported by first class laboratories and workshops, and generally considered in no way inferior to the other constituents of their upper school establishments.

After the usual formalities of the Common Entrance Examination had been successfully completed, I was accepted by Tonbridge. The Headmaster, Charles Lowry, a man of commanding presence and one of the great headmasters of his day, gave me a vacancy in his House. Being two years above the usual age for new boys, I found myself placed in a form on the science side fairly high up the school. This availed me nothing in terms of status which was conferred by the passage of time, and then only if merited by the test of standards related more to the games fields than the classrooms. Having to settle down in entirely unfamiliar surroundings as an insignificant member of a community demanding rigid adherence to long established customs and traditions is a salutary experience of lasting value, not least during the first few weeks in an engineering Works. One's self-esteem may suffer some hard knocks. But the compulsive urge to self-preservation cannot be surpassed as a means of acquiring the virtues of self-reliance, resourcefulness and discipline without which no-one gets very far either at school or anywhere else.

Judged by the standards of my contemporaries, with one exception, my career at Tonbridge was undistinguished. The exception was concerned with the final of the House cricket competition during my last term. I had managed to scrape into the House team as a slow left arm bowler. As such I went in last in the batting order. When my turn came, the head of the House and Captain of cricket C. H. Knott, who later played for Oxford and Kent, was still at the wicket with 186 runs to his credit. The considerable crowd watching the match naturally thought all would be over in a few minutes. My orders were quite simple – to keep the ball off my stumps, score singles only and make sure that Knott had the bowling. The last wicket stand endured for two hours and put on 198 runs, of which I contributed twelve not out! Knott scored 372, a school record not yet surpassed.

Before this one and only burst into prominence, I had been well content to make the most of my last year in the Engineering VIth. Mechanical drawing took up much of my time and earned me the only two school prizes I ever won. Such spare hours as were available, I spent in the Metal Workshops, and there gained valuable experience of hand tools and simple machine tools. It is today often contended that time at school can be better spent elsewhere than in the Workshops. With the first twelve months of so many of the best engineering training courses now spent in an Apprentice Training School detached from the main production shops there may well be some force in this contention. But in 1920, when the invariable custom was for all apprentices to be drafted straight into production shops there to acquire skill as best they could, depending largely on the goodwill of chargehands and craftsmen with whom they worked, there was no doubt that elementary knowledge gained in school workshops was most useful, if only as a means of avoiding the effects of some of the leg-pulling which the men enjoyed to inflict on unsuspecting apprentices. Even today, I am in no doubt that some time spent under supervision, in workshops at school, is more likely to be useful than otherwise.

Though I do not subscribe to the old adage that school days are the happiest days of one's life, I certainly enjoyed my years at Tonbridge and I remain convinced of the benefits which accrue to those who are fortunate enough to spend some part of their school years away from home. Though I left with few regrets, the now familiar scene dominated by the magnificent chapel set among beautiful surroundings overlooking the Head – the 1st XI cricket ground – had imperceptibly exerted upon me, as upon so many others, influences for good of lasting value fully appreciated only in later years. For me, Tonbridge certainly justified its motto – *Deus dat Incrementum*. I owe to the school, founded by Sir Andrew Judde in 1553, and partially rebuilt in 1863 from funds accruing to the Governors from the compulsory sale to the Midland Railway of the land upon which St. Pancras goods yard was built, a debt which can never be fully repaid.

During my last year at school I had to make my choice of a railway company to whom to apply for my practical training. I obtained particulars of their conditions of employment from Crewe, Swindon, Doncaster, Stratford and Derby. Compared with the scheme of training offered at Derby, those at the other Works seemed to be rather restricted in scope. Moreover, whether those under training were designated as pupils or premium apprentices, a fee of £100 to £150 per annum was payable. At Derby, on the other hand, no premium was payable, but the Midland Railway required their Chief Mechanical Engineer's Department privileged apprentices to pass an entrance examination before employment. Knowing, as I did, more of the Great Eastern than of the other companies, Stratford seemed the obvious choice. But on further reflection there seemed no sense in paying a substantial sum per annum for less than was apparently obtainable at Derby for nothing. Furthermore the Midland was one of the larger and more progressive of the railways – and the works at Derby had a very high reputation. I therefore applied to Sir Henry Fowler, Chief Mechanical Engineer of the Midland Railway for employment as a privileged apprentice.

In due course I was called for interview at Derby, a free ticket being sent for the journey via the M. and G.N. Joint Line to Leicester and thence over the Midland main line through Trent Junction to Derby. That free ticket gave me a foretaste of what I have come to regard as the most agreeable perquisite of railway service – unlimited travel at one quarter the normal public fare with an allowance of free passes increasing in number and availability as one progresses upwards in the service. To those who in the fullness of time become Chief Officers, a gold medallion pass is issued, available for life throughout British Railways and on their ships. The value of this privilege cannot be measured. To some, no doubt, it is of little significance. To me and others like me, with an urge to see what is at the end of the line, whether at Land's End or John o'Groats it is of inestimable value. Extending as it does to one's family and to many foreign countries, this privilege contributes much to a full life and enables railwaymen, if they so wish, to see far more of their own and other people's countries than other less fortunate people.

Incredible though it may seem in these present days of easy long distance holiday travel, in 1920 my personal acquaintance with this country was limited to parts of East Anglia, Buckinghamshire and Kent, and that part of London roughly bounded by the principal main line termini. The journey to Derby across the fens of Lincolnshire and on through the undulating Leicestershire farmlands broke entirely new ground for me. It was then that I saw for the first time an ironworks – the blast furnaces of the Stanton Company at Holwell. I remember that I had some difficulty in understanding accents very different from the familiar Suffolk and Norfolk intonations. It was a fascinating journey, but as on so many of our cross-country routes, it took a very long time.

The Locomotive Works at Derby are immediately adjacent to the passenger station, of which in those days, the headquarters offices and the Board Room of the Midland Railway were an important part. On this, my first visit, I was content to stay within the confines of the station and the Works. The main access to the Chief Mechanical Engineer's offices whither I was bound, was by a footbridge from No. 1 Platform, spanning the station and a number of sidings, on which were stabled locomotives awaiting entry to the Works for repairs. I had hoped to catch a glimpse, for the first time, of some of the 3-cylinder Derby Compounds, the pride of the Midland express passenger fleet. There was none in sight, nor were any of the trains passing through Derby while I was there that day, worked by one of the Compounds. However, it was not long before I came to know the Compounds and their anatomy as intimately as anyone could possibly wish.

I, and others, were interviewed by Sir Henry Fowler's assistant in charge of all training, one George Woolliscroft, a benevolent elderly gentleman, a Whitworth Scholar and a magistrate. Whether he was a good engineer I was never able to discover. It was to Woolliscroft we went when seeking an overdue move from one shop to another. But for all his benevolence Woolliscroft could be very elusive. The apprentices at Derby were expected to make a full contribution to the output of the job to which they were allocated – and I suspect that Woolliscroft was sometimes unwilling to risk upsetting Shop Foremen by moving apprentices to another shop just as they were becoming useful. He occupied a ground floor room in the main office block, with two doors, and was apt to leave hurriedly by one door as an apprentice entered by the other. This retreat was once neatly frustrated by a contemporary of mine, a resolute man and no respecter of authority who, seeing Woolliscroft disappearing through his outer door, ran round the block, and confronting his guide, philosopher and friend head on, demanded and obtained his move.

Things are done better today. Transfers from one shop or office to another, after a preliminary period in the apprentice school, are made in accordance with carefully planned alternative courses which afford a wide range of experience and comply with the requirements of the professional Institutions and the Engineering Industry Training Board. The training schemes operating today at all the Main Workshops of British Railways were developed from the original Derby pattern, under the direction of Edgar Larkin whose experience in this field was unsurpassed when he retired a few years ago as Assistant General Manager of the Workshops. To him also should go the lion's share of the credit for the Apprentice Training Schools which in standards of instruction, equipment and amenities are very good indeed.

My interview and examination results were apparently satisfactory for, within a few days, I was offered a privileged apprenticeship at Derby Locomotive Works.

CHAPTER TWO

Apprenticeship and Pupilage
at Derby

1920–25

ON 24th SEPTEMBER, 1920, I entered the service of the Midland Railway at Derby Locomotive Works. My weekly wages were, as I see from my service history card, twenty-two shillings and nine pence per week, made up of seven shillings per week base rate plus fifteen shillings and ninepence war wage addition. At this rate of pay, and with lodgings to be paid for, one was certainly not entirely self-supporting. My father had come to Derby with me on this occasion to see me satisfactorily settled into digs, in regard to which the Works Staff Office gave valuable advice. On the previous afternoon we had been seen by J. E. Anderson, the Works Manager and deputy to Sir Henry Fowler. It was a most friendly interview, during which it was made quite clear that my future progress would depend entirely on my own efforts. This was again emphasised when, after the usual brief preliminaries in the Works Staff Office, I was taken down to the Brass Foundry in which I was to spend the first few months of my practical training, and handed over to the care of the Shop Foreman, F. G. Chambers.

'Little Chambers', as we all knew him, to distinguish him from his brother who was in charge of the Locomotive Experimental Section in the Drawing Office, was an outstanding man who ran his Shop very well. He took his responsibilities to the apprentices committed to his care seriously. We were sent for, from time to time, to receive an encouraging talk in his private office. We were expected to pull our weight in the shop, and Chambers did not hesitate to admonish those whom he thought deserved it. He was, in due course, promoted to the Works Management staff in charge of the Premium Office – so called because the administrative work in connection with piecework payments (the Rowan Premium Bonus system) was undertaken there. Today, the equivalent appointment would be Production Engineer, and Chambers achieved this position at a time when it was most unusual for a shop Foreman to reach managerial rank. The usual route to Works Management was, in those days, through the Drawing Office or from technical assistants' appointments in the Works Manager's Office.

The standard working week in 1920 and for some time thereafter, was forty-seven hours, from 7.55 a.m. to 5.30 p.m., with one hour off for lunch, which the engineering apprentices and pupils were allowed to take at the Railway Institute just over the road from the Station. We were given typical canteen food – not very appetising, but filling and cheap. On Saturdays the works closed at 12.30 p.m., but effective work finished a good deal earlier than the official closing time. I had escaped, by a few years, the 6.00 a.m. start with a pause for breakfast. I cannot think that very much productive work was done at that unearthly hour. While in 1920 there were none of the 'ten minute' tea breaks for shop foremen to contend with, the men were no more anxious to get stuck into the job at the beginning of the day than they are now. Nevertheless Chambers was invariably punctual himself, and there was no slacking when he was in the Shop. Our working week differed only to the extent that privileged apprentices were required to attend classes on two mornings each week at Derby Technical College, conducted as an integral part of the Railway's training scheme, in addition to the usual evening classes.

The Brass Foundry produced about 20 tons of castings weekly, varying in size from washout and fusible plugs up to the solid bronze axleboxes which was the standard type for many Midland locomotives at that time. There were many quite intricate castings to be made, often in oil sand cores, such as drivers brake valves and combination clack boxes, which gave one a valuable insight into the complexities of pattern making. The Shop was well provided with moulding machines for semi-skilled work by which the steady demands for big end and axlebox brasses, coupling rod bushes and phosphor bronze slide valves were met. The White Metalling Shop, adjacent to the foundry also came under Chambers' supervision, and during the time I spent in the Shop, I was given a good run round on all the principal jobs.

I was first handed over as mate to an elderly gentleman, by name Nelson, whose speciality was solid bronze axleboxes. Hand ramming the moulding boxes was strenuous work. And with floor sand everywhere and plenty of fumes, inadequately extracted during the morning and afternoon casting times, a hot bath at the end of the day was a necessity rather than a luxury. Washing facilities, clothes lockers and other amenities of the high standard which men rightly take for granted in any decent Works today were simply non-existent at Derby in 1920.

A generous helping of machine oil, followed by a bucket of warm water shared with one's mate had to suffice. For the first few weeks I brought in a tin of gresolvent to help remove the grime. But it was pinched from the drawer under our bench so regularly that I soon learned there was no future in pioneering the use of detergents! Similarly in the Erecting Shop many months later, it was necessary to exercise much ingenuity in hiding one's bag of tools, lead hammer, chisels and files, originally issued from the shop stores and only to be replaced on a one for one basis when worn out, under engine pit boards or other unlikely places in the hope that they would be there for the next day's work. Even so they were often purloined. The law of the jungle prevailed. It was every man for himself, and I had no hesitation in acquiring someone else's tools to get on with the job.

Nelson's immediate neighbour on the hand moulding benches was one Harold, a long, lanky man who regaled us on Monday mornings with Rabelaisian stories of his weekend amorous activities and the amount of beer he had drunk. Eight pints on a Saturday night seemed quite a usual ration. I was subjected to searching cross-examinations from Harold as to my family background and other personal matters. It was all very good-natured. From Harold and many another like him, I learnt a great deal about the shopmen's outlook on life, about the bosses as seen by those who are bossed, and about the rich variety of the English language – lessons of lasting value which can be learned nowhere else but on the shop floor in direct and daily contact with the men.

Work in the White Metalling Shop gave me my first practical insight into repair operations in contrast to new production. I was aware, in a general way, of the designed use of white metal alloys as bearing metals for lining bearings of all kinds and the wearing surface of axleboxes, crossheads and eccentric straps. But what was quite new to me was the use of white metal as a cheap and convenient 'putting-on' tool to make good wear and recover for further service, such components as hand-fitted square backed axlebox brasses and hornstays that would otherwise have to be scrapped. David Rushton, with bushy eyebrows and a battered bowler hat, the white metalling chargehand, taught me about the procedures for segregating and renovating to the standard analysis the metal melted out from the parts sent in for repairs. Two alloys predominated – No. 1 for bearings subjected to heavy alternating loads such as coupled axlebox brasses (Tin 85 per cent, Antimony 10 per cent, Copper 5 per cent) and No. 3 for bogie and tender axlebox bearings, of quite a different composition (Lead 75 per cent, Antimony 13 per cent, Tin 12 per cent).

The very different composition and high cost of these alloys clearly emphasised the importance of careful segregation to ensure that expenditure on new metals for restoring secondhand melts to the standard analyses was kept within reasonable bounds. Rushton kept a firm hand on this work in the Shop. But there was a constant battle with the machine shop and outstation depots who were not always as careful as they should have been in separating the various grades of mixed bronze and white metal cuttings from machining operations, returned to the shop for renovation.

In the normal course of events, apprenticeships terminated at twenty-one years of age. Thus, I could expect to have three and a half years in the Shops. It seemed to me, after having spent ten months or so in the Brass Foundry, that with the other principal shops in which, as I judged the matter, it was essential for me to work, the time had come for me to apply for a move. My first approach was, of course, to my Shop Foreman. With a good report from him, and a number of visits to Woolliscroft, persistence was rewarded, and I was transferred to the Boiler Shop, where I spent the next six months.

In retrospect, I am sure I was fortunate in having been sent first to a comparatively small shop, and one in which the Foreman was really concerned for the well-being of his apprentices. A quite usual starting point was the Grease Corner, a section of the Machine Shop in which were installed the nut and bolt machines and copper stay lathes. The simple centre lathes, long since replaced by capstans and automatics for boiler-stay and bolt production, were manned entirely by apprentices. Though of course this section of the Machine Shop is a vital link in the production chain of any Locomotive Works, and an essential introduction to the turner's trade, the work was purely repetitive, and there was far less opportunity than in a shop like the Brass Foundry for getting to know and understand, early in one's career, craftsmen skilled in their trades, upon whose goodwill we depended so much for learning all that an aspiring professional engineer would need to know of what goes on in the Shops.

Though each of the Shops in a large Works is a closely knit community in itself, with its own special characteristics deriving largely from the jealously guarded customs and traditions of the craft and the personality of the Chief Foreman, they are nevertheless very much parts of the whole Works in which all that goes to make up everyday life in the Shops conforms to one, general pattern, to which one soon becomes completely accustomed. One gets to know the ropes that matter. There is no problem of acclimatisation in moving from one Shop to another, and I was soon absorbed in the mysteries of flanging, plating and riveting with the men on boiler repairs and new construction.

It was surprising how quickly one became oblivious to the very high noise level which is the constant accompaniment to work in any Boiler Shop. One soon acquires the ability to hear, and be heard, without shouting above the din of pneumatic riveting hammers. There was no lack of heavy hand work in the Boiler Shop on such jobs as hand flanging of copper firebox plates or knobbling copper stays. In later years, copper plates were customarily flanged in 700-ton hydraulic presses, as was always the case with steel plates. But at Derby in 1922, it was the practice for the flanges of copper tube and firedoor plates to be knocked up hot by a gang of men wielding large, long-handled wooden mallets. Copper stay heads too, were formed by hand hammering. Three men worked as a gang, one holding-up, and the other two striking alternate blows with knobbling hammers. This was hard work in cramped suroundings – and woe betide the apprentice who missed his aim and hit the plate instead of the half-formed stay head.

The boiler is the most important main component of a steam locomotive. For upon it depends the power which the locomotive can produce. It is useless to provide adequate cylinder volume ensuring a high starting tractive effort unless the boiler can provide all the steam required to maintain sufficient drawbar horsepower throughout the appropriate speed range at which traffic is operated. The boiler is responsible for a large part of the expenditure incurred in locomotive maintenance. Its condition determined more than any other single factor, the period which locomotives could remain at work between consecutive heavy repairs in C.M.E. Shops, and its characteristics and limitations affected and influenced the whole organisation of the Motive Power Department.

Locomotive boiler building is a fairly straightforward form of heavy engineering production. Neither the general standard of accuracy demanded in building the boiler shell and firebox, nor the high precision work involved in manufacturing and fitting the firebox stays, tubes and mountings were difficult to attain consistently in well equipped shops. But from the first day a boiler is put to work it is acted upon constantly by two destructive forces, one chemical, the other mechanical, the combined effects of which necessitate the boiler being taken out of traffic for repairs in Motive Power Depots or Shops.

The one factor from which most trouble stems is the quality of the feed water which varies widely in different parts of the country. So far as its effect on boiler repairs is concerned, feed waters may be divided into two main categories – heavy scaling waters and corrosive waters. Heavy scaling waters principally affected the firebox plates and stays. Corrosive waters, on the other hand attack the steel portions of the boiler causing wastage and pitting below the water line, due to chemical action.

But even with ideal feed water, deterioration in the fabric of the boiler from purely mechanical causes goes on all the time. This is greatly accentuated with bad water or too rapid cooling down. The flat surfaces tend to move slightly under pressure. The repeated bending action sets up incipient fractures. Apart from this mechanical action steam pressure is raised only as a result of the application of heat. The consequent expansion and contraction is unevenly distributed, and when in service the plates, stays and tubes are in a state of constant movement. The rate of combustion may vary from about 40 to 150 lbs of coal per square foot of grate per hour, the quantity of heat transmitted and the temperature gradient through the plates thus varying in a corresponding manner.

.R. *Claud Hamilton* class.
any years the mainstay of
Eastern express passenger
services

ud Hamilton in her final
Rebuilt as L.N.E. *Class
D16/3.*

that remains of *Claud
ton* – in the author's garden.

4. Two G.E. *1500 Class* 4-6-0s which replaced the *Claud Hamiltons* on the heaviest duties.

5. G.E.R. *1500 Class* rebuilt as L.N.E.R. *Class B12/3* leaving Ipswich on express to Liverpool St.

6. G.E.R. 2-4-2 Tank locomotive – on which the author had his first footplate trip.

7. G.E.R. steamer *Suffolk* on passage down the River Orwell from Ipswich to Harwich.

8. M.&G.N. 4-4-0 The Midland features are unmistakable.

9. M.&G.N. 4-4-0 rebuilt with Derby G7 boiler – the mainstay of the Yarmouth–Leicester expresses.

10. Tonbridge School – from 'The Head' the First XI cricket ground.

11. Locomotive Erecting Shop – Derby Works.

12. Midland three-cylinder compound – built during the author's time in the Erecting Shop at Derby.

One of the twenty-two Stratford-on-Avon & Midland Junction engines, whose tyres had all to be examined to enable a record of makers and cast numbers to be compiled.

One of the two *Tilbury* tank engines used for coal consumption tests on trains with plain and roller bearings.

15. Arrival at Derby after a trip from Manchester in the Indicating Shelter on Compound No. 1011.

16. Holbeck Motive Power Depot, Leeds – from which many locomotives have set out to show their paces over t
Leeds–Carlisle road.

Unequal expansion of the copper firebox and stays in relation to the steel plates and tubes introduces further stresses. The outcome of the stresses to which boilers are subjected is to be seen in the grooving which takes place at the bends of throat and door plates, at the smokebox tubeplate and circumferential seams of the barrel. Copper stay heads and plates are subject to progressive wastage, and cracks appear in copper tube and door plates.

This digression will serve to emphasise the dominant part which repairs played in the output and organisation of the boiler shop of a railway locomotive Works. For every new boiler built, twenty would be given heavy repairs. It will be evident that locomotive boilers must be examined regularly to ensure both safety in operation and the longest possible time in service between one heavy repair in Shops and the next. Inspections at the Running Sheds were undertaken by District Boiler Inspectors – skilled boilermakers controlled from C.M.E. Headquarters. Scarcely less important was the meticulous examination carried out by the Works Boiler Inspector when, as a result of accumulated wear and tear in service, locomotives had to be sent to the Works for heavy boiler repairs.

Repair procedures in general were always subject to detailed instructions issued by the Chief Mechanical Engineer. Nevertheless a wide discretion remained to the Boiler Shop Foremen in deciding the repairs to be done having regard to the age, past history, expected further life and the Works Inspector's report on individual boilers. Sound judgment based on long practical experience was required in reaching the right decisions. Sammy Walters, the Chief Foreman at Derby, as good a boilermaker as anyone could wish for, gave me some weeks with the Works Boiler Inspector, during which, among other things, I became reasonably competent in detecting broken copper stays by the sound produced when their heads were struck by a hammer. I saw too, for the first, but not the last, time, during those weeks, the dire effects which a broken inside connecting rod can have in punching a large and jagged hole in the throat plate and copper tube plate of a locomotive boiler. Steam and scalding water escaping through the hole had blown most of the fire on to the footplate and killed the fireman. This incident, and one or two others like it, no doubt gave rise to the issue of the following 'Locomotive Circular' sent to outstation shops:

Connecting & Coupling Rods 26-1-23
   We have recently had a case when a connecting rod has had a hard spot about 18″ from the little end due to having been heated and quenched. Instructions have been issued that under no circumstances whatever are connecting and coupling rods, or big or little end straps to be quenched after being heated in the fire. In order to ensure that there are no rods in service with hard spots, please arrange for a file to be run from end to end along each rod which goes through your shop, and should any hard spots be

found, please advise me so that steps can be taken to have the rod replaced or annealed. In all cases where rods require to be heated for any purpose whatever, they must be sent to Derby to be dealt with.

The six months in the Boiler Shop implanted in me an abiding interest in boiler repair problems, which, developed over the years, stood me in very good stead when, as Works Manager, one was called upon to give decisions in difficult cases as to whether boilers should be repaired or condemned – and if the former what repairs should be done.

Six months in the Boiler Shop was followed by a similar period in the Materials Test Room where one began to understand, from the practical point of view, the properties of materials, and the physical tests of tensile strength, ductility and hardness laid down in the Railway Company's specifications for the steel from which tyres, axles, boiler and frame plates and all the other component parts are manufactured. The time in the Test Room, filing test pieces and tyre sections for Brinell hardness tests, and assisting generally on the testing machines was well spent. The theoretical courses in Properties and Strength of Materials at the Technical College took on a new and much more significant meaning.

Transfers to the Machine Shop and Erecting Shop followed at approximately yearly intervals. Then it was that I met for the first time the redoubtable Jack Mathers, Chief Foreman of the Machine Shops, who also exercised an overlordship of the Erecting and Paint Shops. He was one of the most influential men in the Works. A stern disciplinarian, with a remarkable command of industrial English, he was held in awe by old and young alike. An interview in his private office was said by one or two of my fellow apprentices to be something of an ordeal. Jack Mathers was commonly thought to have no very high opinion of the general run of privileged apprentices. But I must acknowledge that when he found that I was in his Shop to work, not just to watch, I received nothing but help and encouragement at his hands.

Tom White, the Chief Assistant Foreman, a man of considerable culture and a cut above the average foreman of the time, was responsible for the apprentices in the Shop. He threw me in at the deep end on a 12″ screw-cutting lathe. I remember particularly tender hand-brake spindles with a three-start square thread. Here indeed the elementary knowledge I had gained in the workshops at Tonbridge came in very useful. This was followed by spells on the cylinder and frame fitting sections. Filing and scraping face to face joints for cylinder covers and bedding horn blocks to new frames, were jobs that called for much patience and persistence in satisfying the high standards of workmanship demanded by the chargehands of their gangs.

My last job in the Machine Shop was on the marking-off tables preparing rough castings and forgings for machining, by scribing on them their centre lines, setting marks and the designed finished dimensions. One learnt, by proxy as it were, a great deal about the essential machining processes. Hitherto I had worked at day-rate, or as one among a piecework gang. But on the marking-off tables I worked on my own to individual piecework prices. I soon discovered that there were 'good jobs' on which high bonuses could be earned, and 'bad jobs' on which it took me all my time to earn bare day-rate. On the whole, however, the prices were easy. The official ruling, respected then as now more in the breach than in the observance, was, and still is, that work done should be booked for payment currently. But to the men it is no more than plain common sense that some of the work done in a good week should be held in reserve to help maintain their pay packets at the desired steady level during weeks when 'bad jobs' predominated.

When the time came for me to move on from the marking-off tables, I had a very tidy sum accumulated for work done but not claimed for payment. I proposed, in my innocence, to book this all in one week. I was given to understand, however, by Bill Paulson, the leading hand, that this would be a most unfriendly thing to do, liable to give rise to embarrassing enquiries. Arbitrary cutting of prices on which it might appear that excessive balances could be earned was apparently not unknown. And so I was entirely content to hand over to Bill, for the benefit of anyone to whom he cared to give them, my unclaimed piecework tickets. It was a small price to pay for what I had learned of some of the more devious ways in which piecework systems really work.

Of all the Shops in which we served our time, it was the Erecting Shop which held the greatest interest for those of us who hoped and intended to spend our whole working life with locomotives. Here one discovered how locomotives were built, and even more important, what was involved in pulling them to pieces and making good the effects of wear and tear in service. Six pits on one of the three bays sufficed for new locomotive building. The remainder of the Shop, with the middle roads left clear for wheeling and subsidiary jobs, accommodated sixty locomotives undergoing repairs. During the time I was in the Shop the new engines being built were *Class 2* superheated 4-4-0s, some 0-6-0s with inside Walschaerts valve gear for the Northern Counties Committee, the railway in Northern Ireland owned by the Midland Railway, and the first series of the L.M.S. standard three-cylinder Compounds Nos. 1045 to 1064. The *Class 2* 4-4-0s were, presumably for some obscure accountancy reason, officially classified as rebuilds, although frames, cylinders, motion and, of course, the boiler were all new. As someone put it, 'There was nothing left of the original locomotives except the space between the wheels'.

Almost without exception the locomotives sent into Derby were given heavy general repairs, such light shop repairs as were necessary being done at one of the outstation Shops, all since closed, such as Kentish

Town, Leeds and Bristol. In the days of which I am writing there were virtually no spare boilers. It was thus the universal practice for boilers taken off the frames for repairs to be returned to the same locomotive for further service. As the time taken to repair boilers, about fifty days, was much longer than was needed for rectification to the frames, wheels and other principal parts, it was this which controlled the overall time that locomotives were out of service for repairs. The repair activities as a whole were, however, well organised. They were based on the principle, introduced by Sir Cecil Paget when Works Manager, of fixing times for all operations. Immediately after stripping, frames were taken out of the shop on their leading and trailing wheels to storage sidings, there to remain until brought back for repairs to be completed by the time the boiler was expected to be ready. Thus, available floor space was used to the best advantage, as the erecting pits were occupied only by locomotives on which repairs could continue to completion without interruption.

The Erecting Shop was notified seven days in advance of the date by which it was expected that repairs to each boiler would be completed. With this information available, the Erecting Shop, in their turn, arranged for the appropriate frames to be brought in for repairs and also informed the other Shops, in accordance with a definite schedule, of the dates by which wheels, axleboxes, motion and valve gear, etc. would be required for re-erection. The men in the Erecting Shop were divided into specialist gangs, each doing the same work on all the locomotives under repair. The men moved to the job, rather than, as in later years, the locomotives being moved to the men.

There were, for example, the motion gang, the axlebox and wheeling gang, and the valve setting specialists, with all of whom I worked. Once more I had the opportunity of working on my own to standard piecework prices. They were a good deal tighter than on the marking-off tables, and there was no time for rumination if any balance was to be earned on such jobs as setting slide bars and fitting up cross-heads and slide blocks to the right limits. The shop was reasonably well supplied with portable tools – but hand-grinders for trueing up axlebox guides had not then been introduced. These had to be restored square and parallel by filing – and filing a work-hardened surface about 18″ long by 8″ wide was no easy matter, and inclined to be monotonous! Axlebox bearings and big end brasses were bedded to their journals by hand scraping. Repaired axleboxes, after machining to sizes supplied by the Erecting Shop, were all tried up in their guides, before wheeling. The fit had to be sufficiently tight for the axleboxes to sustain their own weight when pushed up with a pinch bar to the top of the guides – not very scientific, but quite effective in the absence of any machining tolerances or limits of fit on the drawings. All this, of course, was altered in later years. And with the introduction of limit gauges for controlling machining operations to close tolerances, the need for subsequent hand fitting was substantially reduced. Manufacture and repair of locomotive components became, and is, high precision engineering.

The system in force at Derby produced twenty general repairs per week from sixty pits. But with locomotives waiting repairs, stripped frames waiting their boilers and engines in the Paint Shop also taken into account, there were usually from 250 to 300 locomotives, over fifteen per cent of the stock, on the Works at any time – and each locomotive was out of service for about three months. It was not until some years later that the financial advantages which could accrue from providing sufficient spares to ensure that a repaired boiler would always be available for replacement on a locomotive immediately the frames were ready, came to be realised. In this way, the time locomotives are out of service for repairs is greatly reduced. Thus, the availability of the locomotive stock for revenue earning service is increased, fewer locomotives are under repair at any time, and as a consequence fewer locomotives are needed for a given volume of traffic. It is less expensive to have spare boilers available for changing than to have locomotives out of service for repairs an hour longer than is absolutely unavoidable.

A memorandum dated November 1927 prepared for the Works Manager by James Rankin, who twenty years later followed me as Works Manager at Crewe, set out the factors to be taken into account in calculating the economic stock of spare boilers. It was shown that 200 boilers were needed, and, as they became available, operations in the Erecting Shop were reorganised on a progressive basis, with the locomotives being moved down the shop in three stages. The number of locomotives under repairs in the Erecting Shop was reduced from sixty to thirty-nine. In each of the three repair bays, thirteen locomotives were put down. After stripping, the frames no longer had to be sent out of the Shop to await their boilers, but were immediately placed on the first repair stage – the frame section. Five sets of frames were put down to be worked on; the next stage known as the boiler section carried four locomotives; and the final stage, known as the motion and wheeling section, also took four engines. Under this system four locomotives were moved on, and four moved off every three days. And as there were five frame pits, three locomotives were erected in nine days, and the fourth in twelve days. There was thus flexibility, and time was available without disrupting the working, for new cylinders to be fitted if necessary. The output was eight locomotives per week from the thirteen engines in each bay, or twenty-four in all. The final outcome of the new system was that the number of engines on the Works was reduced by seventy-five per cent to no more than about sixty-five, the time under repair came down to twenty days, and including locomotives under repairs at outstation Shops, the percentage of the stock out of service for Shop repairs was seldom more than five per cent.

The theoretical part of our training was undertaken on two mornings each week, supplemented by evening classes at Derby Technical College. The college was a rather seedy building in the centre of the town, very different from the present college. This is a magnificent building now adorning what used to be Markeaton Golf Course, at the opening of which thirty years later by the Chairman of the British Transport Commission I was destined to be an official guest.

The college ran courses especially for the Midland apprentices. They were I suppose, reasonably good, judged by contemporary standards before the National Certificate schemes, sponsored jointly by the professional Institutions and the Ministry of Education were established. But I was not impressed by the calibre of the teaching nor by the objectives at which the courses apparently aimed. It seemed to me that if I were to reach the goal I had set myself in the time which I judged to be available, namely to pass the Associate Membership examinations both of the Institution of Civil Engineers and the Institution of Mechanical Engineers before the end of my apprenticeship, the Technical College courses would have to be supplemented by a lot of reading on my own account in the evenings. It is true that courses of training which involved obtaining academic qualifications equivalent to, and indeed more useful than an external university degree, concurrently with practical experience in the Shops, did involve doing things the hard way. This, however, was the pattern followed by the majority of embryo engineers fifty years ago. Those who today serve a two-year graduate apprenticeship after obtaining a university degree, or better still, those who choose the $1 - 3 - 1$ course with a year in the Shops before and after university, can count themselves extremely fortunate in having more time at their disposal to develop wider interests and pursuits, without prejudice to their chosen career. Nevertheless, demanding of spare time though it is, I cannot too strongly urge those who have not the discipline of full-time academic courses to goad them on, to pass, or obtain exemption from, the essential Institution examinations as early in their careers as the regulations allow. Otherwise, competing demands on time and energy, almost certainly more agreeable than swotting for exams are bound to arise. And if this important step is too long delayed there is a very real risk that it will never be taken at all, as many young men have found to their cost when seeking appointments for which membership of a professional chartered Institution is an essential qualification.

Sir Henry Fowler took a close personal interest in the progress of his pupils and apprentices. It was his custom to summon us all, once a year, to a meeting in the Works Canteen at 8.00 a.m. on the chosen day, and to deliver what today would be described as a pep-talk, on the advantages of service in his Department, of which we were exhorted to take full advantage. The Chief Mechanical Engineer always made a deep impression on his audience, as much perhaps by the sense of surprise that Sir Henry himself was on the job so early in the day, as by what he had to say.

Regular reports were submitted on our work both in the Shops and at the Technical College on the basis of which one was sent annually to our parents, signed personally by Sir Henry. As a further test, all of us were required to sit an examination conducted by the C.M.E. Department each year for a prize given by the Midland Railway Directors. I came first in this examination three years running, which I mention only because, as a result Sir Henry promoted me in September, 1923 to be one of his pupils. This involved a further twelve months training until twenty-two years of age, and attendance at courses in metallurgy at Sheffield University.

In most large industrial organisations there are always a variety of interesting odd jobs cropping up, often urgent, though for which it is not always easy to find men from among the permanent staff. These jobs can provide excellent experience during the later months of training, and I was most fortunate in the number which came my way. I was told one morning by the Shop clerk to report to the Locomotive Drawing Office for some unspecified work. Herbert Chambers, the Chief Draughtsman to whom I reported, was elder brother of the Foreman who gave me such a good start in the Brass Foundry. He was a first rate locomotive man, who had spent all his time on the Midland. Work in the Drawing Office tended to fluctuate sharply, and this was one of those times when everyone was fully occupied. Would I mind helping a draughtsman engaged on a new design of Walschaert's valve gear for three 0-6-0 engines to be built for the Northern Counties Committee railway in Ireland?

All well-equipped locomotive drawing offices had a full size valve motion model on which the valve events from new or modified designs could be checked throughout the whole working range with greater precision than is possible from ellipses derived only from the drawings. I had two separate periods of some weeks setting-up and taking readings from the model, work which encouraged me to find out more about valve gear design by writing a paper on Walschaert's valve gear,* which was accepted for presentation at meetings of the Graduate Section of the Institution of Mechanical Engineers. Through the good offices of Sir Henry Fowler, the Chair at the London meeting was taken for me by Sir Vincent Raven, the last C.M.E. of the North Eastern Railway before amalgamation.

Back again to the Shops for a few months when I was sent off by the

* R. C. Bond 'The Walschaert Locomotive Valve Gear' *Institution of Mechanical Engineers*, 1923.

Works Manager to Stratford-on-Avon, of all unlikely places. One of the small railways absorbed into the Midland Division of the L.M.S. was the Stratford-on-Avon and Midland Junction Railway. This little line traversed some of the most unspoilt parts of the counties of Northampton and Warwick from junctions with the Midland and L. & N.W. at Ravenstone Wood & Blisworth to Broom Junction on the Midland line from Barnt Green to Aschurch. The records maintained of their locomotive stock, a varied assortment of 0-6-0s and one 2-4-0 — twenty two in all, were judged to be quite inadequate by Midland standards. In particular, no information was available regarding the makers and cast numbers of locomotive tyres. I was sent to gather this information by personal inspection of the markings stamped on every tyre in service. People were rather sensitive about tyres in those days. Fatigue flaws sometimes leading to tyres breaking in service were not uncommon. One of the Compounds, travelling at high speed on an express passenger train broke and shed a driving tyre. Nothing worse befell than the delay occasioned by obtaining a replacement locomotive. It was one of those incidents, not unfamiliar to railwaymen, which could have been, but by sheer good fortune, was just not a serious accident. All tyres from the particular cast were immediately withdrawn from service. But two, shown in the records, were apparently missing. Once again I was borrowed from the Erecting Shop to inspect all the Compounds at the Motive Power Depots, and either find the tyres or satisfy the Works Manager that they were no longer under a locomotive.

From 1921 to 1926, thirty-seven fatigue failures occurred on the Midland Division. A statistical analysis of all the 216 failures of locomotive tyres on the L.M.S. from 1921 to 1933 undertaken by the Research Department, established a clear relationship between fatigue failure and locomotive wheel arrangement. The basic assumption was that tyres are fatigued by impact forces imposed when passing over rail joints and crossings. On this hypothesis, the wheels of a locomotive that will suffer most are, firstly, the leading wheels, since they do not have the track 'laid down' for them by any preceding wheels, and secondly the driving wheels, because they have an unsprung mass nearly twice that of other coupled wheels of the same size. Hence for a given vertical acceleration set up at a rail joint or crossing, the impact load will be about twice that on other coupled wheels. It would therefore be expected that failures would occur most frequently on driving wheels that are also leading wheels; next on driving wheels that do not lead and leading coupled wheels that are not drivers. These expectations were borne out in practice. The complete freedom of bogie wheels from fatigue failures was attributed to their relatively small unsprung weight — $1\frac{1}{4}$ tons per pair, compared with 4 to 5 tons per pair for driving wheels — and to the much greater stiffness of bogie wheels resulting from the same section tyres and rims being used on bogie wheels as on the much larger diameter coupled wheels. This assessment was confirmed by the fact that failures are most frequent on the large driving wheels of express locomotives, but never occurred on the small leading and driving wheels of eight-coupled freight locomotives. Changes in design and workshop practice introduced over the years included elimination of set-screw and rivet fastenings which required holes to be drilled in the tyres, deep triangular section wheel rims, built-up instead of cast balance weights, and closer tolerances and finer finishes on wheel rims and tyre bores. These measures were completely effective. Tyre failures were virtually eliminated long before steam gave place to the newer forms of motive power.

These two jobs chasing tyres, took me out all over the Midland Division. Days and nights at the Running Sheds waiting for engines to come in off their workings gave me a wonderful opportunity to see at first hand something of what work with locomotives in service is really like.

Further experience on work controlled from the Drawing Office, this time by the Test and Experimental Section, came along in the shape of two series of tests in service, one with a train of passenger coaches fitted with roller bearings working on the Tilbury Section, and the other with one of the superheated Compounds, No. 1011 between Derby and Manchester. With the formation of the L.M.S. group an accomplished fact, the Lancashire & Yorkshire dynamometer car was now available. It was used for the first time on the Midland for both these tests. The usual L. & Y. crew brought the car down from Horwich to Manchester, Victoria, where it was handed over to us 'foreigners' from Derby who travelled with it through the night down to Shoeburyness.

Although scarcely so intensive as the steam service worked by the Great Eastern into Liverpool Street, the morning and evening peak service operated over the L.T. & S. section of the Midland between Southend and London stretched the available facilities to the limit. The trains, often thirteen coaches non-corridor stock weighing close on 350 tons, were worked by non-superheated outside cylinder *Class 3* 4-4-2 tanks of L.T. & S. design, with no more than 20 square feet of grate and 17,000 lbs tractive effort. They were excellent engines – far better in proportion to their size than the 4-6-4 tanks designed by Whitelegg during the last phase of the Tilbury's independent existence.

The object of the trials was to ascertain the reduction in coal burnt hauling the roller-bearing train compared with the normal consumption on trains with standard plain bearings. Two locomotives, Nos. 2177 and 2179 were used throughout the tests; my part therein was to ride on the footplate, observe the working of the locomotives and record their coal consumption. Two double trips between Shoeburyness and London, one in the early morning and one in the evening peak hours were worked each day for a fortnight. It was in the layover time after the up morning trips that I was first introduced to bacon grilled on the firing shovel held in the open firehole door – and very good it was.

The middle of each day after weighing off the coal remaining from the morning trip, and re-coaling for the evening turn was mine to do as I pleased. Some days I spent riding on locomotives, including the large 4-6-4 tanks, which being too heavy to run into Fenchurch Street, were used to and from Barking on the through trains over the District Line from Ealing Broadway. On other days, I explored as much as my legs and the local bus service permitted in the time available, of the lovely Essex coast and marshes of Foulness Island bordering the Maplin Sands.

Coal burnt hauling the test trains was roughly 50 lbs per mile. But so far from there being any saving with the roller-bearing train, there was an average increase of 3·69%. This result was so unexpected that a further test was run between St. Pancras and Leicester, this time with Compound No. 1034, specially fitted with a Westinghouse pump for working the air-braked Tilbury trains. The results were the same – there was no reduction in work done in hauling the roller-bearing train and coal consumption was greater. These trials certainly demonstrated the excellence, from the point of view of rolling resistance, of the standard white metalled pad lubricated carriage axlebox bearing. Roller bearings are of course, quite rightly always used today in new locomotives and rolling stock, but for quite other reasons.

This was a memorable fortnight, not least because it was the first time I had a footplate pass in my pocket. I made very good use of it; and I shall not forget the return journey to Derby, after a weekend at home, on the Sunday midnight train from St. Pancras. One of the conditions attaching to the issue of footplate passes is that they shall be used 'only when absolutely necessary for the proper performance of duty. . . .' On this occasion I interpreted my duty fairly widely, and found myself with a friendly crew on one of the *700 Class* 4-4-0s.

All seemed set for a good run, but half way through Belsize tunnel, five miles out, a gauge glass burst. The automatic shut-off valve did not work. The cab was filled with steam and scalding water. I judged I was in the way, and got out on the foot-framing round the outside of the cab, until, after what seemed a long time, the gauge cocks were closed with the help of the coal pick. The unfortunate fireman's hands were badly blistered – nevertheless my offer to fire for the rest of the trip was politely declined, and we duly arrived at Derby only a few minutes late.

The 3-cylinder Compounds were originally built as saturated engines working with a boiler pressure of 220 lbs per square inch, cylinders 19″ × 26″ and coupled wheels 7′ 0″ diameter. When later these engines were superheated, the boiler pressure was reduced to 190 lbs per square inch, with no alteration in dimensions. In this condition the engines were often unable to keep time on their regular jobs. Boiler pressure was therefore raised to 200 lbs per square inch. Trouble was still experienced on certain trains, notably on the heavy gradients over the Peak between Derby and Manchester. Calculations showed that to develop the same power and tractive effort as a saturated engine with a cut-off of 57 per cent in the high pressure cylinder equal to the seventh notch on the reversing gear, a superheated locomotive would require to work in the eleventh notch, giving a cut-off in the high pressure cylinder of 75 per cent. No wonder the superheated engines lost time. Clearly more power was required.

A series of comparative trials on express passenger trains between Derby and Manchester with three locomotives, Superheated Compound No. 1011, Saturated Compound No. 1017, and *Class 4* Superheated Simple No. 997 was therefore arranged. Two alternative ways of obtaining more power from the superheated compounds were tried. First, live steam was admitted by a booster valve under the driver's control, direct to the low pressure cylinders. The alternative, ultimately adopted as standard, was to reduce the lap of the H.P. valve from $1\frac{1}{16}''$ to $\frac{11}{16}''$, thus increasing the port opening and cut-off at any position of the reversing gear. In either case, power was increased by about 10 per cent, but whereas the use of live steam direct to the L.P. cylinders increased coal consumption quite significantly the reverse was found to be the case with the modified H.P. valve gear.

Indicator diagrams were taken from the H.P. and one of the L.P. cylinders of 1011. My part in these tests was to ride in a shelter fixed alongside the smokebox and assist with the indicating. The diagrams were taken by Frank Sutherland. He was one of the best judges of a locomotive I have ever known. He was a delightful man to work for, meticulous in all he did, sometimes even to the point of exasperation. His nephew, Graham Sutherland was, for a time, a contemporary of mine at Derby. He was not, I think, happy in the company of locomotives. The fame he has won as an artist is surely proof that he was right in not staying very long with us at Derby.

Working in an indicating shelter is certainly exciting. The heat from the smokebox is only partially dispelled by the violent draughts that swirl around the narrow space in which one works. There were many tunnels and sharp curves on the route over the Peak between Derby and Manchester. We were always glad to be out in the fresh air again after nearly two miles of Dove Holes tunnel, usually so full of smoke that the glow from the cab window was often obscured. Sparks bounced back off the tunnel roof and the noise was deafening. Riding over the front buffer beam, one soon came to know the rough spots in the road. There was a particularly bad lurch coming down the bank round the curve into Haddon Tunnel. Taking diagrams and changing cards is a tricky job at high speed. Fortunately for the quality of the diagrams we were more concerned to know what was happening in the cylinders when climbing the bank to Peak Forest, and most were taken around 40 miles per hour.

In his book *The Midland Compounds*,* O. S. Nock has given a detailed account of the results of these trials. Suffice it to say here that the modified H.P. valve gear was found to be the solution to the problem of obtaining the additional power required. Instructions were given for all locomotives to be modified accordingly when they came into Shops. It was thus all the more surprising that this alteration was not incorporated in the new engines, 1045 to 1064, built shortly afterwards. Instead, the old H.P. valve gear was retained, the cylinders were increased in diameter by $\frac{3}{4}''$, and the coupled wheels were reduced 3" in diameter to 6' 9". It was thought that these changes in dimensions would produce equally satisfactory results. In fact this was not the case. As the diameter of the high pressure piston valve and the size of the low pressure slide valves were not increased to correspond with the greater cylinder volume it was odd that anyone expected the excellent results from 1011 to be reproduced by the new locomotives. Moreover trouble was experienced with their steaming and there was a spate of bent coupling rods. It was not long before the cylinders of the new engines were linered to the old standard diameters and the H.P. valve gear modified. This indeed was one of those cases which demonstrate the folly of making significant changes in essential dimensions in a series of locomotives without first ascertaining their effects by trials in service.

Extremely welcome as these special jobs were, they did sometimes tend to interrupt preparation for the Institutions' examinations. Nevertheless this work had to go on, and I had been greatly helped in this by a change which I had made quite early in my time at Derby, from rather unsatisfactory 'digs' to the home of a solicitor practising in the town. George Eddowes lived in a large house, and his wife seemed to enjoy taking one or two paying guests. From a situation in which any sort of congenial social life was completely absent, I was introduced to a large circle of most agreeable friends. I owe much, not only to the lifelong friendship which the Eddowes family and mine have enjoyed but also to the encouragement which Evelyn Eddowes, acting in *loco parentis*, gave me in sticking to the work without which examinations just do not get passed, when other more attractive alternatives were available. To round off this part of my story, the Preliminary and Associate Membership examinations of both

* O. S. Nock 'The Midland Compounds' *David & Charles, Dawlish* and *MacDonald, London.*

Institutions, the Civils and Mechanicals, were passed in the sequence and by the dates I had planned. On the results of the Civils examination, I was awarded the Bayliss prize of the Institution.

CHAPTER THREE

Inspection at
Contractors' Works
[1924–28]

ALTHOUGH THERE WAS ABOUT twelve months of my pupillage still to run, I had, as events turned out, virtually come to the end of the normal run of practical work in the Shops. The number of new locomotives authorised by the L.M.S. Board during the years immediately following the formation of the company was beyond the capacity of the railway shops alone. In consequence, large orders were placed with private builders. Supervision of these contracts was a Derby Works responsibility delegated to the Production Office whence I was transferred to undertake the inspection of the new locomotives during construction at the various Contractors' Works.

Over the first five years during which orders were placed outside, 700 locomotives were built for the L.M.S. by private contractors. In addition 716 locomotives were built in the Company's Works. With the exception of ten 0-4-4 tanks of Caledonian origin, all were either Midland types, or in the case of the *Royal Scots* and *Garratts*, designed under the direct and detailed supervision of Herbert Chambers, Chief Locomotive Draughtsman at Derby. It would have been surprising had it been otherwise for the locomotives ordered in 1926 and subsequently, after Sir Henry had succeeded George Hughes as Chief Mechanical Engineer. But when the first series of orders was placed, Hughes of the L. & Y. Railway was still in charge at his headquarters in Horwich. On the basis of the twin principles that it is the responsibility of the Operating and Commercial Departments to specify the loads to be hauled and the timings to be observed, and of the Chief Mechanical Engineer to interpret those requirements in terms of locomotive design, and bearing in mind:

(i) that there was an obvious need for more powerful locomotives for the West Coast route express passenger services;

(ii) that both the L.N. & W. and the L. & Y. Railways had relatively large four-cylinder 4-6-0s in service – the *Claughtons* and the Horwich *Class 8s* respectively, backed up by a considerable number of *Prince of Wales* 4-6-0s; and

(iii) that the Midland had nothing larger than *Class 4* 4-4-0s and only fifty-five of them at that (forty-five three-cylinder Compounds and ten two-cylinder Simples),

it might have been expected that the orders placed in 1924 and 1925 would have been rather differently constituted.

But two factors working together proved decisive in settling the pattern of locomotive building on the L.M.S. during the early years. First, the Midland form of traffic operating organisation was immediately adopted throughout the new Company. In this, a Motive Power Department, separate from the Chief Mechanical Engineer and owing prime allegiance to the Operating Superintendent is responsible for locomotive running and day-to-day maintenance in the Motive Power Depots. Simultaneously, J. E. Anderson, previously Deputy C.M.E. of the Midland and Works Manager at Derby, was appointed Superintendent of Motive Power in the new organisation. He had been Chief Draughtsman before taking charge of the Works. He was a man of strong views, and undoubtedly it was he rather than Fowler himself, who dictated the locomotive design policy of the Midland Railway. The powerful influence which he continued to exert on locomotive design in his new appointment was naturally towards perpetuation of the Midland types he knew so well. Secondly, the results of three series of dynamometer car trials conducted by the C.M.E. department to assess the relative merits of the more important types of express passenger locomotives played right into the hands of the Operating and Motive Power Departments, dominated as they were at the time by Midland men.

The operating principles upon which the express passenger services of the two main trunk-route constituents of the amalgamated company were based differed considerably. On the L. & N.W. Railway heavy trains were the order of the day. While maximum loads to be taken without assistance over the various routes were laid down for each class of locomotive they were not always strictly observed. The drivers had been brought up in a tradition which demanded that they should take and keep time with whatever was hooked on behind them.

In L. & N.W. days double-heading was by no means uncommon but the engines were often thrashed along the road and coal consumption was heavy. By contrast the Midland express passenger timetable was based on a frequent service of comparatively light trains which, if heavier than the very moderate loads laid down for each class of engine in the Loading Tables were invariably double-headed.

Though the loads permitted to be hauled without assistance on the Midland, compared with the tonnage, *Claughtons, Princes* and *Georges* were expected to take, were sometimes the subject of derisive comment in North Western circles, nevertheless they were soundly based and were soon applied to the whole of the L.M.S locomotive stock. Whatever the form of motive power, it is clearly desirable that the loads to be hauled should be determined on sound scientific principles and on the results of tests in service. Though no longer of more than academic interest, it may be worth recalling the system of steam locomotive power classification originated by the Midland Railway, and applied with some refinements to the whole of the L.M.S. locomotive stock.

The method adopted used a curve deduced from experiments on the L. & Y. Railway giving mean effective pressure, expressed as a percentage of the boiler pressure for various piston speeds. The M.E.P. depends, of course, not only on the size of ports, steam pipes, etc. but also on the ability of the boiler to supply an adequate quantity of steam. It was therefore necessary after working out the tractive effort at the selected speeds in accordance with the above curve, to make sure that the boiler could supply sufficient steam. The speeds selected for this purpose were twenty-five miles per hour for freight engines and fifty m.p.h. for passenger locomotives.

The method of ascertaining the maximum tractive effort for which the boiler can provide steam was as follows: Assuming a maximum combustion rate of 130 lbs of coal per square foot of grate per hour, and an actual evaporation of 6·15 lbs of steam per lb of coal, the boiler will generate 800 lbs of steam per square foot of grate per hour. Assuming also steam consumption per horsepower-hour as 25 lbs and 20 lbs for saturated and superheated engines respectively, boiler power equates to 32 and 40 horsepower per square foot of grate.

The power of L.M.S. locomotives was therefore based on cylinder tractive effort and boiler capacity; the lower of the two ascertained figures being used for classification purposes. The original L.M.S. classification scale was as follows:

Class	Passenger T.E. in tons at 50 m.p.h.	Freight T.E. in tons at 25 m.p.h.
1	1·5—2·0	2·85—3·60
2	2·0—2·5	3·60—4·35
3	2·5—3·0	4·35—5·10
4	3·0—3·5	5·10—5·85
5	3·5—4·0	5·85—6·60
6	–	6·60—7·35

As specific performance improved over the years in conformity with the development of detailed design it became apparent that a mean effective pressure curve 20 per cent higher than that originally used corresponded more closely to the results from contemporary indicating and dynamometer car trials. The classification system was modified accordingly, and in the absence of anything better, was initially applied to all the locomotives inherited by British Railways at nationalisation. Nevertheless there were some anomalies particularly in respect of mixed-traffic locomotives, and in 1949 a new and more rational basis of classification was evolved in which free area through the tubes, as well as grate area was taken into account in assessing boiler capacity of passenger and mixed traffic locomotives.

Freight locomotives were assessed on the lower of two values: (i) Nominal tractive effort at 85 per cent boiler pressure, and (ii) Adhesion weight divided by 4·5 as representing the maximum drawbar pull sustainable at low speeds.

The immediate result of the adoption throughout the L.M.S. of the Midland system of power classification and train loading was a great increase in double-heading on the Western Division main line expresses. Although at this distance in time, with departmental reports and internal correspondence which would establish the facts no longer available for scrutiny, it seems probable that this was accepted as only a passing phase. There is little doubt that it was intended to re-organise the Western Division services on Midland principles. What is beyond any doubt is that the dynamometer car trials carried out between Leeds and Carlisle, and Preston and Carlisle in 1924 and 1925 to ascertain the coal, water and oil consumption and engine performance of Midland Compounds in comparison with *Claughtons Prince of Wales*, Midland *990*s and *Caledonian* 4-4-0s and 4-6-0s when hauling trains of 300 and 350 tons, established beyond question the economic superiority of the Compounds over all the other contenders even when hauling and keeping time with loads a good deal heavier than the normal permitted maxima. Therein seems to lie the justification for the large orders for Midland Compounds which was placed by the L.M.S. between 1924 and 1926.

An admirable account of all these tests is to be found in O. S. Nock's book on the Midland Compounds. I was fortunate in taking part in some of them, assisting with coal weighing and riding in the dynamometer car on a number of occasions. A spirit of intense, though friendly, rivalry persisted throughout. On every trip staff in the car not otherwise occupied and distinguished visitors alike, including George Hughes himself who joined us one night at Hellifield, crowded round the instrument table watching the traces of drawbar pull, speed, and power development while climbing to Blea Moor or Aisgill. I have many memories of these trials over one of the hardest main lines in the country. But none is more vivid than the firework display put up by the *Caledonian* 4-4-0 doing her best with 300 tons up to Blea Moor. Never before or since have I seen such a rain of incandescent coal from a locomotive chimney.

Until it became clear to them that the Western Division express passenger train services could not be re-organised on Midland principles, the Operating and Motive Power Departments were no doubt satisfied that, with the locomotives they already had, a substantial increase in the stock of Midland Compounds would meet their requirements for some time ahead. Hughes and Fowler, however, both seem to have had doubts. E. S. Cox* has told us of the schemes for large 4-6-2 express passenger and 2-8-2 freight locomotives which were developed both at Horwich and Derby during the first three years after amalgamation, and how they came to nothing.

First, in 1923 and 1924 proposals were prepared at Horwich for four-cylinder simple 4-6-2 and 2-8-2 locomotives. In due course, both were re-schemed as three-cylinder engines, allegedly at Anderson's instigation. Quite independently, Derby had done some preliminary design work on a three-cylinder Compound 4-6-0. Immediately after his appointment as Chief Mechanical Engineer, Sir Henry stopped all work on the three-cylinder proposals at Horwich, and had them re-started as four-cylinder Compounds. By this time, early in 1926, the Operating and Motive Power people themselves became convinced of the need for larger locomotives. But Anderson did not like what the C.M.E. intended to build to meet the traffic requirements. There followed the series of events, less incredible today than they seemed at the time, which led to the cancellation of orders for four-cylinder Compound 4-6-2s, after work had actually started in the Shops, and to the design and construction of the *Royal Scots*. A *Castle* class locomotive loaned from the Great Western had proved beyond doubt the ability of a well designed 4-6-0 to do all that was needed on the L.M.S. at that time. Here indeed was apparently a case of a Chief Mechanical Engineer allowing his responsibility to be usurped. It was not until Sir William Stanier came to the L.M.S. from Swindon in 1932 that the un-questionable right of the C.M.E. to decide how the requirements of the Traffic Departments should be met in terms of locomotive design was firmly re-asserted at Euston. It is, of course, quite beside the point that Herbert Chambers and the North British Locomotive Company did what was required of them exceedingly well. The *Royal Scots* as originally built, and as later modified by Stanier, were magnificent engines.

For a variety of reasons, some stemming from the change in motive power from steam to alternative forms on the railways of the world, others from the urge of nations hitherto dependent upon Great Britain for their locomotives to be self-supporting, the private locomotive building industry in this country has been steadily declining in size and importance

---

* E. S. Cox 'Locomotive Panorama' Vol. 1, *Ian Allan, London.*

over many years. For some time the English Electric Company had been the only firm in Great Britain from whom a railway could obtain complete locomotives, steam, diesel or electric with everything pertaining to them designed and built within one organisation. In due course it was announced that the Vulcan Foundry Locomotive Works, part of the English Electric Group of Companies, would cease building locomotives. This indeed was a sad state of affairs, for it marked the virtual extinction of an industry of which this country was the world pioneer 150 years ago. It will, no doubt, be said that a major contributory factor to the decline of the industry has been the policy consistently followed by our railways, before and after nationalisation, of building their own locomotives, only resorting to contractors when demand outstripped capacity of their own shops. Be that as it may, I personally have never had any doubt, having been both sides of the hedge, that the railway's policy of building the bulk of their own locomotives is wholly correct from their point of view, notwithstanding that other countries have relied on contractors rather than their own Shops for new construction.

At the time of which I am writing, however, the early 1920s, the industry had enjoyed some years of relative prosperity overcoming the arrears in demand for new locomotives which had built up during the 1914–18 war. There were fifteen or so firms engaged in locomotive building. Some, such as the North British Locomotive Co., the Vulcan Foundry, Beyer-Peacock's of *Garratt* fame, and Robert Stephenson's were long established in the industry. Others, for example, Beardmore's and Armstrong-Whitworth's had turned to locomotive building when their traditional production of armaments was no longer required. The orders placed by the L.M.S. were distributed widely. In the interests of early delivery two or three firms were often engaged at the same time in building one type of locomotive. In all, over a period of four years, I was concerned with inspection at the Works of thirteen companies, ten of them concerned with locomotives and three with Sentinel steam railcars.

What better opportunity could there be for a young engineer to widen his knowledge and experience of workshop organisation and manufacturing methods, which differed quite significantly even between the two works of one company formed by amalgamation many years earlier.

Apart from the *Royal Scots* and *Garratts*, the detailed drawings for which were completed by the contractors, all the locomotives ordered by the L.M.S. were to existing designs for which all drawings were available for issue to the builders. In addition to the specifications for raw materials to which all purchases whether for use in the railways' own Shops or by contractors, had to conform, the contracts for new locomotives were governed by comprehensive specifications and codes of practice for particular parts and assemblies. These set out, in considerable detail, the tests to which boilers, cylinders and other parts had to conform. In some cases, the workshop processes to be followed were precisely laid down.

It might well be thought that little scope existed for an inspector to exercise his own judgment. But no specification can cover every contingency, and there was one thing conspicuously lacking. None of the drawings issued from Derby in those days had manufacturing tolerances shown upon them. Everything relating to limits and fits resided only in the heads and notebooks of Shop Foremen and Chargehands at Derby. Just as the best way to learn about some new subject is to write a paper about it, so, also, there was no better way of finding out what were the correct amounts of play in motion parts, for example, than to be asked by contractors' foremen (sometimes, I felt, with their tongues in their cheeks) what my requirements were in this matter. My invariable answer was 'Follow your standard practice'. A quick visit to the Shops at Derby on the following Saturday morning soon proved whether or not the railways' and the contractors' limits coincided sufficiently to allow my answer to stand.

Just as the real function of railway signals is to keep trains safely on the move, not to stop them, so the job of an inspector is to help, and not hinder, production. He must, of course, secure strict compliance with the specifications and drawings in all essential matters. But there are many borderline cases, and the essence of the job is to know what can be allowed to go, and what cannot. Due largely to the contractors' relative unconcern with performance and maintenance matters after successful completion of 1,000 miles in traffic, views sometimes differed. However, I remember only one case in which my decision was not immediately accepted. This concerned twelve connecting rods which, due to a mistake in the contractor's drawing office, were forged two inches too long. I pointed this out to the Works Manager, a very pig-headed man, who paid no attention. In time, of course, after some of the rods had been machined, the error was acknowledged. Without seeking my permission, which I should certainly have withheld, all the rods, machined or otherwise, were heated and jumped to the correct length. There was no furnace large enough to normalise them. And, therefore, I condemned the rods at once. The matter was referred to Derby and I was summoned to see Sir Henry. He heard, with some astonishment what I had to say, and immediately upheld my decision.

One other similar case, illustrating contractor's lack of understanding of what matters from the point of view of subsequent repairs, arose in regard to a boiler. I noticed, when asked to pass a completed frame for alignment prior to wheeling, that some rivets at one corner of the foundation ring and some boiler stays had been filed to give sufficient clearance for the boiler to be lowered into place. The Erecting Shop Foreman was not pleased when I insisted on having the boiler lifted to find out the cause of the trouble.

The Works Manager was, at first, even less pleased when, having found that the trouble was due to twist in the firebox throatplate, I would not allow matters to be rectified by tilting the boiler laterally in the frames with a tapered liner at the smokebox tubeplate and non-standard expansion angles. But he quickly accepted that with boilers changed from one engine to another at general repairs his solution to the problem was unacceptable. In any case, it was not a very difficult job to eliminate the fault at its source.

These were isolated instances, and in general the standard of workmanship, particularly at the larger, old established works, was very good. But no inspector, however vigilant could hope to see everything which might be called in question if the builders were minded otherwise. Thus it was essential to establish and maintain a relationship of mutual trust and understanding with the management, and men, with whom one was in daily contact at the various Works, particularly as the contractors' own inspection arrangements were not then very highly developed. This was not difficult, for without exception, the firms seemed very well disposed towards their customers' resident inspectors. Nevertheless I received much friendly help and advice from consulting engineers' inspectors – senior men of long experience, notably those employed by Rendel, Palmer & Tritton, and the Crown Agents for the Colonies.

As well as being an invaluable supplement to one's normal practical training, these years of inspection afforded many opportunities for meeting in the Works or at lunch in the Directors' dining room, men at the head of their profession on whom heavy responsibilities rested. I call to mind particularly, Sir Hugh Reid, head of the North British Locomotive Co. and his Chief Works Manager, one 'Tiny' Anderson – a giant of a man who seemed to me to permit his managers at Hyde Park and Queens Park Works too much freedom in their choice of production methods. Why, for example, until we required otherwise, did Queens Park screw boiler stays in from the inside firebox, while Hyde Park followed a diametrically opposite practice? Then there was Alec Campbell a man of great charm, and the Alcocks, father and son, whose firm, The Hunslet Engine Company, alone seems to have weathered the storm which has hit the private locomotive building industry. I recall Greg of Nasmyth Wilsons, a Crewe trained man, who averred that L. & N.W. locomotives were nothing but cast iron and lampblack! And his assistant at the time, Robert Arbuthnott, a life-long friend, later a Director of the North British Locomotive Co., who did so much for the British locomotive industry. Finally, though by no means least in the influence they had on my career were F. S. Whalley and A. J. Lane, Managing Director and Works Manager respectively of the Vulcan Foundry. Whalley had served his time at the Vulcan Works. After some years on the Indian State Railways he returned to manage his old Works with conspicuous success during very difficult years. He was a man of the highest integrity to whom, I owe a great deal. Lane was one of the best among the many Works Managers I have known.

The private locomotive builders had perforce to rely for the bulk of their output on orders placed by overseas railways. Thus there were nearly always foreign orders in progress alongside our own engines and I was able to study at close quarters the designs of a wide variety of broad and narrow gauge locomotives, so different in many of their details from those with which I was familiar. Few of the foreign railways for whom British firms built locomotives were constructed to our standard 4' 8½" gauge. Consequently special arrangements, which took the form of multigauge rollers built in to an erecting pit together with a short length of multi-gauge track, were provided to enable a sufficiently comprehensive test in steam to be carried out on completed locomotives. The usual test consisted of two to three hours running with the driving wheels on the rollers.

Thereafter, the coupling rods were fitted for a short run on the multi-gauge track into which was laid a minimum radius curve on which clearances and throwovers could be verified. The roller test was very convenient for making a thorough check of the motion and valve gear when running. By placing a hand on appropriate moving parts it was easy to feel any tendency to knock. It was important, however, never to put one's fingers where there wasn't room for them. I learnt this lesson the hard way long after I should have known better. My left thumb nail bears the marks to this day, of having been torn out by an outside valve spindle crosshead and guide of *Royal Scot* No. 6110 when under steam test on the rollers.

The contractors' Works were for the most part situated sufficiently near Derby for my work to be done by daily visits. But others were further afield. Stephenson's at Darlington, the North British and Beardmore's in Glasgow involved longer stays away from headquarters and opportunities for exploring new country. There were few evenings during the summer months when, with orders on any of the Scottish Works, I was not to be found on one of the railway's steamers sailing from Greenock and Gourock over the beautiful waters of the Clyde. There were other agreeable interludes in the normal weekly routine. An order for five 2-8-0 freight engines for the Somerset & Dorset Line placed with Robert Stephenson's coincided with the celebrations, organised by the London & North Eastern Railway, to commemorate the centenary of the opening of the Stockton & Darlington Railway. I was thus able to see a pageant of locomotive history and development which has never been surpassed. Locomotives, ancient and modern moved in steam slowly past stands filled by thousands of spectators on their way to exhibition in the Works yard at Faverdale. The Summer Meeting of The Institution of Mechanical Engineers, in the Presidential year of Sir Vincent Raven, was held in Newcastle at the same time – altogether a great railway occasion.

The contractors were responsible for arranging delivery of their locomotives, either in steam or dead, to specified Works or Motive Power Depots. As a general rule the engines were sent individually in steam to the nearest motive power shed. Most of the 400 freight shunting tank engines were, however, delivered dead in trains of four or five locomotives and whenever possible I rode with them. There were many night trips from Glasgow and Leeds which enabled me to ride on a varied selection of Caledonian, Midland and L. & N.W. freight engines. Over-warm axleboxes on the new locomotives, which had to be doctored with cylinder oil were not uncommon.

The longer journeys sometimes involved a night at one of the footplate men's barracks provided by the Companies at many of the larger running sheds. My recollection of these establishments is that they were comfortable, spotlessly clean and very well run. It was the normally accepted practice on long main line express duties for men to work a train out from their home station, spend the night away and work back next day. One hundred and twenty miles or therabouts was regarded as the basic day's work, with anything above this paid for at 15 miles per hour. As the trains involved were averaging anything up to 50 miles per hour or more, these were lucrative turns of duty with a good night in comfortable quarters at the end of the day. I sometimes wonder whether the agitation which arose in later years for the abolition of lodging turns was entirely to the liking of the men in the top mileage links.

As was to be expected, there were very few troubles with the engines allocated to the Midland Division to whom they were entirely familiar. Things did not always go so smoothly on the Western Division. 'Midlandisation', which was anathema to Western Division men was in full swing. To them Midland locomotives were both strange and unwelcome. It was rightly deemed important that I should keep closely in touch with the new engines during their first 1,000 miles running to ensure that any complaints of inferior workmanship should be followed up immediately. I recall a visit I paid to Crewe Works soon after the first batch of *Class 4* 0-6-0 engines arrived there from one of the contractors. I was received with the utmost courtesy by the Works Manager, F. A. Lemon, an out-and-out Crewe man. The only complaint, conveyed to me by James Denning, the Assistant Works Manager, was that the Contractors were making too good a job of non-essentials (he quoted in particular, polished buffer heads) compared with the practice at Crewe, who were building the same type of hated Midland engine at the time! If that was all that was wrong, clearly I had no cause to worry. I was indeed much more concerned, first that the *Compounds* and later the *Royal Scots* should live up to expectations.

The 'Scots' were quite the most important locomotives for the inspection of which I was responsible. Here were fifty locomotives more powerful than anything then running on the L.M.S. built to a new design straight off the drawing board, and intended to be the mainstay of the Western Division passenger services.

By the time the first of them was delivered on 14th July, 1927, the early antagonisms between Derby and Crewe had become less acute, and these engines were just what the operating people wanted. Apart from one or two isolated cases of seized motion due to an inadequate gap in the piston valve rings, causing the valves to bind in the liners, and some leakage from stays and tubes, these engines performed magnificently from the start. I rode on them whenever I could on my weekly journeys to and from Glasgow. They were essentially simple and straightforward locomotives. Most important of all their steaming was beyond reproach.

The Compounds, on the other hand were the first express engines of Midland design to be allocated to the Western Division. They did not take kindly to the rather heavy handed treatment which was the lot of *Claughtons, Princes* and *Georges*. The way in which the Compounds should be handled was clearly not understood by all the Western Division men with whom, quite unofficially, I rode. Compound working on these engines depended on the regulator being opened on to the second valve to shut off the auxiliary live steam supply to the low pressure cylinders. This was often not understood. Nor was the fact appreciated that every notch of the reversing gear on a Compound denotes a much greater overall ratio of expansion than on a simple expansion engine. I recall one journey very clearly. It was from Liverpool, Lime Street to Crewe with one stop at Runcorn. Starting away from Runcorn at the bottom of the two-mile bank at about 1 in 115 up to Sutton Weaver the driver opened the regulator on to the first valve only and immediately wound the reversing gear to notch 6, halfway to mid-gear. We had a full boiler and were blowing-off. Naturally, our progress was extremely slow. After a few hundred yards I persuaded the driver to push the regulator right across and drop down into full-gear. He was apprehensive as to what would happen to the water level in the boiler – but I was able to reassure him. With one injector on, the regulator wide open and in full gear we sailed up the bank in great style to the pleased astonishment of the driver. Here at least was one Western Division convert to the Midland Compounds. I fear, however, that when they first went to the Western Division the outstanding merits of the Compounds were not always appreciated. In Scotland, on the other hand, the men took to them at once, and they were soon keeping time with loads for which Midland men would undoubtedly have expected a pilot.

The amount of inspection to be covered naturally fluctuated quite widely over the four years. The intervals between one year's programme and the next was profitably filled for me by further locomotive testing. There were series of trials over the London, Manchester and Bristol roads with a *Class 3* 4-4-0 No. 777 fitted with two alternative types of exhaust injector, a *Class 2* No. 332 with different designs of super-heater elements, and two *Compounds,* No. 1099 with a modified design of brick arch, and 1059 fitted for oil burning, of which we had some experience during the 1921 coal strike. I rode with most of the Derby top-link men and came to know them well. Three of them, I remember specially. Wright Eyre Poole with his smartly trimmed beard, overalls always clean and his cap attached to a black cord of the kind used in other circles for monocles, was always a joy to ride with. On the 10.47 a.m. from Derby to St. Pancras, arriving 1.30 p.m. and out again at 2.25 there was no time for a meal after turning and fire-cleaning. It was Poole's invariable custom to eat a banana as soon as we had settled down after leaving St. Pancras to be followed by a pipe of his horrible herb tobacco, a fill of which I always had to smoke. Poole was a very good driver. Then there was Varney, a tall sardonic man, who called down terrible curses on any yard signalman who delayed his prompt return to the shed after the day's work. And Crabtree who used to run for miles sitting on the reversing screw facing across the cab and only occasionally glancing at the road ahead. Sad to say, he was killed some years later in a collision at Ashchurch, and I was not altogether surprised to read in the official report that he had run by all his signals at danger. It was with Crabtree I was riding on the oil-fuel tests with 1059 when we nearly came to grief. Between Loughborough and Barrow-on-Soar a bridge over the river was being renewed two roads at a time. We were approaching at normal express speed when, from my usual position behind the driver, I saw our road sharply slewed to the goods road span of the bridge. I shouted to Crabtree who slammed on the brake, and by sheer good fortune we got by with nothing worse than a severe lurch through the reverse curves. It was on 1099, diverted from our London job due to some minor mechanical defect, to the Bristol turn, that for the first time I fired an express passenger train. Though we kept time, I was nearly dead by the time we arrived back in Derby.

Above all, there was the diversion provided by the General Strike. I can offer no new thoughts or comments on the political and economic factors which led up to those unforgettable events in 1926. What may perhaps be of some interest is a short account of ten days on the footplate as a fireman under rather unusual circumstances.

There was never, during my time at Derby, any question of apprentices or pupils being asked or expected to join a Union. We were, rightly in my opinion, accepted without question as being 'company's men.' Thus no conflict of loyalty could arise. Reporting for duty as usual at the office, I was asked whether I would be willing to volunteer as a locomotive fireman. There was, of course, only one answer – most certainly – YES!

Two other apprentices and myself were forthwith taken by the Manager of the Carriage Works in his car to Leicester Motive Power Depot. There for the duration of the strike we lived in a sleeping car stabled in the shed yard, feeding in the Refreshment Room on No. 3 Platform. It was all splendid experience, but the hardest ten days I had ever spent. My mate was a regular driver who refused to go on strike. Our day started at 5.00 a.m., preparing our engine, a super-heated *Class 2* 4-4-0 for a tender first trip to Loughboro' to bring a load of mill girls into Leicester. After breakfast in the Refreshment Room we worked a passenger train to Bedford. A short visit to the shed for turning and fire-cleaning prepared us for the return trip home. It was, of course, a matter of honour that we should never be short of steam. The only untoward incident was once, when throwing a shovelful to the front of the firebox preparing for Sharnbrook Bank, the shovel slipped out of my hand into the fire. This had obviously happened before – my mate, with a broad grin told me to fetch the spare shovel which he had prudently secreted at the back of the tender. By the time we had dropped the fire, cleaned out the ashpan and smokebox and coaled for the next day's work it was usually well past midnight.

My roster was changed for the second week, during which I had a senior locomotive inspector, one Daniells, as my driver. The day started with a trip to Derby, then back to Kettering via Leicester, and finally home via Manton and Melton Mowbray. During this week I realised one of my ambitions, for I spent the whole time driving the super-heated *700* which was assigned to us. Apart from one day when I came into Melton Mowbray a little on the fast side, my judgment of the brake was, I was told, quite promising.

All in all, it was a grand ten days, both on the footplate and during the few off-duty hours. There was, I remember, a good deal of innocent fun and games with the Refreshment Room girls, who did a magnificent job in seeing that we were well fed. Only once did I leave railway premises during the strike. Towards the end of the time we were running short of soap and towels. Something had to be done about it. Requests to the District Locomotive Superintendent, a bachelor who was in the habit of doing his laundry in his office, produced no result. So Ross Campbell, a Derby apprentice who had come over to Leicester with me suggested that he and I should get out through the pickets and pay a visit to the drivers' lodging house, there to obtain what we needed. It was not known whether the lodging house keeper was on strike or not. It transpired that he certainly was, for the place was deserted. We climbed in through an open window, purloined a good supply of soap and towels and made good our escape back to the shed.

Financially, of course, the strike was not unprofitable. We were paid the rate for the job which, with overtime, came to a good deal more than my normal pay. I learnt much that was new to me about railway operating. The company took care to keep us informed of the general progress of events. So that those things, of so much significance at the time, shall not be wholly forgotten, I have included in an appendix a copy of a news bulletin issued by the L.M.S. management, and of one among many notices which were issued to the footplate crews. The receipt, too, of a letter and certificate from the Company, which is reproduced in Appendix C, was justifiably, I think, a matter for some satisfaction. After it was all over, arrears of sleep to be made up, and back to inspection!

CHAPTER FOUR

Three Years out of the
Railway Service

ON THE OFFICIAL TERMINATION of my time as a pupil, I was appointed to the fairly nondescript grade of temporary assistant works inspector. After two years, I was promoted to the permanent staff at a salary of £260, raised a year later to £300 per annum. Though inspection at contractors' works was coming to an end, the prospects for further interesting experience in the Works Managers Office at Derby were good. I was much concerned at the time with completing my qualifications for Corporate Membership of the Institution of Civil Engineers. This involved submitting some original designs and working drawings. As I saw no immediate likelihood of going into the Drawing Office, nor indeed had I any wish to leave the main stream of works activities, I sought and obtained Sir Henry Fowler's permission to do some design work in the Locomotive Drawing Office, outside normal working hours. Here, I met for the first time E. S. Cox, an immigrant from Horwich, with whom later on, before and after nationalisation, I was destined to work ever more closely as the years unfolded. He, and Edgar Larkin, also in the drawing office at the time, both played important parts in the development of locomotive design and workshop organisation respectively on British Railways.

I produced designs for a taper boiler to replace the standard G 9AS boilers carried by the Midland Compounds, and a set of coupling rods for an hypothetical four-cylinder 4-6-0. The drawings and supporting calculations, with Sir Henry's signature appended, sufficed to give me Section C of the 'Civils' examination. Out of hours also, I was much involved as Honorary Secretary of the Railway Engineering Club. Derby had been the headquarters of all engineering activities of the Midland Railway, and remained so for the Midland Division of the L.M.S. Railway. The Engineering Club strongly supported by the chief engineering officers held regular meetings for the presentation and discussion of technical papers. An associate section of the Club gave the keener apprentices excellent opportunities for getting themselves known and overcoming their natural diffidence in standing up and speaking at meetings attended by their elders and betters!

Altogether life on the railway at Derby was most satisfying and enjoyable. Away from the Works, living as I did with a family established in Derby for many years, there was much congenial social activity outside my immediate railway circles. Nevertheless I was impatient for faster progress. There were, it seemed to me, rather too many men in the C.M.E. Department just ahead of me too near my own age. Unless I made a move I saw myself waiting too long for dead men's shoes. I had recently received an offer of an appointment as an Assistant Works Manager at the Vulcan Foundry. I knew the Works and its people well. They built good locomotives and enjoyed a high reputation in the industry. I discussed the offer I had received with Sir Henry, as always most accessible to his young men. Having heard what he had to say, I decided, though with some misgivings, to accept the appointment and resign from the service of the L.M.S. Railway. In writing accordingly to Sir Henry I expressed the hope that 'in a few year's time it may perhaps be possible for me to return to the service with a considerably wider experience'. This hope I also expressed verbally to R. W. Reid, a Vice-President of the L.M.S. Executive, whom I knew personally quite independently of railway affairs. Robert W. Reid, a Scot, was a railway mechanical engineer by profession. Before his appointment to the Executive Committee of the L.M.S. he had been Carriage and Wagon Superintendent of the Midland Railway. He was an engineer of great ability and a brilliant administrator. But for his untimely death at a very early age he would probably have exercised a dominating influence on railway affairs nationally right up to and indeed beyond, the time of nationalisation in 1948.

Whether at a time when it was almost unheard of for anyone, once having left the railway service, to be re-engaged, it was even remotely reasonable to hope that I could return later, is certainly open to doubt. That my hope was in fact realised three years later may support the conclusion that the risk I was taking was justified. Unless, when young, one is prepared to take risks and stake everything on one's hopes, backed by self-confidence, nothing very much is likely to be achieved. But there is a world of difference between a calculated risk, and one that is quite incalculable. The risk, I took in leaving the L.M.S. in 1928 fell into the second category, and as I came to realise later, I had not thought out sufficiently carefully the possible consequences of the step I had decided to take. That, as things turned out, I gained from the move I made, there is no doubt. But it might well have been otherwise. Had I not been able to return to the railway I should never have experienced the full measure of satisfaction and happiness which a lifetime in railway mechanical engineering has bestowed upon me.

Many years later, as chairman of a selection committee set up to interview candidates for one of the railway's University scholarships, or a place in the graduate training schemes, I was rather dismayed by the small proportion of those applying who clearly wished to follow their career in mechanical engineering on the railway, to the exclusion of all else. Most were concerned only to obtain what they knew to be a first class course of training. Thereafter, it seemed, they would be equally content in following their chosen profession in almost any one of the many varied fields embraced within mechanical engineering. There were, however, some exceptions – potential dedicated railwaymen. To such young men fortunate enough to find themselves where they want to be, with both feet firmly on the ladder I would say 'Count your blessings, and think twice before risking sacrifice of the long-term objective for the sake of a possibly illusory short-term gain'.

One more round of visits to contractors' works where orders for the L.M.S. were still in progress, ended my first eight years of railway service. As it was going to be some time before I should again have a footplate pass in my pocket, I fixed up a final trip on the *Royal Scot* from Carlisle to London. The *Royal Scot* locomotives on which I had spent so many strenuous months in Glasgow, and which I felt to be peculiarly my own, were limited to 420 tons on the 300 mile non-stop run to Euston. With anything above this on the up journey, a pilot had to be taken to Shap. On the day I travelled we had a heavy train, and as pilot, a Lancashire and Yorkshire *Class 8* 4-6-0, on which I rode the thirty-one miles to the summit. The two engines made light of the job, but the assisting engine did not, I fear, contribute a great deal to the proceedings. She was not steaming and when she hooked off at Shap the water was nearly out of sight in the bottom of the glass. I climbed up on to the *Scot's* footplate with considerable relief, and off we went non-stop to Euston. It was a thoroughly comfortable journey with good coal and plenty of steam, though the engine twice exhibited the bad riding habits for which the *Scots* acquired a reputation in their early years. Coming round the curve to Winwick Junction, where I glanced with mixed feelings at the Vulcan Works, we developed a series of heavy rolls, and south of Kilsby tunnel on straight track, I had my first experience of quite severe hunting. Coal consumption of the *Scots* was commendably light. But firing 31 square feet of grate over 300 miles of fast running is hard work by any standards, and I well remember the forthright expression of relief as the fireman finally threw his shovel into the nearly empty tender as we came over the top at Tring, a few minutes before time on a sunny afternoon in April.

The Vulcan Foundry, which I joined on 1st May, 1928 as an assistant works manager, was founded in 1830 by a Mr. Charles Tayleur of Liverpool. The firm described themselves as 'Manufacturers of all kinds of steam engines, sugar mills, boilers, &c. &c.' Robert Stephenson was a partner before his appointment as Engineer-in-Chief of the London and

Birmingham Railway. Sir Daniel Gooch and W. M. Kirtley, who later became Locomotive Superintendents of the Great Western and Midland Railways respectively were for some time employed at the Vulcan Works. Sir Daniel's younger brother, W. F. Gooch, came from the South Devon Railway to manage the firm in 1864 and stayed nearly thirty years. He was followed in the appointment by Sir William Collingwood, home from the Indian Railways, who presided over the firm's activities from 1892 for the next thirty years.

Growth of the works from small beginnings was steady and continuous. When I became a member of the staff, the firm employed about 2,500 men and had capacity for building 250 locomotives and 100 spare boilers per annum. Over the many years that I have known the company there seldom seems to have been a time when new shops or offices, or extensions to existing facilities were not being built. During the last seventy years of its independent existence, many of them very difficult years for the locomotive industry, the company owed its success very largely to Sir William Collingwood and members of his family. F. S. Whalley a son-in-law, and Gerald Collingwood, Sir William's youngest son, both of whom served their time at Newton-le-Willows rejoined the firm after some years of service on Indian railways; and both successively held the appointment of Managing Director. Though it was a public company, the Vulcan Foundry was in many ways very much a family concern. During the years when I was most closely in touch with the firm, the Works Secretary was a Collingwood cousin – Arthur Collingwood Lermit, a cheerful character and a good friend, who served the company well.

The works management organisation was simple and entirely straightforward as befitted an establishment of medium size, confined to manufacturing a simple product with which everyone concerned was entirely familiar. Up to the time of which I am writing the works had built nothing but conventional steam locomotives, which, though they naturally varied in their details, were essentially the same in regard to the manufacturing processes involved. Day-to-day control of the Works, was a very personal matter in the hands of the Works Manager himself.

Until my arrival there had been three assistant works managers, each of whom exercised general supervision of all that went on in a group of similar shops. W. E. King, a Swindon man, a cynic of few words, with a sardonic sense of humour, was the senior assistant. He supervised and coordinated the work of the foremen in charge of the boiler, erecting and tender shops. The two others, Darbyshire and Chard were responsible in a similar way for the machine shops and the forge, smithy and foundries respectively. In addition, Darbyshire had some responsibility for piecework prices on the machine tools. Chard, a Welshman from the Taff Vale Railway was in charge of the materials test room and daily analysed samples of the feed water for the works Lancashire boilers.

The techniques of modern scientific management were comprehended little, if at all; but in the circumstances of the time the Works was probably none the worse for that. There was no Production or Process Planning Office. The foremen and leading hands were their own progressmen. Inspection and quality control, functioning independently of the shop foremen, as they are known today, were conspicuous by their absence. As the customers all employed experienced resident inspectors the management no doubt considered it quite unnecessary for the firm to incur the cost of an inspection organisation of their own. Unfortunately I have no records to remind me what sort of control was exercised over workshop overhead expenses. In effect everything pertaining to the day-to-day management of the works was done personally by the Works Manager and his assistants with virtually no clerical or junior technical assistance. Even the Works Manager himself had no personal secretary.

That so small an organisation could and did produce the desired results is a reflection of the generally high level of competence of the foremen and the skill of the craftsmen. It demonstrates too, how very much easier it is to run a Works confined to new construction than one of the same size engaged both on new construction and repairs, with the latter predominating to the extent, say, of absorbing 80 per cent of the total man-hours expended.

The Works Manager, to whom as the fourth and junior member of his team I acted as personal assistant, was A. J. Lane. He had served his apprenticeship at Derby, and before coming to the Vulcan Foundry had been an inspector for the Crown Agents.

Apart from F. S. Whalley, the Managing Director, Lane was the dominating personality at the Vulcan Foundry. He was inclined to be dictatorial, and would brook no interference from any quarter in what he regarded as his preserves. He was prone to exaggeration and never at a loss. He was a flamboyant character addicted to *plus fours* in the Works on Saturday mornings. He was neither concerned nor, I think, very interested in the problems of locomotive design, maintenance and operation, but as a production engineer he was first class. He would have been successful in managing any sort of manufacturing activity. Paper work was anathema to him – and he spent the minimum possible time in his office. By example, he taught me that the right place from which to manage a Works is in the Works itself in personal contact with men and machines on the shop floor – not sitting in an office chair. This was a lesson I never forgot. It was the foundation upon which I built my own activities as a Works Manager later on. Two other valuable lessons Lane taught me. First, that it is usually better to ask people to do what you want them to do – not to tell them. And, secondly, that so long as you get done what you want to get done, it matters little who receives the credit.

Whereas at Derby a visit from the Works Manager to the Shop in which one was working seemed to be rather an infrequent event, quite the reverse was the case at the Vulcan Foundry. Lane paid at least one visit to every Shop each day. The routine scarcely ever varied. Working hours for the works managerial staff were the same as for the men. Lane always arrived in his office shortly after 8.00 a.m. He was soon down in the Shops for the morning tour. The assistant managers, already out in the works met Lane in succession and accompanied him through the Shops for which they were respectively responsible. Every chief foreman was, of course, on parade. Progress was reviewed, problems were discussed and decisions given on the spot. Commendation or criticism were dispensed as necessary. It was all very simple and effective. After the tour we, the assistant managers, returned one by one, to the office which we shared, there to enjoy a brief respite and a smoke. The civilising influence of a cup of coffee in the middle of the morning was unheard of in those days.

As personal assistant to Lane there were few activities in the Works with which I was not concerned in one way or another. It was invaluable experience; though inevitably somewhat limited in scope, it would not have satisfied me for long. I missed the daily contacts with design, maintenance and operation of locomotives which are part and parcel of life in the Chief Mechanical Engineer's department of a railway company. As some compensation I spent many evenings in my rooms working out what possibilities existed for developing more powerful three-cylinder Compounds within the British loading gauge, and scheming out a large three-cylinder 4-6-2 – indications of where my true preferences lay. I certainly could never have summoned up any sustained interest in the purely commercial considerations involved in scrambling for orders, which loom so large in the activities of purely manufacturing concerns. I was, however, soon to be immersed once again in a predominantly railway environment supervising on behalf of the firm, erection of the mechanical parts of electric locomotives for the Great Indian Peninsula Railway in Bombay.

Thirty-five miles inland from Bombay at Kalyan Junction the Great Indian Peninsula Railway divided into its two main routes serving the interior of India. One, the trunk line to Agra and Delhi continues in a north-easterly direction, the other turns south-east to Poona. Both have to surmount the coastal barrier of the Ghat Mountains involving very heavy gradients and severe curves. On the mountain section of the route to Poona, over the Bhore Ghat, the line rises 2,100 feet from sea level in only sixteen miles between Karjat and Khandala. Owing to the gradients involved and the rugged nature of the country, the line was originally built with a reversing station halfway to the summit. Operation of trains was both difficult and expensive – indeed it would be difficult to imagine a route over which the particular merits of electric traction could be exploited to greater advantage. Train loads with steam locomotives were severely limited both up and down the Ghat section, and banking was of course essential.

The suburban passenger services from Bombay to Thana and Kalyan had for some time been electrified at 1500 volts direct current and operated by multiple-unit trains. Contracts for the main line sections of the complete electrification scheme to Igatpuri, on the line to Delhi, and to Poona, involving conversion of nearly 300 single track miles and construction of a power station at Kalyan and new maintenance depots, were let in 1927.

An important part of the scheme was the elimination of the reversing station on the Bhore Ghat. This involved a re-alignment two miles long, with a ruling gradient of 1 in 37, and three tunnels through solid rock of a total length of 1,500 yards. Train loads were able to be substantially increased and the capacity of the line was doubled.

Forty-one freight and three passenger locomotives were initially ordered for the main line services. It was with the former that I was directly and intimately concerned for a period of fifteen months. The main contractor for these freight engines was Metropolitan Vickers of Trafford Park. The mechanical parts of these locomotives were designed, and ten sets were built, by the Swiss Locomotive and Machine Works of Winterthur, Switzerland. The remaining thirty-one locomotives were ordered from the Vulcan Foundry, to the Swiss designs.

The specification and conditions of contract governing the supply of these locomotives were drawn up by the Consulting Engineers to the railway, Messrs. Merz and Partners of London, who were unrivalled in the field of electric traction schemes. The main contractors were, of course, required to accept responsibility for the satisfactory performance of their locomotives and to make good any shortcomings arising either from design or workmanship during the first twelve months in service. Although the Vulcan Foundry were in no way responsible for the design of these locomotives, either generally or in detail, they were apparently regarded as having assumed, in respect of the mechanical parts, all the obligations which the main contractor had perforce to accept under the conditions of contract. It therefore followed, at any rate in the minds of some of the parties concerned, that any components which failed to perform satisfactorily due to faulty or inadequate design would fall to be replaced at the expense of the builders of the mechanical parts. This was, no doubt, reasonable enough in the case of the sub-contractor who had designed the locomotives. But to the Vulcan Foundry who were only required to work strictly to drawings and specifications issued to them, this view of the matter seemed very much a case of 'Heads I win – tails you lose' – and was naturally unacceptable. Certain components, as I shall recount later, did give such trouble in service that they had to be modified or entirely replaced. Inevitably, there were acute differences of opinion as to whom should bear the costs incurred, which gave rise to an action in the High Court before a settlement in favour of the Vulcan Foundry was reached.

The freight locomotives were designed to haul trains of 1,000 to 1,600 tons single handed over the level coastal section at a speed of 35 miles per hour. A second locomotive was provided for banking up the mountain grades at 18 miles per hour, and for assisting with regenerative braking coming down. They were also intended for banking passenger trains up the Ghats at 35 miles per hour. The locomotives, of double bogie design with a 0-6-0 + 0-6-0 wheel arrangement, had a nominal tractive effort of 68,800 lbs and weighed 123 tons. They closely resembled some engines well tried in service on the Swiss Federal Railways, and their details conformed to European rather than British practice.

Each bogie carried two 650 h.p. motors, mounted rigidly in the frames and driving through pinions on to a geared jackshaft and thence through connecting and coupling rods. An important part in transmitting the heavy alternating loads was played by the jackshaft bearings. These were steel castings in halves, lined throughout with a tin base white metal, and jointed, in the worst possible place, on the horizontal centre line. They were the source of much trouble in service.

With the object of reducing flange forces at the leading wheels when rounding curves, diagonally opposite inner corners of the two bogies were connected through bell cranks by tubular links and a cylinder containing volute springs. When the load in the linkage, due to pivoting on curves, overcame the heavy initial compression of the springs the bogies were assisted in taking up different angular positions relative to the body, without exerting excessive lateral pressure on the rails. That, at least, was the idea, but this mechanism gave a good deal of trouble in service, and on some locomotives from which it was removed mileage between tyre turning was not adversely affected.

The drawgear and buffers were mounted on the bogies and thus all traction loads were passed via the pivot centres through the body underframe structure.

The body as a whole involved a form of lightweight construction with which all locomotive builders are thoroughly familiar today, but which was quite new to the Vulcan Foundry when these locomotives were built. As might be expected, the workmanship and finish of the first few bodies were not entirely beyond reproach. This was particularly unfortunate as it gave rise to a good deal of adverse criticism from the main contractors and Consulting Engineers when the locomotives arrived in India. Comparisons, unfavourable to our locomotives, were inevitably made with those supplied by the Swiss Locomotive Works who had been building electric locomotives to their own designs for many years.

Until certain enterprising shipping companies, notably Belships and the Clan Line, built and equipped some of their ships with large derricks of sufficient capacity to lift complete locomotives on board from the dockside, it was necessary for steam locomotives for export to be dismantled after test for shipment. Engine and tender frames were unwheeled, boilers lifted and cabs removed, all for transport as separate consignments. Subsequent re-erection was undertaken entirely by overseas railways in their own Shops. The electric locomotives for the G.I.P. Railway were, however, required to be re-erected in India by the contractors, who were also responsible for 300 miles trial running before submitting the engines for inspection and acceptance for service, by the Consulting Engineers, on behalf of the railway company. A bay in the erecting shop of the G.I.P. Works at Parel, a suburb of Bombay, was allocated to the contractors, who were responsible for recruiting locally such artisan staff as they needed. These men were employed and paid, not by the railway company, but by the contractors themselves. Metropolitan-Vickers, who had undertaken similar work in South Africa and were familiar with all that was needed, established a complete shop and administrative organisation at Parel under an erection superintendent sent out from home. He was assisted by a team of young engineers and skilled fitters and electricians under whose direct supervision the locally recruited Indian men worked.

Whether because they were not fully informed of all that would be expected of them in re-erecting and handing over their locomotives for service, or because they were relying on more assistance from the main contractors than could reasonably be expected, the Vulcan Foundry only sent out one man with the first locomotive. He was Joe Roberts, a chargehand erector, and a most competent and reliable man. He had much experience of delivering locomotives to the home railways and keeping an eye on them for the first 1,000 miles in traffic during which the builders were responsible for rectifying any minor defects which might arise.

I had a very high regard for Joe; I knew him well, as he had delivered to Derby many of the locomotives for the inspection of which I had been responsible at Newton-le-Willows. He was, however, completely out of his depth in attempting to tackle, virtually single-handed, the technical and administrative problems awaiting him in Bombay.

Apart altogether from the main work of organising and managing the re-erection of the mechanical parts, in step with the installation of someone else's electrical equipment – a full-time job in itself, much time had necessarily to be spent out of the Shop, some miles away at the Docks supervising unloading and arranging transport of locomotives by rail to Parel on well-trucks, which were seldom available when wanted! Add to all this, supervision of trial running and preparation of locomotives for final inspection by the consulting engineers, and it will be appreciated what an impossible burden it was for one man alone to undertake in a foreign country, a horrible climate and with native labour no more than about 25 per cent efficient judged by British standards.

Before many weeks had elapsed the inevitable happened. Re-erection was taking far too long; and complaints were made that we were holding up the main contractors in their electrical work and causing serious delays in handing engines over for service. Clearly, something had to be done.

I was sent for by the Managing Director. He explained the situation and asked me to go out to India immediately, find out what was really wrong, put things right, and re-establish cordial relationships all round. It was, I was told, unlikely that I should need to be in India for more than two or three weeks – in fact I was there for fifteen months! Naturally I accepted without a moment's hesitation. I felt flattered by being asked to undertake what was clearly going to be a difficult job, in which diplomacy was likely to be more important than engineering. I had never been abroad before; as an unattached bachelor I had no ties or family responsibilities, and here was an opportunity of seeing something of the world under the best possible circumstances – an assignment of limited duration with one's job firmly based at home.

The next few days were spent obtaining tropical kit including, in my ignorance, a large topi of quite the wrong sort worn, as I was soon to find out, only by Anglo-Indians in remote up-country districts. Within a couple of days of my arrival in India I was wearing the regulation style of 'Bombay bowler!' I sailed from Birkenhead one evening early in January 1929 in the Anchor Line's *S.S. Britannia*, of about 8,000 tons. She was a new and very comfortable ship, typical of passenger liners, which also carried mixed cargo, on the Indian run. Two of our locomotives were stowed away down below. The main propulsion machinery of the *Britannia* was of special interest as a Bauer-Wach exhaust turbine coupled by an hydraulic coupling to the triple expansion engine could be brought into operation to extract a little more energy from the expanded steam on its way to the condenser. I was asked to find out as much as possible about the hydraulic coupling and its mechanism, in view of possible future application of the principle to diesel locomotives, in which the firm were then beginning to take a keen interest.

The voyage to Bombay was wholly enjoyable. Three weeks of enforced idleness at sea in glorious weather, apart from a couple of days crossing the Bay and one day hove-to in a storm south of Sicily, I found very much to my liking. There was a full passenger list, with many attractive and care-free young ladies, known, as I was to learn later, as the 'fishing fleet', who came out to India each year for cold weather visits to relatives and friends. My cabin companion, going out for the first time to make a career in commerce in the East, and I successfully staked a claim on the two prettiest girls on board and enjoyed their company throughout the voyage. These casual shipboard friendships are, I am sure, much to be encouraged! They can be as harmless as they are enjoyable. Both sides know, in spite of protestations to the contrary, that it is long odds against the separate ways which each must soon take ever again crossing. The *Britannia* called only at Port Said, where for the first time one enjoys, or not, as the case may be, the authentic and unforgettable smell of the East. Everyone went ashore, very early in the morning, to pay the traditional visit to Simon Arzt's world-famous store. Time was short and we were soon back on board for the leisurely passage down the Canal to Suez, the Egyptian State Railway skirting one bank, the desert and camels on the other. Then the sweltering heat of the Red Sea with flying fish for company, the Indian Ocean and finally, twenty-one days from home, alongside Ballard Pier hard by the Gateway of India. First impressions, though often mistaken, are always important. Mine of India were distinctly favourable as our friends insisted on us joining the lunch party arranged for them at the Royal Bombay Yacht Club, a British stronghold whose former glory has long departed. And so after the last farewells had been said, we went our various ways to meet whatever the next day held in store.

The state of affairs generally which I found on arrival at the G.I.P. Railway Works can best be summed up by reference to the first progress report which I sent home. Twenty locomotives had arrived in Bombay and were in various stages of progress.

Whereas Metropolitan-Vickers had built up their staff to 172 men, we had only one-third of that number. One locomotive only was by then in traffic. It had taken four months to erect, and was submitted for inspection twice before acceptance by the consulting engineers. The ten locomotives built in Switzerland were already in traffic. Experience was showing the need for some modifications, which of course had to be incorporated in our locomotives. The necessary work was done for us in the railway shops or other local engineering firms – all of which made for delays to the main job of completing engines for service. There had also been delays due to late delivery of electrical equipment, and it was not always easy fairly to allocate responsibility for final lateness of any particular locomotive. In daily contacts and discussions with the railway and consulting engineers, the Vulcan Foundry, with only one man on the spot, was already at a disadvantage, particularly as the consulting engineers would deal only with the main contractor's people. There were plenty of opportunities for passing the buck, and for 'the pot calling the kettle black'. The Vulcan Foundry's agents in Bombay had done their best to help Roberts in regard to pay and ration matters. But they were not staffed or equipped to do more than this. They were certainly in no position to lend him effective support in matters in which Roberts and Metropolitan-Vickers people did not see eye to eye.

Having weighed up the situation, it was clear to me that four things had to be done at once:

(i) Roberts had to be relieved of everything except supervision of actual erection in the Shops.

(ii) Our staff had to be substantially increased, separated entirely from Metropolitan-Vickers and paid and administered by us.

(iii) All grounds for complaint of our workmanship, justified or not, had to be eliminated as quickly as possible.

(iv) Cordial relations had to be established with the Railway Company and the Consulting Engineers.

I was able quickly to establish most friendly relations with the people who mattered on the railway. I received a warm welcome, both on and off the job, from the General Manager (known in Indian Railways by the odd title of 'Agent') and the Chief Mechanical Engineer, to both of whom I had letters of introduction. They saw to it that whatever assistance I needed at the Works would be forthcoming. Charles Cock, the Chief Electrical Engineer, who twenty years later was to become my opposite number as a Chief Officer in Robert Riddles' team at Marylebone, was equally helpful.

The Consulting Engineers' people, however, were by no means so agreeable to deal with. I was given fair warning of what to expect. Smooth progress of the job as a whole was not helped by the refusal of the Consulting Engineers to deal officially with anyone except the main contractors. Questions for decision on purely mechanical matters had to be submitted through Metropolitan-Vickers' Erection Superintendent. And even he, a tough and wily Welshman who knew the ropes well, often became exasperated by the intransigence of the Consulting Engineers' people in regard to quite trivial matters both mechanical and electrical. The Consulting Engineers' head man in Bombay was reasonable enough. But one of his assistants was particularly tiresome. When, with the best will in the world, we were not willing to accept his decisions and sought a ruling from the chief, a sensible compromise was reached in which the interests of the railway were always fully safeguarded.

The Consulting Engineers' inspectors had a difficult job to do; and true enough they had legitimate grounds for complaint of indifferent workmanship from time to time. My first encounter with one of them, Colin Inglis, a competent electrical engineer, but no great locomotive expert, was not exactly harmonious. To my intense annoyance he refused to pass a locomotive for service after successfully completing trials, on account of some trifling defect to do with pipe clips – and that at a time when life was quite difficult enough without it being made well nigh impossible by inspectors' foibles. However, we soon established mutual respect and a sensible *modus vivendi*. Colin Inglis and I recalled our first meeting together with some amusement and no hard feelings when, thirty years later, he joined British Railways as Chief of Research.

With our staff increased to nearly 100 men, and Roberts giving undivided attention to the work inside the Shops, the general state of affairs soon improved. We suffered occasionally from strikes of the railway shopmen, when it was deemed prudent to send our men home. Some of my staff were members of the Bombay Auxiliary Force who were mobilised from time to time to help quell riots in the mill areas of the city. But these were passing incidents of no great consequence. The erection work should have been quite straightforward, but was in fact seriously hampered by constant trouble with the brake piping on the bodies, and damage to axle journals and crank-pins. Although the pipe systems had been tested with compressed air at the Vulcan Works before the locomotives were prepared for shipment, we were faced with a lot of trouble due to leakages which either had not been made good at home or had developed since. Lap welded instead of solid drawn piping had been used which, combined with some bad workmanship, turned out to be distinctly false economy. Axle journals and crank-pins were always protected for shipment with a coating of black lacquer and a band of inch square wooden battens secured by steel strip. These proved quite ineffective against the damaging effect of humid air and rain. Many of the journals and pins were so badly pitted that they had to be skimmed to make them fit for service. Axleboxes naturally had to be re-bedded, which, with Indian fitters, was an expensive job.

As the bogies of the last fifteen engines were coming out wheeled and with the rods in position, I looked forward to being soon relieved of any further trouble due to damaged axles. How wrong I was! As the whole object of sending bogies out fully erected was to save time and money in India, they were regarded as being ready for service with nothing more than topping-up axlebox keeps and oil boxes. For a time all went well.

Ten locomotives with bogies shipped fully erected had completed trials without so much as a warm crank-pin; they had been in service for some weeks and mileage was accumulating nicely. Doubts which had been expressed in some quarters as to the wisdom of allowing the locomotives into service without first unwheeling the bogies for examination were now felt to be unjustified. They were, in fact, well founded. Before long two hot boxes developed on two successive days – and they had been really hot with all the metal out. The cause was not, as I had hoped, inattention to lubrication by the drivers or maintenance staff, but very rough journals. The outline of the axlebox brass oil groove and the shape of the underkeep oil pad were deeply etched into the surface of the journals. The other axles of these two locomotives were all pitted and rough. There was nothing for it but to unwheel for examination the bogies of all locomotives not yet in service.

I was also faced with a demand that all other bogies which had been shipped fully erected should be examined at Parel by my men, even though they had run many thousands of miles in service without any trouble. I was anxious to avoid this as normal erection would have been completely disrupted. Unfortunately some of the journals already examined were not only pitted but had been filed to remove superficial blemishes before shipment. This was, of course, quite inexcusable and put me in a most difficult position. As a railwayman with experience of inspection in contractors' works I knew the demand was not wholly unreasonable. But I also knew that progress with the overhead wiring was not up to schedule and that there were twenty-five engines available for only eight booked jobs. Stopping engines for examination that were running without any trouble would cause the railway no embarrassment at that time. By contrast this additional work, if carried out in my erecting bay at Parel would completely wreck our programme. Compromise proposals were accepted after a good deal of argument.

The arrival of the monsoon on 2nd June (earlier than usual – I was told 15th June was the standard date!) brought a crop of further troubles. No-one who has not experienced monsoon rains can have any idea of the ferocity of the downpour. Day after day almost without a break, a solid wall of water descends from the heavens. Railways and roads are flooded as a matter of course. Within a surprisingly short time the brown and arid countryside turns green. True, the rains brought some slight relief from the worst of the sticky heat, but they certainly found all the places where the bodies of our locomotives were not watertight. An epidemic of flashovers and other electrical troubles was the result and urgent remedial action had to be taken.

Nevertheless in spite of all the difficulties output was increased steadily to three locomotives per month, and erection time was cut from four months to ten weeks. The new administrative arrangements gave me proper control of expenditure; and cost per locomotive came down by 50 per cent. We worked nearly every weekend, Saturday and Sunday. There were no financial penalties by so doing – overtime and weekend working were paid for at ordinary rates. There was no difficulty in adjusting staff to short-term fluctuations in work – all men were engaged on the basis of 24 hours notice!

Looking further ahead to the time when, with erection still in progress, maintenance work at Kalyan would increase as more locomotives were handed over for service, I reported to the firm that an additional man should be sent out to India. A chargehand erector, familiar with the locomotives, Joe Hindley, came out to join the team. He was worth his weight in gold, the more so as, soon after his arrival, and to our great grief Roberts died in hospital after a serious operation. For some time I had been concerned by his indifferent health. Much against his will, I had to insist that he should go into hospital for treatment. By his death the firm lost a very loyal and conscientious servant, and I, a very good friend.

In spite of the initial delays, completion of locomotives had been consistently ahead of the overhead wiring programme. During their first few months in service, therefore, the locomotives had been confined to relatively short runs mainly over the easier stretch between Bombay and the foot of the Ghats. Apart from breakages of side bearer springs, fitted at the four corners of the body to give lateral stability, which were clearly not strong enough and had to be re-designed, there were no troubles of any real consequence either mechanical or electrical. There had been some cause for concern about jack-shaft bearings. One or two of them, opened up for routine examination, had shown signs of inadequate lubrication. But judgment had to be reserved until experience could be gained with full load trains, and regenerative braking over the severe gradients. Trouble did, in fact, soon become serious, after through running to Poona was introduced. Although in half-a-million miles running only one bearing actually ran hot, all those taken down for examination, both ours, and the Swiss were found to be well on the way to failure. Incipient fusion and cracking of the white metal, some of which was usually dragged up into the oil grooves, pointed unmistakably to ineffective lubrication. This was the more perplexing because bearings, alleged to be of identical design, were said to run trouble-free from one general repair to the next on locomotives working over the St. Gotthard route – which was certainly quite as hard a job as anything on the G.I.P. electrification. Various remedies were suggested and many trials undertaken. The composition of the white metal and grade of oil was changed. The running clearance in the bearings was increased and the shape of oil grooves altered – all the usual things! The problem was still unresolved by the time I arrived home from India. As the general design of the bearings might well become a crucial issue, and contractual responsibility for design was already a bone of contention, it was thought desirable that we should find out, by seeing for ourselves, whether the G.I.P. bearings were, or were not, identical with those said to be perfectly satisfactory in Switzerland. The opportunity presented by a journey to the Continent, to attend an exhibition of German locomotives staged for the Second World Power Conference, was taken for me to pay a visit to the Swiss Federal Railways. Arrangements were made by the Chief Mechanical Engineer for me to visit his Shops at Bellinzona near the Italian border, where the St. Gotthard locomotives were maintained. This suited me down to the ground, and I set out on the first of many subsequent journeys over that magnificent railway from Lucerne through the St. Gotthard tunnel. There were plenty of bearings for me to see. All were obviously giving impeccable service, but not one was identical with the Indian bearings. Their lubrication arrangements were totally different, and many were jointed top and bottom instead of horizontally along the line of maximum load. The G.I.P. bearings were lubricated by the rotation of an annular ring, dipping into a sump, which was supposed to carry oil to the top of the bearing whence it passed through to the bearing surfaces. Not one of the Swiss bearings had this annular ring. All of them, whether jointed horizontally or vertically, were lubricated by a spring supported pad bearing on the underside of the jackshaft, and taking oil from a large underkeep. Here, obviously, were the answers we had been seeking. An essential feature of design was at the root of the problem – my journey to Bellinzona had been well worth while.

I must return now to events in India. The main line electrification to Poona was officially opened on 5th November, 1929 by Sir Frederick Sykes, Governor of Bombay. The arrangements followed the familiar pattern for such occasions. A special train of the white coaches usually reserved for V.I.P.s in Government and railway circles, double-headed by two 4-6-0s, one of which was the G.I.P War Memorial engine *Hero* built by the Vulcan Foundry, conveyed a large number of guests from Bombay to Poona. After the usual speeches, we returned to Bombay hauled by the first of the 4-6-2 electric locomotives, No. 4000, built by the Swiss Locomotive Company and Metropolitan-Vickers. One of our freight locomotives was attached in rear to provide additional brake power descending the Ghats. Everything went very well – hospitality was in accordance with the best railway traditions – and a main line electrification which, at the time, was the most extensive in terms of route mileage of any in the British Empire was successfully inaugurated.

With all our freight locomotives now erected and in service, the centre of gravity of our activities shifted from the Works at Parel to the Running Maintenance Depot at Kalyan. With the jackshaft bearings remaining the only cause of some anxiety, and with the arguments as to who should pay for the design modifications we had been compelled to make to our locomotives, agreed by Metropolitan-Vickers' people and myself to be a matter for settlement by our respective chiefs at home, I felt able to make plans for my return to England. Before leaving, however, I was asked to find out as much as possible about the performance of the new standard steam locomotives which we had built.

Apart from a small number of metre gauge engines built in their own Shops by the Bombay, Baroda and Central India Railway, locomotives for India were designed and built by British firms to specifications drawn up by the consulting engineers to the Indian Government. They followed British practice in all essential features. As would be expected, inside cylinder 4-4-0s and 0-6-0s predominated on the broad gauge lines, supplemented by superheated 4-6-0s and 2-8-0s for the heavier duties. There were, of course, a varied selection of tank engines for suburban services and shunting. On the G.I.P. there were, in addition, a few Atlantics, and twenty very large four-cylinder superheated oil-fired 2-10-0s of 50,000 lbs tractive effort for freight services over the heavy grades.

In common with many other railways, those in India suffered severely from the effects of the Great War between 1914 and 1918. Renewals of capital equipment and maintenance fell seriously into arrears. There was an urgent need during the early 1920s, not only to make provision for growing traffics, but also to handle more efficiently the traffic that was already there to be carried. The need for locomotives more powerful than the standard types then existing was clearly recognised. At the same time it was urgently necessary to reduce the bill for locomotive fuel which, over a period of nine years to 1923 had, on the broad gauge systems, increased by 110 per cent for an increase in engine mileage of only 12 per cent.

One way (and the most obvious) of reducing fuel costs over a period of years would be to increase the proportion of second grade fuel burned, of which there were ample supplies available. The existing locomotives with their narrow fireboxes and relatively small grates would not have been able to produce sufficient steam at an economical rate of combustion with low grade coal. Thus to obtain the necessary boiler horse-power to haul heavier trains and burn second grade coal wide fireboxes and, as a consequence, 4-6-2 and 2-8-2 wheel arrangements were judged to be essential.

In 1924 the Indian Railway Board had appointed a Locomotive Standards Committee to standardise the several modifications introduced into existing types of locomotives, and to prepare diagrams and general specifications for new types required on Broad and Metre gauge systems. Some five years earlier the need for more powerful locomotives had led the Railway Board to agree to three of the Indian railways each ordering two *Pacifics* for trial. Four of these were designed and built by the Vulcan Foundry, and two were ordered from Baldwins in America. The Locomotive Standards Committee prepared diagrams and general specifications for eight new designs, five for the Broad gauge systems and three for the Metre gauge lines. The proposed Broad gauge locomotives comprised three types of 4-6-2s and two 2-8-2s for heavy freight services. In accordance with established practice the working drawings were to be prepared by the builders in collaboration with the Consulting Engineers. The preliminary designs of one of the *Pacifics*, the XB type, was based on information available in respect of the four experimental locomotives built by the Vulcan Foundry. They, therefore, were asked to prepare the designs for the new standard locomotives.

The new locomotives represented a complete break with previously existing standards. Nevertheless, the initial orders, which were in progress at the time I joined the firm, were for quite substantial numbers of engines. There was, apparently, no question of two or three prototypes being tried out on each of the railways requiring new locomotives before placing large orders. Indeed the new locomotives were built before any experience had been gained with the six experimental *Pacifics*. From what I could glean from discussions with Charles Finlayson, the Chief Draughtsman at the Vulcan, I gained the impression that the design of these locomotives suffered from lack of contact with the men who were going to run and maintain them – the Chief Mechanical Engineers of the railways concerned.

In general the designs conformed to the British pattern, but some features of typically American origin were introduced to India for the first time. Grease lubrication for axleboxes, motion and rods was a development for which a good case could undoubtedly be made. Arch tubes, too, were no doubt appropriate, although by no means essential in the new wide fireboxes. But coupled wheel springs arranged on top of the axleboxes seemed to accord ill with plate frames.

It is a matter of history that during their first ten years in service, these locomotives had a very chequered career. As originally built they were anything but satisfactory as vehicles on much of the Indian railways' permanent way. Derailments at speed when hauling express passenger trains gave rise to much anxiety, and there was conflict of opinion as to cause and remedy. The culmination came with the derailment of an XB Class 4-6-2 at Bihta on the East Indian Railway in which over 100 passengers were killed. This disastrous mishap gave rise to a public outcry, and was followed, first by a judicial enquiry, and later by the appointment of the *Pacific* Locomotive Committee under the chairmanship of Sir Alan Mount, the Chief Inspecting Officer of Railways in Great Britain. Sir William Stanier and Stewart Cox served on this Committee together with distinguished French and Indian railway engineers. Their report* is, to my mind, one of the best technical locomotive documents ever written. It is a complete textbook in itself covering an aspect of locomotive design which, to say the least, was somewhat obscure at the time. In its treatment of matters of organisation and the relationships which ought to exist between railways and their consulting engineers and contractors, the report is as valid today as ever it was when written in 1939.

While I was in Bombay some of the small XA type *Pacifics* arrived fully erected for the G.I.P. Railway, and some of the larger XC locomotives for

* Pacific Locomotive Committee Report, 1939 *Manager of Publications, Government of India, Delhi.*

the B.B. & C.I. Railway. Both railways wisely unwheeled their engines and opened up cylinders and valve chests for a general inspection before passing them into traffic. Quite a number of modifications, small individually but considerable in total, were made in the railways' shops before the engines were released. The lines of communication from the owning railway up through the Board and home to the builders via the consulting engineers were obviously not entirely effective. I rode on some trial trips with the XCs but at the moderate speeds we reached there was no sign of any hunting, about which I was soon to hear in conversation with the C.M.E. of the East Indian Railway. Trouble was also being experienced with broken main frames and cross-stays.

To find out how the new engines were behaving on the North Western Railway I went up to Lahore to visit the Headquarters and Mechanical Workshops. Before this I had made only one long railway journey in India, much of it on the footplate of a G.I.P. 4-4-2 to Gwalior to discuss with the State Railway people a proposal for some new locomotives. Two days and nights across the plains of India accompanied by a personal servant and one's own bedding roll prepared each night while the sahib goes off to the dining car, is an experience not easily forgotten. I planned my journey so that I was able to spend a short time in Agra to see the Taj Mahal. No doubt, like many others, I had heard such high praise lavished on this building that I felt certain to be disappointed in the reality. My scepticism was wholly misplaced. The Taj Mahal is quite wonderful. No words of mine can hope to convey the matchless beauty of this magnificent memorial and its setting.

My Managing Director was himself an old North Western of India man, and I was given a warm welcome by the railway community in Lahore. The Production Manager of the Moghalpura Locomotive Works, with whom I stayed, was an old friend, T. G. Creighton, who had served his time with me at Derby. The Works seemed to me to be better organised than Parel, but they were chronically short of spares and renewal boilers. As a result, repairs which could not otherwise possibly have been financially justified, had to be undertaken. So far as the new standard engines were concerned, it was early days and there was not a great deal to be learnt. The general consensus of opinion appeared to be that the capacity of the new engines was distinctly generous in relation to the loads to be hauled. The XE 2-8-2s particularly, could not be given trains appropriate to their power because of the low standard of maintenance of the wagon vacuum brakes and limited length of refuge sidings.

With the few remaining loose ends satisfactorily tied up, I sailed for Liverpool in S.S. *Tuscania* on 13th March, 1930. I saw for myself what I had so often been told was the finest view in India — Bombay Harbour from the stern of a homeward bound liner. I enjoyed the fifteen months I

spent in India, largely because I knew my stay was to be of limited duration. I take less kindly than most to unduly hot weather here at home or
anywhere else. But whereas here one may complain, knowing that cooler
days will not be long delayed, moaning about the heat in a tropical climate
is pointless and one quickly learns to live cheerfully in a constant state of
dripping perspiration. The job I had to do was mine alone to make or mar.
I had to make my own decisions – I was too far away to be able to 'Ask my
Dad!' – with due regard, not only to the effect which they would have on
other people's work on the ground, but also to safeguarding the firm's
financial interests at home. It was in every way first rate experience of inestimable value to a young man early in his career.

Away from the job life was most agreeable. My railway friends were
most hospitable. With the Visitors' Book at Government House duly
signed and two or three weekends spent, as custom decreed, dropping
cards on the right people, invitations were quickly forthcoming. After
some weeks in a hotel and a rather nasty boarding house, I was invited by
two friends, to share their bungalows during the temporary
absence of wives in England. One H. D. Ash was an engineer and a
very keen yachtsman. T. E. S. Bell, who in recent years has done so much
for the Benevolent Fund of the Institution of Mechanical Engineers, was a
permanent resident and I became the third in a very congenial 'bachelor'
establishment. The hub of European social life, when I was in Bombay in
the palmy days of the British Raj, was the Yacht Club, of which Ash was a
prominent member. He owned one of the local Seabird class of racing
dinghies and was a first rate helmsman. After a few probationary outings,
Ash invited me to crew regularly for him in the weekend sailing races. I
know of nothing which takes one's mind so completely off everything
except the job in hand than racing a small boat. At a time when I seemed to
be spending my days arguing with the main contractors or fighting the
consulting engineers' people, the Saturday races in Bombay Harbour,
followed by hot tea laced with whisky as the sun went down over the sea,
were a most welcome relaxation.

During the slightly cooler winter months after the monsoon, I was
drawn, not unwillingly, into the customary round of social activities –
dinner parties and dances, culminating in the brilliant function of the
Byculla Ball traditionally honoured by the presence of the Viceroy. Swim-
ming at Breach Kandy and Juhu Beach, tennis and golf at the Gymkhana
Club, but above all sailing most weekends kept me fit, apart from two
short attacks of dengie fever, throughout my stay in India. It was all very
pleasant while it lasted; but any slight leanings I might have had to a
career overseas and the life of an exile in a foreign country, were effectively
extinguished. Before leaving the L.M.S. to go the Vulcan Foundry I had
considered the immediate attractions of service on one of the overseas

railways which before the Wind of Change, recruited their officers from the United Kingdom. I did, in fact, decline an offer of an appointment as an assistant locomotive superintendent on the Sudan Government Railways; and after what I had found in India I was glad that I had done so. I could not help being impressed by the dominating topic of conversation among my friends in Bombay. It was always 'When do you go on leave?' This preoccupation with the next leave, understandable though it was, seemed unconsciously to develop, as a permanent feature, the same attitude of mind to the job which afflicts disgruntled men nearing retirement which impels them to mark off the days on their calendar. With changes, at relatively short intervals, in the occupancy of senior posts as a dominant part of life in the administration of a service run by Europeans in an overseas tropical country, it must be difficult to achieve continuity and efficiency in implementation of Board policy. A career in essentially alien surroundings, however much cushioned by incidental compensations would not have suited me.

Back at the Works, I was soon immersed once again in the daily routine of locomotive building. The post-war boom in new construction had come to an end, and new orders were hard to come by. Nevertheless there was no lack of interesting developments in hand, including the construction of a boiler for the Buenos Aires Pacific Railway built entirely from stainless steel. The well-known troubles arising from bad water were particularly acute on this line, but as one boiler only was built in stainless steel, this remedy was presumably not found to be economically justified. Certainly the problems encountered in building this boiler, notably in flanging the firebox plates and achieving steam tightness were formidable.

At this time too, diesel traction was beginning to appear over the horizon as a serious competitor to the conventional steam locomotive. No enterprising manufacturer, with an eye to the future, could afford to ignore this development. The choice of a suitable diesel engine for rail traction, from among a number of designs already well established in industrial applications, was probably not a very difficult matter. Uncertainty lay far more in the choice of a reliable means of transmitting the high powers necessary for main line railway service. Any form of transmission avoiding the use of electrical equipment, which they did not manufacture and with which they were unfamiliar, naturally had certain attractions for steam locomotive builders preparing for the diesel revolution. The Vulcan Foundry were contemplating building a main line diesel locomotive as a speculative venture.

I was therefore sent over to Berlin to see an exhibition of German Railways' rolling stock, included in which was a diesel locomotive with compressed air transmission. The locomotive, having a 4-6-4 wheel arrangement, a starting tractive effort of 26,500 lbs and weighing 122 tons, was powered by a 1300 h.p. MAN diesel engine driving a twin cylinder double acting single stage compressor. The compressed air was delivered to two outside cylinders of normal steam locomotive design. Without too much stretch of the imagination, this engine could be regarded as a conventional steam locomotive with the boiler replaced by the diesel engine and compressor.

The report which I made on this locomotive, and the trial trips in which I took part with the diesel hauling a dynamometer car and a 2-10-0 locomotive fitted with counter pressure braking equipment to maintain constant speed and power, certainly makes interesting reading today in the light of what has actually happened in the development of diesel traction over the last thirty years. I was not a very good prophet. I must have been unduly influenced by the immediate attractions of a locomotive which, getting rid of the boiler and all its troubles, nevertheless retained much that was familiar and well understood. I did draw attention to extreme congestion and lack of accessibility in the power unit compartment, and some other unsatisfactory design features, not all of which have even yet been wholly eliminated in modern diesel locomotives. I found that this locomotive was simple to handle. I expressed the opinion that it would be quite satisfactory from an operating point of view. This was probably true; but with three sets of cylinders, pistons and valves and the losses inherent in three stages of energy conversion, efficiency could not be very high. Maintenance costs could scarcely have been less than for equivalent steam power. However, it was a most interesting locomotive, the design of which I was able to discuss not only with Dr. Wagner, the Chief Mechanical Engineer of the Reichsbahn, but also with Professor Lomonossof, the great Russian Locomotive Engineer. The former was at pains to point out that this locomotive was the first of its kind – it was not a perfected design. Lomonossof was entirely non-committal on the prospects of compressed air transmission.

Remembering, too, the Kitson-Still locomotive which ran for a short time on the L.N.E.R., it is remarkable how much time and ingenuity were expended, during the early years of diesel traction, in attempts to develop alternatives to electric transmission. Diesel-electric locomotives may not be exactly simple pieces of equipment, but they and their counterparts with straightforward hydro-dynamic transmissions have succeeded by the logic of hard economics, albeit after a good deal of pain and grief, in deposing steam locomotives from the position of unchallenged supremacy in railway motive power which they had held for more than 100 years. This is something which the more exotic designs of diesel locomotives could never have done.

There were other locomotives of great contemporary interest included in the exhibition which was staged in a new running shed of unusual design. The pit roads were arranged longitudinally down the shed, but instead of the usual large end doors, locomotives entered and left the shed on two cross-traversers giving access to all the pits. Smoke extraction plant was installed, and a flexible hood for attachment to the locomotive chimney was provided over every engine position. Here indeed was proof that steam locomotive depots did not have to be the dark and dirty slums that ill-judged parsimony condemned so many of them to become. Far less money than was so lavishly expended a few years later on new diesel depots would have been a very sound investment at some of our larger steam sheds.

The locomotives which attracted most attention were two super-high pressure types and a freight engine equipped for burning pulverised brown lignite coal. The Germans arranged footplate trips for me on these engines to Magdeburg and back. One of the high pressure types was a Schmidt-Henschell three-cylinder Compound 4-6-0, the boiler of which generated steam at three different pressures – 1400 lbs per square inch in a closed circuit water tube firebox, 950 lbs per square inch for feeding to the inside high pressure cylinder, the exhaust from which mixed with steam at 250 lbs per square inch, generated in the boiler barrel passed to the two outside cylinders. The ill-fated locomotive *Fury* No. 6399 built for the L.M.S. by the North British Locomotive Co. was fitted with a boiler of the same design. During early trial running one of the high pressure water tubes burst, killing . the fireman and injuring the inspector in charge of the trials, my friend Frank Pepper who in earlier years had helped me on inspection, and with whom when work was slack at the N.B. Works, I had tramped many happy miles beside the Scottish Lochs. Neither the German locomotive nor *Fury* were able to produce the overall economy resulting from higher thermal efficiency which was the objective of the design. Indeed *Fury* never got the length of revenue earning service in her original form, but as 6170 *British Legion* re-built by Stainer, she became the forerunner of the taper boilered *Royal Scots,* one of the best locomotives ever to run on our railways.

During the three years that I had been with the Vulcan Foundry some important changes had taken place among the ranks of the Chief Officers of the L.M.S. Railway. Robert Reid, the engineering Vice-President of the Executive had died. In his place, the Board under the chairmanship of Lord Stamp appointed Sir Harold Hartley, an Oxford Don from Balliol and a Fellow of the Royal Society who, as a Brigadier-General, had been Director of Chemical Warfare during the Great War. Sir Harold, who in later years I came to know well, was a man of abounding energy, whose wisdom, experience, and an indomitable spirit which refused to be daunted by a crippling physical disability, enabled him to exert a powerful influence over affairs of national importance in science and the engineering profession right up to the time of his death at the advanced age of 94 years.

Alone among the four group companies, the L.M.S. inherited from their three principal constituents a mechanical engineering organisation in which the responsibilities for locomotives and carriages and wagons were discharged by two quite separate departments. This they retained for eight years. But on 1st January, 1931 the two departments were amalgamated, a course which subsequent experience has consistently proved to be eminently sensible. Ernest Lemon, the Carriage and Wagon Superintendent, a locomotive trained man, a brilliant organiser and a production engineer of outstanding capacity was appointed in charge of the combined department. He supplanted Sir Henry Fowler, who (to use Sir Harold Hartley's own phrase) 'moved over to research'.

Sir Henry Fowler, whose interests tended as much to the academic fields of metallurgy and engineering education as to locomotive design and operation was well qualified to assist Sir Harold in setting up the Scientific Research Department, a new venture so far as the L.M.S. was concerned. Nevertheless, I remember that I and some of my contemporaries at Derby who owed so much to Sir Henry (notably my close friend Martin Herbert who became the first head of the Research Department) convinced as we were that short of a seat on the Executive there was no appointment in the service of the L.M.S. of greater distinction than that of Chief Mechanical Engineer, were sorry that our old chief being then over 60 years of age did not retire but was apparently content to be shunted on to what we felt was rather a side line.

Sir Henry was a man of wide interests and probably played a larger part in professional activities outside the immediate railway field than any of his brother C.M.E.s. Though much had been done to rationalise and improve the locomotive stock of the L.M.S. during his term of office as Chief Mechanical Engineer much remained to be done – and there were certainly those who, given half a chance, would have taken delight in overturning the policy of 'Midlandisation' which was anathema to them. If Fowler was not to continue at the head of the combined department Ernest Lemon was the only possible successor from within the service at that time.

The changes wrought by Edward Thompson when he followed Sir Nigel Gresley at King's Cross would have been as nothing to the convulsion which would have occurred in L.M.S. locomotive design policy had Beames from Crewe been appointed to succeed Sir Henry. Whether, had he stayed longer as C.M.E., Lemon would have been able to judge between the radically different ideas on locomotive design held by his deputy, Beames on the one hand, and Symes, his principal locomotive assistant on the other, and provide the L.M.S. with a new standard range of more powerful locomotives which it so badly needed, is a fascinating question which can now never be answered.

Equally fascinating to me, and just as insoluble, is the question whether, if the events I have recounted had not occurred, I should ever have been invited to return to the service of the Railway to which I was so deeply attached. However that may be, I received, at the end of April 1931, completely out of the blue, a letter from the new C.M.E. It was so typical of the man, brief and to the point – 'I shall be pleased if you will please call and see me when you are next in London'. Was this the opportunity to rejoin the L.M.S. for which I so fervently hoped? I made it my business 'to be next in London' – at Euston, within a very few days. Lemon took me along to be introduced to the Vice-President. Sir Harold Hartley questioned me about my responsibilities as an Assistant Works Manager at the Vulcan Foundry – and after a most friendly interview, I was invited to come back to the C.M.E. Department of the L.M.S. in a managerial appointment at one of the Works – unspecified at the time. I was not able to accept the invitation there and then; I explained that I was bound by a three year agreement with the Vulcan Company which had still some months to run, and from which I should have to obtain release. Through the kindness of the present General Manager at the Vulcan Works, I have been able to refresh my memory about this agreement. It was, perhaps, a rather one-sided affair. The firm could dispense with my services at one month's notice at any time. By contrast, the employee was only able to leave of his own accord after three months' notice at the end of the three year period. However, Fred Whalley was very understanding. He knew well where my interests really lay, and I rather think he had received a letter from Ernest Lemon.

Be that as it may, the Vulcan Board agreed to my request to terminate my engagement, and within a few days I received the letter from Euston appointing me as Assistant Works Superintendent at the Locomotive Works at Horwich, whither I went on 19th May, 1931.

I was more than content with a modest increase in salary. At least it was all salary, payable without any strings. At the Vulcan Foundry my remuneration had been compounded of two parts – a basic £350 per annum plus a sliding scale bonus on output which varied from ten shillings per locomotive for the first thirteen engines completed per quarter, up to twenty-five shillings 'for all engines over fifty completed per quarter, as certified by the Company's cashier for the time being.' This was no doubt an admirable arrangement so far as the firm was concerned – forerunner of the productivity bargains so fashionable today. But as the output of locomotives depended far less upon the efforts of the Works Manager and his assistants than upon the success or otherwise of those whose job it was to secure orders in the first place, the pros and cons of such a bonus system could certainly provide an interesting subject for debate!

To say without qualification that I was glad to be leaving the Vulcan Foundry would give a wrong impression. I was glad beyond measure to be returning to railway service and that was the root of the matter. No longer should I have to watch the *Royal Scot* and the Manchester–Llandudno Club trains passing the works as an outsider. Away from the Works, the Vulcan 'family' – the firm had many of the attributes, good and not so good, of a family concern – were most hospitable people. Already knowing them well, and many of their friends also, from my time as an inspector at the works, I had been drawn in to all the agreeable diversions open to an unattached bachelor. In common with most other communities, large or small, there were the occasional ruffles on the generally placid surface. Sometimes more than a little tact and diplomacy were needed to steer a course between the Scylla of being asked, when dining with Mr. & Mrs. A., what I thought of Mr. & Mrs. B., and the Charybdis of the same question from the opposite direction a few weeks later!

With examinations finally surmounted, time was available for developing wider interests. Liverpool and the North Wales coast were within easy distance. I found myself roped in to the parties which on winter Saturdays packed themselves into motor cars and crossed the Mersey to run miles following the Cheshire beagles over the country dominated by Beeston and Peckforton Castles. All in all very enjoyable, but entirely secondary to the main stream of my ambitions, which I was soon to be able to resume.

Those three years with a locomotive building firm had given me most valuable experience to which, of course, the time in India contributed a great deal, not least in rooting firmly in my mind the conviction that the four phases of locomotive engineering – design, construction, operation and maintenance – must be treated as one comprehensive whole – they cannot be viewed in isolation. This may seem so obvious as not to require even mentioning. And yet from the way in which some railway organisations have been fragmented in recent years, the principle seems to require restating once more! In practical terms it comes down to this; that one chief officer, and one alone, must have the ultimate overall professional responsibility.

I became convinced, too, of the advantages, at any rate in terms of career opportunities, stemming from the sheer size and command of resources possessed by a nationwide organisation. The scope for rapid promotion is so much greater, the benefit of which, to my mind, far out-weighs the disadvantages said to arise from the alleged impersonality of large undertakings.

Though it is now over forty years since I left the Vulcan Foundry, the close ties early established have never been broken. During many visits when the Works were building diesel and electric locomotives for British Railways, I was always made welcome as a member of the 'family'. I was particularly pleased when, as Chief Mechanical Engineer of British

Railways, I was invited by my old friend, Gerald, last of the Collingwood family, and Managing Director, to present the awards to apprentices at one of the annual prizegiving ceremonies.

CHAPTER FIVE

Return to the Railway Service

THE LOCOMOTIVE, CARRIAGE AND WAGON works of the Lancashire & Yorkshire Railway had originally been situated at Newton Heath on the outskirts of Manchester. In 1886 all activities were transferred to a new Works at Horwich, a small town midway between Bolton and Chorley. The Works had been laid out in open country, unhampered for space by any other industrial buildings, under the shadow of Rivington Pike, a hill dominating the landscape, from the summit of which Snowdon to the south and Blackpool Tower to the north-west are often clearly visible. Apart from Eastleigh on the Southern Railway, Horwich was the youngest of the large railway works.

The town of Horwich, which virtually owed its existence to the coming of the railway works, is rather a dreary place, with no pretensions whatever to any architectural merit in its terraced houses so typical of the Victorian era. Electric trams rattled their way from Bolton along Chorley New Road, past the main entrance to the Works, with the Fire Station at the gates and a green oasis of lawn and garden in front of the offices.

The most prominent features in the landscape of so much of the industrial belt of South Lancashire, stretching across from Manchester through Bolton and Wigan, are factory chimneys and the waste tips and winding gears at colliery pit heads – a rather unlovely prospect. But the general drabness of Horwich was redeemed by a stretch of unspoilt country to the north stretching from the nearby village of Rivington over the moors to Blackburn and beyond up to the Trough of Bowland. Immediately to the west of the town, Liverpool Corporation Waterworks owned a wide tract of country in which had been built reservoirs, forming lakes below the wooded slopes of Rivington Pike. There were also many hundreds of acres of parkland, originally owned by Lord Leverhulme, since given over to Horwich Urban District Council and preserved inviolate from any building. If I had to live in the industrial areas of Lancashire there were few better places to be than the outskirts of Horwich at Rivington where, when I married eighteen months later, I found our first home, a small cottage with a stream running through a woodland garden, on the Waterworks Estate.

The station, with a large and ugly corrugated iron carriage shed was in keeping with the rest of the place. A single platform with the minimum of amenities, not far from the works sufficed for the traffic of the branch from a triangle junction at Blackrod on the direct route from Manchester and Bolton to Euxton Junction on the West Coast main line. There was a surprisingly good service of through trains to and from Manchester. The journey time was sufficiently short to permit my new chief, G. N. Shawcross, often to slip down for lunch with his brother officers in the Headquarters Mess of the old L. & Y. Railway at Hunt's Bank, Victoria Station. To supplement the through service a steam rail motor ran a shuttle service up the branch from Blackrod.

The three years during which I had been away from the L.M.S. had been a period of intense activity in standardising, after exhaustive and detailed analysis, the best of the many diverse practices inherited from the constituent companies. In his address to the shareholders a few years earlier Sir Josiah Stamp had pointed out that 'rationalisation on any amalgamation requires first, time for comparison, deliberation, and choice; second, a period of transition and execution; and third, an ascending period of realisation'. The year 1931 was well within the ascending period of realisation.

The beneficial effects of enlightened rationalisation, measured by increased efficiency and economy, were felt nowhere more than in the realms of locomotive maintenance and operation. At amalgamation in 1923, the L.M.S. had a stock of 10,316 locomotives, comprising 393 different classes. When I returned to the company's service, the number of engines had been reduced to 9,032 – a reduction of 12 per cent, with a fall of only half this amount in the engine miles run. The criteria by which the efficiency of the maintenance organisation can best be judged in relation to expenditure, are threefold. First, there is availability, the percentage of total time that locomotives are available for working traffic. Next, there is the percentage of the total stock under and awaiting repairs at any time, and finally, the mileage run between successive heavy repairs. Availability had been increased substantially to 85 per cent. The number of locomotives under repair in the main Works had been reduced from 8 per cent to something under 4 per cent, with a corresponding reduction in the number of days out of traffic under repair.

Mileage between repairs for passenger locomotives increased by 10,000 miles to 66,000 miles, with a similar improvement for freight engines. The cost of shop repairs came down from 4·70d to 4·28d per mile. All this added up to economies measured in hundreds of thousands of pounds at a time when the pound sterling was many times its present value.

The organisation and progress of locomotive repair had been radically improved. Control of the input of locomotives to shops had been centralised at C.M.E. Headquarters. Budgetary control of all expenditure and individual costing of repairs were firmly established and paying handsome dividends. Progressive systems of repairs, with adequate stocks of spare boilers, had been introduced in the four main works. About a year before I went to Horwich, Shawcross had reported in glowing terms to the Chief Mechanical Engineer on the re-organisation of locomotive repairs, which he had undertaken. The resulting economies, which Shawcross specified under three heads, were considered satisfactory and apparently exceeded his expectations. They were

    (i) Reduction in number of locomotives under repair in the Shops;

    (ii) Direct savings in wages paid; and

    (iii) Increased capacity of workshops for more repairs.

Many repairs hitherto done at the Sheds were sent into the Works, with considerable net saving in expenditure; and space was made available for any other work that might come along. Shawcross concluded his letter by saying that 'the re-organisation has been an unqualified success, and Horwich Works, as a result of it, is one of the most efficient in Great Britain'.

This was probably true. Horwich was as good as the other L.M.S. Works at the time, particularly in the use of limit gauges and standard step sizes for the reconditioning of components worn in service. The machine shop was one of the best in the group. Boiler repair procedures were closely controlled and Horwich was early in the field with copper welding. Initial examination of parts before repairs was firmly established under the control of an inspection department reporting direct to the Works Manager.

In a more general way some of the former glory of Horwich had departed with the transfer of departmental headquarters to Derby. When George Hughes was appointed first Chief Mechanical Engineer of the L.M.S. he naturally established his headquarters organisation on his home ground at Horwich. There it remained for a short time after Sir Henry Fowler, who never moved from Derby, succeeded Hughes. I well remember Martin Herbert and I, ignorant as we then were of the idiosyncracies of large organisations and the doctrine of personal responsibility of the man at the top for everything that happens, good or bad, deriving mild amusement from the letters which Sir Henry at Derby used to write to himself at Horwich, copies of which were distributed for action in the office at Derby in which we were working at the time.

The principles by which Horwich had been guided for many years are set out in a paper by the late Colonel H. E. O'Brien one time Works Manager, delivered to the Institution of Locomotive Engineers in October, 1920.* They are as valid today as when they were first enunciated. The most important among them sank deeply into my mind and later influenced my thinking on more than one occasion. It is worth repeating here; O'Brien wrote 'It should be noted at the outset that the main objective of the management of a railway locomotive workshop is essentially different from that of a commercial manufacturing works; the engineering management of a commercial engineering works desire to see a constant expansion of their shops, while in the case of the railway management their desire should be to see a constant shrinkage of the shops brought about by

    (i) Improved methods of manufacture

    (ii) Improved organisation.

    (iii) Rectification of errors of design and material with the object of reducing renewals and repairs to a minimum.

It is possible to effect this because the capital expansion of the locomotive stock is very slow on English railways, and therefore the capacity of the Works should more than keep pace with the demands if the management is progressive, in spite of the increased weight and power of the more modern stock. The number of locomotives on the L. & Y. Railway had only increased from 1,326 to 1,645 in the last 20 years. The aim of every railway management should therefore be to effect improvement in the cost of repairs at a greater rate than the capital expansion, so that far from requiring additional shop room, increased floor space will steadily become available in the existing shops while the number of employees remains constant or even decreases.'

This was indeed a principle which guided the Chief Mechanical Engineers of the L.M.S. They applied it with conspicuous success for twenty-five years from amalgamation to nationalisation. This same policy was followed no less energetically, and with even greater scope, when at nationalisation in 1948 British Railways inherited eighteen main and five subsidiary locomotive works and nineteen carriage and wagon works. Such was the way in which progress was sustained that when, some years later, a few people from outside the railway service, who were presumably considered more enlightened than those whose life's work had been to run railway workshops, were brought in to key positions in the organisation, plans were already in existence to close down fifteen locomotive and six carriage and wagon works, and concentrate their activities in a smaller number of the more efficient establishments.

In the wider context of the national economy 1931 was in a period of trade depression and economic unrest. Moreover the effects of road competition were being increasingly felt by the railways. Though a fall of £5

* H. E. O'Brien 'The Management of a Locomotive Repair Shop' *Journal, Institution of Locomotive Engineers, Vol. X No. 45.*

million, equal to 7·35 per cent in the gross receipts of the L.M.S. Railway had been more than matched by a reduction of 7·79 per cent in expenditure there remained a compelling need to reduce costs, without sacrifice of efficiency, by every available means. As one among many innovations, the techniques of comparative analysis of workshop methods and costs were introduced throughout the C.M.E.'s Department. A Committee of Works Managers, of which S. H. Whitelegg from Horwich was a member, was set up to examine and compare the methods in use at each of the works for manufacturing the multitude of spare parts needed for the maintenance of locomotives and rolling stock. It was Whitelegg's absence from Horwich which created the gap I was appointed to fill. The activities of the Committee stimulated intense competition between the Works. In broad outline, the policy followed was to concentrate the manufacture of each item examined at the works with the lowest overall cost, unless one or other of the more expensive works was able, after modification to their methods, to continue production at or below the lowest cost. Much ingenuity was displayed by the works in their determination not to lose jobs to one of the others.

Of course there were the occasional fiddles. One of the most colourful personalities, who I met for the first time at Horwich, was Herbert Yates. A bluff, good hearted Lancashire man, fat and rubicund with an addiction to bright yellow waistcoats, he had a powerful vocabulary well suited to his job in charge of the 'black' shops at Horwich. A Pels forging machine, just the thing for upsetting the ends of spring top plates, had recently been installed. Yates was determined that this job, for the whole of the department, should be concentrated at Horwich; and to make quite sure he quietly arranged with the Millwrights Shop Foreman that the machine should be put down in a shop with substantially lower overheads than the forge. Not strictly orthodox perhaps, but as the direct wages and materials were lower at Horwich than elsewhere the company was not out of pocket! Nevertheless the various alternative methods of allocating overhead charges of expensive machines was clearly a question of some importance if slightly questionable methods of exploiting local conditions were not to mislead the committee in making their decisions on the allocation of jobs between competing works.

Ernest Lemon was a great believer in setting his Works' standards to achieve rather better than current performance. For locomotive repairs the target he set, soon after taking charge, was 100,000 miles between general repairs – roughly double the mileage then being achieved from one heavy shop repair to the next. Except in the comparatively few cases of engines being sent into the Works for some specific defect – for example to change the boiler after a lead plug failure or to repair collision damage, repairs of a kind which do nothing to liquidate mileage run – it had been the general practice for all locomotives sent in to L.M.S. mainworks to be given a complete general overhaul, irrespective of whether the condition of the firebox or wear of tyres and axleboxes was the determining factor in calling the engine into shops. Whereas in the case of the boiler and firebox wear and tear are related to hours in steam, it is mileage run which is the dominant factor for the rest of the locomotive – the frames, wheels, axleboxes and motion. The relationship between hours in steam and mileage run naturally varied widely depending upon the class of locomotive and the services upon which they were engaged. The rates of accumulation of wear and tear for the boiler and mechanical parts by no means always conveniently coincided to the extent that both were fully rundown at the same time. It follows that neither time nor mileage, by themselves are satisfactory bases for deciding when steam locomotives need to be sent into Shops.

Actual physical condition, ascertained by a thorough examination after a pre-determined period in service is the only satisfactory criterion on which to base decisions.

The need to renew copper firebox stays was, more often than not, the deciding factor in calling engines into the Works. The wastage of the rivetted heads, which made renewal necessary, was always a serious problem of locomotive maintenance, so much so that in 1929 the four group companies commissioned the British Non-Ferrous Metals Research Association to make a thorough investigation of causes and possible remedies. Martin Herbert took charge of the work under the supervision of a committee with Sir Henry Fowler in the chair.

When the research started it was commonly held that the main cause of copper stays wasting was burning of the copper, which implied a high temperature for the stay heads. Scouring by solid fuel particles carried in the gas stream was also thought to contribute. Accurate measurements in service showed that the surface temperatures of stayheads were comparatively low (300–350°C), and the effects of scour was much less than expected. At the same time a factor hitherto disregarded, was identified which seemed to account for most of the trouble. As engines cool down in the running sheds leakage frequently occurs from stays in certain parts of the firebox. Water with a high chloride content seeps past the screw threads and spreads over the inner surfaces of the firebox and stay heads. The action of this solution causes the oxide skin, normally hard and strongly adherent to be detached, thus exposing fresh metallic surfaces to oxidation when the engine is next put into service. Although stays are screwed tightly into the firebox plates and are watertight under hydraulic and steam tests, plastic deformation due to compressive stresses in the plates and stays when the engine is in steam results in permanent distortion of the stay holes. On cooling down the copper, stressed beyond its elastic limit, fails to return to its original dimensions. Small gaps occur between the threads and leakage paths are formed.

Herbert's work* established beyond doubt that the wastage of stay heads was due to the combined effects of alternating periods of oxidation during running followed by leakage in the sheds. To mitigate the trouble remedies in two main directions were suggested. It was clearly necessary to obtain a material for the stays with an inherently greater resistance to oxidation, and to find means whereby the thermal stresses causing distortion and leakage could be resisted either by modification to design, or by using materials both for stays and plates with superior elastic properties.

Trials with stays made from various grades of high tensile cupro-nickel alloys, and from steel, were initiated. Knowing my interest in his work, Herbert had given me copies of all his reports. Shortly before I went to Horwich, all this experimental work was centred there. I was thus able to pick up the threads of all that had been going on. T. F. B. Simpson, who had been transferred from Barrow when the Furness Railway Works there had been closed, looked after this work for Shawcross, to whom he had direct access. As he was given to interfering in Works management matters, and did not welcome my arrival on the scene, we soon crossed swords. Once he understood and accepted that what he had got away with in the past was not acceptable to the new incumbent of the No. 2 position in the organisation, we got along splendidly. In later years, in the Outdoor Machinery Department, and particularly as Locomotive Works Manager at Derby, Fred Simpson did a magnificent job. Unfortunately, he never seemed able to eradicate a tendency to disregard official instructions for obtaining authority for expenditure, and other matters which he found inconvenient. He certainly got things done; but not infrequently he involved his chiefs in some difficult whitewashing exercises! He will always be remembered with affection by his many friends in the railway service, not least for his untiring efforts on behalf of the Derby Railway Orphanage.

Reverting to the theme of locomotive maintenance as I found it when I returned to railway service, the policy of general repairs every time did keep things nicely in step and ensured a uniformly high standard of maintenance. Nevertheless work was sometimes done, either to the boiler or the mechanical parts, when some potentially useful service still remained. As a means of eliminating this wasteful expenditure and extending the time and mileage between general repairs the L.M.S. introduced what were called service or intermediate repairs in which boilers were repaired on the frames, and the amount of work done to the mechanical parts was governed by specified limits of wear below which components were allowed to run for a further period without attention. Full advantage

* Locomotive Firebox Conditions: Gas compositions and temperatures close to copper plates. *Institution of Mechanical Engineers*, 1928.

was thus taken of the cumulative effect of improved methods of boiler maintenance in the shops and sheds, to which the copper stay research made a significant contribution. The emphasis tended to shift from firebox condition to that of the mechanical parts as the main factor in deciding when engines should be sent into Works. Greater flexibility was thereby imparted into the system, and money was saved. But it was not until Stanier introduced steel, and later, monel metal stays in place of copper in his new standard boilers that the periods obtained between each consecutive service or intermediate repair were approximately equal, and substantially equivalent to the mileage which it was possible to obtain from the mechanical parts between one repair and the next.

These developments in engine repair policy, and much else besides, were new to me, and had to be thoroughly absorbed. To Midland men Horwich and its locomotives had always seemed rather remote. Apart from the standard mixed traffic 2-6-0s — the 'Crabs' — which became known and admired from one end of the L.M.S. to the other, and a few of the Hughes four-cylinder 4-6-0s drafted to the West Coast main line, Horwich locomotives seldom wandered far from the lines of the railway for which they had been built. I now had to get to know them as thoroughly as I knew the Midland engines. I had previously had little experience of staff and labour relations. Lane kept this important part of Works management very much to himself. At Horwich however it was part of the Assistant's job to take the chair at Works Committee meetings. It so happened that, thirty-seven years later, the last meeting I had with a Works Committee was at Horwich when, as General Manager of British Railways Workshops, I met the men at their request to reassure them, so far as I honestly could, on the future of their Works.

In addition to their main purpose of repairing and building locomotives, carriages and wagons, most railway works have other responsibilities extending beyond their own immediate boundaries. Horwich was no exception. The Works Fire Brigade was a case in point. It was the town's only fire fighting service, and in addition, the brigade manned the fire train for which a locomotive was always available in steam to answer calls to fires on company's property, anywhere on the old L. & Y. system. Calls were, to me, surprisingly frequent — although more often than not they were to Ince Moss, not very far from the Works, to damp down the Civil Engineer's refuse tip which seemed unquenchable.

The Works too, are the focal points from which a heavy maintenance service for a wide variety of plant and equipment spread all over the system, is provided. I was ignorant of the geography of our outdoor machinery districts on the Central Division, as the old L. & Y. Railway was now known, an omission which had to be repaired by journeys, sometimes on the footplate, to the boundaries of the division.

I was once more deeply involved in railway work and with domestic responsibilities possibly not far away, I had neither the time nor the inclination for other distractions. Whilst at the Vulcan Foundry I had been persuaded by some of my friends to join their Territorial Army Unit – the 5th Battalion Manchester Regiment with headquarters at Wigan. I found myself as the junior subaltern of the machine gun company under another locomotive engineer, Robert Arbuthnott of Nasmyth Wilson. On the whole, it was an ill-considered and unsuccessful venture. I was glad of the opportunity presented by my return to railway service to resign my commission. My brother officers seemed to bear me no ill-will, realising, no doubt, that I was unlikely ever to become an ornament to their unit. I salved a slightly guilty conscience by reflecting that the railways had played a vital part in the 1914–18 war. They would undoubtedly play a vital part in any future conflict. And though it would be for someone else to decide, I reckoned I was likely to be of more use to the country helping to run railway Works than doing anything else.

It was good once more to be able to get about the country with free passes and privilege tickets. There were few weekends when I was not going somewhere in the Company's trains or ships. I had a good reason for wishing to make frequent visits to Northern Ireland. Since returning from India I had been seeing as much as separation by the Irish Sea allowed of my sister's closest friend Jean Holmes, a regular summer visitor to my home in Suffolk. While I was still at Newton-le-Willows we had dined together at the Adelphi in Liverpool before she set out on a six-month visit to a brother in Ceylon. It was six months too long so far as I was concerned. Nothing was said that evening, but we both felt fairly certain that within a short time after her return we should be engaged to be married. That indeed was the outcome of yet one more weekend in Northern Ireland. High on the hills above Glynn, overlooking Larne Lough, the essential question was asked and answered to my intense satisfaction. The job of house hunting which was to continue with little respite over the next fifteen years, began on my return to Horwich next morning.

Jean Holmes and I were married in the spring of 1932 at the country town of Antrim on the shores of Lough Neagh. No-one could have wished for a more cordial welcome than that which I received from my 'in-laws'. Their home was a cheerful place constantly full of young people. My mother-in-law was beloved by all who knew her. On both sides of the family interests were largely centred, apart from the daily job of work, on games and outdoor pursuits. My father-in-law, an Irish Rugby football and hockey international, was the local solicitor to whom country folk from miles around came for help and advice, and were not disappointed. The garden of 'Ferrard', the family home, adjoined the N.C.C. railway station. The level-crossing gates were conveniently in sight. More than once, as I came to find out later, trains were kept waiting when a shout from Alec the gatekeeper warned the stationmaster of the tardy arrival at the double, of a member of the Holmes family on their way to Belfast. It was all delightfully friendly and Irish. For me, life took on an entirely new dimension, and for twenty-five years, almost to our silver wedding day, until her untimely death, Jean and I were as happy as any two people have any right to be!

It was during my time at Horwich that William Stanier, the stranger from another railway, for whom all of us in the engineering departments of the L.M.S. came to have a deep respect and affection, was appointed Chief Mechanical Engineer. Lemon moved up as a Vice-President of the Executive for the Commercial and Operating Departments. My first encounter with our new chief was brief in the extreme, entirely devoid of ceremony and a trifle daunting. It took place during Stanier's first visit of inspection to Horwich. I was not summoned by Shawcross to his office. Instead, without any preliminary warning, the door of my room opened – Lemon and Stanier peered in, but came no further than the threshold. 'That's Bond' was Lemon's remark – a curt nod from Stanier, and they were gone.

Stanier was a perfectionist in all that he did and required of other people. He demanded the same high standard of technical competence and workmanship to which he had been accustomed at Swindon. He was a Great Western man through and through. But, unlike some of his colleagues, his awareness of engineering progress and development was not bounded by the narrow confines of his own railway. He had an open-minded approach to all the technical and administrative problems which faced him in the formidable task of rejuvenating the locomotive stock of the largest of the four group companies.

Stanier's appointment naturally caused a considerable stir in railway circles. Before the formation of the group companies it was not unusual for a C.M.E. to be appointed from another company. Since 1923, however, such an appointment was unprecedented. The reasons which led to Stanier being invited to leave Swindon and the manner of his coming to Euston have been recorded elsewhere. Suffice it for me to say that his appointment set the course of mechanical engineering policy on the L.M.S. for the next twelve years, and had a decisive influence on the course of events for at least a further fifteen years into the era of nationalisation.

Each of the locomotive and carriage works of the constituent companies which formed the L.M.S. Railway had their own iron and brass foundries. Some of them were small and not very efficient. While it can be argued that foundries are essential to any well equipped Works engaged on maintenance, there was obviously a case to be examined for concentrating the manufacture of castings such as permanent way chairs needed in very large numbers but having no direct connection with rolling stock maintnance activities. A scheme had already been prepared, no doubt at Beames' instigation, for concentrating the production of chairs at Crewe. But Stainer had other ideas which were conveyed in broad outline to the Works Managers principally concerned – Crewe, Derby and Horwich – at a meeting in Crewe in October, 1932.

The cornerstone of the plan was that all permanent way chairs, together with brakeblocks and locomotive firebars for the whole group, excluding Scotland, hitherto made in relatively small quantities at a number of works, should be made at Horwich. To enable that to be done on the floor space available, all other locomotive and general iron castings made at Horwich were to be transferred to Crewe. The foundry at Earlestown Wagon Works was to be closed and their work sent to Horwich. At Derby, the locomotive general castings, except cylinders, were to be made in the Carriage and Wagon Works foundry which was also to take over production from Wolverton Carriage Works. The iron and chair foundries at Derby Locomotive Works were to be converted into a new brass foundry for making the whole of the non-ferrous castings required by the English divisions. This was a bold and imaginative scheme which, though it could only be brought to completion, step by step, over a considerable period of time, accorded well with the needs of a situation as seen through the unbiased eyes of a new C.M.E. with no inherited leanings towards any one of the Works now under his command.

All of the Works involved were required to make their own plans and financial estimates for their part of the comprehensive project. We at Horwich had to prepare a scheme for the manufacture, by mechanical means, of 8,000 tons of brakeblocks, 3,000 tons of firebars and 50,000 tons of permanent way chairs per annum. Shawcross asked me to take this on as a full-time responsibility with the Machinery and Plant Assistant. This suited me very well. Whitelegg had recently returned to Horwich from his stint on the Manufacturing Costs Committee. Thus, there were two of us in the one job, with all the possibilities of friction inherent in such a situation. Whitelegg was of course, at that time, senior to me, a fact which I freely acknowledged in my attempts to arrange with him a sensible division of responsibilities between us. The foundry job solved the problem so far as I was concerned and kept me very busy until my promotion to Crewe a few months later.

Horwich had been making chairs for many years, turning out about 11,000 tons of castings each year. Repetition work of this kind should have been ideal for machine moulding. But with no shortage of men willing to do the heavy work involved, it had not been possible to make an economic case for superceding the traditional hand methods by which a gang of four men with no equipment except patterns and moulding boxes, a pile of sand, a watering can and a couple of wheelbarrows made 300 chairs per day, year in and year out, casting them and wheeling them out to the fettling shop. Such broadly was the situation at Crewe and Derby also.

The price charged to the Stores Department per ton of chairs delivered during a representative 4-weekly period in 1932 varied only from £3 7s 8d at Derby, £3 5s 10d at Crewe, and £3 4s 8d at Horwich. The metal mixture cost alone accounted for over £2 per ton within the total. Direct wages per ton were 10s 4d at Crewe and 9s 11d at Derby and Horwich. Clearly there was little scope for large savings arising only from concentration at one Works, with the existing hand methods of production continuing in operation.

For the contemplated output of 50,000 tons, over 2·6 million chairs had to be produced each year – 10,500 every day. Surely with such an output moulding machines backed up by sand preparation and distribution plant, continuous casting conveyors and mechanical means for knocking out and disposing of the hot castings could not fail to be an economic proposition? Such indeed was the confident prediction made by the firm of foundry experts who, having already made the original proposals for Crewe, Stanier had sent along to us at Horwich. Under their guidance Shawcross and I, accompanied by Ernest Millington, the chief metallurgist from Derby went to see a number of mechanised foundries in Northern France and Belgium. We were impressed by what we were shown, and came home satisfied that a fully mechanised plant could give us what we wanted.

We went to work at once preparing a scheme based on what we had seen on the continent. We calculated that five continuous casting units would be needed to cope with the full output. We made it clear, however, to our contractors that one unit only on which experience could be gained and economies proved (or otherwise) would be installed in the first place. Heavy capital expenditure was involved – we had to be sure of what we were doing.

Shawcross was, in any case, rather tight-fisted where money was concerned. He was never anxious to put up schemes involving capital expenditure if they could possibly be avoided. He seemed oblivious to the damage which that philosophy would ultimately do to Horwich. Here, however, he was acting under instruction. But even so, obtaining his agreement to submit for authority the proposals developed for us by our advisers was made easier by a case being fought out at the time in the High Court. The Austin Motor Co. was being sued by an American Company for the balance of a fee due to them as engineering works advisers on the re-organisation of the foundries at Longbridge. The re-organisation was supposed to save £16,000 a year. Apparently it had done nothing of the sort. Instead of obtaining a saving the firm was worse off than before. So far from reducing labour costs the result of the re-organisation had been to increase them.

This was a cautionary tale I was not allowed to forget! This, my first contact with a really large scheme involving radically different methods of production from those to which we were accustomed, soon convinced me of the need to subject all proposals, however attractive at first sight, to a rigorous, even hostile, scrutiny against the background of our own shop floor experience. Clearly, there was an obligation placed upon me, which I had no hesitation in imposing on others in later years, to be quite certain that what I put up to Shawcross to send to the C.M.E. for which he, Shawcross, not I, would have to accept responsibility was right. I was confirmed in this view of my obligations by a day spent in the mechanised foundry at Eastleigh Works on the Southern Railway. It could certainly not be taken as a foregone conclusion that sufficient savings would be forthcoming from the schemes we were proposing for Horwich to justify the capital expenditure involved.

Parts of the comprehensive foundry plan were put into effect, but the largest single project – the mechanised plant at Horwich was not completed for another 15 years!* During the intervening years a number of alternative proposals were considered with Crewe as the preferred location for the mechanised foundry. I was to be much concerned with the seemingly endless discussions on the scheme and its ramifications, both at Crewe and Derby, right up to the time when it was finally authorised for Horwich in 1947.

Without my having the slightest inkling of what was in the wind, Shawcross sent for me one morning to tell me, with suitable congratulations and expressions of regret, that I was to go to Crewe as Assistant Works Superintendent in succession to Robert Riddles. A letter had been received from Beames, the Deputy Chief Mechanical Engineer, informing Shawcross that Riddles was going to Euston as Stanier's locomotive assistant in place of S. J. Symes, who had been appointed Chief Stores Superintendent.

This was the first of three occasions that fate decreed that I should follow in Riddles' footsteps. Though it would have been a quite redundant question, I was not asked whether I would be willing to move to Crewe. I was merely told after the event that I had been appointed and would go to Crewe forthwith! The simplicity and discipline of it all is in strong and faintly amusing contrast with what has to happen today. There was none of the paraphenalia of advertised vacancy lists and selection committees.

This promotion to Crewe, coming so comparatively soon after my return to the railway service, was of course, a matter of considerable satisfaction. I went home at once in my fourth-hand Austin 7, to break the

* S. A. S. Smith 'The British Railway Mechanised Iron Foundry, Horwich' *Journal, Institution of Locomotive Engineers*, 1955.

good news to Jean. How fortunate I was in my wife, who then, and always in the years ahead, when told of yet another move, merely said 'Splendid – when do we go?' More than once in recent years moves I had planned to make from one Works to another, giving promotion to really first class men, were frustrated because a wife refused to face the domestic upheaval involved. More than once I felt tempted to say 'Go where the railway wants you to go or get out' – but of course that is not the answer today.

The two years at Horwich were excellent preparation for wider responsibilities. They were also very enjoyable. Our small cottage in the country, inconvenient though it was, with neither gas nor electricity laid on, suited us very well. We had made many good friends. But while Horwich, at the end of the branch from Blackrod was rather off the beaten track, Crewe was 'the centre of the universe' – the focal point of everything that happened on the West Coast route from Euston to the north. Though Derby and Horwich might have been reluctant to concede the point, Crewe was after all the most important of the L.M.S. Locomotive Works, with a wide range of activities in addition to the main job of building and repairing the most important locomotives. As the first Midland man to be appointed second-in-command at Crewe, I took up my new duties with some trepidation and a firm resolve not to offend against North-Western traditions.

Most of the cities and towns in which the principal railway Locomotive and Carriage and Wagon Works are situated would look very much as they do today if a railway works had never been built there. Some towns, however, owe their very existence and character to the fact that a hundred or more years ago, one of the early railway companies found the locality a convenient place in which to establish their workshops. Crewe is, I think, the most completely 'railway' town that I know – not even excepting Swindon. It is of course, less so today with Rolls-Royce and other firms providing alternative sources of employment. But at the time when I first went to Crewe, and indeed over all the years since 1843 when the Grand Junction Railway closed their shops at Edge Hill and moved to Church Coppenhall, the parish in which the town was originally built, Crewe, depended for its prosperity and development entirely upon the L.N.W.R. and its successor the L.M.S.

In addition to building houses for their work-people, the railway provided all the civic amenities which a growing community would need. They built schools and a Mechanics Institute, which in later years became a social club, the president of which was always a senior railway officer – usually the Works Manager. The railway owned the Town Hall. They built a parish church and paid the parson's stipend. They built and ran a hospital, and provided the town's water and gas supplies, for which the Works Manager was wholly responsible until quite recent times. To celebrate the Golden Jubilee of Queen Victoria in 1887 — a year in which the redoubtable F. W. Webb was Mayor, the company presented the town with its municipal park.

For many years the town itself, let alone the Works, was virtually governed and run by the railway. Benevolent dictatorship from Euston would, I suppose, best describe the situation. Though in due course the town came to manage its own affairs, like any other borough, railway influence remained very strong, as I soon found out for myself. There was among the foremen and men in the Works a strong sense of pride in Crewe and a firm loyalty to the company on whom they, and often their fathers before them, had depended for their livelihood.

I knew my new chief, F. A. Lemon, both personally and by reputation. He had received me some five years earlier with kindness and an old world courtesy which was typical of him, when I went to Crewe to see how the new Midland locomotives, for the inspection of which I had been responsible at contractors' works were faring on the Western Division. He had a reputation for irascibility, caused no doubt by the deafness from which he suffered. He had a sharp tongue; and certainly did not mince his words in dressing down anyone who displeased him. More than once in the years ahead, senior foremen, less tough than some of their colleagues, were to come into my office, white faced, and shaking with fury or emotion, to receive comfort at my hands! Lemon never used a fountain pen. He signed his letters with an old-fashioned, sharp pointed nib. There was a story, probably true, that one morning when he had been more than usually irked by someone's stupidity, Lemon stuck his nib through the paper he was signing. He threw the pen away in disgust, exclaiming to Richard Darroch, one of his assistants, a most gentle and cultured man, 'Even the pens have gone to hell!'

The Chief Mechanical Engineer of the L. & N.W.R. was responsible, not only for the locomotive works and outdoor machinery throughout the system, but also for locomotive running. Lemon had spent some years in the Running Department and had been manager of the Dundalk, Newry and Greenore Railway in Ireland, owned by the North Western. Thus he had a wide general engineering and railway experience, and by inclination he took a close personal interest in all the many non-locomotive activities for which he was responsible at Crewe. There were few days on which Lemon did not visit the Sawmill and Joiners Shop, both conveniently near the main office building, in which oak keys and ferrules were made by the tens of thousands on automatic machines for the permanent way. Wooden signal boxes, level crossing gates and the platelayers barrows knocked together on jigs at an incredibly low price were staple items of output. The signal shop and the millwrights, which did a great deal of work for the Marine Department at Holyhead, the Gas Works, the pumping station and reservoirs for the town's water supply ten miles away in the country at Whitmore, all received their full share of attention from my chief. All of this meant that his assistants could, and indeed were expected, to devote most of their time to the general run of locomotive activities in the Works. But woe betide anyone, who, with the best possible intention of not wanting to worry the chief, failed to tell him, before he found out himself, of anything that looked like going wrong. In all the five years that I was his assistant I never had a wrong word with Lemon. Harmonious relations at work were combined with personal friendship with his family from whom, as indeed from many others, we received a warm welcome as newcomers to the railway community at Crewe.

I could not have been sent to Crewe at a more interesting time from the point of view of locomotive design and development on the L.M.S. Stanier had been Chief Mechanical Engineer for 18 months. The first of his new locomotives, a 2-6-0 mixed traffic type for duties similar to those undertaken by the Horwich 'Crabs' were beginning to emerge from Crewe, closely followed by the class for which we had all been waiting – the four-cylinder 4-6-2 express passenger engines of which three had been authorised for building. The first of them, No. 6200 *Princess Royal* had only recently gone into service when I arrived at Crewe. The second, *Princess Elizabeth* was nearing completion in the Erecting Shop.

The appointment of someone from another railway as Chief Mechanical Engineer was probably the only way of stopping once and for all, the guerilla warfare between Derby and Crewe. That the new chief came from Swindon also ensured, or at least justified a confident expectation, that the new engines, which it would be his prime responsibility to produce, would emulate the high standards of Swindon locomotives and would contain some, or perhaps all the design features which, though virtually unchanged since the days of the great G. J. Churchward, had for many years assured pride of place in British locomotive performance to the Great Western Railway.

Swindon design had already had a profound influence on locomotive development, both on the L.M.S. and L.N.E.R. – and less directly on the Southern too. The interchange trials between a Great Western *Castle* and a Gresley A1 *Pacific* arranged after the two locomotives had been exhibited beside each other at the Wembley Exhibition in 1925, demonstrated the advantages of long lap valves and long travel valve gear so convincingly that Gresley modified all his *Pacific*s accordingly. The *Castle* which the L.M.S. borrowed in 1926 met contemporary traffic conditions on the West Coast main line so well as to lead directly to the production straight off the drawing-board of the first fifty *Royal Scots*. In the light of later events a note attached to the report of the tests with the Great Western engine makes interesting reading. It was as follows:

It will be noted that the rates of combustion and evaporation were in no way exceptional, whereas the coal and steam consumptions were very good and this would seem to indicate that the efficiency of the G.W. engine results from the engine and economical accessory fittings. As a result of this the boiler is well able to produce the steam required at a low fuel consumption. It is noted that full advantage is taken of: high boiler pressure, long valve travel, exhaust injector, top feed for injectors, pump for vacuum brake, good air space between firebars, efficient ashpan damper gear. The rate of combustion was fairly high, but at the same time combustion was very good, as indicated by the low coal consumption, and it was also noted that very little black smoke was ejected from the chimney.

Nothing was said in this report about the most distinctive external characteristic of Great Western locomotives – the taper barrel boiler. The original *Royal Scot* boilers, with their large diameter parallel barrel, were always excellent steamers. However, it soon became known that Stanier's new locomotives were to have domeless tapered boilers, practically identical in their form of construction and details with standard G. W. boilers. Though relatively expensive in first cost, they were known to have an excellent maintenance record and to be capable of running large mileages between heavy repairs. The gently curved shape of their Belpaire fireboxes and generous water space round the sides of the firebox undoubtedly influenced their maintenance performance far more than the conical shape of the barrel.

I had always been particularly interested in the thinking behind the design of taper boilers. Was the nominal diameter of the barrel to be regarded as that at the smokebox tubeplate or the throat plate? The masters do not seem to be of one mind on this question. In replying to the discussion on his paper on 'Large Locomotive Boilers'* Churchward speaks of the front of the barrel being narrowed down into the smallest diameter in which the tubes could be spaced. In articles on Locomotive Boilers which Sir Henry Fowler and S. J. Symes wrote in *Railway Engineer* in 1924, they have this to say about taper barrels:

'The end of the cone towards the smokebox of the boiler is made to the nominal diameter of the boiler barrel, while the end which is attached to the throat plate is considerably larger in diameter. The axis of the cone is lifted at this end so that the bottom portion is horizontal. By this means a considerable increase of steam and water space above the centre line of the boiler and round about the tubeplate is obtained at the expense of a comparatively small increase in weight.'

As generous water spaces round the sides of the firebox and between the outer rows of tubes and the barrel are essential to ensure unimpeded circulation in the areas of maximum evaporation, it is the diameter at the throat plate that is of prime importance. A parallel barrel no larger in

* G. J. Churchward 'Large Locomotive Boilers' *Proceedings, Institution of Mechanical Engineers*, 1906.

diameter than necessary to accommodate the required number of tubes in the smokebox tubeplate would be quite inadequate. And thus it seems to me that the diameter at the throat plate should be regarded as the nominal diameter of the barrel – the coned barrel being credited with a reduction in weight. The Swindon boilers tapering quite sharply from the throat plate to the smokebox and boiler backplate did provide water surface area and steam space where they were most needed, and utilised a given weight of material more efficiently than the simpler parallel boiler. Desirable though these characteristics are, they were shown to be quite secondary in importance from the point of view of evaporative capacity and locomotive performance to a sufficient number of tubes and flues of the right proportions, granted, of course, adequate grate area and firebox volume in the first place.

I think we all viewed with considerable misgivings Stanier's original adherence to low degree superheating – misgivings which were soon shown to be fully justified. It is true that the major part of the economy in coal and water consumption possible from superheating is secured if the steam is just hot enough to ensure that the temperature of the cylinder walls is slightly above the saturation temperature at working pressure, thus avoiding initial condensation. One must assume, I think, that Churchward and those who followed him knew as well as anybody else that cylinder efficiency could be further increased by using steam temperatures higher than the minimum needed to avoid condensation. Why it took Swindon so many years to take advantage of this fact must now always remain a matter of conjecture. Perhaps it was that with coal consumption in relation to work done generally lower than the contemporary average due to good steaming boilers, first rate cylinder and valve gear design able to utilise high boiler pressure efficiently at early cut-off, any further gains were considered to be not worth while having regard to the difficulties which other people had encountered with valve and cylinder lubrication with highly superheated steam. Be that as it may, Stanier's original adherence to low superheat on a railway which had learnt to live with the problems associated with really hot steam, put some of his new locomotives at a considerable disadvantage.

It was particularly unfortunate that the new three-cylinder 4-6-0s – the *Jubilees* as they came to be known, came out before the *Class 5* two-cylinder 4-6-0s. The former were intended to be an improved development of the *Baby Scots* which had already established an enviable reputation for themselves, notably on the Birmingham two-hour expresses. The new engines were virtually *Baby Scots* with a different boiler which, whatever its other merits, wouldn't steam. The limitations of low degree superheating are always sharply accentuated when associated with indifferent steaming; and in this the new engines were no exception. The

Class 5 two-cylinder engines, by contrast were a resounding success from the start. Above all they steamed freely, though like the *Jubilees*, and indeed the *Princess Royal Pacifics*, their performance as a class was much improved by successive developments in their boilers, later batches of which had increased firebox volume and free area, improved tube ratios and larger superheaters. They were so much better than anything of comparable power which the L.M.S. possessed at that time, that the inherent limitations on efficiency imposed by low degree superheating were relatively unimportant so far as the first batches of *Class 5s* were concerned.

It was quite another matter with the *Jubilees*, which as originally built were just not up to the jobs for which they were required. The first thing was to make the boilers steam. It seemed that the Swindon formulae for smokebox, chimney and blastpipe dimensions were unsuitable for three-cylinder locomotives.

Orders came in to the works for new blastpipe caps of reduced diameter. Instructions were issued for jumper tops to be wedged down and smokebox baffleplates to be removed. More radical alterations involving new copper and steel tubeplates and superheater headers followed soon after. Material had to be ordered and the work pushed through the Shops, taking precedence over everything else. The men responded magnificently, working round the clock, as they always did at Crewe when the reputation of the department was at stake.

I followed with intense interest the various dynamometer car tests and boiler efficiency trials which were undertaken with the 5X class locomotives during these years. Tests with two parallel boiler engines Nos. 5517 and 5540 and two *Jubilees* Nos. 5553 and 5554, both with two-row superheaters between Wolverhampton and Euston on accelerated timings of 1 hour 50 minutes showed up the deficiencies of the new engines. Their steaming was indifferent and coal consumption was 10 per cent higher than with the *Baby Scots*.

In view of the great importance of locomotive fuel consumption Sir Harold Hartley had appointed a committee in 1930 to consider the combustion process in locomotive fireboxes and the possibilities of saving fuel. New methods for analysing the smokebox gases and evaluating the amount of unburnt fuel were devised. Developed under the supervision of Dr. Lewis Dale, head of the chemical division of the Research Department, they enabled a complete heat balance of a locomotive in service to be drawn up. Thus it became possible accurately to compare the efficiency of boilers of different designs. The locomotives to be tested were equipped with indicator shelters and experimental apparatus at Crewe. Though not always welcomed by C.M.E. headquarters who were inclined to think that all locomotive experimental work was their monopoly, the gas analysis work which Martin Herbert's people did was a most valuable supplement to more conventional dynamometer car trials.

When fitted with larger superheaters and improved tube ratios, the taper boilered locomotives were as good as their predecessors. They did in fact become very good engines on express passenger work all over the system.

Swindon had always enjoyed a high reputation for good workmanship and finish on the locomotives they built. It was very soon plain that the new chief would be satisfied with nothing less than he had been accustomed to in the past. Methods new to the L.M.S. were introduced for finishing journals and axlebox bearings. Wheel centres, re-designed to give a much stiffer rim, had to be machined to higher standards than those to which we had been accustomed. New techniques had to be learned. Stanier's engines had hollow cast iron piston heads screwed on to the rod – something quite new to us, which took some time to get right. In boiler-making too, there were significant changes, both in the shops and sheds, upon which Stanier insisted.

Tubes were in future to be expanded on the water side of the tube plates. Copper ended flue tubes, with steel ferrules were replaced by tubes screwed into the firebox tubeplate, demanding a very high standard of machining. Crewe Works and one or two of the Western Division sheds already had some 5 years experience of steel firebox stays in the *Royal Scots*, but their widespread introduction in the new taper boilers caused one or two troubles. Broken steel stays were not always easy to detect. I remember very well the consternation caused when, after a *Class 5* 4-6-0 came on to the Works for repairs with a badly bulged firebox due to broken stays, Riddles quite rightly stopped all *Class 5s* until their fireboxes were specially examined.

We were perhaps more caught up at Crewe than at other Works in the anxieties which arose from the troubles, small in themselves, but large in the context of departmental politics, with new locomotives from which so much was expected. Stanier had gained the wholehearted loyalty and respect of his own staff. But there were subversive influences elsewhere, unhelpful to the new engines, against which Riddles, as Stanier's principal assistant, waged implacable war.

It was specially important that the two *Pacifics* should be universally acknowledged as doing well. They were for some time plagued by minor troubles. The smokebox regulator, combined in one casting with the superheater header, was a perfect pest. Distortion from temperature differences made it very difficult to keep the regulator valve steamtight. Great Western engines had their smokebox regulator valve castings quite separate from the superheater headers. Hot bogie boxes and outside slidebars were other troubles which brought the engines back to the

Works more often than was good for their reputation – particularly after an unfortunate Press demonstration run from Euston, when 6200 had a hot box which entailed a 45-minute late arrival at Crewe. There was, too, the remarkable case of one of these engines working the Up Merseyside Express non-stop from Crewe to Willesden, developing a hot inside big end near Rugby. The brasses disintegrated. The resulting knock loosened the big end cotter and gudgeon pin, both of which fell on to the track. The rod, now free, was shot out on the ground through the narrow space between the leading and trailing bogie wheels. This sounded such an extraordinary story when I heard it over the 'phone from the Motive Power people, that I went off to Rugby on the first available train to see for myelf the extent of the damage to the engine, by that time safely in the shed. Some new parts were obviously going to need putting in hand in the Shops forthwith. How the connecting rod got itself out on to the track without derailing the locomotive we shall never know – it was one of the classic 'might have beens' of which those outside the service seldom hear anything.

Riddles gave me verbal instructions – Lemon was away ill at the time – that the *Pacifics* were not to be taken on the Works if any minor defect was within the competence of Crewe North Shed to put right. Whatever may have been the state of relationships in high places at Euston, we at Crewe 158 miles away worked in close and friendly contact with our opposite numbers in the Motive Power and Operating Departments. Though I forget now what exactly the trouble was, I was asked one morning to take 6201 on the Works for some minor job which would have taken the Shed a couple of days, but which we could do and have the engine back in traffic the same day. As it seemed to my simple mind that the object of the exercise was to keep these two engines out of service for the shortest possible time, I readily agreed and the job was done by lunch time. Somehow or other Riddles heard that 6201 was back on the Works. He was soon on the telephone demanding an explanation. He was in no way mollified when I told him the engine was already back in traffic. I was sharply instructed kindly to obey orders in future. A useful lesson on the need to pay attention to politics in high places, however obscure the reason for so doing.

Lemon's illness lasted for many weeks, during which I found myself, for the first time, in charge of Crewe Works. Enjoying my chief's confidence, as I believe I did, one saw to it that affairs were carried on as he would wish. Nevertheless there is a real difference between being second-in-command and in temporary charge of the whole outfit, even though it may be for a matter of weeks rather than months. Questions which the Chief Clerk might reasonably be excused for keeping for the chief's return from a normal holiday period had to be decided. Walter Evans, a chief clerk of the old school in the days before lady secretaries for Works Managers would have been considered quite the thing, was a tower of strength, upon whose advice one could rely. Weekly meetings with Arnold Bentley, the local head of the Chief Accountant's Department, to discuss current expenditure in relation to budget and decide action thereon, had now to be dealt with direct, instead of by instructions conveyed to me by Lemon.

Other new responsibilities of quite a different kind came crowding in upon me at this time. Our first child – a daughter – was born on 11th September, 1934. I was far more fussed about this happy event than was my wife. A 'phone call from the doctor announcing Angela's safe arrival about 11 o'clock in the morning lifted a load from my mind.

The news having been relayed to the Works Manager's house, I was bidden by Mrs. Lemon to let the locomotives look after themselves for the rest of the morning and come along to celebrate.

For the first time I found myself on the list of officers whom the Operating people had to notify by telephone, at any hour of the day or night, of serious accidents on the Western Division. My wife and I seldom patronised the cinema, but on the evening of 28th September, 1934, we left our new daughter in the care of Jean's sister and went to see some special film now long forgotten, at a cinema we had never before visited. I was astounded half way through the performance to see a flash appear on the screen announcing that I was wanted on the 'phone by the Traffic Control Office. It was, I suppose, a routine drill to telephone all places of entertainment if a call on the company's 'phone to one's house was unanswered. How else, even in Crewe, where one's movements seemed to be of more than ordinary interest, could I have been tracked down?

There had been a bad collision at Winwick Junction. The 5.20 p.m. Euston to Blackpool had run into the rear of a local train. A number of passengers had been killed. An Officers' Special was leaving Crewe for the site in half an hour. I was uncertain whether it was the usual custom at Crewe for the Works Manager to go to accidents – but as it seemed to me better that the question 'What is he here for?' should be asked rather than 'Why wasn't someone from the Works there?' I hurried off to the station and joined the special train. The Winwick collision was wholly due to a signalman's error. The engine of the express, a *Prince of Wales* No. 25648 *Queen of the Belgians* though buried under the twisted remains of three or four telescoped coaches was virtually undamaged, and not derailed. In fact, it left the site in due course under its own steam. No help in the shape of men or equipment was needed from the Works on this occasion – nor was the mechanical condition of the locomotive in any way involved. Nevertheless the Winwick collision impressed on me the questions which might be at issue in other circumstances. Whenever reasonably possible after this, I went to serious mishaps of which I was notified by Control. There was nearly always something to be learnt from a design or maintenance point of view. Being at the site, watching the breakdown gangs at work was always interesting and added to one's general knowledge and experience as a railwayman. Sometimes the evidence of one's own eyes was invaluable for subsequent use at the accident inquiry, when conflicting departmental interests were involved.

As the steaming troubles with the three-cylinder 4-6-0s were overcome and with the *Class 5* 4-6-0s and 2-8-0s welcomed everywhere, the early doubts about the new engines completely disappeared. The *Pacifics* of which eleven more, including No. 6202, the turbine locomotive, were built in 1935, were doing splendid work. The turbine locomotive, often known as the 'Turbomotive', an abbreviation almost as offensive as 'British Rail', was, I think, the most successful unconventional steam locomotive ever to run in this country. I was fortunate to be concerned with its building, which involved many visits to the Trafford Park Works of Metropolitan-Vickers, who designed and made the turbines and gear transmission. Sir Henry Guy, who later became the Secretary of the Institution of Mechanical Engineers, was in general charge of the project. I was much impressed by the high standard of workmanship and later by the meticulous care which Guy took during discussions in my office, in probing and analysing the cause of early troubles in service with some of the turbine and transmission components with which we were unfamiliar. The turbine locomotive covered nearly half a million miles in revenue earning service. This might well have been very much more but for long periods out of service during the war years, when absolute priority for munitions production made it impossible to undertake repairs to the turbines and transmission. The experience which we gained with 6202 seemed to me of such wide interest that I wrote a paper* for the Institution of Locomotive Engineers giving an account of the first ten years of service. In 1952 Riddles decided that the cost of new turbines, which by then were needed, could not be justified. The decision was therefore taken to rebuild 6202 as a normal four-cylinder locomotive. I was glad to be able to persuade J. F. Harrison, who was by then in charge at Derby, to make one or two alterations to the drawings which certainly enhanced the appearance of this grand engine when she emerged from Crewe in her new form.

The middle nineteen-thirties were the years when competition from internal air services and the private motor car on long distance journeys began to be seriously felt. With each new issue of the timetable faster express services were introduced. The *Princess Royal Pacifics*, together with the *Royal Scots* were able to meet all demands. Regular double-heading was virtually a thing of the past. But more was yet to come. A new train, to be named the *Coronation Scot* planned to cover the 401½ miles

* Ten Years Experience with the L.M.S. 4-6-2 Non-condensing Turbine Locomotive 6202 Paper 458, *Journal, Institution of Locomotive Engineers, Vol. XXXVI No. 191.*

between London and Glasgow in 6½ hours was to be introduced in the 1937 summer timetable.

For the purpose of obtaining data for the timings of the new train, a dynamometer car test with one of the first two *Pacifics* hauling a train of seven coaches weighing 219 tons, non-stop from Euston to Glasgow in 6 hours, returning the following day, was planned to take place on 16th and 17th November, 1936.

I was much concerned, literally at the last moment if a postponement of carefully laid plans was to be avoided, in the preparation of 6201 for the test runs. In his biography of Sir William Stanier, O. S. Nock* has already told my story of the spare main steam pipe joint ring, which in response to an urgent telephone call from Riddles, was obtained from the Stores at Crewe on a dark and wet Sunday evening and handed to the driver of a train bound for Euston. It does not need to be repeated here. I was more than content to see 6201 come through Crewe three minutes before time the following day, and ten minutes early at 95 miles per hour past Minshull Vernon, where I had taken my wife to see the train pass on the return journey.

Five new streamlined *Pacifics* with appreciably higher steaming capacity than the *Princess Royals* were built at Crewe for working the *Coronation Scot* trains. It seemed from the drawings which I saw on their way to the Shops, that there were not likely to be any unduly difficult production problems. The steel and copper throat plates were just about as large as the presses could accommodate, but we had already learned a lot about deep flanging when building the latest version of *Princess Royal* boilers. Time was short and we were certainly going to be very busy in the pattern shop, foundry and millwrights, producing a complete set of new boiler flanging blocks, to say nothing of new cylinders, wheel centres and general iron and steel castings.

Nothing was allowed to stand in the way of turning the new engines out to time. Late evening visits to the Shops to see how things were progressing on the night shift were part and parcel of our daily routine, and sustained the drive to meet the promised dates. The engines went together beautifully in the Erecting Shop. It was the final finishing that caused the pain and grief! Lemon insisted that the hexagon heads of the scores of externally visible set screws fastening the streamlined casing plates to the crinoline irons should all be precisely in line when finally tightened up – no easy job. And we spent a long time one Sunday morning in the Paint Shop deciding exactly how the four silver stripes painted along the sides of the streamlined casing were to be brought smoothly over the compound curves, to a neat point between the buffers. The final result

---

* O. S. Nock 'William Stanier: An Engineering Biography' *Ian Allan, London*, 1964.

was worth all the time and trouble. The engines were both good in
themselves and good to look at. A letter from Sir William, reproduced
below, of which Lemon sent me a copy, gave all of us at Crewe much
pleasure and satisfaction.

F. A. Lemon, Esq.   From: C. M. E.'s Office,
Crewe.   Euston
                                                  30th June, 1937.

Dear Lemon,
    I think that with the results of yesterday's trials, and with the results that we have ob-
tained up to the present with the four engines which are now out of the works, that I
should write to you of my appreciation of the work that has been done at Crewe under
your direction in the construction of the locomotives.
    I have in my short time with the L.M.S. made a great many demands on both the
designers and the Works, but none have been so great as that which I have asked to be
done in the building of the latest *Coronation* engines.
    The short time available for their building has meant, I know, long hours of work, not
only for the men, but for you and your staff, and to the men and to you and your foremen,
I am very grateful.
    The results that we have so far obtained prove that the workmanship has been of the
very best, and I am sure that in no part of the world have any locomotives been turned out
with a greater degree of accuracy in measurement.
    I should like you to convey to all those concerned on your staff, and to the men, my very
great appreciation and thanks for what they have done, and for maintaining the prestige
of our Department in this great railway.

                    Yours very sincerely,
                    W. A. Stanier.

    High praise and generous indeed. 'Yesterday's trials' to which the
C.M.E. referred was the special demonstration run from Euston to Crewe
and return, on which No. 6220 *Coronation* reached a speed of 114 miles
per hour coming down the bank from Whitmore, and returned from Crewe
to Euston in 1 hour 59 minutes at an overall average speed of 79·7 miles
per hour. The electrics do no better today. Of course, they do it every day
and several times a day – but let those fine performances of the steam era
not be forgotten. The five *Coronation Pacifics* and thirty-three engines of
the same class which were built later were Stanier's masterpiece. To me
they represented all that was best in British locomotive engineering.
    Though in my recollections of these years the new locomotives seem to
have been our main preoccupation, this was only partially true. Like all
other railway works something like 85 per cent of the man-hours worked
at Crewe were on activities directly concerned with repairs to locomotives
and general railway engineering equipment. There were too, always
schemes of improvement in progress in the Works, notably at this time the
re-equipment of the Steel Foundry with pulverised coal-fired melting fur-

naces. Pulverised coal may be all very well if properly confined. But fed from a central plant through flimsy pipes over considerable distances to the Forge as well as the Steel Foundry, it was the most prolific source of dust and dirt that it has been my misfortune to encounter.

Labour relations at Crewe were generally very good, largely due to the influence of Horace Andrews, the secretary of the Works Committee, at meetings of which I frequently took the chair. Andrews held strong views inclining to the left; but he was always reasonable and absolutely straight. He staunchly upheld the interests of those who had elected him, but he was a stickler for constitutional procedure though impatient of petty debating points. He saw more clearly than some of his colleagues that the well-being of the men in the Works was ultimately dependant on the prosperity of the Company for which we all worked.

As it seemed to me likely that such further promotion as might come my way would be in Works rather than in other sections of the Department, I involved myself as fully as possible in the broader aspects of works ad-ministration, such as staff relations, systems of payment by results and organisation generally – in a word the management of men as distinct from the purely engineering aspects of locomotive design, construction, maintenance and performance which interested me so much.

I was fortunate in being appointed as a member of a committee set up by the C.M.E. to report on the pay and conditions of service, in all L.M.S. Works, of that important body of men between the craftsmen and the foremen – the work examiners, piecework setters and progress inspectors – who had put in a claim for salaried status. This was most valuable experience towards preparing me for what I hoped might be the next move – to find myself in charge of one of the smaller Works when one of the Works Managers retired.

But though man may propose in his own mind, the Chief Mechanical Engineer disposes! I was sent for by Stanier at Euston towards the end of 1937 and told that, subject to the approval of Sir Nigel Gresley, to whom he was taking me at King's Cross in a few minutes, I was to become Superintending Engineer to take charge of the design, construction and running of the Locomotive Testing Station to be built as a joint venture by the L.M.S. and L.N.E.R. at Rugby. Sir Nigel was most cordial in ap-proving my appointment.

Returning home that evening I turned over in my mind the pros and cons of this unexpected turn of events. On the credit side, it was probably a compliment to be given responsibility for an entirely new enterprise that would be much in the public eye – the more so as Sir Nigel Gresley, the principal advocate of the need for a stationary testing plant in Great Bri-tain might well have wanted one of his own men. I should be reporting direct to the two Chief Mechanical Engineers, and through them to a joint committee of directors of the two Companies. There was a reasonable increase in salary, welcome at any time, particularly so just then, with our second child expected within a few months! There was no denying that I should miss the restless activity and the sense of urgency in a large Works, which I found so stimulating. Was not the new job rather restricted in scope — a little too specialised? Above all, might it not become a backwater? The railways had carried on quite successfully in the past without a locomotive testing station; and could continue to do so in the future. They certainly could not do without locomotive Works. Thus I had some reservations, but I deemed it wiser to keep them to myself. In any event the way ahead for the next two or three years was clear enough. I was deeply interested in locomotive testing and performance. The new experience which I should gain in the design and construction of the testing plant itself, and the buildings, would be invaluable. Here was a project which would be mine alone to bring into successful operation as soon as possible. Then I would seek the first opportunity to return to the flood tide of essential activity — the main workshops organisation of the department.

So my first five years at Crewe ended with some regrets. We were however, to continue living within the precincts of the Works for a further eighteen months, though working at Euston returning home at weekends, until progress with the Testing Station made a move to Rugby essential. We had become completely absorbed into the railway community at Crewe. Outside working hours there were few weeks, particularly during the winter months, when we were not involved in some social activity directly connected with the Works, culminating in the annual dinner and dance of the Workshop Supervisory Staff Association, to which the C.M.E. and his family were always invited. All this we should miss when the time came to move our home. No-one, least of all perhaps myself, could have foreseen that the fortunes of war would bring us back among these familiar surroundings before another five years had passed.

CHAPTER SIX

Rugby Locomotive Testing Station

[1937–39]

THE DECISION OF THE BOARDS OF THE L.M.S. and L. & N.E. Railways jointly to build a Locomotive Testing Station similar to those which had been operating for some years in America, Germany and France, was a fitting tribute to the persistence of Sir Nigel Gresley. Ten years earlier, in his Presidential Address to the Institution of Mechanical Engineers in 1927, Gresley had urged the need for a national testing station if Great Britain was to remain in the forefront of locomotive design and development. As a result a committee under the chairmanship of Sir Alfred Ewing was set up by the Department of Scientific and Industrial Research to examine the matter. The Committee, on which the railway companies and the private locomotive builders were represented, reported in favour of the project. But by the time they did so, economic conditions compelled postponement of any action. Sir Nigel Gresley returned to the attack in a further paper to the Institution of Mechanical Engineers in 1931.* A new committee appointed in 1934 confirmed the previous findings, though some of the former intending participants in the scheme did not then feel able to contribute to the cost. But Gresley, backed up by Sir Harold Hartley, had made his case: the two companies decided to proceed on their own.

Tests and comparative trials have always played an important part in locomotive development. One may call to mind, for example, the Rainhill trials on the Liverpool and Manchester Railway in 1827. Probably the first vehicle on a British railway equipped as a dynamometer car to measure locomotive drawbar pull was a four-wheeled van put into service on the Great Western Railway about 1879. Other railways followed suit some years later. It is a comparatively simple matter to measure the power output of a locomotive at any particular point in a journey, if indicating gear is fitted to the engine and a dynamometer car is attached between the locomotive and the other vehicles in the train. What is much less simple is to establish a scientific basis on which to relate the measurements so obtained to the dimensions and design features of the locomotive, and the

---

* H. N. Gresley 'Locomotive Experimental Stations' *Proceedings, Institution of Mechanical Engineers, Vol. 121*, 1931.

various resistances to motion overcome by the power produced.

The principal objectives of locomotive testing, apart from straightforward comparative trials between one type of locomotive and another, are twofold – first to assess the effects of changes in design on performance and efficiency in terms of fuel consumed in relation to work done, and second, to determine the relationships between loads hauled, speeds and fuel consumption. Thus locomotive testing work as a whole falls into two broad groups providing information for those responsible for design and operation respectively. They can conveniently be described as Design Efficiency Testing and Performance Efficiency Testing. The former includes:

(a) Verification of scientific data on which design is based.
(b) Assessment of the effect of modifications to design on performance and efficiency.

The latter embraces:

(a) Determination of loads and timings in relation to locomotive capacity and efficiency; and
(b) The effects of different methods of working and of varying states of repair.

The history of steam locomotive development is one of sustained improvement in power and efficiency to which the contribution made by indicating and dynamometer car tests in normal service was very important. Valuable though they were for etablishing the broad relationships between power, speed, fuel consumption and work done, deciding loads and timings appropriate to the capacity of locomotives over a given route, and assessing design changes, the results of such tests were necessarily average values reflecting the widely varying conditions of normal service. Speed, gradient, curvature, wind and weather are all subject to random variations. The power output of a locomotive on a normal journey is thus correspondingly variable; and is affected by the human element in driving and firing. Thus it is not possible in normal service testing to derive characteristic curves of coal consumption, steam rate and power in relation to speed, cut-off and steam temperature, nor to establish the connection between draught, gas flow and steam flow over the whole operating range – in a word, to plot the relations between all the interdependent factors which together determine the whole pattern of locomotive power and efficiency.

As design becomes more efficient thus reducing the scope for further improvement, and as the need to utilise locomotives in traffic as effectively as possible became ever more insistent, testing methods must become more accurate and closely controlled. It is essential for correct conclusions to be drawn from either design or performance efficiency testing that each separate factor influencing the results should be isolated, strictly controlled and maintained at constant values for the duration of each test. Therein lies the justification for locomotive testing stations, and for equipment such as Mobile Testing Units or brake locomotives to enable tests to be carried out on the line under constant conditions, particularly as regards speed – or, as developed under the title of the Controlled Road Testing system at Swindon, at constant rates of firing and evaporation. Design efficiency testing can be carried out with equal accuracy on the road or at a stationary test plant – but usually more conveniently at the latter. Performance efficiency trials must of necessity be undertaken on the road. As S. O. Ell of Swindon has pointed out,* the two complementary methods of testing provide the link between the thermo-dynamics of the locomotive and the dynamics of the train.

At the time of my appointment as Superintending Engineer of the new testing station, the offices of the two Chief Mechanical Engineers to whom I was now jointly responsible, were within a stone's throw of each other – at Euston and King's Cross respectively. I might well have been asked to go to King's Cross. But I was glad to be given accommodation at Euston and invited to join their private lunch club at Maples by L.M.S. men I already knew well. Rather naturally, I tended to regard myself still as belonging to the L.M.S. But I was reminded of my rather unusual joint status by being given a London & North Eastern silver pass – and the meetings of the Superintending Committee of Directors were held in the Board Room at Marylebone under the chairmanship of Andrew McCosh – who presided over the Locomotive Committee of the L.N.E.R.

Though for the previous six years I had enjoyed the advantages of a private office, I was more than content to share at Euston a room with Stewart Cox. He was then Personal and Technical Assistant to the C.M.E. and was amongst other matters much concerned with the policy and methods of locomotive testing so far as the L.M.S. was concerned. Thus was established a close relationship which was to continue with the utmost harmony, and identity of outlook on the many problems which it fell to us to deal with together for the next thirty years.

In order to provide a channel of communication with the C.M.E. Department of the L.N.E.R., and as he put it, 'To keep an eye on what I was doing' Gresley deputed a member of his personal staff at King's Cross, Roy Hart-Davis, to give me whatever help I needed in obtaining information about L.N.E. locomotives, for which provision would need to be made at Rugby. This was for me a most agreeable arrangement. Roy Hart-Davis was a personal friend of long standing. We had first met through a mutual friend in Norwich, when Hart-Davis was Assistant District Locomotive Superintendent there. He was unique among railway

* 'Developments in Locomotive Testing' S. O. Ell. *Journal of the Institution of Locomotive Engineers Vol. 43* (1953) No. 235.

mechanical engineers. He was a bachelor, and fastidious in his personal affairs to a remarkable degree. He was an accomplished horseman – and during his years in London was a member of the Metropolitan Mounted Police. He had a distinguished war record in Burma. He inherited Sir Nigel's roll-top desk and when, in later years, I was able to secure his appointment as secretary to the committee on the system of electrification to be adopted by British Railways, and he had to move to Railway Executive Headquarters, his only stipulation was that he should bring his own office furniture with him from Doncaster. Not for him the standard office equipment of the day. He was something of a mystic – and I remember well an evening when, knowing I was taking a night train to Scotland, he telephoned me at home urging me to get into the train, and close the door, before it started moving. I heeded the warning and did as I was bid. Roy Hart-Davis is unhappily no longer with us. I salute his memory. He was a firm friend, and a delightful companion on the journeys to Paris and Berlin where we went to visit the French and German testing stations at Vitry and Grunewald.

With due regard to all that we had learnt from our visits abroad, I went ahead with the preparation of plans and estimates for our new plant. My proposals were based substantially on the layout of the French station at Vitry. General arrangement drawings were made for me in the Locomotive Drawing Office at Crewe by Frank Onions, a senior works plant man, who I knew would produce a first class job.

In his paper on Locomotive Experimental Stations in 1931, Gresley made the point that the plant, which he then proposed should be built in this country, should reproduce conditions on the road more closely than was the case with the stations operating abroad. This was to be done by surrounding the locomotive under test in a wind tunnel. The idea was not to simulate the air resistance of the locomotive on the track, but to reproduce the effect of a current of air into the ashpan. It was intended that the power for driving the fans to produce the wind should come from the locomotive under test. So instead of the usual method of power absorption by hydraulic brakes, a combination of electric generators and brakes connected together through bevel gearing was proposed. Presumably as a result of the experience gained from the tests with *Cock O' the North* at Vitry in 1934, Gresley was satisfied that the wind tunnel idea was neither necessary nor desirable. Be that as it may, there was no question of a wind tunnel being included in our plans. The provision of a wind tunnel would have implied confusion of thought as to the types of test for which a stationary plant is pre-eminently suitable and those for which controlled conditions out on the line are preferable.

It was important that our new plant should be able to accommodate not only all British steam locomotives then in service, but also any which might be built in the future. I had it in mind, too, that with some additions to instrumentation, the plant should be capable of testing electric, diesel or gas-turbine locomotives. It seemed to me not unlikely that 4-6-4s, 4-8-2s and even 2-10-2s might be built before many years were out. Our plans, therefore, made provision for seven sets of roller units on which the wheels of the engine under test are supported. The foundations and main girders supporting the equipment were made long enough to accommodate an eighth roller unit if ever that were needed in the future. Five Froude hydraulic brakes, each capable of absorbing 1200 horse power throughout a wide speed range up to a maximum of 130 miles per hour, were specified. The roller units were designed to carry an axle load of 30 tons. With the hydraulic dynamometer capable of measuring tractive efforts of up to 40 tons, we had made ample provision for the future.

My ideas for the main building in which the plant was to be housed were strictly conventional. A steel-framed brick building with a trussed roof and girders for a 15 ton overhead crane seemed to me to fill the bill very nicely. But of course I was no expert in civil engineering construction. It had already been decided that the buildings and the foundations for the testing plant would be designed by the Chief Civil Engineer of the L.M.S. and constructed under his supervision. The welded steel arch design produced by the office at St. Pancras was admirable in every way. It provided just the right solution to the difficult problem of supporting the smoke corridor high in the roof from which a steel chimney movable longitudinally, had to be suspended.

Alongside the main building, which included a sound-proofed control room and workshop facilities for plant maintenance, there was to be a locomotive preparation shed in which I proposed to instal a 35 ton wheel drop. We should thus be able to deal with hot boxes without having to rely on the Motive Power Depot or the C.M.E. erecting shop. They could however, be called on for boiler washing or any special repairs which might arise. It seemed sensible that we should be reasonably self-supporting, so I made provision in the office building for a small chemical laboratory in which coal samples could be analysed and calorific values determined.

With the civil engineering side of the project safely in the hands of the L.M.S. at St. Pancras, I gave much thought to the question of how best to deal with the design of the equipment of the testing plant itself. Frank Onions and his men at Crewe, with some increase in staff, could have undertaken the work. Competitive tenders for the various items would have been involved. The more I thought of it the less I liked this solution to the problem. The hydraulic brakes, around which the whole of the plant would have to be designed, were to be obtained from Messrs. Heenan and Froude of Worcester. They were the only British firm with any experience of equipment for locomotive testing plants. All the many items, from the foundation grillage to the coal handling and water measuring apparatus, would need to be compatible with each other and function as one comprehensive assembly. Clearly this was a case for one main contractor only to be responsible for design, construction, and erection of the whole plant, in conformity with the specifications which I had prepared, and which had been approved by the two Chief Mechanical Engineers and the Superintending Committee. To my great relief my recommendation that Heenan and Froude should be appointed main contractor was accepted.

There was in any case a considerable job of co-ordination to be done with the civil engineer's department laying the tracks giving access to the site, the building contractors, electricity and water supply authorities, and Messrs. Heenan and Froude.

Both Stanier and Gresley maintained throughout a close personal interest not only in the general progress of the work, but in the many details of design upon which I sought their advice. Stanier was always approachable. I had been given to understand from some of my L.N.E.R. friends that Gresley was not easy to talk to – but I found quite the reverse to be the case. Once the contracts for the plant had been let, I had a great deal of travelling to do, not only to Worcester, but also to sub-contractors works. There were plenty of opportunities for trips on the footplate. One such journey was down to Scotland on a streamlined *Pacific* hauling the *Coronation Scot* non-stop from Euston to Carlisle. More I think, than on any previous journey, I was impressed by the desirability of fitting speed indicators to all express passenger locomotives. After many miles in the eighties along the Trent Valley from Tamworth 55 miles per hour round the curve at Stafford No. 1 seemed deceptively slow. Few serious accidents have been caused by excessive speed. Nevertheless a speed indictor, if not a recorder, was obviously becoming essential if speed restrictions were to be accurately observed as average booked speeds increased. I happened to mention this journey in conversation with Gresley at one of our weekly meetings. He expressed a wish for me to ride on his A4 *Pacifics* hauling high speed trains – and having done so to give him my impressions. I rode from King's Cross to Newcastle and back on two of the newest A4s. What magnificent engines they were. I remember watching the speed recorder under the fireman's seat showing a steady 95 miles per hour for miles on end. The riding of both engines were generally first class, but coming down from Stoke tunnel to Grantham, and on the return journey somewhere near Hitchin, the engines each suffered an attack of severe rolling – so much so that on both occasions steam was shut off and the brakes applied. All this I reported to Sir Nigel, suggesting that the Great Western bolster bogie which Stanier had brought with him from Swindon had much to commend it. Gresley listened intently to what I had to say. Did I think that Mr. Stanier would let him have drawings of the L.M.S. *Pacific* bogies? The drawings were of course supplied. In due course a number of L.N.E.R. engines were fitted with side-bolster bogies.

Gresley was an ardent admirer of French locomotive engineering. As our plant at Rugby was to be based largely on the layout at Vitry, with some important modifications shown by experience to be desirable, Sir Nigel arranged with the General Manager of the French National Railways for the engineer in charge of Vitry to be available for advice and consultation if required. I did not particularly welcome this arrangement, which was soon terminated. The Frenchman was a volatile character, whose ideas on advice and consultation did not altogether coincide with mine. He was apparently much involved in political activities in his native country. And when on one of his visits to London he asked me to acquire a revolver which I was to smuggle into France on my next visit to Vitry, I felt the time had come for us to part company! An embarrassing situation was neatly resolved, with the approval of the Superintending Committee, by a tactful letter and a substantial payment for services rendered.

An important addition to the plant at Rugby, which experience at Vitry had shown to be essential, was equipment for damping out the longitudinal vibrations arising from the unbalanced reciprocating forces, particularly with two-cylinder engines. The forces applied by a steam locomotive to the recording equipment of a stationary testing plant or dynamometer car is the resultant of two quite separate components due (i) to the steam pressure acting in the cylinders and (ii) to forces set up by unbalanced reciprocating parts. The first varies above and below a steady mean value, but always acts in one direction. The second varies from a maximum positive to a maximum negative value once in each revolution of the coupled wheels. The second component can at high speeds reach a value many times in excess of the steady mean tractive effort. Although occurring as an accelerating and decelerating force, it is a matter of common knowledge that the heavy fluctuations are not recorded on the dynamometer and are not passed back to the train. The explanation of this apparent anomaly lies in the fact that the frequency of the disturbing forces is many times greater than the natural frequency of the elastic sytem constituted by the locomotive and train. But the natural period of oscillation of a stationary testing plant is very different. During early tests at Vitry with a two-cylinder 2-8-2 locomotive the disturbing forces coincided with the natural frequency of the plant. Resonance was set up and the locomotive and plant were thrown suddenly into violent oscillation.

It was obviously important that we should know the conditions under which resonance might arise at Rugby, and what should be done to suppress it. I enlisted the help of the mathematics section of the Research Department to make an exhaustive analysis of this whole fascinating problem. As a result design parameters for the drawgear assembly and damping mechanism were established which would always ensure suppression of resonance at any speed at which locomotives were likely to be tested.

The German railway people whom I met during my visits to Berlin were no less helpful than the French in giving us information and arranging for me to be present at tests on the plant at Grunewald or out on the line to Magdeburg. Yet occasionally symptoms of the underlying tension of those years before the war came to the surface. It was during my visits to the continent at this time that I first came to regret that I had not been compelled, however unwillingly, to become reasonably fluent in at least one foreign language. I could manage passably well in France – but not in Germany. On my second visit to Berlin I took with me Ellis Brown, then one of the technical assistants at Euston, who spoke German fluently. He had German friends in Berlin, whom we invited to dine with us one evening. The conversation inevitably turned to international affairs, and went on until the early hours. Surely, we argued, civilised nations could compose their differences without once again going to war. Brown's friend was not unhopeful. Not so his wife – she argued vehemently that nothing would do but that Germany should regain her lost colonies, and if that meant war – so be it! It was a frightening evening and boded ill for the future. Roy Hart-Davis and I had another uncomfortable encounter returning from a visit to Amsler's works in Switzerland. Our route from Schaffhausen lay through Germany to Singen, where we were to join the international express to Calais. The Nazi official who examined our passports at the frontier station obviously wanted us to leave the train. He spoke no English and we firmly declined to understand any German – words or gestures! I told Roy that, short of physical force, we would not budge from the train. It was an early morning workman's local, the passengers in which, we could see, were becoming so impatient at the delay that the passport gentleman retired defeated. The train went on its way to Singen with us in it, and thus the episode ended. But we certainly felt a sense of relief when we left Germany that evening.

As well as taking a share in the testing plant at Rugby, the L.M.S. had authorised the provision of a new dynamometer car and three mobile units for constant speed testing on the line. These new facilities made it necessary to review the organisation and control of locomotive testing as a whole. This work had hitherto been the sole responsibility of the C.M.E. Department. But the design of the automatic electrical control of speed, which was the novel feature of the mobile testing units, was due to Dr. H. I. Andrews, a member of the Research Department – who were the initial sponsors of this new equipment. Though Rugby would be firmly rooted within the Chief Mechanical Engineer's sphere of influence, there was the complication of joint ownership with the L.N.E.R. And in any case Rugby would never have been authorised but for the support from Sir Harold Hartley – the 'father' of the Scientific Research Department. The possibilities for argument and inter-departmental rivalry were obviously quite considerable.

On the analogy that it was a settled principal of L.M.S. organisation that such functions as accountancy, purchasing of materials and control of stocks were the responsibilities of departments independent of those in which the accountable activities and consumption of materials took place, a memorandum was submitted suggesting that all locomotive testing should become the responsibility of an independent authority, either the Research Department or an autonomous inter-departmental committee. Only so, it was said, would testing be put on a scientific basis and unbiased results obtained. Strictly objective results from the two new forms of testing, directly reconcilable with each other were obviously necessary – but to have handed the work wholly to the Research Department would have been unacceptable to the C.M.E. Department, and quite rightly so. Though I have always been a firm believer in the need for a separate scientific research department as an essential part of a large railway system, here was an example of the way in which the Research Department sometimes acted against their own true interests by attempting to grab other people's work for themselves. Even today I doubt whether this lesson has been fully learned. But there is another side to this coin which should never be forgotten. The down-to-earth engineers on whom responsibility for design and safety of everything that runs on the railway ultimately rests, must keep their own theoretical knowledge polished and up to date. And they must have on their staff first class men of an academic standard at least equal to that of their opposite numbers in the Research Department.

The discussions on organisation took place before I was appointed to Rugby. By the time I arrived at Euston, a joint testing committee had been set up. A sensible division of work between the new facilities had been agreed. Rugby and the Mobile Testing Units would be regarded not as rivals, but complementary to each other. There were, however, deep divisions of opinion as to the details of testing procedure in which the protagonists were usually Stewart Cox and me on one side and Dr. Andrews on the other. D. W. Sanford, who followed me as Superintending Engineer at Rugby, took a prominent part in our discussions. He had a truly scientific, yet intensely practical, approach to all engineering problems. He was an accomplished mathematician; and had an unusual facility for making his mathematics understandable to others less gifted than himself. He was an excellent foil to Andrews, who had an equally scientific, but less practical approach to locomotive testing – a subject on which, however, he was very well informed, particularly in regard to the methods followed by the Germans and Russians. He argued his case with pertinacity, though always with good humour and took no offence at the nickname of Ivan the Terrible which Sanford bestowed upon him.

The arguments in committee were largely on the methods to be adopted to eliminate errors in determining coal consumption which could arise from differences in the weight and condition of the fuel on the grate at the beginning and end of a test. A further matter which aroused acute controversy was whether the characteristic curves of performance and efficiency should be based on indicated tractive effort or drawbar pull. Though final decisions on some of the questions would have to wait until we had some experience with our new equipment, there was a sufficient measure of agreement to enable me to start on the preparation of a code of practice for design efficiency testing at Rugby. I was much helped in this work by further visits to find out how the continental railways dealt with the matters about which we had been arguing. From what Stewart Cox and I saw at Vitry, it was evident that the French methods of gauging the amount of fuel on the grate left a great deal to be desired. We concluded that to ensure an acceptable degree of accuracy in coal consumption figures, at least three tons of coal would need to be burnt in each individual test, thereby reducing errors to a negligible amount.

French methods of constant speed testing on the line were also of considerable interest. We travelled in the dynamometer car between Laroche and Les Laumes on a test at seventy miles per hour with a four-cylinder 4-6-0 fitted with a Velox boiler — an oil-fired forced circulation steam generator capable of being ready for work as quickly as a diesel engine. Indeed, the locomotive with its driving cab at the front end was an attempt to achieve with steam some of the advantages of diesel locomotives. Some 4-6-4 diesel-electric locomotives, one of which we saw at Laroche, was already in main line service in France. The ease with which two old locomotives equipped with counter-pressure braking maintained the speed constant was most impressive. This test provided an interesting comparison with one I had attended a short time before with a B17 class 4-6-0 between York and Darlington in which speed was controlled in the same way.

We were accompanied throughout this visit to France by Monsieur Leguille, the C.M.E. of the East Division, who had been a member of the Indian Pacific locomotive committee. The French were probably ahead of everyone else in the work they had done in studying the behaviour of locomotives as vehicles on the track and measuring the complex forces involved. Footplate trips between Belfort and Troyes on a four-cylinder compound 4-8-2 and thence to Paris on a 4-6-2 over a road on which sharp curves of thirty chains radius with 6" cant were taken at seventy miles per hour without any signs of nosing or rolling, gave us convincing proof of the effectiveness of the values chosen for the initial and final loads on the side control springs of the bogies and trailing trucks of these two locomotives.

Though the visits which I had to pay to Worcester and places north of Crewe made it possible for me to spend an occasional night at home mid-week, weekends with my wife and family were a pleasure not to be lightly sacrificed. But the chance of taking part in a special test run with one of the L.M.S. *Pacifics* No. 6234 *Duchess of Abercorn* was too good to be missed. The engine had recently been fitted with a double blast pipe and chimney, the effects of which were to be ascertained by a dynamometer car test one Sunday from Crewe to Glasgow and back with a train of twenty vehicles, weighing 604 tons at the fastest current timings. The engine put up a magnificent performance, particularly on the return journey. Coming up the Clyde Valley in a raging wind and a snowstorm she averaged 63·4 miles per hour from Symington to Beattock Summit.

Drawbar horsepower was between 1800 and 2000 over long distances, with a maximum of 2500. The overall time from Glasgow to Carlisle with 604 tons was only one and a half minutes longer than the scheduled time of the 297 ton *Coronation Scot* train. The outward trip from Crewe had been good enough in all conscience, with 132 miles from Winsford to Carlisle covered at just over sixty miles an hour. The remainder of the journey on to Glasgow was equally noteworthy, though not without some anxiety. The train was booked to stop at Beattock for water; but someone decided that we should run non-stop to Symington instead. A contemporary account of this day's test refers to the fact that we lost a little time coming down from the Summit. And no wonder – the warriors on the footplate were trying to conserve what little water they had left. When we stopped at Symington, the tender was empty and the water was out of sight below the bottom of the gauge glasses. While the driver and fireman were busy at the water column, 'Uncle' Sutherland, who was riding as footplate observer, was making frantic efforts to get an injector started. He succeeded just in time – it was touch and go as to whether the fire would have to be dropped.

During the early spring of 1939, the headquarters of the C.M.E. Department were moved once more back to Derby. The C.M.E. himself and a small personal staff remained in London. Construction of the Testing Station buildings and the massive reinforced concrete foundation for the plant had reached a stage at which it was appropriate for me to move to Rugby. The office block had scarcely been started. Temporary accommodation was found for my clerk, a typist and myself, in which we set about all the administrative jobs involved in setting up a completely new organisation. The summer of 1939 was overshadowed by the growing international tension. The hopes of maintaining peace were clearly fading.

For some time previously we had all been receiving instructions on air raid precautions. For some reason, which was never very clear to me, I was required to attend a course in London on camouflaging buildings. I knew that if war broke out work on the Testing Station would be suspended at once – but what lay in store for me in that event I had no idea.

Though she was most unwilling to go, I sent Jean and the children over to her home in Northern Ireland during the last week in August. There perhaps they might escape the devastating air raids we all expected within a few days. I had promised to go over to Ireland for the weekend and set out from Rugby on Saturday evening 2nd September in a train to connect at Crewe with the Ulster Express for Heysham and the night boat to Belfast. It was a weird journey. The train was virtually blacked-out. The normal compartment lights had been replaced by dim blue bulbs. There was a violent thunderstorm going on outside – and the nearer I got to Crewe the less happy I felt about redeeming my promise to spend the weekend with my family in Ireland. Anything might happen within the next twenty-four hours. Shipping services might be suspended without warning. I might be stranded on the wrong side of the Irish Sea just at a time when the least one could do would be to be on the job ready for whatever instructions might be forthcoming. By the time the train drew into Crewe, I had made up my mind. I had to return to Rugby. I arrived back in the middle of the night. The street lights were still on – war had obviously not yet been declared. I heard Chamberlain's fateful broadcast on Sunday morning in my car on the way over to fetch our maid back to Rugby from her home in Nuneaton. The lights went out that night, not to be switched on again for five years.

Back in the office early next morning I received a call from The Grove, a large house in the country near Watford, which had become the wartime headquarters of the L.M.S. I was to stay in my office to receive further orders from the Deputy C.M.E., C. E. Fairburn, who, with Stanier half way across the Atlantic, returning from New York, was in charge of the department. When they came, after a delay which tried my patience to the utmost, the orders were as welcome as they were unexpected. I was to go to Glasgow as Acting Mechanical and Electrical Engineer, Scotland, in place of Robert Riddles who was being seconded to the Ministry of Supply as Director of Transportation Equipment. Fairburn asked me to meet Riddles for breakfast at Euston next morning, come out to The Grove to see him, and be prepared to go to Glasgow by the mid-day train. And so with time only to pack a bag and shut the front door, leaving my clerk to close down the office, my appointment as a joint officer of the L.M.S. and L.N.E. came to an abrupt end. I was once more to be back in the main stream of activity essential to the running of a railway, in peace or war.

CHAPTER SEVEN

The War Years:
St. Rollox and Crewe

[1939–1946]

THE NECESSARY PRELIMINARIES to taking up my new appointment in Scotland were soon completed. They were short and to the point. From what Riddles had time to tell me during breakfast at Euston, it was clear that affairs at St. Rollox were in good shape. It would be up to me to gain the confidence of the staff who served Riddles so well, and keep them so! The instructions I received from Fairburn, sitting behind a packing case as an improvised desk in an otherwise bare room at The Grove, were equally straightforward. I was to report to the Chief Officer for Scotland – one, John Ballantyne – in Glasgow the following morning. After that, get on with the job, and good luck!

The journey to Glasgow gave me plenty of time to reflect on what the future might hold in store. At the time of the formation of the L.M.S. Railway and for some time afterwards there were located at each of the main locomotive works, a Divisional Mechanical Engineer who was responsible, not only for the Works and Outstation Locomotive Shops, but for all outdoor mechanical engineering, except carriage and wagon activities. As each of the mechanical engineers in charge of the English divisions retired, the responsibilities of their successors were, with one or two exceptions, confined to the management of the main works and outstation shops. Control of outdoor machinery work was exercised direct from C.M.E. headquarters.

In Scotland, however, the original organisation continued unchanged, with the Mechanical & Electrical Engineer responsible for all departmental activities, including carriage and wagon work, north of the Border. The department in Scotland was thus a small scale replica of the department as a whole, an arrangement which accorded well with the autonomy in local management which Euston delegated to the Northern Division. To give some idea of what my new responsibilities would entail – there were two main Works, St. Rollox in Glasgow for locomotives and carriages, and Barrassie, down on the Ayrshire coast, for dealing with heavy repairs to wagons. Stock allocated to the Northern Division consisted of 1,290 locomotives, 4,700 coaches and 64,000 wagons. Subsidiary works at Inverness and Kilmarnock made a significant contribution to the output of locomotive and rolling stock repairs. Outdoor carriage and wagon work was organised in five districts controlled from Glasgow. There were quite large wagon repair shops at Perth and Motherwell, and smaller shops and depots spread about the country. A similar organisation with four areas spanning the country from Stranraer to Thurso and Kyle of Lochalsh looked after the maintenance and preparation of new works schemes of everything embraced within the title of outdoor machinery.

The department was also the responsible authority for fire protection at all the company's property. I see from my records that when I took over from Riddles, the department had a staff of 4,841. Annual expenditure was running at about £1.5 million. The weekly output of repairs was – locomotives 12; carriages 50; and wagons, heavy repairs 140; light repairs 1,650. It was all going to be of intense interest. Probably fairly straightforward under normal conditions, though I had everything to learn about carriage and wagon work. But under wartime conditions, of which I was given a grim reminder that night, it was anybody's guess. The city was black and silent, but something unusual seemed to be happening when I walked into the foyer of the Central Station Hotel. There were tired looking disconsolate people, some wrapped in blankets milling around. I presumed there must be an air raid warning in force. But I was wrong – these were some of the more fortunate victims of war – survivors from the torpedoed *Athenia*.

The new job was a challenge I felt ready to meet. Moreover, war or no war, the prospects of living within reach of some of Scotland's most magnificent country was most enticing. From the many months I had spent twelve years earlier inspecting locomotives built by the The North British Locomotive Co. and Beardmore's, I already knew Glasgow well. The Firth of Clyde, the lochs and mountains had cast their spell upon me. Any excuse to visit the west of Scotland during the intervening years had been good enough. My wife was half Scot; she had been at school in Helensburgh and had many friends in Scotland. We could look forward to a warm welcome in our new surroundings.

All L.M.S. affairs in Scotland were, subject to general policy direction from London, controlled by a local committee of directors, some of whom were members of the main L.M.S. board. General management was in the hands of the Chief Officer for Scotland, to whom I reported the next morning. I knew John Ballantyne only by repute. A Scotsman who had come up the hard way, he was said to be a man of few words, of shrewd commercial judgment and not inclined to suffer fools gladly. As members of his team, the departmental officers owed allegiance to the Chief Officer, Scotland, as well as being directly answerable to the head of their department in regard to their professional responsibilities. They attended the monthly meetings of the Scottish directors, to whom they presented reports on the work of their department. These arrangements were eminently sensible and worked well. I soon learned what the Chief Officer wanted from the C.M.E. Department in his territory; and I knew how Mr. Stanier wished the departmental responsibilities to be discharged. I received instructions, appropriate for each to give, direct from both my masters. But no conflict of loyalty arose. John Ballantyne had a healthy respect for his engineers and was far too wise to want all instructions to them to be issued in his name. Too often today it seems that what should be quite straightforward lines of communication down functional channels are twisted unnaturally to satisfy a theoretical management principle that instructions to the members of his team may only be issued in the name of the manager himself. Presumably this is done to bolster up the principle that no man can serve two masters. But everyone knows that in a complex organisation like a large railway system with all-line departments and geographical areas, many people in authority must inevitably serve two masters. But they serve them, in different ways, and with sensible men no conflict need arise. In my experience, a system which requires instructions from chief engineers to members of a department for which they are held professionally responsible, to be issued through area managers unqualified to understand the questions at issue, merely to maintain a principle, which is in any case an illusion, is not sensible.

John Ballantyne did not detain me long. I was soon on my way to take over the reins at St. Rollox. I was conducted by the commissionaire, with all due ceremony up to my room on the first floor, there to meet William Aikman, the chief clerk, and Miss Armour, my personal secretary. Aikman was a man of strict principles, wide learning and much experience in the railway service. He exerted considerable influence at St. Rollox and was held in respect by the staff. He looked after the interests of his chief with unremitting care. He took a fatherly interest in all our affairs – but was always most correct in his manner of offering advice. With his subordinate staff he was sometimes tactless and dictatorial. He was inclined to be quick tempered. On one occasion, so it was said, the Works Manager, hearing sounds of conflict, went in to Aikman's office to find him nearly throttling one of his minions! Another story which Aikman told me himself was an amusing sidelight on his character. It was apparently a long-standing custom that the policeman on the beat in Springburn Road covering the Works entrance, was given a free pass each year. There was a boilerhouse chimney near the road inclined to belch black smoke, about which the bobby made complaints at the office. He was told that if he made a nuisance of himself Aikman would stop his free pass!

I owed a great deal to William Aikman who was to be my guide and philosopher for close on two years, and a friend for very much longer. When he retired three of his old chiefs, Ivatt, Riddles and myself gave him a farewell lunch in Glasgow, with George Bellamy, who had followed me as Mechanical Engineer in Scotland. I was well served, too by Miss Armour, a gentle kindly soul inclined to be emotional – but nothing was too much trouble for her in seeing to my needs.

The Works Manager at St. Rollox was S. H. Whitelegg, for whom my arrival as his chief could not have been very welcome. He had not been very co-operative when we found ourselves virtually in the same job together for a short time at Horwich, six years earlier. This was no time to stand on ceremony. I went in to Whitelegg's room next door to mine, shook hands, and asked him to arrange for me to meet all the chief foremen, and the chairman and secretary of the Works Committee before the morning was out. It was just as well to get off the mark quickly and start as I meant to go on.

For the first time I found myself a member of a team, on an equal footing with the others, whose job was to run a railway system serving a part of the country whose contribution to the war effort would be particularly dependent on rail communications. My intense interest in everything that goes to the operation of a railway was immediately engaged. I acknowledge, with gratitude, the friendly welcome, and help I received from my new colleagues, Scots and Sassenachs alike. We were about equally divided. We lunched together in the Chief Officers Mess at the Divisional headquarters adjoining Buchanan Street Station. Many matters were settled over the lunch table without the need for writing letters to each other. I usually sat next to the Civil Engineer, A. W. McMurdo, a good Scot who, for the first few weeks, had little more to say to me than 'Good Morning'. But when he found that I had Scottish connections and a genuine affection for his country, invitations to join him on tours of inspection in his coach to such places as Oban, and Kyle of Lochalsh, where I had departmental outposts, were freely offered and accepted.

The transition from peace to war conditions proceeded remarkably smoothly. For at least two years the problems that would arise in the event of a major European war had been under discussion between the Ministry of Transport and the Railway Companies. It was known by the time of the Munich crisis that in a serious national emergency the railways would be brought under government control. A Railway Executive Committee consisting of the railway general managers was appointed in September 1938. It met regularly for the next twelve months. And so when on 1st September, 1939 the Minister of Transport issued the Emergency (Railway Control) Order taking them over, the railways were ready. The Minister appointed the Railway Executive Committee to be his agent for giving directions under the Order, and instructed the railways to carry on as usual. This we did, only more so, for the next six years.

Though from the very beginning the consequences of war pressed in upon us, massive air raids and widespread destruction, which everyone expected, did not materialise. There was a feeling of surprised relief that nothing worse than rationing and the blackout had so far to be endured. There no longer seemed any good reason why we should not take steps to resume a normal domestic life. My wife returned from Ireland to get on with the job of house hunting. I set off from the office one evening late in October to drive down to Stranraer to meet her. Ninety miles in pitch darkness with nothing but the miserable little slits in the headlamp masks for light was, certainly for the first time, a novel experience.

Houses to rent were hard to come by. We were fortunate to find a furnished house, vacated by a refugee family returning to Glasgow, in Bridge of Weir, twelve miles from the city in the Renfrewshire countryside. Away to the north Ben Lomond dominated the landscape. On clear days from our new home at the highest point in the village we could see Ben More and Stobinian, and to the west the hills and moors leading down to the sea. With the first weekend spent building a wall of sandbags to protect the windows of a room which was to serve as an air raid shelter, we were ready to meet the worst that Hitler could, and no doubt soon would, do. A chance meeting in a local shop with a girl whom Jean recognised as a school friend of some fifteen years earlier, was the beginning of a close and enduring friendship with the Stewart family, Frances and Henry, through whose kindness we were soon made to feel anything but strangers in a strange land.

A great deal of preliminary work on the utilisation of capacity in railway workshops for the production of munitions of war had been done during the years before 1939. Some government work was already in hand before the outbreak of war. But it was not until the spring of 1940 that orders for munitions of all kinds – tanks, aircraft, guns, bombs and shells and Bailey bridging components, to name but a few of the items produced – leading finally to over eighty per cent of all staff in L.M.S. Works being engaged on war production, were received on any large scale. In the meantime there was more than enough to keep us busy on normal railway work. It was not long before I received orders from Euston to do whatever was necessary to bring down the number of engines under and awaiting repairs, then standing at 5 per cent of the stock, to no more than 4 per cent. The miles made good by heavy repairs were roughly in balance with the miles being run. Output of repairs had been keeping pace with requirements. There were however, too many locomotives stopped waiting shops, some of which had been standing out of service a long time. A modest increase in the number of repairs per week should soon produce the desired result.

Output was increased by five engines per week, though without any reduction in the percentage out of service. Dissatisfaction with our apparent inability to do what was asked of us, which I expressed to Henry Fowler, son of my old chief Sir Henry and my assistant in charge of locomotive repairs, drew forth the reply that the Motive Power people were up to their old game frustrating our efforts by sending running engines into shops instead of those already stopped 'unserviceable at the sheds' — and moreover, the output of light repairs from the sheds was very much less than usual. I tackled my opposite number in the Motive Power Department, R. F. Harvey, another ex-Midland man, who undertook to restore the output from his depots at Polmadie, Carlisle and Perth, to the usual level. I reported accordingly to Euston, which, rather to my surprise, brought me a mild reproof from the C.M.E., who did not like classified repairs being done at the sheds. Far more important, however, was a letter which he sent to the Chief Operating Manager pointing out that there was not much hope of the Works getting down to 4 per cent if his people would not co-operate by giving preference to stopped engines in making their weekly allocation of repairs for the shops.

Second only in importance to increased output of repairs to locomotives and wagons, was the need to secure the utmost economy in the use of all kinds of material. A detailed review of repair practices was instituted at all the Works. Some relaxation of standards, hitherto regarded as inviolate would be permitted. Renovation of secondhand material from rolling stock under repairs had long been a highly developed part of our departmental organisation. A central depot at Derby for reclaiming non-ferrous metals had been in operation for many years. Many new steel components were made from scrap axles and tyres forged down to convenient sizes. The shops were generally self-supporting for supplies of cast iron, steel and non-ferrous scrap required in the foundries. No less than 19,000 tons of scrap arose from the maintenance activities in the C.M.E. Works and depots of the Northern Division during 1939. Nothing was sold which could be economically processed for further use. Equally nothing was taken for granted and the review of existing methods produced some useful new ideas for further economies.

An equally critical eye was passed over outdoor machinery and new works schemes. One which it was decided should go on was for cranes and conveyors for unloading two million tons per annum of iron ore for Colville's steel works from 10,000 ton ships into railway wagons at General Terminus Quay by the Broomielaw. A twenty-four hour turnround time for the ships was one of the conditions to be met. Transporters or cranes were the obvious alternatives. But if the latter were chosen, were they to be slewing or luffing cranes? This was a scheme in which Riddles had taken a close personal interest. He was convinced that the right solution was to use luffing cranes incorporating in their structure, a hopper into which the ore grabbed out of the ship, would be discharged, passing thence to conveyor belts and so into trains of special wagons to run a shuttle service between the quay and steelworks. The outdoor machinery people at Derby headquarters had different views. Notwithstanding the harmonic motion of the luffing mechanism, they felt that the swing developed by the loaded grab would be great enough to make a clean discharge into the hopper a very chancy affair. Riddles had told me of this difference of opinion and warned me that, with him out of the way, an attempt would almost certainly be made by Derby to have the whole question on which a decision had already been given by the C.M.E. re-opened.

Sure enough, within a very few weeks I received a letter from Derby suggesting 'that the whole question should be discussed afresh with me or my people'. Derby proposed that new tenders should be invited on a revised specification so drawn as to leave the type of plant offered to the discretion of the tendering firms. Clearly a delicate situation was about to arise! The conclusion that luffing rather than slewing was the right principle had been reached only after exhaustive investigation, including visits, sometimes with the Derby people, who were now trying to rock the boat, to Barking and Fulham Power Stations, where luffing cranes were successfully doing a similar job to that which we had to do in Glasgow. On the face of it there seemed to me no valid reason why the decisions already reached should be called in question. But the matter having been raised, the responsibility for confirming or varying the recommendations made to the C.M.E. and the Chief Officer for Scotland, was now mine. After much reading of papers and a good deal of devil's advocacy with my Outdoor Machinery Assistant, George Thomson, a first rate man who had been concerned with the scheme from its inception, I had no hesitation in repulsing the attack from Derby, and taking on the scheme unaltered from where Riddles had left it. Unfortunately, developing war conditions compelled postponement. It is beside the point that when, many years later, the scheme was completed, transporters, not cranes, were provided for unloading the ships.

To the duties entailed in running a divisional mechanical engineering department in peace time, there were added many additional responsibilities under war conditions. Air raid precautions and an organisation for covering emergency repairs to plant and equipment at depots, stations and docks in the vulnerable area were established and working smoothly, though it was some months before they were subjected to anything like a full scale test. As quite a separate matter, we were asked to make a detailed review of the firefighting arrangements, with particular reference to water supplies at railway properties throughout Scotland. This arose as a consequence of a proposal I had submitted to the Scottish directors for a

33,000 gallon water tank and booster pump to augment pressure in the fire mains serving the Stores Department and Carriage Paint Shop at St. Rollox. They were vulnerable buildings some distance from the remainder of the Works.

There we had already provided three mobile fire pumps and 40,000 gallons of water in spare tenders spread about the Works in case the fire-mains were put out of action. There were over 100 L.M.S. fire brigades in Scotland with a peace time complement of 900 trained men, now augmented by a similar number of volunteer auxiliary men. The efficiency of our firefighting organisation was something of which, in normal times, we were justly proud. The report drafted for me by the Fire Superintendent, Wishart, a lugubrious gentleman who was inclined to ascribe every little fire to a 'dropped light' satisfied me, and in turn the Scottish Committee, that we were ready for any emergency.

In carrying on as usual, as we had been enjoined to do, there was much that was anything but 'usual' during the next eighteen months. We were much concerned with the provision of special trains for the movement of troops. A. E. Milne, my Outdoor Carriage & Wagon Assistant, suggested that a visit with him to Greenock might prove interesting. We were there to see the arrival of the first Canadian contingent welcomed at Princes Pier by the Lord Provost of Glasgow throwing a generous supply of oranges to the astonished soldiers as they came alongside. The identity of the new arrivals had been well concealed. Many of the onlookers thought they were British soldiers returning from France. A well kept secret, too, was the passage down the river of the *Queen Elizabeth* from Clydebank to the Tail of the Bank. Wholly unreliable rumour had fixed the date for a Sunday afternoon in February 1940. Along with hundreds of others we betook ourselves to a hillside overlooking Dumbarton Rock to see the ship pass by. It was a fruitless journey – but a reliable tip a few days later from a source with whom our operating people were in constant touch, made a visit with R. F. Harvey to Bowling signal box on the banks of the Clyde, worthwhile. What an astonishing sight it was to see the great grey ship pass majestically by on her way to sea.

The Observer Corps had a post on the golf course not far from our house, manned on the night that Hess arrived a few miles away on Eaglesham Moor, by a friend who, like many others, was baffled by the sound of a fighter aircraft, so different from that of the bombers to which they were becoming accustomed.

Unusual indeed, but so was the weather during the early wartime winters. For days deep snow drifts blocked all main lines between England and Scotland. Trains were snowed up near Carstairs. Noel Phillipps, the Operating Manager, living not far away went off to supervise the clearance of the line and got snowed up himself in the wilds of the Upper Clyde Valley.

Even down on the shores of the Firth that had seen no snow for years, the station at Largs was virtually submerged with a couple of engines off the road at the entrance to the tunnel.

With all the difficulties imposed by wartime conditions on railway operating, it was remarkable how well the services were maintained. There were of course, delays caused by the blackout and sporadic air raid warnings, but serious interruptions were few and far between. Nevertheless, the Scottish officers were required by the Operating Vice-President, at Euston, Sir Ernest Lemon, to meet regularly to see what could be done to improve matters. The good old hardy annual – late arrival at Carlisle of trains from the south was often prayed in aid – not without justification – for unpunctual running in Scotland. Many down expresses approaching Carlisle were delayed due to the platforms at Citadel Station being occupied by military special trains held for the purpose of feeding the troops. Some general improvement in timekeeping was to be expected from raising the maximum permissible speed from sixty to seventy-five miles per hour, and from a relaxation of the limit imposed during air raid warnings. Maintenance of locomotives, engine casualties, time lost in running due to unfamiliar grades of coal and shortage of engine tools came in for their full share of attention at our meetings, matters with which the department was directly concerned.

The customary freedom from serious mishaps on the line was well maintained, though there were two accidents on successive days in March 1940, which necessitated journeys to the site. The first involved two freight trains between Slochd Summit and Aviemore. Twenty-two of the thirty-one vehicles of a double-headed train from Perth to Inverness broke loose due to a broken drawbar hook on a private owner's wagon, as the train came to a stand on the 1 in 70 gradient at the summit. They ran back for ten miles, covering the distance in about twelve minutes. A following train, already on its way, could not be warned, and was hit by the runaway wagons near Carr Bridge Station. The crew of the leading engine, an old Highland 4-4-0, which ended up laying on its side at right-angles to the single track, buried under a pile of demolished wagons, were killed instantly. The train engine, a *Class 5* 4-6-0, behind which was another pile of smashed wagons, was virtually undamaged – I remember the front buffer beam was slightly bent. We cut up the old 4-4-0 into furnace size on the spot.

We had barely sorted things out at Carr Bridge when we had to go north beyond Inverness to a passenger train derailment between Tain and Edderton on the shores of Dornoch Firth. It was my first journey on the line to the far north. I was resolved to go there again – to Georgemas Junction and Thurso in less strenuous times. This I did years later. The *Royal Highlander* to Inverness, the next night in Thurso, the third in Kyle of Lochalsh; MacBrayne's steamer to Mallaig, and back in the sleeper to King's Cross – three days of Britain's most beautiful scenery, part of it seen from the footplate. How fortunate are railwaymen who use aright their benefits in kind! The derailment was one of those unsatisfactory cases for which there was no one clearly identifiable cause. The six vehicles of the train were all off the road. The tender of the *Class 5* 4-6-0 hauling the train was derailed to the inside of a gentle curve of eighty-five chains radius, but was still coupled to the engine, which remained wholly on the rails. The track which had been relaid with new material only two years before, was in generally good condition, except for two lateral displacements of about 2″ first to one side and then to the other. As the drivers of the derailed train and of the one before it both stated that their engines rode perfectly smoothly, the slight displacements were assumed to be a result and not the cause of the accident. The engine had run only 5,300 miles since service repairs and was in good condition throughout. Tyre profiles and axlebox clearances were entirely satisfactory and the wheels were true to gauge. As there was nothing in the condition of the engine to give a clue to the cause of the mishap, I told the shop foreman at St. Rollox to get it back into traffic at once. That, of course, was a stupid mistake. It occurred to me later, in time to countermand my instructions, that if there was to be a Ministry of Transport Inquiry the Inspecting Officer would wish to examine the engine himself. In spite of the trainmen's assertion that the train was travelling at only 35 miles per hour, we thought that with two of the derailed vehicles upside down with their bogies in the air, the speed was over rather than under the permitted maximum of 50 m.p.h.

After much verbal sparring we concluded that the derailment was due to oscillation of the tender initiated by some slight irregularity in the track and accentuated by the passage of the locomotive at excessive speed, thus causing the right leading tender wheel to climb the rail. Attention was drawn to the boggy nature of the ground and to the severe alternations of frost and thaw to which the district had recently been subjected. No departmental susceptibilities were seriously offended! Two days away from the office ended with a hectic journey back from Inverness, not, as was usually the case on those occasions, in an officers special, but on the regular afternoon express. Relaxation over a cup of tea was rudely disturbed by the violent riding of the dining car — one of the old Caledonian Pullman cars — coming down the hill from Druimachdar summit. Unduly sensitive as perhaps we were at the time, Harvey went forward at the first stop to warn the driver to watch his step, and on arrival at Perth, for the first and last time on which it was necessary to do so, I exercised my authority in this respect and had a red label immediately placed on the offending vehicle.

One further accident enquiry brought me in contact with the Scottish legal system and the formidable Jim Figgins, the general secretary at the time, of the National Union of Railwaymen. It was a fatal accident enquiry at which I had to give evidence into the death of a fireman seriously injured on the footplate by a firebox explosion on one of the streamlined *Pacifics* No. 6224 working the 10.00 a.m. Glasgow–Euston on 10th September, 1940. The train had been compelled to stop at Law Junction short of steam, and after restarting, the water level was allowed to fall so low that both lead plugs fused, the crown of the box was severely scorched and a tear three feet long and a foot wide took place in the left-hand side top bend of the copper firebox plate. The force of the explosion was shattering. The smokebox door was blown open and one of the streamline casing doors was found fifty yards away in a field beside the line. The firebars were forced downwards towards the ashpan, the damper doors of which were badly distorted. The firedoor and the tender coal space doors were torn off and blown on to the permanent way. The severity of the blow through the firehole could be judged from the appearance of the tender which looked as though the plates had been sand blasted. The boiler had been washed-out and given a full inspection the day before the accident. It was in first class condition, as were the injectors and water gauges. It was unhappily a simple case of mismanagement on the footplate. This was, to me, a particularly interesting case, as I had seen one almost identical in cause and effect on a Great Indian Peninsula 2-10-0 ten years earlier.

Though technical development and experimental work had obviously to be suspended unless it made a direct contribution to the war effort, there was still time for the occasional investigation of proposals for improving locomotive design and performance. One such was a new system for burning pulverised coal, submitted by a Scotsman, one Symington MacDonald. Mr. Stanier asked me to see him and report on his ideas. Experiments with pulverised coal firing had been undertaken in Germany some years before the war. No difficulty was found in obtaining a sufficiently intense heat release per cubic foot of firebox volume to generate all the steam required. The Southern Railway converted one of their mixed traffic 2-6-0 locomotives to burn pulverised coal which was unsuccessful.[*]

The case put forward by MacDonald was based entirely on his contention that pulverised fuel firing had never been properly applied to locomotives because the conventional locomotive boiler is unsuited to this type of fuel. A burner placed in the firebox cannot be arranged to give a long straight flame which in MacDonald's opinion was essential if troubles from blockage of tubes with ash and slag, and heavy wear of the refractory lining in the firebox was to be avoided. From our knowledge of the previous trials and from information we were able to gather from the Fuel Research Station, it seemed clear that the earlier tests had failed for the two reasons mentioned, which might well be overcome if the fuel could be burnt in a long furnace tube. The advantage of increased efficiency at the higher rates of firing and the use of lower grades of coal which the successful development of pulverised fuel

[*] 'Locomotive Adventure' Vol. 2. H. Holcroft, *Ian Allan. London.*

firing might well bestow, were certainly worth exploiting if this could be done without incurring penalties in other directions.

The question which I had to consider, therefore, was whether the design of boiler proposed was likely to be a practical proposition. It was a combination of a Lancashire and Locomotive boiler. A long combustion flue, about three feet in diameter was disposed within the barrel, with the fuel burner placed at the smoke-box end. The flue was connected to an ash chamber arranged rather like an ordinary firebox. The products of combustion passed into the ash chamber and thence through tubes and flues back to the smoke-box and chimney. To maintain the same free area through the tubes as with a conventional boiler the barrel would have to be much larger in diameter. This objection was countered by the assertion that as pulverised fuel could be burnt with about one-third less excess air than needed for normal coal firing the free area could be correspondingly less. In claiming that his boiler could produce the same amount of steam with a much reduced free area and tube surface the inventor was falling into the same error which resulted in more than one of the revolutionary experimental locomotives of earlier years being complete failures.

In addition to savings in fuel costs varying from 20 to 45 per cent, it was claimed that if pulverised fuel could be successfully applied to locomotives, only 20 per cent of passenger trains and 10 per cent of freight trains would need two men on the footplate. Considerable reductions in wages costs would thus be secured. It was evident that there was little understanding of the facts of life of railway operation.

I came to the conclusion that a boiler designed in accorance with Mr. Symington MacDonald's ideas of the same external diameter as the *Coronation* Pacific boilers would produce no more steam than the G7 boilers on L.M.S. *Class 2* 4-4-0 locomotives. It would be better, or so it seemed to me, even accepting the superiority of the straight flame idea, first to make further attempts to overcome the difficulties of burning pulverised coal in ordinary boilers. In any event we could not, under war conditions, embark on a large scale development programme for an entirely novel design of boiler. Much, I fear, to the disappointment of the inventor I reported accordingly to the C.M.E.

Nothing daunted MacDonald returned to the attack two years later, by which time I was no longer in Scotland. In 1946 he raised the matter again, when I was once more involved. There was then no obstacle in the way of developing revolutionary new ideas, if they held out any promise of economic success. But with conventional boilers giving efficiencies of 70 to 75 per cent under normal working conditions, a small margin only remained for further improvement. Stewart Cox and I did not feel justified in recommending the expenditure that would have been involed in developing MacDonald's ideas. We may have erred on the side of caution, but in the light of subsequent events I think we were probably right.

All this was no more than a little light relief from the increasingly urgent impact of the war on all our work. There was no question of taking any leave during the summer months of 1940. Even supposing it would have been permissible to be away from the office for as much as a week at a time, one would not have felt justified in doing so. In any case, our usual holiday haunts, our parents' homes in Northern Ireland and on the Suffolk coast, were too far away and virtually inaccessible. The Tarbet Hotel on Loch Lomond side was as far as we had gone for an occasional weekend when any of the meagre ration of petrol for private motoring was available. I had seen much of the Highlands but always from the train on one or other of our special inspection trips. Now an opportunity arose to get deeper into the hills by road. My friend Stewart had to go up to the borders of Argyll and Inverness to inspect some standing timber and invited me to go with him. We planned to spend two days away from home, Saturday and Sunday of the first weekend of September, 1940, with one night at Dalmally under the shadow of Ben Cruachan. We were back on Clydeside in well under twenty-four hours! All went according to plan on our outward run. We had dined well at Dalmally Hotel. The war seemed a long way off when I retired to my room for the night. Undressing slowly I was vaguely conscious of the church clock striking, and as one does, I counted the hours. When my counting had reached fourteen I came to with a jerk! It was not the clock – it could only be the church bell ringing the invasion signal. Within a few minutes the local Home Guard Commander arrived at the Hotel – his rendezvous point. Yes, it was the invasion warning. I 'phoned my office in Glasgow – yes they had received the message – with instructions to immobilise the port facilities at Stranraer! I told the office that I should be on my way back at one. It was a moonless night, bright starlight but black as ink when we set off on the hundred mile run to Glasgow. Road blocks at strategic points were all manned by armed Home Guardsmen anxious to do their duty to the limit. Dawn was breaking as we reached the shores of Loch Lomond at Tarbet. Our final encounter was on the bridge over the River Leven at Alexandria. I gently pushed aside the muzzle of a rifle inserted through the lowered window on my side of the car by a drunken Home Guardsman, while his mate examined our identity cards. The final act in this bizarre weekend was a further 'phone call to the office from a roadside kiosk. It was all a false alarm – everything had been cancelled.

With much relief and a good deal of laughter we made our way to Erskine Ferry, crossed the river and arrived outside our house before seven o'clock in the morning. Stones thrown at our bedroom window roused an astonished wife. The church bells had not been rung in Bridge of Weir!

Though it was not until the early spring of 1941 that Scotland was seriously affected by air-raids, two incidents, quite unrelated to each other, brought home to us the ordeal that people in less fortunate localities had nightly to endure. Lord Stamp, Chairman and President of the L.M.S. Executive was killed by a direct hit on his home near London. He had been in Glasgow only a short time before, and paid a visit to St. Rollox Works. This was my first and only meeting with this great man, who, had he lived, would surely have been a dominating influence in all the preliminaries to the nationalisation of the railways only seven years later. Josiah Stamp was a kindly man, who was able to put any of the less exalted of his staff completely at their ease. His retentive memory and powers of observation impressed me greatly. During his tour of the Works, a special purpose machine tool caught his eye. He asked me how long it had been installed, as he did not think it had been there on his previous visit some years earlier. He was indeed correct. By his untimely death, the nation and the great company which he had so brilliantly led suffered a most grievous loss. There are, I suppose, few today who remember the moving tribute to Lord Stamp's character and achievements, which we heard from the Reverend George McLeod of Iona at the Memorial service in Glasgow Cathedral.

We expected a visit from a cousin journeying north to the Orkneys, to join her husband serving there in the Royal Air Force. She did not arrive as expected, and as Manchester where she lived, had been heavily bombed the night before, we were concerned for her safety. The railway police in Glasgow went to considerable trouble to find out that my cousin's house, though empty, was undamaged. We heard much later that she had left Manchester Exchange Station, bombed and still burning after the raid, and quite oblivious of the anxiety she was causing us, had decided not to break her journey in Glasgow.

With the German air offensive on England in full swing, an attack on Glasgow and Clydeside could surely not be long delayed. It came with all its fury during the full moon period of March. Three nights running the bombers came with their hateful unmistakeable drone, minutes only after the sirens had sounded. Clydebank and Dalmuir bore the brunt of the attack. Oil tanks were hit the first night, and burning for days were a perfect marker for the next attacks. High up above the valley as we were at Bridge of Weir, we had a grandstand view of the performance being enacted six miles away. Parachute flares hung in the sky, and the flash of bursting bombs was followed by a perceptible wind on our faces as the blast wave reached us. The ground defences seemed to be putting up a good show judging from the shell bursts in the sky and streams of red tracers flying upwards. As it seemed scarcely possible that trains would be running after such a night I went up to the office next morning in my car, returning home that evening down the Dumbarton Road through the worst hit areas as far as Erskine Ferry. It was a gruesome journey. Tenement buildings were lying as heaps of rubble in the roadway. Overhead wires hung festooned around abandoned trams, and rows of small houses were still burning.

The next full moon it was Greenock's turn. By then I had gone to take over at Crewe, perforce leaving the family to fend for themselves. When I returned briefly for the weekend, I found they had been taken in by kind friends after a parachute mine had come down unpleasantly close. We, in our turn, now had a mother and son, refugees from Greenock, temporarily living with us. The husband, a Naval Petty Officer, arrived home from sea to find his house in ruins and his wife and son missing. Such scanty information as he could glean from neighbours brought him to Bridge of Weir in search of his family.

A few days before the raids on Greenock, I had received a confidential letter, handwritten by Mr. Stanier, telling me he had decided the arrangements at Crewe must be revised. He had asked F. A. Lemon, my old chief there to retire; and he wanted me to take charge of Crewe Works.

I derived much satisfaction from the presumption that I would not have been given charge of the most important of the L.M.S. Locomotive Works unless the powers-that-be had been reasonably satisfied with our performance in Scotland during the past eighteen months. Nevertheless, as I told the C.M.E., I should, like my predecessors who had returned south, leave Scotland with some regrets. By common consent, the job at St. Rollox was regarded as one of the best in the department. Headquarters was 400 miles away, and if only because of the Scottish Committee of Directors, we enjoyed a greater measure of independence than at the English Works.

Things were going well in the Works and in the department generally. I had a first rate team of assistants and a Works Committee who were more than usually co-operative in discussing and reaching agreement on the staff problems that had to be settled. True, I should have no misgivings in regard to these two matters at Crewe. Special training schemes for machinists and acceptance of labour dilution mitigated the worst effects of shortage of skilled men. Everyone was working at least fifty-six hours per week. Locomotive and rolling stock repairs were in a healthy state, and we were doing a full share of government work on tank components and bridge trestle units. More government contracts were being negotiated, particularly at that time repairs to Spitfire aircraft at Barassie. We had successfully resisted a proposal from Derby to close down, in the interests of economy, part of Kilmarnock Works. Locomotive and crane repairs would have been transferred to St. Rollox, a sound idea in peace time of course. But when St. Rollox or any of the English Works might at any time suffer serious damage and loss of capacity, it seemed to me that the balance of advantage was heavily in the direction of retaining every square foot of floor space that we had, and filling it with more government work. We had devised and put into operation, a comprehensive system of machine tool loading and were fairly confident of the reliability of our delivery promises.

Though small compared with the production lines at Derby and Wolverton Carriage Works for the manufacture of aeroplane wings and repairs to Hampden and Lancaster bombers, the Spitfire project at Barassie was, I believe, the only one in which completed aircraft were prepared for service and flown away from the Works. An airstrip was built on a golf course next to the Works requisitioned for us by the Air Ministry. The wagon paint shop was converted into a repair shop for wings and fuselages and as the scheme developed under George Bellamy, two hangars were built by the runway for final assembly.

Production and inspection staff totalling over 500, half of whom were women, turned out nearly 200 aircraft. I was sorry not to be able to see the first repaired aircraft fly off from our private aerodrome, but regrets or no, to Crewe I had to go to take over from Arnold Lemon.

My arrival at Crewe during the first week of May, 1941, coincided with one of the series of air raids on Merseyside. The sirens sounded, punctually it almost seemed, at the same time for six nights running. As my family were still in Scotland, I spent the greater part of these first six nights in the air raid control centre of the Works, a dugout just in front of the main offices. It was as good a way as any of getting to know the details of the Air Raid Precautions Organisation and the people who were in charge. There had been one or two quite minor attacks on the town which had done little damage. But it was to me one of the unsolved mysteries of the war why Crewe, as important a rail traffic centre as any in the country, with the Works engaged on vital production, to say nothing of Rolls-Royce just alongside, and two ordnance factories within the bombing margin of error, was not constantly subjected to heavy attacks. I certainly never dared to hope that we should be let off so lightly as we were.

I returned to Crewe with the great advantage of knowing the Works intimately. Even more important, with one or two exceptions, I knew the people and they knew me. Though from the discussions which took place at the monthly meetings of Works Managers, held at Derby usually with Fairburn in the Chair, I knew that Crewe had not been meeting their commitments, I had no inside information as to the causes of their difficulties. Clearly my first task was to find out exactly what was the state of affairs.

Knowing as I did from my experience as second-in-command for five years the very high standard of efficiency the Works had reached under Lemon's management, what emerged from my preliminary review of the general position concerning the output of locomotive repairs, Government work, particularly tanks, and new locomotive construction which took me a month to complete, was to say the least disconcerting. Things were really in rather a muddle. It was not difficult to diagnose the root cause of the trouble. The long established tradition at Crewe was always to take on anything and everything that was offered; and having done so, to do whatever was necessary, come Hell or high water, to ensure that commitments would be met.

Crewe had remained true to their traditions in taking on the work. They had been unable to build up their resources to correspond. In the face of all the wartime difficulties, this was understandable, and indeed excusable. What was inexcusable was the failure to disclose the true position.

No one man, however able, can run a large Works single handed – indeed it is foolish to try. I have myself been criticised by colleagues and assistants for keeping too much in my own hands. But my experience in charge at St. Rollox and earlier at Crewe and Horwich had at least taught me that running a Works is a team effort. Without good assistants, upon whom one can rely implicitly, it is an impossible job. I suspected from all I could sense of the general atmosphere in the Works, and from what I gleaned from my daily contacts with my staff and foremen on the shop floor, that some staff changes would be necessary. I put the position bluntly to Fairburn, who took the necessary action. John Bagguley, a cheerful character whom Stanier had brought from Swindon was sent to Crewe as my assistant. I was indeed fortunate – I could not have had a more loyal and hard working principal assistant.

The main items of output Crewe was required to produce were:
    (i) Not less than forty locomotive repairs per week,
    (ii) Four Mark V Cruiser Tanks per week,
    (iii) New locomotives at the rate of three per fortnight;
with priority accorded to these three 'activities' in the order in which they are stated above. Concurrently with this work, there was the boiler building programme, both for renewals and new locomotives to be maintained. The actual rates of output from the beginning of the year had been:
    (i) Locomotive repairs – thirty-six per week,
    (ii) Cruiser Tanks – 1·6 per week, with staff then on the assembly lines sufficient only for an output of two tanks each week,
    (iii) From the beginning of the year only ten new locomotives had been turned out.

The background to the locomotive position on the L.M.S. at the time, was that during 1938 the number of repairs turned out had been only sufficient to make good 84 per cent of the engine miles run. The number of engines under and awaiting repairs actually increased. In September 1939, in spite of some months of overtime at all the Works, the number of engines for repairs had risen to $8\frac{1}{2}$ per cent of the stock, with 370 locomotives stopped unserviceable at the sheds. Clearly with the prospect of greatly increased traffics in view this state of affairs could not be allowed to continue. It was decided therefore to suspend new locomotive building entirely, where it interfered in any way with repair output. Repairs were to be stepped up by twenty-two engines a week, to give a total output of 105 weekly. The action taken was effective and within the first year of the war, the locomotives under and awaiting repairs were down to 4·4 per cent with only thirty-one stopped at sheds. Crewe had been turning out thirty-six repairs per week.

With the engine repair position restored to health, the possibility of resuming the locomotive building programme was considered by Headquarters. After a review of the available capacity on machine tools at Crewe and Derby, the conclusion was reached that some new locomotives could be built without detriment to engine repairs, or to existing commitments for government work. But there were three important provisos:

    (i) that all key machines should be treble shifted to work twenty-four hours per day seven days per week, not only at Crewe and Derby, but at the other Works also;

    (ii) that the necessary additional staff would be obtainable; and

    (iii) that there would be no increase in government work.

The conclusion also rested on the reasonable assumption that in assessing the machine hours available for new locomotives, Crewe had taken fully into account the first priority, capacity needed for stores stock order production. It was assumed, too, that though in arrears, the work on the various programmes at Crewe was reasonably in balance. Unfortunately this was not the case. All this was going on while I was still in Scotland. We did, in fact put twenty-two machines in St. Rollox on treble shift. But as the men at Crewe objected to the loss of hours per man which treble shifting entailed, compared with double shifts of $62\frac{1}{2}$ hours per week, the arrangements had to be discontinued after a short period.

When I took over at Crewe the number of staff employed was 6,440. For some time before the outbreak of war, members of the 155th Railway Workshop Company of the Royal Engineers and other reservists and territorials, had been recalled to their units. Nearly 500 men had left to join the Forces by the middle of 1941. Moreover, we had loaned nearly 400 men, under pressure from government departments, to other firms, 300 of them to Rolls-Royce for stepping up the output of Merlin engines for fighter aircraft. These losses of staff, many of whom were skilled men, naturally had a serious effect on output, for in addition to locomotive work and other railway demands, the amount of work the company was being urged to undertake for the government had greatly increased and was still increasing. The loss of men had been compensated to some extent by increasing working hours from 47 to $62\frac{1}{2}$ per week. This was equivalent to

1,430 additional men – but it was nothing like enough to enable us to meet our commitments. I estimated that we needed a further 2,150 staff, knowing that we were faced with further losses of young men to the Forces, that the nett increase in staff over the previous three months had only been about twenty, and that dilution and the employment of women was then making little progress. It was obvious from the point of view of staff numbers, if from no other, it would take some time to build up output to the required level. In fact, available machine tool capacity was a further controlling factor.

Comprehensive machine loading statistics of the kind which I had found quite indispensable at St. Rollox for ensuring that we did not bite off more than we could chew, had not hitherto been compiled at Crewe in sufficient detail. It took some time to assess the situation and build up the essential statistics. Before they were complete it became clear that assistance from other Works was needed on some categories of machine tools, even if no new locomotives were built.

The position as a whole which emerged from my investigation was very clear. There was not the slightest immediate prospect of building any new locomotives and at the same time producing the promised output of repairs and cruiser tanks. In time, of course, providing the necessary staff could be recruited and some additional machine tools obtained, the full requirements could be met. For the present, with the output of repairs increased to forty per week, it would have to be either tanks or new locomotives – not both. It was as simple as that, and at the time, tanks had to take precedence at Crewe.

The Mark V Cruiser Tanks – the Covenanters – had been designed at Derby under Ivatt's direction. J. W. Caldwell, who later became Chief Draughtsman at Derby and was responsible for the detail design of the L.M.S. *Class 4* 2-6-0s, surpassed in ugliness only by Bulleid's austerity 0-6-0s, was in charge of the tank design office. It says much for the versatility of railway trained designers that Caldwell and his men were able to take on unaided an entirely unfamiliar and complex armoured fighting vehicle. The L.M.S. Railway acted as the parent company of a consortium, of which the English Electric Company and Leyland were the other members, for building the tanks. We worked together very harmoniously. There was, I think, little to choose between us so far as building new tanks was concerned. But when it came to a programme of heavy repairs and modifications, we were playing on our home ground! English Electric Stafford, were very pleased to let us have their share of the repairs in exchange for some of our new vehicles. The first four tanks for modification arrived under their own power and caused quite a sensation in the town. Output was built up to twenty per week. Within two months 150 had been dealt with and returned to their army units. Before tank construction was finally displaced in August 1942 in favour of new locomotives, Crewe built 161 Covenanter tanks as well as thirty hulls of another type for completion at Horwich.

Though we had been doing quite well with engine repairs, the output had to be increased by a further 10 per cent. Existing facilities were already stretched to the utmost – or so it was said. A study of all causes of failure to conform to the time schedules laid down for each of the six repair lines in the Erecting Shop soon revealed that we needed more portable equipment of all kinds – grinders, drills, cylinder and piston valve boring machines and welding plant – in the shop. Electric plug points for the new equipment were increased from fifty to 250! We needed too, an additional 50 ton overhead crane in one of the bays to permit wheeling of locomotives at the same time as a boiler was being lowered into a repaired frame. There had always been a balancing night shift in the Erecting Shop and in order to beat the blackout, we built a light-trap outside the traverser opening so that engines for repair could be brought in at any time during the day or night.

No repair organisation, however well equipped in other respects, can function effectively without adequate stocks of spare parts available on demand. This may appear so painfully obvious as not to need stating at all. Nevertheless, it was a matter which required constant attention. My Chief Foremen already knew of my insistence on stock orders receiving first priority at all times. There was room for improvement in the system of control and progressing of these orders. Changes were made, the success of which owed much to the establishment at the same time of all planning and production control functions, hitherto separate, in one large office.

We were at this time running into a cycle of heavy frame repairs. Crewe locomotives had never had really adequate main frames, and the situation was now aggravated by increasing trouble with cracks in the high tensile frames of the standard *Class 5* 4-6-0s. A stock of spare boilers had long been regarded as indispensable for reducing the time out of traffic of locomotives undergoing repairs. If, as was now the case, heavy frame repairs were taking up to a fortnight for engines which were due out of the Erecting Shop in six to eight days, why not spare frames? It seemed to me entirely logical to apply to frames the same argument as for boilers. We obtained authority to build three sets of frames complete with cylinders, dragboxes, and all other fittings, one for *Class 5* 4-6-0s, one for L.N.W. G1 0-8-0s, and one for the standard *Class 4* 0-6-0s, these being the most numerous classes in which interchangeability could be fully exploited. These spare frames abundantly proved their worth – but as a means of reducing the days on Works they were considered slightly 'offside' by some of my friends on other railways with whom I compared notes, and who were sometimes inclined to be sceptical, not to say envious, of our engine repair results.

Another innovation, so far as locomotive repairs were concerned, was a weekly telephone conference between the central shopping bureau at Derby and each of the Works. Some classes of engines were allocated to more than one Works for maintenance. And remembering the loss of availability caused in Scotland by taking engines out of traffic for repairs instead of giving preference to stopped engines, it seemed to me probable that we might be taking engines in out of traffic from the Western division, when individual locomotives of the same class maintained at another Works were standing stopped at sheds. Why not co-ordinate shopping at all Works by means of a telephone hook-up similar to the daily conference between the four traffic operating divisions?

I was assured by Stanley Parkhouse, my opposite number in charge of the Operating Department at Crewe that the necessary telephone facilities could be made available. Derby headquarters liked the idea. It was adopted, and has persisted, with beneficial results all round.

The output of locomotive repairs steadily rose to an average of forty-one per week for many months – a record which I believe still stands. It was not enough merely to achieve the desired output of repairs. Expenditure on locomotive maintenance both in shops and at the sheds was subject to the same close scrutiny to which we were all accustomed in normal times. The financial arrangements made with the government when the railways came under control provided that revenue receipts and expenses of the controlled undertakings would be pooled, and to each would be paid, with certain qualifications, the average of its nett revenue for the years 1935 to 1937. Provision was made for standardisation of charges for maintenance including renewals, on the basis of the average of the charges made in the basic period, subject to adjustment for altered conditions. Thus, it was essential to know how expenditure incurred on locomotive maintenance during the war years was related to actual costs during the base years 1935 to 1937 inclusive. The matter first came to a head when figures for expenditure during 1941 became available for discussion at the monthly Works Managers meetings. Overall repair output was down by 3 per cent compared with the base years, but expenditure at a common price level was up by 16 per cent. There were wide variations in the figures as between one Works and another. Crewe, for example, had turned out 2 per cent more repairs but expenditure was up by 29 per cent. By contrast, at St. Rollox expenditure was higher by 35 per cent, but repair output was up by 18 per cent. The results at Derby and Horwich showed similar variations. Explanations were demanded from each of us in charge of the Works. They varied as widely as the figures themselves – but were reconciled and made comprehensible for Fairburn, and indeed for all of us, by Stewart Cox in a detailed analysis of a mass of figures at which he was so adept. At the end of the day, the increase in expenditure for which explanations were required amounted to £1·8 million – a lot of money in those days. Part of the increase was due to higher output, and part to higher costs per repair. War conditions contributed to the increases under both heads – but so also did L.M.S. locomotive policy in the immediate pre-war years. The average miles run between consecutive heavy repairs fell quite sharply during the war, due undoubtedly to the heavier work the locomotives were called on to perform.

The number of repairs required was increased also on account of the in-flux of new engines during the base years, many of which had not then fallen due for their first repair. By the war years they were all coming up for heavy repairs. These new engines (of which 1,254 were in service in 1941), had much improved efficiency and operating potential. They ran higher mileages between repairs, but did it in less time which had an im-portant bearing on the frequency with which they fell due for Shops. They were larger and more complex than the locomotives they had replaced. 4-6-0s had taken the place of 4-4-0s. Small 0-6-0s had been replaced by 2-8-0s. And 2-6-2 and 2-6-4 tank engines had taken over from 4-4-2s and 0-4-4s. There were more wheels and axleboxes to be repaired – and there were more superheated engines in the stock. The money and man-hours expended on each repair to the new engines were inevitably higher than for the smaller and simpler – though less effective – locomotives they replaced. We at Crewe were particularly affected by the new locomotives, most of which were allocated to us for maintenance. Their impact on our repair costs will be appreciated from the information tabulated overleaf comparing significant data from the base years and 1941.

Though we all knew in general terms why locomotive maintenance was costing more than during the base years, something more specific was demanded by headquarters. Financial values had to be attributed to each of the factors affecting the final result. But for the very detailed informa-tion we had available from the individual costing system put in at the in-stigation of Lord Stamp in the early days of the L.M.S., the task would have been virtually impossible. As it was, it was an easy matter correctly to apportion the excess expenditure between the effects of war on the one hand and L.M.S. policy on the other. I spent a lot of time on this, as I had to convince myself, beyond any reasonable doubt, of the soundness of the explanations before sending them forward to Derby. In this, as in so many other financial matters, I received invaluable assistance from Arnold Bentley, the Works Accountant and his staff in giving me figures not necessarily in the standard form, but compiled so as to bring out the salient points of my arguments and render them proof against the searching cross-examination by which Fairburn was apt to test his Works Managers' assertions.

Locomotive Repairs – Crewe Works

	Average 1935–37	1941
Total number of locomotives repaired	1,818	1,846
Average lightweight per locomotive repaired	56·1 tons	58·3 tons
Large 3 and 4-cylinder engines repaired		
4-6-2	25	54
Royal Scot	133	119
3 cyl. 5X	159	193
Garratt	17	38
	334	404
Standard *Class 5* 4-6-0s repaired	112	227
Total:	446	631
Number of new cylinders fitted	52 pairs	157 pairs
Number of new tyres fitted	3,435	3,805
Number of engines coming in for first – i.e. less expensive – repair	171	65
Number of new locomotives allocated to Crewe for maintenance	170	Nil
Number of locomotives scrapped	228	10

The increase in output was achieved only by unremitting pressure in exploiting to the maximum possible extent the agreements made with the Unions for dilution of skilled grades and the employment of women. There was at first a good deal of resistance to dilution and much work otherwise suitable, was too heavy physically for women to undertake. Nevertheless the difficulties real, or imagined, were overcome. At its peak, the number of women employed in the Works at Crewe rose to over 1,000 from a peacetime figure of virtually none. The girls proved extremely versatile and adaptable. Many were engaged on work hitherto regarded as the prerogative of fully skilled tradesmen – and very well they did it. Others, tougher than their sisters, took the driving of heavy steam hammers and drop-stamps in their stride. Rest rooms and other amenities had to be provided to standards laid down by the Welfare Department. Some problems naturally arose. It was an unusual and amusing spectacle to see Fairburn bullied and badgered in his own office in the presence of all the Works Managers, by a deputation of lady welfare supervisors led by their formidable chief, Miss Catto from Euston.

No less interesting, though in quite a different way, was a Works Managers' meeting at Derby taken by Sir Harold Hartley, in Fairburn's absence due to illness. We wondered what sort of a meeting it would be, chaired by a remote Vice-President from Euston, a scientist associated in the minds of the Works Managers more with the Research Department, that tiresome and slightly redundant interloper, than with the down-to-earth engineering departments that got on with the jobs that mattered. Sir Harold surprised us all. He started the meeting by propping up his watch in front of him. He had done his homework thoroughly; and disposed of the agenda with easy competence. He sent us off home earlier than usual to our various Works with his reputation much enhanced. Thirty years later, Sir Harold delighted in reminding me of that wartime Works Managers' meeting.

As the tides of war began to turn, the prospective demand for new locomotives for service in the Middle East and Europe, as D-day approached, became ever more insistent. The War Office wished the railways to have a large stock of standard freight engines which could be requisitioned for service overseas at any time. It had been decided that all heavy freight engines built should be Stanier's 2-8-0 type. These excellent engines were built not only at Crewe, but at Swindon, Doncaster and Brighton, as well as by contractors. The *Austerity* 2-8-0 and 2-10-0 locomotives, for the design of which Robert Riddles will always be remembered, came later.

Crewe had turned out only five new engines in 1940. This was increased to fourteen in 1941, but only because machining had already been completed, and there was some delay in receipt of new material for tank production. Apart from the priority which had to be given to tanks, an impediment to the output of new locomotives was the work involved in preparing engines for service overseas. 150 L.M.S. Standard 2-8-0 freight engines were earmarked for service in Egypt and Persia in 1941. Eighty-seven of them were dealt with at Crewe, of which forty-three had to be fitted with Westinghouse brakes and converted to burn oil for hauling trains of supplies to Russia over the Persian Railways. Not all of these engines reached their destination. Of the final shipment of twelve, four loaded as deck cargo went over the side in heavy weather. The remaining eight in the hold were seriously damaged and had to come home for repairs. Later we had to deal with American army 2-8-0s, 400 of which were used in this country before being sent overseas. They had to be fitted for working vacuum braked trains and modified in other respects for service here at home. Our share of this work amounted to seventy-four locomotives. These engines provided a most interesting contrast to normal British practice.

Just as Churchward incorporated some typically American features in his standard Great Western locomotives, so post-war design on the L.M.S. was influenced by such good features as drop-grates and self-cleaning smokeboxes of these American locomotives.

While cancellation of breaking-up programmes had afforded some relief, we were short of something like 500 locomotives for service on British Railways as a whole – apart from what might be wanted overseas. The first signs we had at Crewe of the increasing need for new locomotives were urgent demands from the wartime headquarters at Watford to know how many additional machine tools and staff we should need to give an assured output of two 2-8-0s each week, without any reduction in repairs or output of tanks and other government contracts. If we could gain general acceptance of treble shift working the answer was twenty-four machines – if not, then we should need sixty-nine new machine tools. At 33,000 man-hours per locomotive, we should require 800 additional staff, of whom at least 450 would have to be men. Clearly some change of policy was in the wind. But neither machine tools nor men were easy to come by. Based on past experience there seemed to be little prospect of building up the staff to the required level. But new locomotives had to be constructed. So the Railway Workshops capacity committee, which for the first two years of the war had been exhorting us to accept ever more government work now had to go into reverse and relieve us of everything which stood in the way of new locomotive building. Another committee was set up to scour the country for boilermakers to be drafted back to locomotive shops.

Some idea of the change-over from direct government contracts to locomotive work may be gained from the table opposite, which shows the allocation of staff to the various activities at Crewe in November 1941, six months after I took over, and toward the end of the war three years later.

With new locomotive building once more in full swing, the ban imposed early in the war on building any express passenger locomotives was relaxed. We built four more streamlined *Pacifics* in 1943, the centenary year of the establishment of the Works at Crewe. There were, of course, no celebrations, but we did not allow the centenary to be forgotten. The Chairman of the Company, Lord Royden, paid us a visit and was I think, favourably impressed by what we had to show him.

Though attention was naturally focused mainly upon everything which affected our main items of output, other productive resources were filled to capacity and developed to the maximum extent which available floor space made possible. The three foundries had never been busier. An existing 4 ton drop hammer was moved from the Old Works and installed alongside two new 3 ton hammers for the production of tank brake band stampings. New furnaces fired from a self-contained coal pulverising plant gave us a complete new stamping shop.

Crewe had a long history of steel making; both castings and ingots from open hearth melting furnaces for rolling into rails, tyres and blooms. The foundry had always been kept thoroughly up-to-date, and though we had our troubles from time-to-time, turned out very good castings. The open hearth melting plant had been closed down in 1932, not because it could not turn out good steel at the right price, but because heavy expenditure which the Company did not wish to incur, was needed to modernise the rolling mills and other plant for converting ingots into useful products. Fortunately the furnaces, two 45 ton and two 70 ton, had been left intact. It was decided that they should be put into working order and held as a standby in case of need. It was not long before the Ministry of Supply asked for the plant to go into production. Two of the four furnaces were melting when I arrived on the scene. But output was hindered by a prohibition on tapping after dark. The plant had of course, been blacked out, and though the arrangements had been passed as satisfactory by the Home Office, complaints from the local police about glare from the furnaces when tapping at night, became so serious that restrictions had to be imposed pending further blacking out.

Many of the men who had previously worked on the furnaces were no longer in the service. But there were enough still in the Works to man one

Division of Staff – Crewe Works

	15th November, 1941		9th December, 1944	
Locomotive Repairs		2,241		2,930
New Locomotives		62		981
New Boilers		129		66
Boiler Repairs		292		351
Stock order manufacturing	930		1147	
Foundries	251	1,396 1,396	226	1,560 1,560
Signal work	170		153	
Points and Crossings	45		34	
Miscellaneous work for other Railway Departments		663		814
		4,783		6,702
Tank manufacture		1,089		—
Aircraft components		69		—
Ammunition		16		—
Guns and Carriages		80		—
Miscellaneous		278		17
Melting Furnaces		181		17
		1,713		34
Total Staff at Work		6,496		6,736
Staff absent		352		499
Total Staff on Books		6,848		7,235
Total Man-hours		384,784		375,422
Hours per man per week		59·23		55·73

furnace and to form a nucleus for training others directed to us from out-side. Herbert Yates, an old friend from Horwich, was my Steel Works Manager. His shadow had grown no less with the passage of time, nor had his picturesque use of the English language mellowed. He did a great job in building up the output of 7 ton ingots for rolling into ships plates to 1600 tons a week. Opening up the 'Melts' as they were known, was to me one of the most fascinating war jobs we were asked to undertake. In all, something over 150,000 tons of steel were made. I always enjoyed watching a heat being worked and tapped. Here indeed was a really skilled job in contrast to some of the so-called skilled work, which, with the minimum of training, women were doing without difficulty.

As the output of ingots increased, transport problems arose. Paths had to be found for special trains of fifty wagons to be worked direct to steelworks in Scotland. This was just one more of the daily problems associated with the number of wagons on the Works. In those days, in spite of constant pressure to reduce them, the number of traffic wagons within our boundary was seldom less than 1,500. The Works, the Stores and the Traffic Departments were all involved. There was any amount of scope for passing the buck!

Euston became impatient in April 1942, as their successors have many times since. On instructions from the President received via the C.M.E., I was bidden to hold a meeting 'To enquire into and report upon what is required to avoid the large accumulation of wagons standing under load in and outside the Works – to be considered from the point of view of regula-tion of traffic and the physical layout'. Any of my readers who have worked at Crewe will no doubt recognise this hardy annual with some amusement. Then, no doubt as now, it was simply a question of deploying sufficient labourers on unloading wagons. Then, though we had occasional assistance from soldiers sent in to help, sufficient labourers were just not to be had.

In a closely knit community where so many of the men were required by the Essential Work Order to remain at their normal peace-time employ-ment and with the astonishing freedom from heavy air raids, life in Crewe seemed to be little changed from the pattern with which we were already familiar. Everything was centred on the railway. In spite of the long hours in the Works time had to be found to discharge the outside obligations which by tradition devolved upon the Works Manager. Chairmanship of the management committee of the Peace Memorial Hospital, of the Webb Orphanage and of the Mechanics Institute Social Club, all in their different ways kept one in touch and aware of the needs and opinions of people, railway and non-railway alike, upon whose help and goodwill so much depended in maintaining good industrial relations within the Works. All the purely social activities, the fetes and the sports in the summer and the Christmas parties at which the Works Manager's wife was expected to play a prominent part, were, of course, suspended for the duration. But there were other jobs to be done, and Jean, a qualified radiographer, was soon called in to help in the X-ray Department of the Hospital, until, with the call-up of our nursemaid to the Works as a crane driver in the Boiler Shop, this was no longer possible.

Soon after coming to Crewe one of the company's houses situated within the Works area, no more than two minutes walk from my office was made available to us. The garden ran down to a door in a high wall built of brick and old stone railway sleepers, on the other side of which ran the main rail traffic artery through the Works from the Old Works entrance at the North Junction to the Steel Works and Erecting Shops over a mile away. The double track line with its background of trees on which new engines built at Crewe were always photographed was at one time the main line to Chester and Holyhead. Now it carried the daily trains of wagons loaded with fuel and raw materials for the west end of the Works.

Along it passed the locomotives for repairs. One of the two roads formed a convenient shunting neck. We certainly lived on the job within sight and sound of the Works, which on the whole, was a great advantage under the conditions then existing. One night each week, when on fire-watching duty, to which everyone was rostered, I slept on a most comfortable camp-bed put up in my private office. Two minutes walk from my home at 10.00 p.m. was a much less tiresome business than a journey in from the country, which was the lot of some members of my fire-watching team. And I could get home for breakfast without any difficulty!

Only once were the sounds of shunting at the bottom of the garden more than I could stand. Towards the end of the war I went down with pneumonia, which to my lasting regret prevented me from attending a meeting at Euston when Field Marshal Montgomery addressed L.M.S. officers about the vital role which the railways would have to play in the preparations for the invasion of Europe. I must have been rather ill for a normally agreeable railway sound to get on my nerves as it did. Be that as it may, the yard foreman, Jack Gee, responded to a 'phone call from my wife and took his shunting elsewhere for a few days.

Though not exactly a country walk, many a quiet stroll on summer evenings out of the garden door and down through the Works to see some special job, or over Eagle Bridge past the 'Melts' to the cooling ponds where a heron or Jack Gee were often to be found fishing, gave Jean and me exercise and relaxation. Not that I needed much of the former, as I suppose I walked something over three miles in and about the 160 acres of the Works nearly every day – though I used the 'cab' – a vehicle of unique design hauled by a 0-4-0 tank locomotive for my visits to the far end of the Works.

In spite of the abnormal anxieties and pressures of the time, managing a large Works, so far as labour relations are concerned was, I believe, a good deal easier during the war than today. There are always some awkward customers. And there were the familiar feuds between the craft and non-craft unions. But there was in general an underlying unity of purpose transcending purely sectional interests. Nearly everyone was imbued by the need to get on with the job. My Works Committee was certainly not docile, but it was not interested in putting forward the sort of trivial matters which can be so tiresome today. On the other hand, they were not willing to fall in with the theory fashionable at the time which we were enjoined by headquarters to discuss, that the men's representatives should be identified with decisions on matters which had hitherto been firmly regarded as management.

Their job, as they saw it, was to look after the men's interests. Mine was to manage the Works. This suited me admirably – we understood one another completely. I could always rely on the Chairman and Secretary to step in and deal with any incipient trouble which might be brewing.

During my five years in charge of Crewe I had only one strike, and that of short duration affecting about 1,200 men in the Erecting Shop. On the morning the Works re-opened after a Christmas holiday during a period of severe frost, the cast iron main supplying the Erecting Shop with compressed air fractured without warning. Rather than send the men home pending restoration of supplies, we scoured the surrounding district to hire mobile air compressor sets with considerable success. But of course production was disrupted to some extent and for a week the men were unable to earn the normal piecework balance. Having rather rigid views on the meaning of payment by results, I declined an application for payment of average earnings. The men downed tools and I was summoned to Euston to see G. L. Darbyshire, the Chief Officer for Labour and Establishment. Would I not relent and change my decision? After all, it wasn't the men's fault that the main had broken. No – but it wasn't the management's either – and had piecework balance to be earned – or were average earnings now to be regarded as a right under all circumstances? It was obvious that I was not going to be supported. It was better to change my own mind than have it changed for me! I remember we reached the sort of so-called reasonable compromise which, over the years, has caused the spiralling of bonus earnings, and brought the straightforward piecework system into such disrepute.

The war moved inexorably on through D-day to the climax of total victory. With the final outcome a foregone conclusion for many months past, the ending of hostilities in Europe made very little immediate difference to the daily round in the Works. Even the lifting of the blackout, blessed relief that it was, made less impact in May with 'summer-time' in force, than if hostilities had ended during the winter months. It would, of course take some long time fully to return to normal conditions – and normal conditions would never again be quite what they had been before September, 1939. In the meantime a steady flow of engine repairs, the first priority at the end of the war just as it had been at the beginning, continued unabated.

Undramatic though the changes were, no-one who lived through those war years can ever forget the feeling of relief that hostilities in Europe and over Britain were at last ended. Celebrations there were in abundance, though I remember little about them, except the bonfires on VE night and a mammoth tea party organised by the Works Committee in Goddard Street canteen for the children of the men and women in the Works, at which I was required to address the assembled multitude.

The changeover from tanks to new locomotives, which had been smoothly accomplished many months before ensured that there was no sudden break in new production, as might otherwise have been the case. Though longer term developments had necessarily been held in abeyance, anything contributing to improvements in organisation, costs and production methods had been pushed ahead with undiminished vigour stimulated by constant pressure from Fairburn, who was adept at the gentle art of extracting the utmost from us all by playing one Works off against the others.

An important contribution to greater efficiency of production was the adoption in all the main works of a uniform system of limit gauging with standard manufacturing tolerances, and fits, appropriate to locomotive work. A committee drawn from the Works, Drawing Offices and Inspection Department, of which I was chairman, spent many months on this fascinating work. The use of limit gauging and the methods of dimensioning drawings had hitherto varied widely at the four main locomotive works. By the time we had finished, every renewable part and mating component had tolerances prescribed on the drawings. A standard system of dimensioning drawings was adopted, and all the many thousands of gauges brought under proper control. Interchangeability between components manufactured at different works was really achieved, with substantial savings in fitting and assembling costs.

A further contribution was the work done on locomotive frames. The three spare frames to which I have already briefly referred, were a great help in turning engines out to time, but they did nothing towards eliminating the troubles and expense of cracked and broken frames. This was a problem which had grown in proportion as the power of locomotives had increased. Age, too, was clearly a factor in the situation. It was a menace which we tackled first by a statistical analysis of records extending back many years to try and identify the reasons why some frames seldom gave any trouble while others were always doing so.

Why, for example, were the *Royal Scots* so prone to cracking when the

5X class 4-6-0s, with a practically identical design of frame, was virtually trouble free? Should the frame structure as a whole be as rigid as it was possible to make it? Or should it be deliberately designed to be flexible and able to give to the complex stresses arising from the steam pressure in the cylinders and from the vertical and lateral forces imposed by running at speed over track to which the terms flexible and rigid could not be applied in any absolute way? Tests to measure the stresses imposed were undertaken with a *Class 5* 4-6-0 and the Research Department was called in to assist with laboratory work and a complex mathematical exercise on the stress distribution in the frame assembly. Repair procedures, particularly welding, were greatly improved under the supervision of L. G. Bird, my Erecting Shop Foreman, a genial despot in his shop, and a stickler for good workmanship. He soon convinced us that if a frame once welded, cracked in the same place again, it was far better to weld in a new piece of plate than repair a crack a second time. Thus was developed the practice of holding in stock pieces of frame plate cut to standard sizes ready for immediate use. The superiority of horn-blocks, compared with separate guides in giving support to the frames at the top of the axlebox gaps, one of the most vulnerable points, was clearly demonstrated, as was the importance of tightly fitted horn stays with large mating surfaces which would not work loose in service. The changes in design and workshop practice arising from these investigations were applied with most beneficial results to L.M.S. locomotives, and later to the British Railways standard engines.

An event, surely unique, must conclude my account of these hectic years. It had no direct connection with the war, but was a consequence of it. The Prime Minister visited Cheshire during his election campaign of 1945. He travelled to Crewe in his special train, and on arrival paraded through the town perched up on the back seat of an open motor car. The people turned out to cheer with great enthusiasm. While on the Western Division, the Prime Minister's train was officially in the care of the Operating Superintendent at Crewe, then Colonel James Watkins, later to become General Manager of the London Midland Region and a Member of the British Transport Commission. James Watkins was one of the great railway operators trained in the true Midland tradition. He had a distinguished army record in the 1914–18 war, and rendered no less distinguished service in helping to run the railways in the second world war. He was a near neighbour of mine, and called in to say he was going out during the evening to pay his respects to the Prime Minister – would I care to go with him? The train was stabled for the night on a single track branch line between Harecastle and Sandbach, a few miles out in the country from Crewe. The stabling point was supposed to be a closely guarded secret – but someone had obviously been talking. Going in where angels might fear to tread, Watkins caused a message to be delivered to

Mr. Churchill enquiring for his comfort, and suggesting that a brief appearance would be much appreciated by the considerable crowd which had gathered by the line side. We did not have long to wait. The great man, followed by his retinue, emerged in the famous blue siren suit and embroidered carpet slippers. Walking down the track to where the crowd was waiting, the Prime Minister delivered a short impromptu speech. This done, the procession returned to the train, with the Operating Superintendent and Works Manager bringing up the rear, to be regaled by the staff for the rest of the evening with large whiskies and sodas.

The war years had brought important changes in the ranks of the mechanical engineering chief officers of the L.M.S. Sir William Stanier, who had been chairman of the Mechanical Engineering Committee of the Railway Executive Committee since Sir Nigel Gresley's death in 1941, was appointed one of three scientific advisers to the Ministry of Production in 1943. Fairburn, who had been in charge of the day-to-day running of our department for some time, followed as chief when Sir William retired from railway service in 1944. Fairburn had but a short time in which to exercise full authority as Chief Mechanical and Electrical Engineer. Increasingly afflicted by ill-health, he died towards the end of 1945. He had come relatively late in life, from the English Electric Company to the L.M.S. as Chief Electrical Engineer. When, shortly after his arrival on the scene, the two departments were amalgamated, Fairburn became Sir William Stanier's deputy. His training and experience differed in almost every important respect from that of his contemporaries. He was one of the first, if not indeed the first, graduates from the engineering school of Oxford University. Alone among the C.M.E.s whom it has been my good fortune to know, he always carried a small slide-rule in his pocket. He had a stern sense of duty, and had little sympathy with such long established traditions as inter-railway or departmental golf matches in working hours. He was thorough in all he did and expected his staff, both at headquarters and in the Works, to be likewise. He was generous in his praise – but devastating in his condemnation of what he judged to be slackness or inefficiency.

He had a more ruthless and strictly commercial outlook on life than that to which we had been generally accustomed. To Fairburn should be given much of the credit for the massive contribution which the L.M.S. Workshops made to the war effort, particularly in the repairs to aircraft damaged in combat. He deserved and gained respect, but not, I think, affection as did Stanier and Ivatt after him. I had much to thank Fairburn for. Had he lived the C.M. & E.E. Department of the L.M.S. would have been efficient. Of that there can be no doubt; but I have often wondered whether it would have been any more efficient than Stanier made it or than it remained under Ivatt's kindly and benevolent rule.

The news of Ivatt's appointment as Chief Mechanical and Electrical Engineer was received with great satisfaction throughout the Department. He was held in high regard as an engineer of wide experience and deep common sense by all to whom, as principal assistant, he had given guidance and direction. The staff changes consequent upon the new appointment were quickly made. I had speculated on the possibilities and hoped that further promotion might come my way. Ivatt has told me since how he sent for James Rankin, Locomotive Works Manager at Derby, to discuss his intended appointments with him. 'I want Bond with me here' he said – 'But who is to go to Crewe?' 'Why not me?' replied Rankin. And so it was decided. Everything was settled with Mr. G. R. T. Taylor, the chairman of the Locomotive Committee of the Board, in advance of official procedure, down to the salaries to be paid, marked on Ivatt's proposed organisation chart in Mr. Taylor's well-known green ink. 'Normal channels' in the Staff Department did not wholly approve of this simple, though unconventional way of getting things done! Thus I was soon to leave Crewe for the second time and move on to work in Derby after an interval of eighteen years. I received on 31st January, 1946, a personal note from the new C.M.E. informing me that as from the following day I had been appointed Mechanical Engineer (Locomotive Works) at his headquarters at Derby, to supervise and co-ordinate the activities at all the Locomotive Works of the Company.

There was no-one to whom I would rather have handed over Crewe than James Rankin. Derby Locomotive Works had flourished under his charge. We had worked together previously at Crewe, which he knew well, having been there as second assistant in F. A. Lemon's time. The only doubt was whether his health would enable him to stand the pace. He would have a good assistant in Maurice Burrows, who had been sent to me when John Bagguley moved on to Outdoor Carriage and Wagon work. Most of the other assistants and chief foremen who had served me so well were still in active service. I left Crewe happy in the knowledge that the Works, which had come to mean so much to me, would be in most competent hands during the difficult times ahead.

CHAPTER EIGHT

The End of an Era:
Derby Headquarters
1946–48

IVATT'S APPOINTMENT as Chief Mechanical Engineer coincided with the time when it was possible to resume a full programme of development of locomotive and rolling stock design, and to pick up the threads of many important projects which had perforce been abandoned at the outbreak of war. Those of us fortunate enough to be directly involved at headquarters in this resumption of normal technical activity were assured of work of the greatest possible interest. The railways were still under government control and likely to remain so for some time ahead. The end of the first world war had brought the amalgamation of twenty-three principal companies into four large groups. The aftermath of the recent conflict might well bring similar and even more far-reaching changes. But those were problems for others to worry about. Our job was the familiar one of continuing to provide and maintain the locomotives, rolling stock and general engineering equipment to meet the present and prospective requirements of the operating and commercial departments of the L.M.S. Railway.

As Mechanical Engineer (Locomotive Works), I became responsible for co-ordinating and exercising general supervision of repairs, new locomotive and boiler building and all other production from the four main locomotive works at Crewe, Derby, Horwich and St. Rollox, and their subsidiary shops at Rugby, Bow, Inverness and Kilmarnock. At headquarters I took charge, with three excellent assistants, of the Locomotive Shopping Bureau, Boiler Inspection, and the Locomotive and Boiler Building and Cutting-up programmes. I thus inherited from Ivatt the responsibilities which he, as Principal Assistant for Locomotives, had hitherto discharged, except design, technical development and testing. This important work he placed under the direct control of Stewart Cox.

Ivatt did not approve of the one-over-one type of organisation with a deputy having no direct personal responsibilities between himself and those in charge of the various functions which had been the general pattern in Stanier's time. He preferred to deal direct with each of us to whom he had given responsibility for the main sections of his Department.

Nevertheless in an organisation in which the heads of the various functions are of equal status, difficulties can arise when, in the absence of the chief, there is nobody officially recognised as his deputy and empowered to act on his behalf. These difficulties were apparently realised for after six months in my new appointment, I was designated Deputy Chief Mechanical Engineer. This was indeed as welcome as it was unexpected. Included among some routine papers which Ivatt's personal clerk brought me in one morning, was a private letter from the chief informing me of a rise in salary. I made some brief appreciative comment and passed on to other matters. Obviously something more was expected. 'Haven't you noticed who the letter from Mr. Ivatt is addressed to?' I was asked. I glanced at the envelope. Only then did I see it was to the Deputy Chief Mechanical Engineer. In a note which Ivatt circulated to his assistants notifying my appointment, he made it clear that the division of duties in his headquarters would remain as before. But it was essential that I should be kept informed of everything that was going on. Thus the only difference so far as I was concerned was that to a compulsive inclination to keep in touch with everything, there was added a duty to do so, for the discharge of which I had to rely on the help of my colleagues most freely given.

When the more urgent preoccupations of the war had become less insistent and time could be found to think about the future, much good work was done by Stewart Cox at Euston, and T. F. Coleman, the chief draughtsman at Derby, in preparing for a full resumption of design and development as soon as circumstances made this possible. The general situation was that we already had a first rate series of standard locomotives which had more than kept pace with the demands for higher speeds and heavier loads in express passenger service before the war. Looking further ahead to a demand which might have arisen had there been no war, a preliminary scheme for a locomotive to haul 500 ton trains between Euston and Glasgow in 6 hours was already in existence. This was an enlarged *Duchess*, a streamlined 4-6-4 with 300 lbs per square inch boiler pressure, 70 square feet of grate and, of course, a mechanical stoker. A further step along the hard road to higher thermal efficiency and greater power from the conventional steam locomotive was to have been taken by building two experimental 4-6-2s, authorised in 1939 generally similar to the *Duchess* class. These two engines would have had a boiler pressed to 300 lbs per square inch, steel firebox with thermic syphons, a steam temperature of 750°F., better draughting and a steam circuit more generous than had already been provided with such good results on the existing *Pacifics*.

A most valuable contribution to the future had already been made by rebuilding, from 1942 onwards, first, two 5X 4-6-0s, and later some of the

Royal Scots with taper boilers based on the design fitted to 6170 *British Legion*, itself rebuilt from the high pressure Schmidt-Henschel locomotive *Fury*. The rebuilt 5X engines became *Class 7* in the power classification, equal to the *Scots*. Their steaming troubles were finally cured. The *Royal Scots* themselves, good engines though they always were, were still further improved by the re-building. A cylindrical smokebox resting on a saddle cast integral with the inside cylinder overcame the difficulty of maintaining the original Midland design of smokebox airtight. New main frames and cylinders, together with a bolster bogie, steel axleboxes and improved spring gear all played their part in improving performance. The first two 5Xs and ten of the *Scots* were rebuilt during my time at Crewe. They were virtually new locomotives. An interesting sidelight on these engines was that just as the compounds had done years before and the *Britannias* were to do in the future, they gave us some trouble for a time with bent coupling rods. Sanding gear was in due course fitted at the trailing coupled wheels, but whether it was this or more careful handling by the drivers which soon cured the trouble is a debatable point.

With plenty of modern and efficient express passenger locomotives in service, with clear ideas already formed if something even larger was to be required, and a greatly increased number of standard 2-8-0s for heavy freight traffic available, what further needs might remain to be filled, and along what lines should future development proceed? In a report which he wrote on steam traction policy, Stewart Cox, while recognising the growing part which electric and diesel traction would play in the future, quite rightly emphasised that, as steam traction would almost certainly be with us for at least a further 20 years (he was writing in 1942), every effort should continue to be made to improve the efficiency and reduce costs of operation and maintenance of steam locomotives.

He suggested that the post-war traffic of the company could be dealt with by eleven locomotive classes. Two of them only, a 4-6-4 for express passenger services and a 4-8-4 for mixed traffic duties, were to be completely new designs. A *Class 4* 2-6-0 in replacement of obsolete 0-6-0s for a wide range of freight services over routes denied to 2-8-0s, was to be derived from the standard 2-6-4 tank engines. For the rest, it was proposed that Stanier's existing designs should continue to be built, modified as to details in whatever respects experience in service (monitored by a staff of mechanical inspectors appointed for the purpose) showed would lead to higher availability and greater mileage between repairs. The war years had driven home, as never before, the lesson that with locomotives which were already economical on coal, further savings in operating and maintenance costs were to be sought more by improving the mechanical performance of existing types than by designing new locomotives which might have a marginally higher thermal efficiency.

Manganese steel liners on axleboxes and hornblocks, drop grates, hopper bottom ashpans and self-cleaning smokeboxes were likely to pay higher dividends than an extra 50 lbs on the boiler pressure. This was indeed the right approach and became the cornerstone of L.M.S. post-war steam locomotive policy. It was followed with conspicuous success as may be judged, for example, by the increased mileage between shop repairs obtained from modifications to the *Class 5* 4-6-0 engines. The figures tabulated below for all *Class 5* 4-6-0s sent in for repairs on the London Midland, and Scottish Regions during 1948 and 1949 are typical.

Average mileage from General Repair to first Intermediate Repair

Locomotives fitted with —		
Manganese steel liners	77 engines	108,283 miles
White metalled faces	243 engines	61,240 miles
Percentage increase = 76%		

Average mileage from first to second Classified Repair

Locomotives fitted with –		
Manganese steel liners	41 engines	77,320 miles
White metalled faces	572 engines	55,288 miles
Percentage increase = 39%		

These results were, of course, influenced by other factors such as tyre wear, condition of cylinders, and particularly in the case of second consecutive repairs, the condition of the boiler. Nevertheless they do demonstrate the extent to which good engines could be made even better by a deliberate policy of development and modification based on analyses of performance in service, and in the shops and sheds. The target at which development in general was aimed was 100,000 miles between consecutive shop repairs for all locomotives, and for the most important express passenger and mixed traffic types 100,000 miles per annum – by no means unattainable.

The need for medium power freight engines, foreseen by Cox, was provided for by Coleman also in the types of locomotives which he proposed should form the future L.M.S. standard classes. In retrospect it may perhaps be of interest to see tabulated together the two series of locomotives, one suggested by E. S. Cox, the other by T. F. Coleman, for meeting the future traffic needs of the L.M.S. Railway.

Proposed L.M.S. Standard Locomotives

Tender engines	Power Class	New Designs E. S. Cox	Existing Standards	New Designs T. F. Coleman
Passenger	9	4-6-4		
	8		4-6-2	
	7		4-6-0	
Mixed Traffic	9	4-8-4		
	7			2-6-2
	5		4-6-0	
Freight	8		2-8-0	
	4	2-6-0		0-6-0
Tank Engines				
Mixed Traffic	4		2-6-4	
	3		2-6-2	
	2			0-6-2
Freight	8			2-8-4
Shunting	—		0-6-0	
			0-4-0	

It is a matter of history that of the new designs in the above table only the *Class 4* 2-6-0 was ever built, and then under Ivatt, in a form which differed somewhat from the original idea of derivation from the existing 2-6-4 tanks. They were not, at first, very good engines due to a badly proportioned double chimney. With this replaced by an effective single chimney they became a most useful class, eventually built in some numbers by and for the Eastern and North Eastern Regions as well as the London Midland.

At this time, various groups of small locomotives kept in service under war conditions required to be replaced. For the first time, Ivatt reversed the almost universal policy of catering for the lighter duties by down grading engines no longer capable of doing the work for which they had originally been built, or as the Motive Power people often seemed to want, by perpetuating obsolete designs, by producing completely new types of *Class 2* locomotives a 2-6-0 tender and a 2-6-2 tank. These excellent little engines were modern in every way, incorporating for light duties all those features which had proved of value in larger locomotives. They became, in due course, two of the classes in the final range of B.R. standard steam locomotives.

Vain speculation though it may be, one cannot help wondering whether any others among the proposed new designs would have been built if nationalisation had not engulfed us, and the L.M.S. had continued as an independent company for a few more years beyond 1948. I am inclined to think not. There is not much doubt that by the time a need for the *Class 9* 4-6-4 and 4-8-4 types might have arisen it would have been met by the diesel locomotives which Ivatt built. Coleman's three-cylinder 2-6-2 would have been a beauty, and an admirable replacement for the Horwich 2-6-0s. But here again, diesels, singly or in pairs would have filled the bill.

It was during the four or five years immediately preceding the outbreak of war that the challenge of diesel traction became a factor of significance in the motive power scene. The L.M.S. had pioneered the introduction of diesel locomotives in this country. After extensive trials with various types of shunting locomotives they had by 1936 evolved a standard design with a 350 h.p. English Electric engine and electric transmission. It was proved beyond doubt that diesel power was technically suitable and economically superior to steam for shunting. Diesel traction for a wide variety of main line services had been successfully developed well beyond the experimental stage in the United States and some European countries. The use of diesel locomotives, particularly on services in which it was possible to run high mileages per annum was growing rapidly in the United States.

Diesels might even prove to be an adequate and less expensive alternative to electrification on all but the most intense services for which electric traction alone would suffice. With the full resumption of technical development in every field, it was most desirable for us to find out by actual trials in service whether the advantages claimed for diesel traction in main line service were attainable under British conditions, different though they might be in regard, for example, to cost and availability of coal and oil supplies. Judging from recorded experience and propaganda from the other side of the Atlantic they seemed to be considerable and could certainly not be ignored.

I was in at the building of the prototype L.M.S. main line diesels Nos. 10000 and 10001 from early days. The inception of the project and the technical features of these locomotives have often been described. I do not need to repeat them here. These locomotives should be remembered for the excellence of their design and performance in service for nearly twenty years. They, and the somewhat similar locomotives which Bulleid put into service on the Southern Region soon after nationalisation were the forerunners of the present diesel fleet. Their design had more than a little influence on some of our later locomotives.

Ivatt took an intense interest in everything pertaining to these locomotives. He brought to bear upon the design of their mechanical parts his instinctive flair for sound engineering, and Derby was the obvious choice of building works. Much would depend upon close collaboration between the Works, Drawing Office and Headquarters, all within five minutes walk of each other. I was given the job of taking the chair at the many meetings to co-ordinate design, supply of materials and power equipment from the contractors and production in the Shops. There was much to be learnt in building the underframe, body and fabricated bogies.

17. The first of 500 locomotives inspected under construction at contractor's works.

18. One of the first three *Garratts* – for Midland coal traffic between Toton and Brent.

Midland design at its best – heavy freight locomotive built for the Somerset & Dorset Joint Railway by Robert Stephenson & Co. at Darlington at the time of the Railway Centenary.

20. The most important inspection job. One of the *Royal Scots* as originally built. David Gibson, a celeb:
Caledonian driver, with whom the author rode many hundred miles, is on the footplate.

21. The *Royal Scots* in their final form – as rebuilt by Sir William Stanier.

22. A Midland compound as developed for service throughout the L.M.S.

23. Midland *Class 3* 4-4-0 No. 777 on which the author carried out coal and water consumption tests.

24. Electric freight locomotive for the Great Indian Peninsula Railway – ready for shipment from the Vulcan Foundry.

25. (Left) Saturday afternoon relaxation in Bombay.

26. Operation over the Ghats between Bombay and Poona after the inauguration of electric service.

27. Our first home – 'Spring Cottage', Rivington. An oasis in the heart of industrial Lancashire.

28. Jean.

29. On leave – relaxing in the heather at Kyle of Lochalsh.

The second of nier's *Pacifics*, cess Elizabeth — the motive which earned author a rebuke — and mmendation — from Robert Riddles.

Princess Elizabeth the record breaking -stop run from ton to Glasgow, 16th November, 1936.

One of the 'might beens' — a Southern ion *Merchant Navy* ught to a stand out mishap after a oken driving axle.

33. Sir William Stanier's Turbine Locomotive – built at Crewe in 1935.

34. The Turbine Locomotive – rebuilt as a normal four-cylinder locomotive, No. 46202, *Princess Anne*.

35. Sir William Stanier's masterpiece. The first of five streamlined *Pacifics* for working the *Coronation Scot* trains.

36. Sir William A. Stanier, F.R.S.

37. The silver stripes on which much time was spent. The first three *Pacifics* outside the Paint Shop at Crewe.

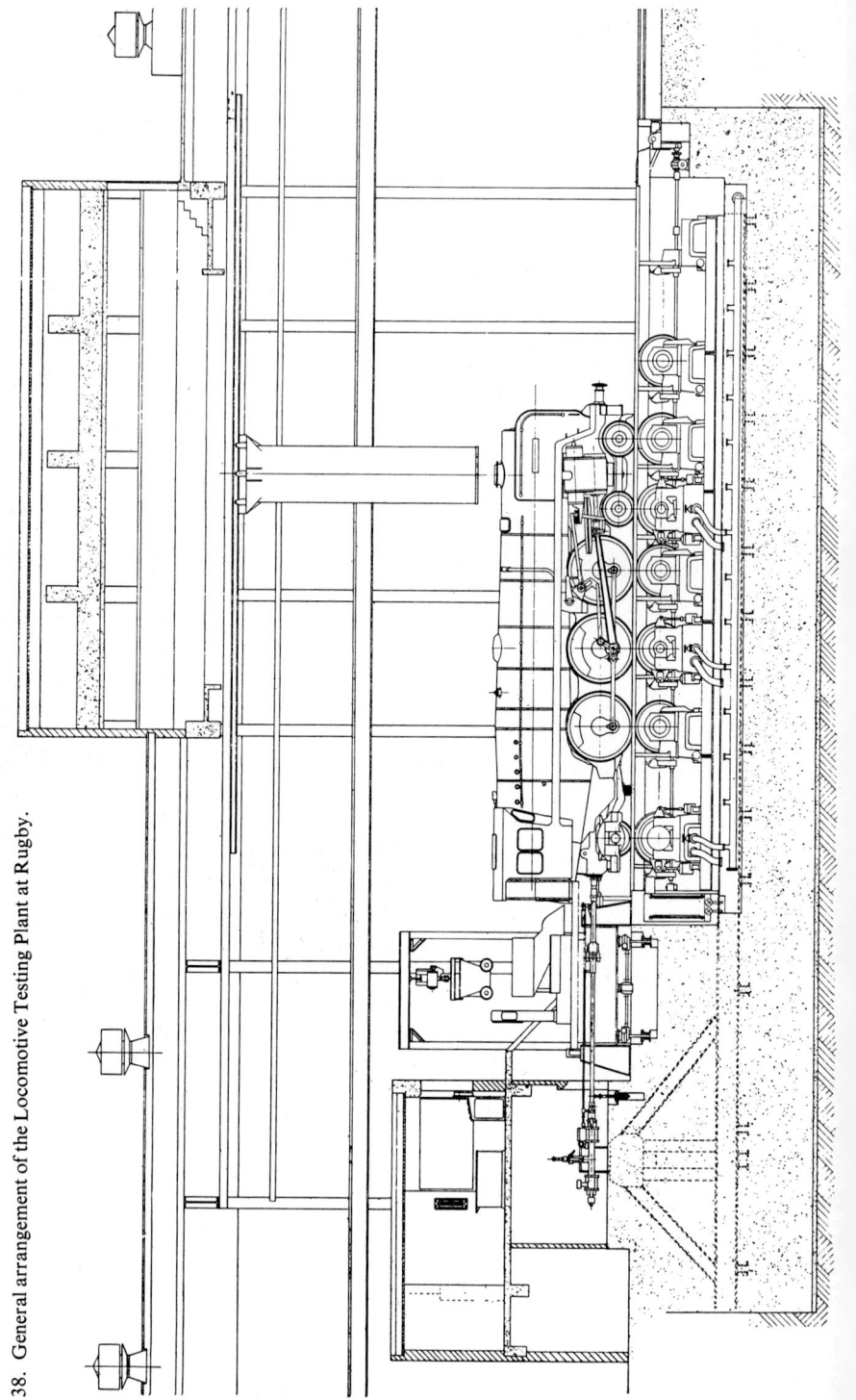

38. General arrangement of the Locomotive Testing Plant at Rugby.

39. The Locomotive Testing Station – when work was suspended at the outbreak of war in September 1939.

40. The Locomotive Testing Plant completed and in use.

41. The dire result of shortage of water — the bulged fire box crown torn off the roof stays of L.M.S. 4-6-2 No. 6224.

42. Spitfire fuselages under repair at Barassie.

43. A *Covenanter* tank – of which 161 were built at Crewe.

44. *Matilda* tanks, the hull plates of which were machined at Crewe, being assembled at Horwich.

A contrast in freight locomotives.

45. L.M.S. Standard *Class 8* 2-8-0 prepared at Crewe for service in Persia.

46. American 2-8-0 for U.S.A. forces in Europe, modified at Crewe for temporary service on Britain's railways.

49. The pioneers of mainline diesel traction on British Railways: L.M.S. 10000 and 10001 hauling the *Royal Scot* from Euston to Glasgow Central.

50. Three of the locomotives on which the author rode on American railroads:

Pennsylvania Railroad: Express Passenger Electric Locomotive, tractive effort 73,000 lbs, total weight 205 to

Delaware and Hudson Railroad: 2 cyls: 24½″ × 32″, 6′ 3″ coupled wheels, total weight 342 tons, boiler pressure 285 lbs/sq. in., grate area 96·2 sq. ft., tractive effort 62,040 lbs.

New York Central Railroad: 2 cyls: 22½″ × 29″, 6′ 7″ coupled wheels, total weight 300 tons, boiler pressure 275 lbs/sq. in., grate area 82 sq. ft., tractive effort 43,440 lbs.

51. The tragic end to 46202 at Harrow.

The locomotive Works Manager, Eric Robson, brought up on carriage and wagon work had wide experience of building all-steel coaching stock. He was able to guide the boiler and erecting shop foremen through many a difficult production problem. Time was of the essence. The days of the L.M.S. were numbered. Whatever happened we were determined that one of the diesels should be finished before the curtain descended. Robson was not one to let the grass grow under his feet. The job was done with three weeks to spare.

This far-sighted project was a first class example of what can be done by whole-hearted co-operation between experts in their own particular fields. We knew far more than any contractor about locomotive design from the railway point of view. The English Electric Company knew far more than we could hope to know about the design of diesel engines and electric transmissions. The locomotives would give us the experience in daily service needed to assess the potential benefits of diesel traction under British conditions. They would at the same time provide private manufacturers with a 'shop window', as it has often been called, enabling them to compete more effectively in what was clearly becoming an important world market. For myself, the experience which I gained was of great value when, not many years later, it fell to my lot as Chief Mechanical Engineer at British Railways Headquarters to press on with the introduction of diesel traction at a rate which nobody in their senses in 1947 would have either thought possible, or likely to be justified financially.

No. 10000 was driven out of the Paint Shop by Ivatt himself to the cheers of a large crowd of the men who had helped to build her, during the first week of December 1947. The plain black finish with aluminium painted roof and bogies suited the diesel well. Instead of the usual gold leaf transfers, the number and letters 'L.M.S.' in stainless steel were riveted to the body sides. We did not intend that the origin of the first main line diesel locomotive built by a British railway company should be easily forgotten. To make assurance doubly sure, the letters were cast as a monogram in the aluminium floorplates of the engine room compartment. A trivial matter perhaps, but symptomatic of the pride we felt in the company which over a quarter of a century from the turbulent days of amalgamation had built up a reputation second to none among the railways of the world.

A week of trial running was followed by the first journey to Euston for inspection by the Board. It was a great occasion, memorable also because standing alongside the diesel was one of the last two *Pacifics* built by the L.M.S. there to be named *Sir William A. Stanier F.R.S.* by the Chairman of the Board, Sir Robert Burrows.

Our old chief was present to participate in the traditional unveiling of the nameplate. It was, and is, unusual for a Chief Mechanical Engineer to be thus honoured during his lifetime. One of the L.N.E. streamlined A4 *Pacifics,* No. 4498 had been named after Sir Nigel Gresley while he was still in office. What more appropriate than that one of the *Duchess Pacifics* should be named after Sir William Stanier? I was glad to have had some part in the choice of name for 6256. It was decided in the train somewhere between Derby and Crewe during a journey with Ivatt and Riddles to see the new engine under construction.

The *Duchess Pacifics* were the finest of all Stanier's locomotives. But he would have been the first to acknowledge the improvements in detail which Ivatt made in the last two built. Roller bearing axleboxes with manganese steel liners throughout, a re-designed back-end and cast steel trailing truck, rocking grate and hopper ashpan all played their part in giving us more miles between shop repairs and higher availability.

The use of oil as an alternative to coal as locomotive fuel was forced on our attention, not only by our trials of diesel traction. Owing to increasing stringency in the supply of locomotive coal the railways were asked in 1946 to reduce consumption by one million tons per year, by converting some engines to oil firing. The planning of the scheme involving conversion of 1229 locomotives, provision of sixty-three oil storage and fuelling depots, and 4,000 oil tank wagons, was handed to a committee of C.M.E. people from the four companies, with Bulleid from the Southern, in the chair. Ivatt deputed me to take this job in hand for him. Everything had, of course, to be done with the utmost urgency; but within a few months after only ninty-three engines had been converted, the fuel supply situation had apparently so radically altered that the job was stopped! Nevertheless we gained some useful experience. From the operating point of view, oil burning was quite successful, the locomotives converted steaming, if anything, rather better than before. Firebox maintenance costs were rather higher. We reckoned that on a heat content basis, 68 lbs of oil were equivalent to 100 lbs of coal. At the then existing prices of coal at 0.29 pence per lb and oil at 0.81 pence, fuel costs with oil were roughly $2\frac{1}{2}$ times more than for coal firing. It would have been an expensive business had it continued long – but the sudden change of policy made one wonder what people were about!

It was a well established custom on the L.M.S. for senior officers to be sent to the United States from time to time to see for themselves how other people tackled problems very similar to their own. My turn came in the autumn of 1947. It had been decided that the foundry scheme with which I had been concerned at Horwich, and Crewe should be completed – in particular that the chair foundry at Horwich should be mechanised.

Existing plans were brought up-to-date, but we were not happy about the methods proposed by the foundry contractor for clearing moulding boxes containing two red-hot castings and several hundredweight of sand from the continuous casting conveyor. Any failure to keep pace at the knockouts would be ruinous to output. We knew from Mr. Taylor, chairman of the Locomotive Committee that this particular problem had been solved in American mechanised foundries by high frequency vibrating screens. As, he said, it was in any case high time that I should be sent to see what was happening in America, a view with which I heartily agreed, arrangements were made for me to accompany the Chairman and Robert Riddles, for whom a visit to Canada and the United States had already been arranged.

This was my first visit to America. It was bound to be of the greatest interest. My departure was fraught with some anxiety. The evening before I was due to leave for Southampton, a jar of fruit which my wife was bottling burst in her face. I felt I should have to postpone my journey, but the damage was not serious and Jean was insistent that I should go as planned. Crossing the Atlantic in the *Queen Elizabeth*, fully restored to her normal standard of luxury from wartime troop carrying, was something to be remembered at a time when food at home was still rationed and austerity of one kind and another remained the order of the day. One had almost forgotten that menus of the kind with which we were presented on the *Queen Elizabeth*, and indeed wherever we went in America over the next four weeks, had ever existed. But that apart, five days at sea in the world's largest liner culminating in a first sight of the Statue of Liberty and the Manhattan skyline glinting in the early morning sun, were very much to my taste. That it took us over three hours in a slowly moving queue to complete immigration formalities at Pier 91, notwithstanding the V.I.P. treatment we received, was no more than slightly tiresome, and a reminder that we were in someone else's country which had its own ways of doing things!

In the course of twenty-five days in Canada and the United States before sailing home from New York in the *Queen Mary*, I travelled nearly 4,000 miles by train visiting the headquarters and locomotive works of eight railroad companies, in addition to mechanised foundries in Detroit, the Works of the American Locomotive Company and Baldwins, and the Electro-Motive division of General Motors building diesel locomotives at Le Grange, Illinois, a few miles out of Chicago. Plans did not work out quite as originally intended. Half way across the Atlantic, Riddles received a cable from Ivatt congratulating him on his new appointment as the member of the new Railway Executive responsible for mechanical and electrical engineering throughout British Railways.

Another telegram instructing him to return to London to take up the new appointment arrived in New York almost as soon as we did. Things were certainly moving into the new era of nationalisation faster than some of us had realised.

My first impressions of North American railroads, influenced no doubt by the magnificence of Grand Central Terminal, with its star-spangled dome, were very favourable. Long distance passenger travel in Canada and the United States was still predominantly by train. Internal air lines were then more a spur to the railroads to provide faster, more luxurious trains, than an immediate threat to passenger revenues. Certainly with two exceptions, when the riding of sleeping and dining cars was really bad, speed, comfort, cleanliness and punctuality of the trains in which I travelled, were as good and sometimes better than the best we had achieved in the halcyon years before the war.

My objectives, in addition to the general one of learning something about American railroads and locomotives and the specific one of production methods in mechanised foundries, are quite simply stated. American motive power was at a vital crossroads in the way ahead. Though steam locomotives still predominated, diesels were challenging their supremacy. I wanted to find out as much as possible about the operation and maintenance of diesel locomotives in main line service, and to assess their probable future position in relation to steam and gas-turbine locomotives. I wanted to learn more about the very advanced unconventional designs of steam locomotives, one at least of which was still being actively developed; and on locomotive design and workshop practice generally to ascertain what features in contemporary American developments could be applied with advantage to our own immediate problems.

Out of a total of 42,500 locomotives on United States railroads there were 5,600 diesel units in service. Three thousand of them were shunters — in U.S. parlance, switchers. But there were something like 1,000 locomotives in various combinations of two, three or four units in main line service. The trend was plain to see from the number of new engines put into service during the previous two years. The figures are given below:

	Locomotives put into service			Locomotives on order
Type	1945	1946	Jan.–July 1947	August 1947
Steam	109	83	63	20
Electric	–	—	2	4
Diesel	534	480	417	782
Total	643	563	482	815

In Canada a close watch was kept on the trend of events across the border. Both the Canadian Pacific and the Canadian National had run diesel locomotives experimentally and the latter had recently decided to work the traffic on Prince Edward Island entirely with diesel-electric locomotives. Opinion in Canada was at that time quite definite that unless diesels could be rostered to work at least 20,000 miles per month they would not be financially justified. Doubts were expressed whether all the diesel projects in the United States had really achieved the economies claimed. High hopes were entertained by both Companies that the development of motive power for main line services in Canada would proceed direct from steam to gas turbine propulsion without an intermediate diesel phase.

In the United States some railroads had gone over completely to diesel traction. Those operating west of Chicago were unlikely to order any more steam locomotives. The case of the Santa Fe was typical. They had last bought new steam locomotives in 1942, but had several main line diesels on order. On the Eastern roads also, the number of diesel locomotives was increasing. Proximity to the coal mines and the fact that so much of their revenue came from the carriage of coal made diesel traction less attractive to the Eastern lines than to the Western and Southern companies. Although costs on a uniform basis had not long been available for comparison with steam operated services, there was little doubt among American railroad men that, when traffic conditions permitted diesels to attain the high annual mileages of which they are inherently capable, their use had been economically justified.

Probably no place in North America was better known as a true railway town than Altoona, the centre of Pennsylvania locomotive development, the site of the world-famous locomotive testing plant, and one of the few railway Works which built their own locomotives. Two or three days in the Works there, with a visit to the Horseshoe Curve only a few miles away, would be well spent. I had seen a triple-headed passenger express and a freight train of 125 cars fighting its way up the bank with four 2-10-4s, two in front and two in the rear, on my journey down the Horseshoe from Chicago. An hour or so by the lineside would not be without interest. Altoona was indeed the Crewe of North America. The shops full of massive locomotives being repaired with hardly a boiler off the frames and new front end sections being welded on to cast-steel locomotive beds, reflected some of the differences in American and British design and practice. Interesting though they were, the shops at Altoona, and indeed the others I visited, were not so well organised as our own.

I was particularly interested to see the locomotive testing plant. The code of practice which I had drawn up for Rugby owed a great deal to the methods employed and the test bulletins issued from Altoona. I was hopeful that there would be some new ideas of value to us; but in this I was disappointed. A 2-10-0 built by the Lima Locomotive Co. for the Polish State Railways was on the plant undergoing complete performance tests in accordance with the well known routine.

The Pennsylvania had adopted a cautious attitude to diesel traction, but had recently ordered forty 6,000 h.p. triple unit locomotives. It was particularly interesting to be told that the scheme for extending their existing electrification from Harrisburg to Pittsburgh and Cincinatti had been shelved indefinitely in the expectation that diesel traction would meet all future traffic requirements with less capital expenditure than would be incurred by further electrification.

No railroad had done more to develop and utilise the maximum possibilities of conventional steam locomotives than the New York Central. None had more carefully attempted to assess the merits of the two forms of traction on accurately ascertained and strictly relevant facts. In passenger services over 928 miles between Harmon and Chicago during 1946, six of the latest *Niagara* class 4-8-4 locomotives were rostered to work three trains daily in each direction in competition with twin-unit 4,000 h.p. diesels. They averaged 862 miles per day throughout the trial period. The diesel locomotives covered an average of 904 miles per day. It was estimated that for a whole year's working the comparison between the two forms of motive power would be as set out below:

	Diesel-Electric	*Steam*
Annual Mileage	324,000	288,000
Availability	74·2%	69·0%

Excellent though these results were for the steam locomotives, costs given to me by the Chief of Motive Power demonstrated that the diesels were superior in this service. The total annual cost per mile with everything included, was 9 per cent less than for the *Niagaras*. While continuing to develop and exploit to the maximum extent the performance and efficiency from their steam power, the New York Central were ordering more diesel main line units.

The locomotive builders had invested large sums in plant and equipment for building diesel locomotives and engines. At Le Grange, General Motors with a capacity of 1,100 diesel units and engines per annum, were increasing production facilities still further. Though the way the wind was blowing was clear enough, the whirlwind was yet to come. Everyone was agreed that the number of diesel locomotives would grow at an increasing rate for some years to come but no-one was prepared to forecast what the ultimate relationship between the alternative forms of traction was likely to be, or when stability would be reached. In the United States, as in Canada, there was a strong view that gas turbines would seriously challenge the diesel engine. I was given plenty to think about as to how matters might develop at home over the years ahead.

Nothing that I saw, or was told about in America caused me to change my opinion long held, that until finally displaced by other forms of motive power, the future for steam traction continued to lie in developing to the utmost the simple, reliable, reciprocating steam locomotive. Three very large steam turbo-electric locomotives, weighing over 400 tons were under construction at Baldwins for the Chesapeake and Ohio Railroad. I saw the first of these in steam at the builders' works. Impressive though it was, this locomotive, which was presumably to be regarded as a reply to the challenge of diesel traction, seemed to me to combine within one locomotive all the major disadvantages of both forms of motive power. It was suitable for running in one direction only and would have to be turned after each trip. Judged on power/weight ratio and length it was in no way superior to diesel-electrics, and from the standpoint of availability it could hardly fail to be adversely affected by the limitations which a coal burning boiler imposes on all steam locomotives, and also by the complexity of its design and construction. This locomotive was hardly likely to contribute anything very significant to the progress of locomotive engineering.

Concerned as I had been with our turbine locomotive at home, I was most interested to find out how the Pennsylvania had fared with their 6-8-6 engine designed in respect of the turbine and transmission on identical lines to our own locomotive. Whereas our difficulties had been concerned with the reversing mechanism and lubrication system these features had caused the Pennsylvania people no trouble. Their problems had been centred on the boiler and firebox. Soon after going into regular service, large numbers of firebox stays were found to be breaking. The trouble was attributed to defective circulation.

Tests conducted with a model firebox fitted with glass observation windows showed a large dead area along the firebox sides. A new boiler was designed with wider water legs and more room under the combustion chamber to ensure adequate circulation – shades of Churchward and his experiments forty years earlier! The Steam Locomotive Research Institute, an organisation sponsored by the principal locomotive building companies under the direction of Lawford Fry, whom I met in New York, were also taking a hand in the matter. They were designing a water-tube firebox for this engine, the working pressure of which was to be doubled to 600 lbs per square inch in an attempt to increase thermal efficiency. Coal and water consumption had been considerably higher than with the P.R.R.'s most modern reciprocating locomotives.

Another innovation to which, as I have already recorded, we had given some attention – the burning of pulverised coal – had been tried out in the United States. Seven of the principal railroads had spent over £200,000 in attempts to perfect a means of burning pulverised coal successfully in locomotive boilers. It had been found impossible to overcome the well-known difficulties caused by accumulation of fused ash and slag. The work had been abandoned. The soundness of the decision not to undertake similar work on the L.M.S. was amply confirmed by American experience.

The lively interest in gas turbines was by no means confined to oil burning installations. Work on development of a gas turbine locomotive to burn pulverised coal had been in hand for two years by the Bituminous Coal Research organisation of the coal industry. Combustion of pulverised coal under pressure, and separation of ash from the gas stream were the main problems to be overcome, on the solution of which all else depended. There was considerable optimism as to the eventual outcome of the project. No other form of coal burning locomotive was considered to have better prospects of competing successfully with diesel traction – but time alone would tell.

Apart from the broad trends of motive power policy, there was much in contemporary American locomotive practice of direct value to our own work at home, particularly in regard to steel fireboxes, roller bearings and feedwater treatment. We were proposing to build two spare boilers for the *Pacifics* with steel fireboxes and thermic syphons. American opinion was almost unanimous that arch tubes or circulators were much superior.

Roller bearing axleboxes for coupled wheels had been widely adopted. Ivatt was fitting roller bearings to the last two *Pacifics* and to twenty *Class 5* 4-6-0s. On two of the railroads which I visited, the Delaware & Hudson, and the Santa Fe, a compromise of fitting roller bearings to the driving axle only had been tried. It was argued that the heavy reciprocating loads which cause knock invariably originate at the driving axle. If by fitting roller bearings to the driving axle only the development of knock can be prevented at its source, the impact loads on the axleboxes of the other coupled wheels will be so reduced as to ensure results as good as from a complete application of roller bearings, with considerable savings in cost. This seemed to me eminently reasonable. Some L.M.S. *Class 5s* and later some of the *Britannias* were built with roller bearings for the driving axle only.

There was no doubt that water treatment, the economic justification for which in spite of repeated attempts we had never been able to prove to the satisfaction of our accountants, was not only worthwhile, but quite essential under American conditions. Properly applied, and above all, properly managed, chemical water treatment in combination with regular blowing down and daily sampling of the water in every boiler, was completely effective in maintaining boilers free from scale, corrosion and priming, thereby saving a lot of money on boiler repairs. Steam locomotive operation as practised in the United States would have been impossible in the absence of effective water treatment. Moreover, I was told by Mr. A. K. Galloway, Chief of Motive Power of the Baltimore & Ohio that correctly treated water was quite essential for avoiding trouble in diesel engine cooling circuits – a lesson which later it took some of us rather a long time to learn.

Galloway was like no other chief officer I had ever met. He worked with the door of his private office always open. Disdaining such refinements as a row of bell pushes on his desk, he summoned his assistants from their large outer office by the simple process of shouting for them at the top of his not inconsiderable voice. He had wide experience of the operation and maintenance of diesel locomotives. He rejected the idea, rather prevalent at the time, that steam locomotive men were constitutionally incapable of mastering the techniques appropriate to the newer forms of motive power.

Facilities for journeys on the footplate were readily arranged though rather more formality was involved than at home. An indemnity absolving the railroad from the consequences of anything which might happen, however unlikely, had to be signed before climbing into the cab. The dominant impression on the footplate of American locomotives was one of unlimited power, without any restriction imposed by the willingness or strength of the fireman.

With one exception my trips were uneventful. The exception was on a Delaware & Hudson 4-8-4, spotlessly clean and in first class order, taking me down from Montreal to Schenectady. Approaching Napierville, where we were booked to stop, I noticed a motor car travelling rather faster than we were on a road running parallel to the track. We were on a righthand curve and I could not see the level crossing ahead. Until the driver, behind whom I was sitting, exclaimed 'We've hit him' I did not associate a slight bump with the fact that the car had failed to beat us to the crossing. It was thrown to the side of the track. Two of the four passengers were dead – the others in a very poor way. We were delayed over an hour awaiting, as required by Canadian law, the arrival of the coroner from St. Jean eighteen miles away. Once on the way again, there was no opportunity of picking up any of the lost time over the single track route down the shores of Lake Champlain through the woods in their full autumn colouring. We had lost our path and were held at crossing stations through which we should have passed without stopping. At one booked stop, a coaling plant built over the main line topped us up in a cloud of dust, with 6 tons of coal. The driver received his crossing orders by a series of written notes – a rather less satisfactory system, I thought, than electrically controlled tablet instruments. The road, severely curved with short transitions into which the engine was inclined to lurch, included many miles of long welded rails, then something of a novelty.

Equally interesting was the run I had over the four-tracked main line of the New York Central on one of their J3 4-6-4s from Buffalo to Cleveland. These magnificent engines from which the *Niagaras* were derived, had 82 square feet of grate, 275 lbs working pressure and cylinders 22_2 diameter. Maximum indicated horsepower was 4700 at 77 miles per hour, and at the drawbar 3700 horsepower at 59 miles per hour. We had a heavy train, something over 800 tons, with which speed was maintained at 80 m.p.h. for miles on end. Unusual in America, the New York Central had installed water troughs – track pans they were called – on their main routes, from which we replenished our very large tender. Steaming and riding was all that could be desired. Returning to the train at Erie, hot, dirty and thirsty, I badly needed a drink, only to be told that drinks could not be served while passing through the State of Pennsylvania. I had to wait until we passed over the border, at nowhere in particular, into Ohio! Even less understandable than some of our own odd licensing laws.

I had my first trip in the cab of a main line diesel locomotive from Chicago to Fort Wayne on the Broadway Limited Express of the Pennsylvania Railroad. The locomotive was a General Motors triple unit rated at 6,000 horsepower. Each unit was mounted on two six-wheeled bogies and powered by two engine-generator sets. Again the impression of unlimited power for hauling the train of 950 tons. Whereas the American Locomotive Company and Baldwins were advocating the use of one diesel engine per unit, General Motors continued at that time, to press the advantages of flexibility which a greater number of smaller power units gives to a locomotive. It was contended that one or more engines could be cut out on easy sections, and that in the event of failure of a power plant, the locomotive can continue on its trip with the minimum of lost time. I had a personal demonstration of this philosophy. Shortly after leaving Chicago it was found that the electrical equipment of one diesel set would not make the transition from series to parallel working. The set was cut-out without stopping and despite the loss of 1000 horse power, we covered 141 miles from Englewood to Fort Wayne in 115 minutes at an average speed of 73 miles per hour. Notwithstanding the advantages of flexibility in such a case as this, I could not help feeling that it would be better to concentrate on removing the causes of failure rather than to minimise their consequences.

I rounded off my footplate trips on a Pennsylvania 4-6-6-4 electric locomotive from Philadelphia to Washington. I was thus able to compare the riding characteristics of an articulated locomotive with those of a twin-bogie locomotive. On the double bogie diesels at speeds up to 90 miles per hour, the riding was superb. On the Pennsylvania electric at the same speed it was good, but more akin to that of a good steam locomotive than to a coach which was the case on the twin-bogie locomotives. Yet one more new slant on footplate drill which I had not come across before, was the invariable practice of the driver of the electric locomotive to move away from his side window to the centre of the cab, whenever a freight train passed us. He insisted that I should do likewise to avoid possible injury from loads shifted out of gauge.

And so on to New York, the *Queen Mary*, Southampton and London, where my wife was waiting for me at Euston Hotel. My first visit to America was memorable in every way, made particularly enjoyable by the kindness and lavish hospitality I had received not only from the railways and locomotive builders, but from cousins of my wife living in Cleveland, with whom I contrived to spend a long weekend in luxurious surroundings. One had so often been told of the differences in physical and geographical conditions as they affect rail transport between Great Britain and North America. They are so obvious as to require no emphasis. What impressed me far more, was the fundamental similarity between the everyday problems to be solved by railwaymen on both sides of the Atlantic.

Back again in Derby, there were only two months remaining before an era would end, and the service which the L.M.S. had rendered to the country would continue uninterrupted in the wider context of national ownership. The last two years had been a time of intense and varied interest. No two days were ever the same. Work on the Locomotive Testing Plant at Rugby was once more in full swing, and among all the other projects on which work had been resumed none was more important than the tests to measure the lateral forces exerted by a locomotive on itself and the track in everyday service. Locomotive engineers naturally had a general understanding of the behaviour of locomotives on the track. But if only because of the elasticity and working clearances of frames, wheels and spring gear, and elasticity of the rails, sleepers and road bed of the track, leading to random variability of the interactions involved, the subject is complex and scarcely amenable to rigid mathematical treatment. It is manifestly clear from everyday experience of railway operation that locomotives can be built to run safely on good track at high speed. The design and maintenance criteria, both for locomotives and track necessary to eliminate risk of derailment are well established. Nevertheless, from time to time, derailments did occur, due more often than not to severe lateral distortion of the track, caused by a locomotive running unsteadily, rolling and swaying from side to side, imposing lateral forces which the permanent way could not withstand. Occasionally, too, excessive flange forces at a single pair of coupled wheels, arising from inadequate guiding from the bogie on a curve could fetch a locomotive partially off the road.

There was the well known case of a *Royal Scot* No. 6131 running through Weaver Junction with a speed limit of 55 m.p.h., at 70 miles per hour, which was safely brought to rest with the leading coupled wheels off the road. Cases such as this were few and far between. Even more exceptional were serious accidents such as the derailment near Sevenoaks of a 2-6-4 tank engine caused by the combination of a locomotive inherently sensitive to track irregularities, travelling at high speed on a road in less than first class condition. In general, the high standards of design and maintenance of British locomotives and track ensured a correspondingly high standard of safety. But there was always room for improvement.

Sir William Stanier had been much impressed, while in India as a member of the *Pacific* locomotive enquiry committee, by the valuable results the Indian Railway Board had obtained from flange force measuring apparatus during their investigations into derailments of *X class Pacific* locomotives. He arranged on his return home for similar equipment to be manufactured to enable tests to be conducted with L.M.S. locomotives. Owing to the war however, nothing could be done until 1945. Preliminary tests with a *Class 5* 4-6-0 showed that the flange forces on this engine, which as a class rode well, were acceptably low and well distributed. These tests were followed by a full-scale series of trials with a re-built *Scot*. Soon after going into service these engines acquired an unenviable reputation for rough riding, a sample of which I had myself experienced on 6127 between Rugby and Nuneaton. Running on straight track at about 70 miles per hour, the engine suddenly seemed to go mad, lurching and banging violently from side to side for no apparent reason, until the driver shut off steam and touched the brake. The original parallel boilered engines were generally good riders. They were inclined to roll a little and like all locomotives, they could sometimes be rough. But there was nothing vicious about them.

The flange force tests with 6120 soon showed that the remedy lay in reducing the strength of the bogie control springs – a reversal of the policy which had been followed since 6131 came off the road at Weaver Junction. Then the initial controlling force of the bogie had been increased from 1 to 2 tons to reduce flange forces at the leading coupled wheels. By increasing the initial control of the bogies of the re-built engines to 4 tons, we had stiffened up the front end too much with uncomfortable reactions at the trailing coupled wheels and footplate. The best overall solution, which, from the nature of the problem is bound to be a compromise, was to use relatively soft springs giving an initial side control load of $1\frac{1}{2}$ tons in combination with friction damping of the bolster slides. The highest degree of safety and lowest maintenance costs, both for the locomotive and track are likely to be achieved when flange forces are evenly distributed and of minimum values over the whole range of working conditions.

The relevance of this work was clearly apparent in the circumstances of the derailment of a down express near Polesworth hauled by one of the streamlined *Pacifics*. We had been having some trouble with broken bogie spring links on these engines. Instructions had been given for all of them to be replaced in a higher grade of steel. We were apprehensive when news of the accident was received in the office that it might have been caused by the breakage of one of the original links. Ivatt and I were soon at the scene, examining the bogie of the derailed engine lying on her side. We were much relieved to find nothing wrong there. The condition of the track, not fully restored to normal standards was the cause of the mishap.

Indeed no two days were ever the same. There was a great deal of travelling to be done on routine visits to the Works, and occasionally on tours of inspection of motive power and outstation depots in an Officers' 'special' with Ivatt, Harold Rudgard, the Superintendent of Motive Power and his operating colleague, Stanley Parkhouse from Crewe. Rudgard was a Midland man born and bred. Parkhouse was as strongly North Western in his origins. Even then the old loyalties had not been entirely submerged. Our private room in the Station Hotel at Holyhead after dinner one evening, when visiting depots in North Wales – with an inspection of the Britannia Tubular bridge thrown in for good measure – was the scene of a hotly contested argument on the relative merits of the two quite different operating philosophies of their old companies.

A monthly visit to Euston with Ivatt, for the meeting of the mechanical engineering committee of the Board was always interesting, and sometimes amusing, as on the occasion when one of the directors, a gentleman of some prominence in national affairs, dozed off briefly allowing his pipe to fall from his mouth with a resounding bang on the polished mahogany table. John Shearman, the Road Motor Engineer, who had served his time at Crewe with Ivatt often attended the Committee with us. He was always a source of humour. The ante-room in which we awaited our summons was adorned with portraits of L.N.W.R. chairmen of Victorian times. 'You know George,' he once said, addressing Ivatt, 'it is a sobering thought that these old gentlemen . . .' – but the sobering thought was more rabelaisian than respectful, and is not for repetition here!

The winter of 1946–47 had brought heavy falls of snow, spread widely over the country. There were blockages on lines in England of a severity normally experienced only on the route to the far north between Inverness and Thurso. Every available snow plough was pressed into service, but there were long delays in clearing some of the lines. Someone had the bright idea that the stream of high velocity hot exhaust gas from an aeroplane jet engine mounted on a flat wagon and propelled slowly into the drifts would get rid of the snow either by melting or blowing it away. The suggestion certainly seemed worth putting to the test. Who provided the jet engines – the Air Force or Rolls-Royce – I do not now remember. But two were borrowed, and some preliminary trials on freshly fallen powder snow were encouraging. The High Peak line from Ashbourne to Buxton was blocked for miles, and being of low priority was likely to remain so for some time – a good place to spend a Sunday in the open air. It was a day of brilliant sunshine, freezing hard. Ivatt and I went out with the special train to see the fun. The snow we were to attack had lain for days. Against it the jets were totally ineffective. All they could do was occasionally to dislodge and hurl into the air lumps as big as paving stones. The heat was sufficient only to cause a slight trickle of water from the wall of frozen snow.

Powerful and efficient though they may be at 30,000 feet and 600 miles per hour, jet engines are not much use for clearing snow drifts. We found out what we went to find out. A good day was had by all concerned; but some arguments arose later as to how the costs were to be divided.

Austerity was slowly becoming less austere. It was permissible once more to celebrate centenaries in the traditional style. One such, to which I was invited, was in celebration of the first maintenance contract between Henry Pooley and Son and the London & North Western Railway Co. approved on 27th May, 1847. Pooley's agreed to 'undertake the entire charge and responsibility of keeping in repair all the Weighing Machines and Weighbridges at all the stations upon your Main Lines and branches.' The souvenir of this occasion with its historical associations and John Bright's words of wisdom, deserves to be remembered.

On more serious matters, mechanical engineering on the L.M.S. was in good shape, ready to meet whatever challenge nationalisation might have in store. Output of engine repairs was running well. Some changes had been made in the allocation for maintenance between the Works to take account of the large influx of 2-8-0 freight engines and to relieve pressure on pit accommodation in Derby erecting shop. Too many large tank locomotives had been causing delays to output. Maintenance of 2-6-2 and 2-6-4 tanks hitherto monopolised by Derby was transferred to Horwich and Crewe respectively. An equivalent amount of work in man-hours was given to Derby by increasing their allocation of *Class 4* 0-6-0s and standard shunting tank engines which took up less erecting shop space. New building programmes were going as well as restricted supplies of steel allowed.

Time was running out, but I had no reason to suppose that the end of our great company would make any immediate difference so far as I was personally concerned. In this I was mistaken. I was summoned to Euston to see Mr. G. L. Darbyshire who, on Sir William Woods' appointment as a Member of the British Transport Commission, had been appointed President of the L.M.S. Executive. I was told that Robert Riddles wanted me on his staff at the Railway Executive Headquarters. I was very content as Ivatt's deputy at Derby.

It was perhaps not too presumptuous to suppose that I might, in due course, achieve my ambition by following him as Chief Mechanical Engineer of the new London Midland Region. I sought and obtained the President's advice. It was quite straightforward, and clearly meant to be accepted. The policy of the L.M.S. Board, I was told, was to co-operate fully with those responsible for setting up the new organisation of British Railways. It was a good thing that ex-L.M.S. men should be appointed to senior positions at Marylebone. And so to Marylebone I should go, where my responsibilites to an ex-L.M.S. Vice-President as his chief officer for locomotive construction and maintenance would be concerned with all the locomotive Works of British Railways.

I reproduce below an extract from the Minutes of the L.M.S. Board, which I hope my readers will feel to be a fitting end to this chapter.

London Midland and Scottish Railway Company

Secretary's Office,
Euston Station.

Extract from the Minutes of the
        Board of Directors
held on the 18th day of December, 1947

At the close of business the Chairman stated that as this was the last meeting of the Board of the London, Midland & Scottish Railway Company, he, and all of the Directors, wished to place on record their deep sense of gratitude to the Officers of all grades for the help that they had given from time to time to each member of the Board, and for their devotion to duty, for their high technical ability, and for their loyalty to the London Midland and Scottish Railway Company at all times, and to the Nation during the recent War.

G. R. Smith,
Secretary.

R. C. Bond, Esq.

CHAPTER NINE

Nationalisation:
The First Five Years
Early Organisation & Locomotive Policy

I SHALL ALWAYS REMEMBER the first day on which the nationalisation of our railways became effective. Out on the line or in the Shops nobody would have noticed the slightest change from the conditions to which they had long become accustomed. Only on those of us appointed to the new Railway Executive headquarters was there any significant impact – and that was not particularly favourable. We whom Robert Riddles had chosen as his team, duly turned up at the old Great Central Hotel at Marylebone, the new headquarters offices on 1st January, 1948. No preparations had apparently been made for our arrival. The rooms we were given as our private offices were totally unfurnished. As the Members of the Executive had been at work for some weeks, and as presumably they had no intention of running the show entirely on their own, they might well have made some rudimentary provisions for their principal assistants. However, someone suggested that we should go over to Euston and scrounge whatever office furniture we needed from the L.M.S. furniture pool. As this was under the care of the District Outdoor Carriage and Wagon Assistant, whose chief until the day before had been Ernest Pugson, newly appointed Chief Officer Carriage & Wagon Construction and Maintenance, it did not take us long to make our selection and arrange for delivery to our new offices.

Riddles based his organisation on familiar lines of three main divisions of responsibility for locomotives, carriages and wagons, and electrical engineering respectively, with a chief officer directly responsible to him for each. He also appointed a senior officer to take the lead in the design of locomotives and rolling stock, and to co-ordinate the work in the drawing offices of the C.M.E.s' departments in the Regions, where it was intended that the actual design work would continue to be undertaken. There was no question of setting up a centralised design office at Headquarters.

Two of the three chief officers, Ernest Pugson and myself, came from the L.M.S. Pugson had been my opposite number on the Carriage & Wagon side of Ivatt's headquarters at Derby. We had known each other for many years and got along together very well. Stewart Cox, in charge of design, also came from Derby. He too, was a close friend and colleague of many years standing. A fourth key man in the new organisation, the administrative assistant, was George Hussey, also from the L.M.S. at Euston headquarters. We knew him well, as he had been concerned in a variety of special investigations touching on our departmental activities. He had a wide knowledge of railway working. Riddles could not have found a better man to minister to the needs of the new team and to establish cordial relations with the other departments with whom we should have to work.

Only two of the senior members of the team came from other railways. Charles Cock in charge of electrical engineering, had been Chief Electrical Engineer of the Southern. He was no stranger to me; we had first met twenty years earlier in Bombay when we were both working on the Great Indian Peninsular Railway electrification. He was, naturally, a powerful advocate of electric traction, and as Riddles also believed that the ultimate replacement of steam traction, when financially justified, should be by electrification, there was no divergence of view on that score. Archie Dent, the senior among the railway road motor engineers, came to us from the Great Western. Important though it is, the work of the road motor engineer is naturally rather separated from the main stream of railway engineering activities. Being concerned with the products of the motor trade, not with those of Swindon, Archie Dent, a most friendly and co-operative person, was in no sense a disruptive influence on the team.

There was, as we heard later, some criticism that the people in charge of the activities in which Riddles himself would be most concerned were all from the L.M.S. On the locomotive side insult was added to injury by the fact that the chief of motive power at Railway Executive headquarters, Harold Rudgard, was also from Euston. Although as an L.M.S. man myself my views may thought to be biased, it seems to me that such criticism was not very sensible. Anyone in Riddles' position, faced with the unenviable task of unifying the designs and practices of four hitherto independent C.M.E. departments, who had no particular wish to be unified anyway, and who would take a lot of convincing that their existing designs and procedures were not already the best that could be devised, would have done the same. For Riddles to have chosen his team from among people whom he did not know, when there were men available whom he did, would have added considerably to the burden of what was in any case going to be a difficult job. In any event, as I was told not long ago by my old chief H. G. Ivatt, who was present, Riddles called a meeting of the four Chief Mechanical Engineers to discuss the proposed new appointments. Names were put forward. It was open to anyone to make alternative suggestions. None that were generally acceptable were forthcoming.

In its broad pattern, the organisation which Riddles established was generally similar to that which had been adopted by the four group companies for their C.M.E. Departmental headquarters prior to nationalisation. There was, however, one important aspect, internal to the departments in which the practice of the former companies had differed. This was in regard to responsibility for electrical engineering. On the L.M.S. and G.W. Railways, the chief mechanical engineer was in charge of all mechanical and electrical engineering activities. By contrast, on the L.N.E.R. and Southern Railway, there were two chief officers reporting independently to the General Manager. These arrangements continued on the corresponding Regions for some time after nationalisation. There are a number of activities, responsibility for which, falls clearly to mechanical engineers on the one hand and to electrical engineers on the other. There are, however, many matters in which the two branches of the profession are both concerned and dependent on each other. Electric and diesel traction, and outdoor machinery plant and equipment, are typical examples in which a combination of mechanical and electrical knowledge and experience are required. Ultimate responsibility in connection therewith had sometimes rested with the mechanical engineer, sometimes with the electrical engineer. There is no rigid technical rule that can be applied in deciding the line of demarcation between mechanical and electrical engineers where both are equally concerned. Depending upon training and general experience, it is possible for either to argue with equal force that his own particular part of the whole exerts the major influence and should therefore have control. Neither in 1948, nor even more so, now, have mechanical or electrical engineers a monopoly of knowledge and experience of those matters particularly identified by tradition with their profession. The most that should be said is that an engineer may have a bias more in one direction than the other.

We had known quite clearly where we stood in regard to these matters in Ivatt's headquarters at Derby. It was obviously desirable that Charles Cock and I should have an equally clear understanding. We did not see entirely eye to eye in regard to the allocation of functions and ultimate responsibility to Riddles in those cases which could be settled in more than one way. Cock had been used to one thing on the Southern; I to something rather different on the L.M.S. I therefore wrote a note to Riddles setting out, in considerable detail, the relationships which Charles Cock, Cox and I agreed should exist between us, and proposing that while ultimate responsibility to Riddles for electric locomotives should be Cock's, diesel and gas turbine locomotives and outdoor machinery should be mine.

Riddles accepted this in principle, but made a quite arbitrary decision that while diesel locomotives with non-electrical transmission should be mine, diesel-electric locomotives were to be the electrical engineer's responsibility. I was not wholly satisfied, but at least this decision made certain that the pros and cons of diesel-hydraulic locomotives would be fully examined on British Railways.

Because of the interdependence of mechanical and electrical engineering it was decided to amalgamate the two departments in those regions in which they had hitherto been independent. This very sensible move made the split between locomotive and carriage and wagon activities, which Riddles insisted on in the Regions, the more inexplicable. Locomotive and carriage and wagon work which certainly had as much in common, though in rather a different way, as mechanical and electrical engineering, had been the responsibility of one chief departmental officer on all the four group companies for many years. It is true that the expenditure incurred on carriage and wagon activities was significantly greater than on locomotive construction and maintenance. A penny saved on a wagon component meant big money because of the numbers involved. It is true, too, that among the locomotive men on the L.M.S. before 1931 there was a slightly superior attitude to the Carriage and Wagon people. But neither recognition of the former nor eradication of the latter (even if it lingered on, which I don't think it did) was, with all due deference to my old chief and friend Robert Riddles, sufficient reason for setting up separate Carriage and Wagon departments in the Regions. Two officers of equal standing in each Region replaced one, and though they continued to use common services for staff and accountancy, at some of the Works where hitherto one Works Manager had sufficed, two were appointed, each with appropriate assistants. I doubt whether this split in the organisation was the best way to make the most of available workshop and other resources. As I shall record later, the departments were re-united in due course.

Another engineering activity directly concerning the Chief Mechanical Engineer in regard to which the Railway Executive inherited different organisations from the four companies was locomotive running – the Motive Power Departments. From the point of view of the job to be done the Motive Power Department, the Locomotive Running Department, the Running and Maintenance Engineer's Office – call it what you will – occupies an indispensable place in the whole railway organisation. It should have a corporate identity of its own. The job to be done can be described quite simply. It is to make locomotives available for working traffic, fully serviced and in sound mechanical condition in accordance with standards laid down by the Chief Mechanical Engineer, when and where they are required by the Operating Department. Whether, in addition, the department also provides the crews to man the locomotives or not, the job as a whole inevitably has two parts, one technical, one non-technical. It is pointless to argue, as has so often been done, which is the more important. Neither can work without the other.

The work as a whole can be organised in three alternative ways, either

    (i) as a department in its own right with a chief officer reporting to the General Manager, or

    (ii) as a department with an officer in charge reporting jointly to the Chief Operating Manager and the Chief Mechanical Engineer, or

    (iii) as a division within the Operating Department or the Chief Mechanical Engineer's Department, organised vertically from headquarters right down to the depots out on the line where the work is done, providing a service to the Operating Department while conforming to technical standards laid down by the Chief Mechanical Engineer.

As a prime responsibility of the motive power organisation is to carry out the day-to-day running repairs to the locomotives in conformity with standards laid down by the Chief Mechanical Engineer, the officer to whom this responsibility is delegated, whichever of the three above alternatives is adopted must obviously be a qualified engineer. In regard to the third alternative the question as to which of the two departments should contain the motive power section had long been a matter of controversy. Strong and divergent views were often held. It really should not have mattered very much which way the decision went, always provided that the man in charge was a qualified engineer. As such he would be competent to satisfy the requirements of both departments quite impartially.

Prior to nationalisation motive power work had been organised on three of the four companies in accordance with alternative (iii) above. But whereas on the L.M.S. and Southern Railways the Superintendent of Motive Power was an officer of the Operating Deparment – but with a direct responsibility to the Chief Mechanical Engineer for technical matters, on the Great Western the position was reversed.

The Locomotive Running Superintendent was an assistant to the Chief Mechanical Engineer, but with a joint responsibility to him and to the Chief Operating Officer for the allocation and distribution of engine power and the preparation of working diagrams for engines and footplate crews. On the London & North Eastern Railway, the locomotive running superintendents reported direct to their Divisional General Manager, but were also responsible to the C.M.E. for maintenance of the locomotives.

If unification was to become a reality, here, obviously, was a case in which one form of organisation should be adopted throughout British Railways. The two Executive members concerned with operating and mechanical engineering respectively submitted their recommendations. Coming as they did, from two different railways their recommendations differed correspondingly. Sir Michael Barrington-Ward, in charge of Operating, advocated alternative (i), with the proviso that the Superintendent of Motive Power should be a fully trained and competent mechanical engineer. Riddles recommended an arrangement which was virtually alternative (ii). The six Chief Regional Officers were asked to express their views. None wished for any change from the organisation to which he was accustomed! Nevertheless, as stated in their first Annual Report, the Railway Executive decided to give the motive power superintendent a separate status, but with a defined relationship to the mechanical engineer and the operating superintendent. In the Regions this meant the adoption of alternative (i). But reference to the Railway Executive diary for 1949, in which the departmental organisation at headquarters and in each of the Regions with the names of the men holding the senior posts, are tabulated, will show that things went on, apparently, precisely as before! There was, however, the one difference which mattered – a chief of motive power at Railway Executive headquarters reporting jointly to the Members for Operating and Mechanical Engineering.

Harold Rudgard was a motive power man to his fingertips. A firm disciplinarian, to whom any hat but a bowler when on duty was unthinkable, he set himself, and expected from others, a very high standard in all he did. Whatever might be printed in organisation charts, the prestige and efficiency of the motive power departments were safe in the hands of the fiery, lovable and sometimes exasperating little man. Essential features of the technical side of a locomotive running department such as periodical and mileage examinations of locomotives, the casualty reporting system and statistical controls, on identical lines to those in operation on the L.M.S. were soon extended throughout British Railways.

Though as independent companies the four railways had each gone their own way on technical matters, there had always been a great deal of consultation, and where obviously necessary, common action in regard, for example, to dimensional standards affecting through running of rolling stock from the lines of one company to another. On the outbreak of war in 1939 the railways were virtually taken over by the Government and run as one system by the General Managers constituted as the Railway Executive Committee. This arrangement persisted right up to the time of nationalisation, and made the transition to conditions of common ownership much easier than it might otherwise have been. Many of the people from each of the four companies who were going to have to work together in the future had already done so in the past. Sub-Committees of the Railway Executive Committee, of which a mechanical engineering committee was one, looked after matters of departmental concern in which common action was necessary in the national interest. First, Sir William Stanier, and later Oliver Bulleid, were chairmen of the M.E. Committee, the members of which were the other Chief Mechanical Engineers. Thus a pattern existed which had worked well for some years on which to build for the future. The new Railway Executive established similar departmental committees.

The Mechanical and Electrical Engineering Committee, with Riddles in the chair, and with his senior officers at headquarters and the regional Chief Mechanical Engineers as members, surveyed and discussed the policies which it was Riddles' responsibility to dictate, subject in certain cases, to confirmation by the Railway Executive in their corporate capacity before instructions were given. Riddles went out of his way to accord to the regional Chief Mechanical Engineers, *vis-a-vis* his officers at headquarters, the precedence to which the positions they had held before nationalisation entitled them. He did his best to enlist their support in all that he and his officers intended to do, and to make the diminution of their powers of independent action as painless as possible. Reactions at the monthly meetings were fascinating to watch. Ivatt, who had been Riddles' chief in former days, quietly exerted more influence than his brethren. He invariably brought common sense and wisdom to bear upon our discussions. He was content in the knowledge that so much of what he had done, particularly in Works organisation and practice on the L.M.S. would continue unaltered. Of the other three C.M.E.s, Peppercorn from the L.N.E.R. and Hawksworth from Swindon, who had never been through the same kind of upheaval as the others at the 1923 amalgamations, accepted the inevitable.

The greatest sense of frustration must have been felt by Oliver Bulleid whose ideas as to the future development of the steam locomotive were so manifestly different from Riddles'. But whatever he may have felt, Bulleid never tried to rock the boat, and saw to it that his staff co-operated fully in all they were asked to do.

With common ownership, and the establishment of the Mechanical and Electrical Engineering Committee as the forum for discussion of all current problems, there was clearly no useful official function which the Association of Railway Locomotive Engineers could perform in future. Continuance in its existing form would have been incompatible with mandatory control from the centre. The dissolution of the A.R.L.E., membership of which was widely regarded by the principal assistants of the C.M.E.s as a coveted honour, was inevitable – but it was, I think, a pity that it was not continued as a purely social association, with the business meetings substituted by a dinner once a quarter. The annual departmental conferences which Riddles held at one or other of the regional C.M.E. departments' headquarters, to which the Chief Regional Officer was, of course, invited did not quite fill the gap.

The means by which unification was to be achieved was quite clear in

Riddles' mind. He set up a number of policy committees, each one of which was required to investigate and report on a specific subject of immediate importance. His officers wrote the remits to each committee, the chairman of which Riddles appointed, usually on our recommendation. The regional Chief Mechanical Engineers were required to nominate one of their people to each of these committees. No time was lost. Within the first week, a committee had been appointed to examine the methods which had been in use on each of the four companies for deciding when locomotives should be sent into the Works for repairs – and to recommend one system for universal adoption in the future. This was, of course, a subject of considerable importance to the whole of the locomotive repair organisation. The remit to this committee was very carefully drawn, and laid down the principles which, based on past experience, we felt to be essential for the future.

They were:

(i) that the decision as to whether a locomotive should be agreed for shop repairs or not will be made by the regional mechanical engineer's H.Q. organisation;

(ii) that such a decision will be based only on the actual condition of each individual locomotive;

(iii) that the stock of locomotives is at all times maintained in first class mechanical condition;

(iv) that the expenditure incurred on the maintenance of locomotives is the minimum consistent with (iii) above; and

(v) that the resources of all Works in each Region and between the various Regions are used to the best advantage.

J. F. Harrison, Peppercorn's principal assistant at Doncaster was chairman of this committee. He was, like so many of his colleagues, a staunch admirer of Sir Nigel Gresley and all his works. He was a dyed-in-the-wool L.N.E.R. man. He professed a profound contempt for L.M.S. methods, a pose we did not have to take too seriously. He was a personal friend of mine; we understood each other very well, and I knew he could be relied on to direct his committee quite impartially in ascertaining facts and making recommendations. The committee recommended unanimously that a Central Shopping Bureau for controlling locomotive repairs should be established at C.M.E. Headquarters in each Region based on the arrangements in operation at Derby.

Other committees, about seventeen in all, were appointed to review the whole field of locomotive construction and maintenance both from their engineering and managerial aspects. Similar steps were taken in regard to carriage and wagon affairs, and design generally. One or two of the more cynically minded among our new associates said to me, 'Why waste people's time with all these committees? You know perfectly well that you are going to introduce L.M.S. methods – why not get on with it, and issue instructions accordingly straight away?' A simple and direct approach, no doubt. It was true that in matters of workshop organisation, particularly the highly developed systems for the repair of locomotives and other rolling stock which the L.M.S. had operated for many years, they were demonstrably ahead of the other companies. But of course there was much more to it than that!

It is one thing to issue instructions, but quite another to get them carried out particularly when they had to be implemented from five regional departmental headquarters in many Works spread all over the country. Any attempt to impose decisions without first ascertaining facts and comparing results would have been doomed to failure. Unless those to whom instructions are to be issued are prepared to concede, though perhaps unwillingly, that what they are asked to do is likely to produce results at least as good as those to which they have been accustomed, nothing is achieved. In any case, though we knew in broad outline, we needed to know in detail what the companies other than our own had been doing. For the members of the committees, the work they were asked to do was a liberal education in itself. As, in most cases they would be directly concerned in implementing the new instructions, the time they spent finding out what each of the companies had hitherto done was very well spent. So much that was going on at this time was reminiscent of the amalgamations of 1923 – but with this difference. In 1923 my contemporaries and I saw the battle for power and influence from afar – from the lower deck, as it were. Now we were in the thick of it, on the bridge beside the captain!

So great an upheaval as was represented by the nationalisation of the railways, to say nothing of the rest of inland transport, was naturally accompanied by many stresses and strains, of which those of us at the centre were acutely aware. The British Transport Commission and the Railway Executive, the members of which were appointed by the Minister of Transport – not the Commission – viewed each other with a good deal of suspicion. The Executive was sensitive to what it regarded as unwarranted interference in their responsibility for management. This came to the surface for all to see in the Minutes of Executive meetings. There were the official Minutes on white paper, which went to the Commission, and the green Minutes which included much else not for the eyes of the superior body.

There were strains too, within the Executive itself. The members were men of long experience in the exercise of power either as General Managers (or the equivalent) or as heads of departments. Coming as they did from different railways they held strong and often divergent views on what was best for the new organisation. Unification, and all that this implied, more often than not extended beyond the confines of individual departments, and thus was the concern of two or more of the Executive members. These inter-departmental problems were submitted to the Chief Officers to sort out.

We spent many hours with our opposite numbers in the Civil and Signal Engineering Departments on this work. Practices differed in regard to such matters as water supplies and outdoor machinery. The lines of demarcation between the various engineering departments had differed quite considerably on the four group companies. Nobody was anxious to relinquish anything for which they had hitherto been responsible. Though naturally concerned to uphold the known views of their members, the Chief Officers, not previously having tasted the joys of unchallenged power in their own right, were perhaps more ready than their elders and betters to agree on sensible compromise solutions without which progress would have been impossible. Right from the start, knowing how much depended on them, the senior officers got on very well together.

It was often thought that promotion in the railway service was painfully slow. It is true that opportunities for moving to appointments carrying higher responsibility arose mainly through retirements of senior men, or waiting for dead men's shoes. But from a position in which one could see the whole picture, it is remarkable how many staff changes occur during each succeeding year. All four of the Company C.M.E.s retired during these first five years. As each one went the new organisation in the Regions separating carriage and wagon from locomotive activities was put into effect.

Kenneth Cook and Hugh Randle, both Great Western men, replaced Hawksworth at Swindon. Life there went on as usual until, sometime later when Harrison moved from Doncaster to Derby on Ivatt's retirement, Riddles decided to take the opportunity of moving people round and bringing a fresh mind to bear at Swindon. Alfred Smeddle who had gone from Darlington to the Southern on Bulleid's retirement, now found himself in charge at Swindon with Charles Roberts on the Carriage & Wagon side. Kenneth Cook was moved to the Eastern & North Eastern Regions as Mechanical Engineer. Randle went to Derby as Carriage & Wagon Engineer.

Moving senior people around from one Region to another was, I believe, a good thing so long as it did not happen too often, and so long, too, as firm control of general policy was exercised from Railway Executive headquarters. Not everyone affected relished being uprooted from their familiar surroundings. One man in particular expressed to me, not altogether facetiously, his conviction that in being moved to another Region he was virtually being 'disciplined' for alleged passive resistance to change.

Dramatic upheavals in local organisation and customs were neither expected nor desired. But the mere fact of a new man asking 'Why?' in regard to practices which had hitherto been sacrosanct certainly did a great deal of good. Kenneth Cook's introduction to Eastern Region shops of the optical methods of lining up locomotive frames which had been so successful at Swindon was one of the good things which emerged. We were not so pleased, however, when he adorned one of the V2 2-6-2 engines with a copper capped chimney, a needless affront to L.N.E.R. susceptibilities which we immediately vetoed! At Swindon, Smeddle soon found himself absorbed into the Western Family presided over by Keith Grand, the Chief Regional Officer at Paddington. It was not in Alfred Smeddle's nature to tear up trees or bash his head against brick walls, but for all that, to him should go much of the credit for pressing on with the work of equipping *Castles* and *Kings* with high degree superheaters and double blast pipes which improved their performance so much during the last days of steam on the Western Region.

Oliver Bulleid and his brother-in-law George Ivatt, were the last of the Company C.M.E.s to go. It is perhaps difficult to imagine two men more diverse in temperament than were these two, subjected as they were to similar early influences, and both ultimately carrying very much the same responsibilities as Chief Mechanical Engineers. Both were indeed 'Master Builders of Steam' so well portrayed in the book of that name, written by the former's son, Anthony Bulleid. His father must often have been up in the clouds exercising his inventive mind on new and original ideas. His uncle was very much down on terra firma. With no pretensions to academic distinction, H.G.I., as we all knew him, was a born mechanical engineer. He was a realist who concentrated on the essentials. His long experience led him unerringly to the right solution of any problem which, when explained in his simple practical language, seemed so obvious. He was completely unflappable, tolerant and kindly, though no-one was ever in doubt as to who was the boss at Derby. He was always prepared to see the best in people. During the many years I knew him, I heard H.G.I. speak disparagingly of only one man for whom he had good reason to have an intense dislike. Just as he himself brooked no interference from Euston in L.M.S. days or later from Railway Executive headquarters in matters which he regarded as his own prerogative, so he never interfered in the work he delegated to his own assistants and staff. He asked people to do things for him, and let them get on with the job. Ivatt was, I believe, quite unconscious of his natural flair for inspiring in all who worked for him, loyalty, respect and affection to a quite remarkable degree. Everyone was sorry to see him go, but as consultant to one of the locomotive building firms, his long railway experience was turned to very good account in the design of some of the best of the diesel locomotives soon to be running on British Railways.

When Bulleid retired he left us an embarrassing legacy in the shape of the *Leader* class locomotives. It will be recalled that in summing up after the lectures on the contemporary state of locomotive engineering given by the four Chief Mechanical Engineers as part of the Centenary celebrations of the Institution of Mechanical Engineers, Bulleid had stated that all requirements for steam locomotives on the Southern Railway could be met by two classes of tender engines and two of tank locomotives. The *Leader* locomotives were to have been one of the tank engine types.

As far back as 1944 a request had been made by the operating people for a modern design of locomotive to replace the M7 type 0-4-4 tank engines. A good deal of correspondence ensued as to whether the operating needs could not be met quite adequately by the Q1 type 0-6-0 tender engines. Apparently not, for it was decided to design a new tank engine suitable for hauling at 50 to 60 m.p.h. trains varying in weight from 256 to 450 tons depending on the route. It is on record that in the early stages of design, it was intended that the new locomotive should be a 4-6-4. But Bulleid decided on something quite radical in conception with the objective of reducing to the maximum possible extent the limitations inherent in conventional steam locomotives.

In his Presidential Address to the Institution of Mechanical Engineers in 1947, Bulleid set out ten conditions which the *Leader* class locomotives were designed to satisfy. They were as follows:

1 To be able to run over the majority of the Company's lines.
2 To be capable of working all classes of trains up to a speed of 90 miles per hour.
3 To have its whole weight available for braking and the highest possible percentage thereof for adhesion.
4 To be equally suitable for running in both directions without turning, with unobstructed look-out.
5 To be ready for service at short notice.
6 To be almost continuously available.
7 To be suitable for 'common use.'
8 To run not less than 100,000 miles between general overhauls with little or no attention at the running sheds.
9 To cause minimum wear and tear to the track.
10 To use substantially less fuel and water per drawbar horse-power developed.

The design of the locomotive was wholly unconventional. It is probably true to say that never before had so many innovations been assembled together in one reciprocating steam locomotive. The principal features of an unusual character were:

(i) The locomotive was carried on two six-wheeled bogies;
(ii) The middle axle of each bogie was driven by a three-cylinder

engine with sleeve valves, mounted in the bogie frames, all moving parts being totally enclosed and continuously lubricated;

(iii) The three axles of each bogie were coupled by chains instead of coupling rods.

(iv) The axleboxes fitted with tapered roller bearings, moved vertically on cylindrical pedestals instead of in horn blocks. Thus there was virtually no side' play, the crank axle assembly being extremely rigid.

 (v) The boiler, generating steam at 280 lbs per square inch, was of a novel design in that the firebox had brick walls instead of stayed water legs. The firebox heating surface consisted of a steel crownplate into which four thermic syphons were welded. The boiler barrel was welded throughout.

(vi) Driving cabs were provided at each end of the locomotive with side corridor communication between each cab. The fireman was accommodated in a separate compartment halfway down the corridor.

(vii) To provide sufficient width for the corridor, the boiler was mounted some inches off the longitudinal centre line of the locomotive.

Innovation enough in all conscience; and yet all the ten conditions could have been met to a greater or lesser extent without any of the unconventional features except the first. Only by providing that all wheels should be coupled would it be possible for the total weight of the locomotive to be available for adhesion. And in a locomotive intended for speeds up to 90 miles per hour this could scarcely have been done otherwise than by a double-bogie design which alone would ensure safe riding as a vehicle on the track.

Five locomotives were included in the Southern Railway's building programme for 1947. Thirty-one more were proposed for inclusion in the 1948 programme. But in view of the quite untried nature of the design, the Railway Executive wisely decided to cancel these further thirty-one engines.

Knowing Bulleid, the originality of the whole design was understandable and only to be expected. What it is not possible to understand is how the detailed work in the drawing office was allowed to get so far adrift that the locomotive came out 20 tons overweight and 10 tons heavier on one side than the other.

The first, and as events unfolded, the only *Leader* locomotive was completed in June, 1949. I went down to Eastleigh very soon afterwards to see this rather extraordinary engine in steam before its departure on a trial trip. Knowing something of the difficulties which faced shed fitters in dealing with day-to-day maintenance of the oil bath and valve gear of

Merchant Navy and *West Country Pacifics* I felt some misgivings as to what was in store for us in shed and shop maintenance of the *Leaders*.

As in the case of Paget's multi-cylindered sleeve-valve 2-6-2 built at Derby forty years earlier, the *Leader* could not be made sufficiently reliable to go into revenue earning service notwithstanding the expenditure of much time and money. Its radius of action was in any case severely limited by its excessive weight and axle-loading. Constant trouble was experienced with breakage of the sleeve valve operating mechanism, and steaming was unreliable. So serious and persistent were the failures during the first three months of trial running that Riddles gave instructions for all work on building the next four locomotives to be stopped pending the outcome of further trials. These continued for a further twelve months. They included two series of dynamometer car tests to compare the performance of the *Leader* with a conventional locomotive of similar power. But it was all to no avail. The tests revealed that coal and water consumption of the *Leader* was about 67 per cent and 47 per cent higher than that of a Southern *U Class* 2-6-0 mixed traffic locomotive. This was due partly to steam leakage past the sleeve valves and pistons, and partly to excessive rates of combustion. The brick side walls of the firebox as originally designed were too thin to stand up to the temperature conditions. They had to be increased in thickness so much that the grate area, originally 43 square feet had to be reduced to 25 square feet. A very sharp blast was necessary to produce sufficient steam and at the high combustion rates involved losses due to fuel discharged through the chimney unburnt were very heavy.

There were other troubles too. After only 6,000 miles the crank axle of No. 1 bogie broke in half, and flaws which would soon have led to fracture were found in the corresponding axle of the other bogie. Working conditions for the fireman were quite unacceptable. The temperature in his cab was often well over 100°F. Conditions became intolerable when the locomotive was running chimney leading owing to a stream of hot air which emerged from the corridor into the fireman's compartment. Thus the engine had to run bunker first and be turned at the end of every trip.

With the best will in the world this could go on no longer. In November 1950 Riddles submitted a report to the Railway Executive which he asked me to draft. It was clear beyond doubt that only by embarking on modifications so extensive as to amount to a complete re-design could the locomotive ever achieve success. Heavy additional expenditure would be involved – and in the end the modified locomotive would offer no sufficient advantage over one of conventional design. There were only two alternatives – to go on spending money to no good purpose, or to scrap the locomotive and the other four on which work had been suspended twelve months before. Riddles really had no alternative. He made a recommendation accepted by the Executive, that the locomotives should be scrapped. Thus history repeated itself. One more among the many attempts to overcome the inherent limitations of the conventional steam locomotive had ended in failure. As in the past, this did not arise through any lack of originality of design. It is simply that within the limits of space and weight available it was proved over and over again there is no more economical or reliable way of using steam power for hauling trains under everyday railway conditions than by exploiting to the maximum possible extent the outstanding merits of rugged simplicity and straightforward design characteristic of the conventional reciprocating steam engine.

Though it must have been a bitter disappointment to him, the decision to scrap the *Leader* did not deter Bulleid from building for the Irish railways, whither he had gone after his retirement from British Railways, an even more remarkable locomotive − the peat burning double-bogie engine with rectangular boiler barrels stayed in all directions. Bulleid invited Ivatt and me over to Inchicore to see and ride on his second edition of the *Leader*. We could not but admire Bulleid's persistence and marvelled as much at his manifest ability to extract money from Boards of Directors as at his unquenchable addiction to technical innovation.

A matter of considerable importance and widespread interest, both in and outside the railway service, was the policy to be adopted in regard to standardisation of locomotives, carriages and wagons to be built in the years ahead. Though it was recognised that alternative forms of motive power would become increasingly important on British Railways in the longer term, it was incontestable in 1948 that steam would remain the principal form of traction in this country for some years to come. Research and development in design and testing, leading to continued improvements in performance and efficiency of the conventional steam locomotive should certainly continue unabated.

The facilities available for this work were greatly increased by the completion of the Locomotive Testing Station at Rugby.

The station was officially opened by the Minister of Transport on 19th October, 1948, at a ceremony, during which Sir Eustace Missenden paid a generous tribute to the two great locomotive engineers, Sir Nigel Gresley and Sir William Stanier, to whom I had been responsible for the design of the plant. A large number of invited guests, among whom was my father, who had travelled down from Euston on a special train, were assembled on the balcony of the control room and round the locomotive on test which, most fittingly, was an A4 *Pacific* No. 4498 *Sir Nigel Gresley*. It was, naturally a matter of intense satisfaction to me to see the Testing Station, on which I had started work eleven years earlier, finally completed.

The dominant position of steam traction on British Railways at the beginning of 1948 will be appreciated from the figures tabulated below:

Route Mileage:	Total	19,631
	Worked by electric traction	894
	Under conversion to electric operation	98
Stock of Locomotives:	Steam	20,030
	Diesel	55
	Electric	16
Power Units:	Electric Motor Cars	1,988
	Rail Cars, Diesel	40
	Steam	3

Over the twenty-five years between the amalgamations and nationalisation, each of the four railway groups had followed a policy of standardisation of locomotive design. The policy was however applied in rather different ways. It was carried to greater lengths on the L.M.S. and Great Western than on the other two groups. On the L.M.S. there were two sharply defined periods when different policies, both of them properly definable as standardisation, were followed. First, there were the years of 'Midlandisation' during which, with one important and a few minor exceptions, all new locomotives were built to Midland designs. The important exception was the Horwich designed mixed traffic 2-6-0. But even this locomotive, when built, was coupled to a standard Midland tender and had a number of purely Midland steam fittings. True, the results of comparative dynamometer car trials to which I have already referred were taken as justification for what was done. In principle this was standardisation by taking one of the constituent company's existing series of standard types and applying them virtually unaltered throughout the group. But with nothing larger than the three-cylinder compounds there was a serious gap at the high power end of the Midland standard engines. I have already recounted how this gap was brilliantly filled for some years by the *Royal Scots*.

During the first year after amalgamation, as E. S. Cox has told us, diagrams were prepared at Horwich for a completely new series of twelve standard types to cover all the traffic requirements of the L.M.S. But Midland influence was too strong, and it was not until Stanier was appointed Chief Mechanical Engineer in 1932 that standardisation by the adoption of a completely new series of locomotives, which owed little to previous constituent companies' practice became the order of the day. The success of this policy in which Riddles, Cox and I had been completely immersed for sixteen years naturally had a profound influence on our thinking on the subject of standard locomotives for British Railways.

On the L.N.E.R. and the Southern also, two distinct periods in regard to standardisation can be distinguished. On the former Gresley, convinced of the superiority of three-cylinder propulsion developed his own Great Northern standard designs. He built new three-cylinder locomotives of pure Doncaster vintage, large and small whenever the need arose. At the same time he did not disdain building engines to constituent companies' designs, without any attempt to standardise renewable details, in those cases where an existing type could clearly meet specific requirements. One calls to mind the Great Eastern B12 4-6-0s and the Great Central *Director* class 4-4-0s, both of which Gresley built for service in Scotland far from their home surroundings. On Edward Thompson's accession to power there was a complete reversal of Gresley's three-cylinder policy except for the most powerful express passenger and mixed traffic locomotives with wide fireboxes. Thompson built a new series of two-cylinder engines and rebuilt several of Gresley's three-cylinder classes with two outside cylinders only. It was a change in direction reminiscent of the upheaval on the London and North Western Railway when Whale slaughtered Webb's Compounds in favour of two-cylinder simple locomotives. Peppercorn continued Thompson's policy, though his own two *Pacific* designs, the A1 and A2 classes owed far more to Gresley than to Thompson's *Pacific* monstrosities! Time, however, was running out and there were relatively few of the eight classes of locomotives, planned by the L.N.E.R. to meet all their operating needs, in service on vesting day.

As to the Southern, it might be concluded that Maunsell had an open mind in regard to certain aspects of locomotive design on which his brother C.M.E.s of the time held very strong views. While perpetuating his own Ashford designs for the smaller mixed traffic locomotives, the larger express passenger types, particularly the *King Arthurs*, even the *Lord Nelsons* and *Schools* class 4-4-0s built under Maunsell's direction derived more from Eastleigh traditions.

Further development influenced of course by continuing electrification proceeded on quite different, and now well known lines when Bulleid arrived from Doncaster as C.M.E. in succession to Richard Maunsell.

Alone among the four companies, the Great Western had suffered no disturbance from the 1923 amalgamation. They had merely swallowed up and digested a number of small Welsh railways whose locomotives were soon either scrapped or fitted with standard Swindon boilers for a further span of life. The G.W.R. had long been the fortunate owners of a complete series of locomotives conceived and brought to perfection by Churchward, highly standardised as to their component parts between the classes. A firmly directed undeviating policy of building locomotives, the design of which was far ahead of general contemporary thinking sustained over a sufficiently long time enabled the Great Western to reap in full measure the benefits of thoroughgoing standardisation. For many years locomotive performance on the Great Western was unequalled in this country. The influence of Churchward's work spread far beyond the boundaries of the Great Western into the drawing offices and Works of the other companies. But so strong was the feeling of Churchward's infallibility in the minds of his staff and successors in office that the rate of further progress at Swindon tended to become slower than on the other companies.

The general state of development of locomotive engineering in Great Britain, Europe and the United States was reviewed in three lectures on Railway Power Plant delivered as a contribution to the Centenary celebrations of the Institution of Mechanical Engineers in 1947. Louis Armand, then assistant general manager of the French National Railways, and Paul Kieffer, Chief of Motive Power of the New York Central System dealt with the trend of events in Europe and America respectively, events which we always followed with intense interest. The lecture presented jointly by the four British Chief Mechanical Engineers on the situation here at home provides an excellent summary of the state of affairs which the Railway Executive inherited at nationalisation.

We on the L.M.S. believed that the conventional reciprocating steam locomotive was still capable of considerable improvement, and that the optimum of maintenance cost per mile and operating availability had not been reached.

Oliver Bulleid, who was in the chair summed up the situation so far as steam traction in Great Britain was concerned, as follows: 'the Southern concentrated on mixed traffic locomotives and expected all their requirements to be met by two classes of tender locomotives and two classes of tank engines. All recent locomotives had totally enclosed continuously lubricated valve gear, steel fireboxes with thermic syphons, improved wheels and clasp brakes.

The Great Western had continued the policy instituted by Churchward in 1902 with improvement in detail. This policy had resulted in exceptional standardisation of parts. Out of 3,860 locomotives, 3,119 were of standard design, divided into twenty classes, all of which carried one of only seven standard boilers.

The L.M.S. had been able to reduce the standard types to ten classes and had introduced a number of improvements to assist availability. They were carrying out trials with roller bearings, poppet valve gears and steel fireboxes in the hope that there would be a further improvement in the time between shoppings.

The L.N.E.R. had eight new standard types which were expected to meet all their needs. Experiments were being conducted on controlled water treatment with the possibility of using welded steel fireboxes; and research was in hand on valve gears and poppet valves.

The rather different alternative approaches to standardisation of locomotive design adopted by the four group companies were all open to us in 1948. Three of the companies owned a comprehensive series of standard locomotives which had proved their ability to meet all their existing traffic requirements. All other things being equal, it would be reasonable to expect that the standard locomotives of any of the companies could, in general, meet the traffic requirements of any of the others. And thus it would have been open to Riddles to have recommended to the Executive the adoption, without further ado, of one of the company's series of standard locomotives as the future standard for the whole of British Railways.

But, of course, all other things were not equal. Elementary common sense required that any series of locomotives to be adopted as the new standard, and built in the years ahead, should be able to run with the absolute minimum of restriction throughout British Railways. Only the L.M.S. standard locomotives as a whole satisfied this condition. The generous width of the Great Western load gauge, deriving from the days of the Broad Gauge, to which their locomotives were built severely restricted the route availability of Swindon locomotives. Many of the L.N.E.R. standard locomotives would have been subject to similar restrictions. Excellent though we ourselves know them to be, imposition by an L.M.S. man of his own company's locomotives as the new standard without first making a detailed appraisal of the undoubted merits of the other companies' engines, would not have been particularly diplomatic, nor indeed very sensible.

Alternatively it would have been possible to allow the Regions to continue building their own locomotives – a policy which was strongly advocated by at least one of the Regional Chief Mechanical Engineers. In the short term, of course, this had to be done to maintain continuity of production of the locomotive building programmes inherited from the companies. Bearing in mind the drawing office work involved and the time required to obtain and manufacture material, it would be at least three years before any new series of standard locomotives could begin to emerge from the Works. Thus, had it seemed remotely likely that within so short a time as seven years a firm policy for the complete displacement of steam traction would be adopted, the only sensible thing to have done would have been to continue building existing classes, though no doubt on a reduced scale. In fact such a radical change did not seem likely. And certainly we could not reasonably have foreseen the breakneck speed at which steam locomotives were to be displaced, resulting in many hundreds of modern engines being scrapped long before the expiry of their normal depreciation life. No less than 1,538 locomotives of the former companies' designs were built during the first three years of nationalisation. But to have continued in this way indefinitely, at a time when the conventional steam locomotive, still capable of further development, was expected to remain the predominant form of traction for many years ahead would not have been acceptable as conforming to the philosophy of complete unification implicit in the Transport Act.

A detailed appraisal of the characteristics of the locomotives inherited from the four companies was quickly put in hand. First, Riddles appointed a committee under the chairmanship of A. W. J. Dymond, a Western Region man, to deal with all matters affecting standardisation of locomotive types and details. The Committee was told that co-ordination was specially desired between common features of steam, diesel and electric locomotives and electric motor bogies. They were asked to prepare a list of renewable details which it was desirable to standardise from the point of view of purchase and manufacture. They were also asked to examine the possibility of selecting one only of the companies' standard types, in each traffic category, for construction until such time as new standard types were designed. As might be expected, with the members' different company loyalties, the committee did not feel justified in selecting one type only in each traffic category for future building. The committee reported that none of the locomotives considered could be excluded on the grounds of inferiority in design or performance. Moreover it was pointed out that the basic requirements of route availability and power characteristics for each type of locomotive for use on all Regions had not then been defined. This, no doubt, the committee thought let them out of a difficult situation. It was recommended that until new standard designs had been prepared each Region should continue to build engines to existing designs, an outcome which was entirely predictable, and on the whole sensible. At any rate, one possible long term alternative to a thoroughgoing standardisation was thereby eliminated.

Secondly, a locomotive testing committee was appointed to organise and conduct a series of dynamometer car tests to record the performance and efficiency of the principal modern classes of existing locomotives. Fourteen types, five express passenger, four mixed traffic, and five freight locomotives were matched against each other in normal services on their own lines and those of the other Regions. The tests lasted more than three months and covered routes as far north as Inverness and as far south as Plymouth. They were the most comprehensive series of trials ever undertaken. As on previous similar occasions, the tests were followed with intense interest and partisan fervour by no means confined to railway staff.

The locomotives which took part, and the routes over which they were tested are set out in the table overleaf.

It was a sound idea, entirely in line with the more enlightened attitude to the disclosure of information, that caused the official report of these tests to be published for all to read. One thing which the tests did was to demolish the idea, held by some opposed to standardisation, that a locomotive designed primarily for service over easily graded routes was

Inter-Regional Dynamometer Car Tests

Locomotives	*Routes*
Express Passenger	
L.M.S. *Duchess Class* 4-6-2	King's Cross–Leeds
L.M.S. Rebuilt *Royal Scot* 4-6-0	Euston–Carlisle
L.N.E. *A4 Class* 4-6-2	Paddington–Plymouth
G.W.R. *King Class* 4-6-0	Waterloo–Exeter
Southern *Merchant Navy* 4-6-2	
Mixed Traffic	
L.M.S. *Class 5* 4-6-0	Marylebone–Manchester
L.N.E. *B1 Class* 4-6-0	St. Pancras–Manchester
G.W.R. *Hall Class* 4-6-0	Bristol–Plymouth
Southern *West Country* 4-6-2	
Freight	
L.M.S. *Class 8F* 2-8-0	Ferme Park (London)–
	Peterborough
L.N.E. *Class O1* 2-8-0	Toton–Brent
G.W.R. *28XX* 2-8-0	Acton–Severn Tunnel
	Junction.
W.D. 2-8-0	Eastleigh–Bristol
W.D. 2-10-0	

Coal Consumption: lbs per drawbar horsepower hour

Express Passenger
L.N.E. *A4* 4-6-2	3·06 lbs/DBHP/hour
L.M.S. *Duchess* 4-6-2	3·12
L.M.S. Rebuilt *Scot* 4-6-0	3·38
G.W.R. *King Class* 4-6-0	3·59
Southern *Merchant Navy* 4-6-2	3·60

Mixed Traffic
L.M.S. *Class 5* 4-6-0	3·54 lbs/DBHP/hour
L.N.E. *B1 Class* 4-6-0	3·57
G.W.R. *Hall Class* 4-6-0	3·94
Southern *West Country* 4-6-2	4·11

Freight
L.N.E.R. *O1* 2-8-0	3·37 lbs/DBHP/hour
G.W.R. *28XX* 2-8-0	3·42
L.M.S. *Class 8* 2-8-0	3·52
W.D. 2-10-0	3·52
W.D. 2-8-0	3·77

inherently unsuitable in hilly country. It was shown beyond question that locomotives indigenous to the south of England were equally effective between Perth and Inverness. From this point of view there was nothing against the production of a series of standard locomotives for service anywhere in the country. Relatively small coupled wheels, provided they were allied to good front end design and long travel valve gear were shown to be no impediment to the attainment of high speeds. The disability suffered by ex-Great Western locomotives from low superheat, shown by analogy from experience on the L.M.S. fifteen years earlier with Sir William Stanier's first series of engines, was demonstrated beyond doubt on Western locomotives themselves. The range of efficiency, as measured by coal consumption per unit of work done, was commendably narrow as shown by the figures tabulated opposite.

It is perhaps interesting to recall that in similar comparative tests on the L.M.S. twenty-five years earlier, to which I have briefly referred in a previous chapter, coal consumptions were on average about 30 per cent higher – a striking testimony to the improvement which had been made in the thermal efficiency of the conventional steam locomotive.

Thus were the facts established. The results of the tests could certainly have been used to support a case for adopting the existing L.M.S. locomotives as they stood as the new standards if Riddles had wished to follow this course. But equally, nothing which emerged from the tests required us to hesitate in the resolve to produce a new series of locomotives combining within them the best of contemporary practice.

While all this had been going on Stewart Cox had been busy formulating proposals for the new standard engines, 999 of which were ultimately built. The last one, a 2-10-0 No. 92220 *Evening Star* was turned out from Swindon in 1960.

The whole fascinating story of British Railways' standard steam locomotives, with the building and maintenance of which I was personally concerned is well told in E. S. Cox's book, and in the two papers which he delivered to the Institution of Locomotive Engineers.

All that I need do here is to recall the main considerations which lay behind the new proposals, and add a few comments on matters of design in which I took a hand.

The main considerations were

(i) that entirely new designs should be put forward whenever a definite step forward in availability and efficiency can be realised,

(ii) that new designs should not be undertaken for their own sake, and that when an existing design offers all that is available from the present state of the art, it should be continued with only detailed modifications,

(iii) that the whole trend should be towards simplification, good accessibility of all parts requiring attention and reduction in time required for repairs and servicing.

One of the original proposals was for a *Class 5* 4-6-2. I felt very doubtful about this proposition. The new 4-6-2 was going to weigh $11\frac{1}{2}$ tons more than the average of the existing *Class 5* engines which it was intended to supercede. The interchange trials had shown the *Class 5* 4-6-0 mixed traffic locomotives to be economical and well able to do the work required of them, with plenty of reserve in hand. I pointed out that the saving in coal which might result from the larger grate area would be almost exactly balanced by increased annual charges arising from the higher first cost due to the increase of 15 per cent in weight. As the larger grate would involve higher standby fuel losses, and the repair costs of the trailing track would not be negligible, it seemed to me that the proposed new *Class 5* 4-6-2 would cost the Railway Executive more to do a given amount of work than did the existing locomotives. I therefore suggested two things – first that the proposed 4-6-2 should be given a rather larger boiler to increase the free area through the tubes and be put into traffic as a *Class 6*, and secondly that a new *Class 5* 4-6-0 combining the best features of existing locomotives should be included in the standard range. These suggestions were accepted.

As the companies had been well provided with express passenger locomotives in the highest power class, there was no immediate need for any of the proposed new standard *Class 8* 4-6-2s – intended to be a four-cylinder locomotive based on the L.M.S. *Duchess* Class. As we saw matters in 1950 however, it seemed likely that the time would come when some of those engines would need to be included in a building programme.

It seemed to me that further thought might well be given to the question of whether these locomotives should have three or four cylinders. Accordingly I suggested to Riddles that an extended trial should be carried out with some L.M.S. *Duchess* 4-6-2s and L.N.E.R. *A1 Pacifics* working side by side on identical services between London and the north, by transferring five *Duchess* engines to King's Cross and five *A1s* to Camden. Repair costs of both classes of engine were individually recorded, and I felt that an interchange of this kind supplemented by a short series of constant speed tests on the line might provide us with valuable information. However, nothing came of this, though other considerations, notably the use of poppet valve gear, led to the adoption of three cylinders when the prototype *Class 8* 4-6-2 No. 71000 *Duke of Gloucester* was built four years later in replacement of L.M.S. 4-6-2 46202 *Princess Anne*, damaged beyond repair in the appalling double collision at Harrow.

Thereby hangs another tale. I have always been a firm believer in the need to visit frequently the Works which came under my general jurisdiction. My responsibilities were now much more extensive than in L.M.S. days. A great deal of travelling was involved in visiting Works spead over the country from Inverurie in the north of Scotland to Brighton and Eastleigh in the south. There were thus plenty of opportunities to indulge my love of footplate riding. There were many classes of Eastern, Western and Southern locomotives on which I had never ridden, to be sampled.

I had a special proprietory interest in 46202. She was the turbine locomotive which I had been so closely concerned with at Crewe, rebuilt as a conventional four-cylinder engine. A routine visit to Crewe Works provided the occasion for a trip on her footplate. Had I not decided at the last moment to save myself a very early start by joining the train at Watford instead of Euston, I should probably not be here now to tell my story. The 8.00 a.m. Liverpool and Manchester express on which I was to travel ran at high speed into the wreckage caused by the collision between an express from Perth and a crowded suburban train standing in the station. The 8.00 a.m. was double-headed on that fateful morning. The driver of the leading engine was killed and though his fireman and the two men on 46202 survived, it was, I think, an odds on chance against a third man on the footplate being so fortunate.

The continuing longer term aspects of the numbers and types of locomotives that would be needed in the years ahead were remitted to a number of Chief Officers – the Ideal Stock Committee – of which I was a member. There was no conflict of view from that source of corporate wisdom! Six of the new standard types were included in the 1951 Building Programme. The operating priority at that time was for locomotives in the upper end of the intermediate power classification. Preference was therefore given to the first batch of twenty-five *Class 7 Britannia* 4-6-2s allocated to Crewe for building. In particular something better than the *Sandringham* and *B1* 4-6-0s was needed for the express services in East Anglia. The L.N.E.R. *A3 Pacifics* would have been the obvious answer but they were too heavy for the old Great Eastern lines. A *West Country Pacific* from the Southern which had been loaned for trial in East Anglia was soon returned with thanks. Before this requirement for a *Class 7* locomotive for the Great Eastern was known, consideration had been given to providing a need for new locomotives in this power classification by discontinuing the rebuilding of the *Royal Scots*. By the end of 1950 sixty of the seventy *Royal Scots* would have been rebuilt. Had there not been a clear need for more *Class 7* engines one could have been created by scrapping the remaining unrebuilt *Royal Scots* as their original parallel boilers required renewal. In the event this procedure was not necessary. Additional expenditure of close on £100,000 would have been involved. As the rebuilt *Royal Scots* had done outstandingly well in the Interchange trials, and were in every way a really good locomotive it would have been wrong not to have continued their rebuilding to completion.

All the Works at which new locomotives were built at the time were given a share of the new standard types. A great deal of thought went into the planning of their production. For the first time, apart from the War years, it was possible to use for the benefit of British Railways as a whole the production facilities available in any of the Works in the most efficient way. This principle of inter-regional assistance, as it was called, saved a great deal of expenditure on patterns, flanging blocks and other production tools. For example Swindon made the cylinders and other iron castings for forty-five locomotives of two different classes being built at three Works on different Regions.

Existing L.M.S. flanging blocks were used for six types of boiler, the plates being flanged on three Regions and the boilers built at six Works. Production of drop stampings, and steel castings was concentrated in a similar way. From time to time, of course, complaints of unsatisfactory workmanship in component parts supplied by other Works arrived at headquarters from those who would like to have done work themselves which had been allocated to somebody else. I had been used to this sort of, mainly good-natured, grumbling between Crewe and Derby for many years. The complaints amounted in fact to very little, but they gave the supposedly aggrieved Works Managers excellent reasons for sending their assistants and foremen to visit and get to know their opposite numbers in Works which they naturally felt were inferior to their own.

The new series of locomotives were, in general, quite straightforward to build. No special production problems of which at least one of the Works did not already have experience were involved. Actual output of new locomotives was still hampered by shortage of steel, the wartime control of which had never been wholly relaxed. Programmes tended to run into the following year before completion – but nothing was allowed to stand in the way of turning out the *Britannias* to time.

The first of the new locomotives, No. 70000, as yet unnamed and painted black, was turned out of Crewe Works on 2nd January, 1951. Within ten days, after a few breaking-in trips, she worked a train of 442 tons, including the dynamometer car, on express timings from Crewe to Carlisle and back the following day. Stewart Cox rode on the footplate on the down journey. An eight minute late start from Crewe was recovered, giving a punctual arrival at Carlisle with a train 22 tons overweight for the class of locomotive. Coal consumption at 3·09 lbs per drawbar horsepower hour, was lower than that of any other class of engine regularly working over the Crewe–Carlisle route.

Riddles and I travelled down overnight from London to be present on the return journey, which gave us the first of many subsequent footplate trips on the new standard engines. Though the *Britannias* rode very well, they were not particularly comfortable on the footplate. They were noisy and very dusty. Unduly stiff springing of the trailing truck made them hard riding at the back end. The cab floor extended back to the tender front which no doubt made firing easier. But the absence of the usual fallplate between engine and tender allowed strong air currents to swirl round the cab, which was draughty and laden with coal dust. Conditions were later much improved, first by canvas screens fitted between engine and tender, and later by reversion to the conventional fallplate arrangement. These were, of course, minor irritations which did not seriously detract from a generally first rate class of locomotive which satisfied the prime and essential requirement – they always had plenty of steam!

The first trip to Carlisle and back was most satisfactory and augured well for the future. There was no sign of the troubles by which we were soon to be beset. The new engines were very well received by the men at Stratford and Norwich. We congratulated ourselves that the first of the new standard classes was off to a very good start. Within a month, however, we were in trouble. I was 'phoned at home, early one Sunday morning in February 1951 to be told that 70000 had broken a piston and cylinder cover, a mishap for which there seemed no discernible cause. Cox and I were over at Stratford within an hour, spares were obtained from Crewe that day, and the engine was back in service very quickly. It soon became clear, however, after further similar mishaps that the *Britannias* were prone to heavy carry-over of water, notwithstanding the sensitive control which should have been given by the multiple valve regulator. Modifications to the main steam pipe inlet, a higher dome cover and a reduction in the highest visible level of water in the gauge glasses soon cured this particular trouble. But worse was soon to follow, and history was to repeat itself. Like Midland compounds and rebuilt *Scots* before them, the *Britannias* started bending their coupling rods. This was a sporadic trouble which usually soon disappeared as drivers became familar with new engine classes. But unlike the other engines, the stresses which bent the side rods on the *Britannias* also loosened the coupled wheels on their axles. This was serious. Seven cases occurred in fairly quick succession.

There was nothing for it but to take all twenty-five engines out of service, a decision which, mortifying though it was, Riddles took without hesitation.

I did little else during the next few days than probing into every detail of assembly of wheels and axles at Crewe. I knew well the Wheel Shop foreman and his men, and had complete confidence in them. Normal methods for pressing on wheels and fitting keys, which had never before given trouble, had been scrupulously followed. What was there unusual on the new engines which might account for the trouble? First, the coupled wheels were fitted with roller bearings. Thus, the wheel seat had to be smaller in diameter than the bearing journal. Next, to save weight, the axles were hollow. Finally, the keys were rather shallower than usual and were tightly fitted top and bottom. We concluded that the hollow axles, with wheel seats ground 1 in 500 taper, were on the edge of being able to withstand the normal pressing on load without deformation. We plugged the ends of the hollow axles, turned the wheel seats parallel, deepened the keyways and hand-fitted the keys with the utmost care. All small things in themselves, but together they were sufficient completely to eliminate any further trouble.

The only other problem which gave us any serious concern was a marked tendency to fore and aft vibration which was noticeable and uncomfortable to passengers in the leading coaches of trains hauled by the new standard engines. The reason for this was at first rather baffling as the percentage of the reciprocating parts balanced followed conventional practice. There seemed no obvious reason for the trouble. However, investigations carried out at Brighton, and also by Swindon, who had some experience of similar vibrations on some of their two-cylinder locomotives, found the trouble was due to excessive static compression of the rear drawhook spring. This, by preventing the drawhook from leaving its stop when the buffers compressed in coupling the locomotive to its train, permitted longitudinal vibrations to be transmitted undamped to the leading coaches. The matter was soon rectified; but it was an interesting example of a simple cause and effect which previously had either been avoided by luck rather than judgment, or ignored!

The new standard locomotives were built over a period of nine years and fulfilled all expectations. From the point of view of thermal efficiency, they were as good as any other locomotives working between the same temperature ranges. They were economical in maintenance costs, and their availability and casualty records, once the initial troubles with the *Britannias* were overcome, left little room for improvement. We deliberately established very close liaison between the building Works and the Drawing Offices, with a view to the Works putting forward suggestions for changes in detail design, leading to reductions in manufacturing and maintenance costs. Well over 100 suggestions for minor design changes were put forward by the Works, many of which were adopted. Plans were made for a more radical review after the first two years experience with the new engines. It was Riddles' expressed wish that if necessary, 'the basic design of components should be considered for changing altogether in order to reduce costs.'

The detailed design of locomotives always was, and probably always will be, to a considerable extent a matter of personal preference and opinion. Among the components which I felt might be radically altered to reduce costs were the multi-valve regulators, the damper operating gear, the reversing gear, the main steam manifold outside the cab, and the vacuum controlled graduable steam brake valve. The multi-valve regulator combined with the superheater header was expensive in first cost, and I had doubts about the alleged greater sensitivity in control amounting to anything in practice. I felt too, that the operating gear for the dome type regulator on the smaller standard engines, with a gland on the side of the boiler barrel, was more expensive to fit in the Shops than the usual arrangement with the stuffing box on the boiler front. The screw operating gear for the ashpan dampers, which was pure Horwich in its origin, had always seemed to be needlessly expensive – and it suffered from the operating disadvantage that the dampers could not be quickly closed to counter or prevent a blowback through the firehole door. The new type of reversing gear, involving bevel gears, roller bearings, and a rotating cut-off indicator, was expensive and probably gave no advantages commensurate with the additional costs compared with the simpler form with the screw in the cab and the long reversing rod.

While the steam manifold outside the cab avoided inconvenience to the footplate crew from occasional steam leakage, duplication of piping and valves was involved, and I questioned whether the additional first cost was justified, having regard to our experience with the simpler arrangement similar to previous G.W. and L.M.S. designs. The new vacuum controlled steam brake gear with a graduable valve was a good deal more expensive than the previous L.M.S. type of driver's brake valve, and made no discernible improvement in brake applications. These and other design features, with longer term implications would have been considered had more time been available before we became engulfed in conversion to diesel traction.

Self-cleaning smokeboxes, rocking grates, and self-emptying ashpans, were features introduced on the new standard engines. They had proved their worth on the L.M.S., based on the experience we had gained with these features on the American 2-8-0 locomotives, which ran for some time in this country, before being sent over to France for service on the Western front after D-day. We needed to be sure that the facilities we were providing on the new engines, admittedly more expensive than the simpler arrangements which were customary in most regional designs, were generally worth while in obtaining a quicker turn round at Motive Power Depots and greater availability for service. We had no doubts whatever about the advantages of manganese steel liners on axleboxes and horn blocks in enabling substantially higher mileages to be run between shop repairs. In addition to the new standard locomotives, nearly 1200 locomotives of previous companies' designs were being fitted with manganese steel liners as they passed through the shops for repairs. On roller bearings, which had been adopted fairly widely on the new standard engines, we were not so certain. Experience on the L.M.S. with *Class 5* 4-6-0s had shown that locomotives with roller bearings on the driving axle only could give as high a mileage between repairs as when all the coupled wheels were fitted. Our doubts of the financial justification of roller bearings for coupled axles were shown by the fact that five of the *Britannias* had been built with roller bearings on the driving axle only, and ten with plain bearings, on all the coupled axles.

All four companies had exercised general control of their stock of locomotives through the medium of annual building and breaking-up programmes authorised by their Board of Directors. There were naturally differences in procedural details, but the principles followed were the same. On the L.M.S., for example, agreement was reached between the Chief Mechanical Engineer and the Operating Department from time to time, that certain classes of locomotives should not have their lives further prolonged by fitting new boilers. Early in each year the Works Managers submitted to headquarters the number of engines in the list of those not to be reboilered, which would normally fall due for a new boiler or require other expensive repairs such as new cylinders during the ensuing two years. At the same time the C.M.E. obtained from the Operating and Motive Power people particulars of any other locomotives it was proposed to take out of stock as being no longer suitable or surplus to traffic requirements, and of the new locomotives needed in replacement of those to be broken up. The principle of annual building programmes was continued after nationalisation until the Beeching era, when this well proved method of control was abandoned in favour of a procedure under which new locomotives were authorised against individual traffic projects. This undoubtedly made it easier to check the economic justification for new diesel motive power in replacement of steam locomotives – but planning of production programmes either in our own Works or at Contractors, became much more difficult.

Once the new standard designs had been established, no further engines of company designs were built. The new locomotives were allocated to the Regions as shown in the table opposite.

Of all the standard classes the two that made most impact on the operating scene were the first and last to be built – the *Class 7 Britannia* 4-6-2s and the *Class 9* 2-10-0s. Both fulfilled a new operating need, as well as being required in replacement of condemned locomotives. The *Britannias* revolutionised the express passenger services of the old Great Eastern lines of the Eastern Region. Their power and capacity was so much in advance of the locomotives they replaced. On the London Midland and Western Regions the *Britannias* took their turn on jobs hitherto covered by rebuilt *Scots* and *Castles*.

New Standard Steam Locomotives
Allocation for Operating

Region	Number of Locomotives
L.M.	348
E.	156
N.E.	63
W.	136
S.	108
Sc.	188
Total	999

There was probably not much to choose between the older and the newer locomotives. There were undoubtedly those who preferred the multi-cylindered *Scots* and *Castles* to the new *Pacifics* which, though much smaller than many two-cylinder locomotives on overseas railways, were perhaps right on the limit for two-cylinder propulsion in high speed services under our conditions. I have often thought what a magnificent locomotive a Mark 2 *Britannia* with three-cylinders could have been!

Although we were well equipped with heavy freight engines in 1948, it was foreseen that sooner or later there would be a need for new locomotives, particularly if it were at last found possible to fit all freight rolling stock with continuous brakes. With the incorporation of virtually all hitherto privately-owned wagons into B.R. stock, a major obstacle to the fitting of continuous brakes to the whole of the wagon fleet had been removed. The existing locomotives for heavy freight traffic had ample tractive effort to haul trains as long as could be accommodated in existing refuge sidings at the low maximum speeds dictated by the limited brake power available. Future development would thus be more in the direction of higher speeds, which universal fitting of continuous brakes would make possible in safety, than of heavier loads. What was going to be needed was more horsepower at speed, not more starting tractive effort. Eight coupled wheels would provide adequate adhesion weight, but they could, with advantage, be rather larger in diameter than 4′ 8′ or thereabouts, then common. A much larger boiler than those carried by contemporary 2-8-0s was the essential requirement. A 2-8-2 with the same boiler as the *Britannias* seemed the obvious answer, and was indeed the first firm proposal for the heavy freight locomotive of the future. A memorandum setting out ten good reasons why a 2-10-0 would not be so suitable was prepared in support of the 2-8-2 proposal. The basis of the argument rested upon the effects of two interdependent limitations imposed by the loading gauge. First, a wide-firebox boiler essential to provide sufficient grate area, and necessarily disposed in a 2-10-0 above the last pair of coupled wheels, would be severely limited in barrel diameter and thus in firebox volume and free area through the tubes. Maximum steam production would thus be correspondingly restricted.

Secondly, it was considered that the absolute minimum vertical space required for the wide-firebox above the coupled wheels would limit their diameter to no more than 4' 10''. Adhesion weight, to which Riddles attached much importance, would be rather more on a 2-10-0. He asked the designers to think again. By the time heavy freight engines were included in a building programme, it had been found possible to accommodate 5 0' diameter coupled wheels. The 2-10-0 won the day.

In spite of all the arguments which were later adduced in favour of the 2-10-0, had the decision been mine to make the new standard heavy freight locomotive would have been the 2-8-2. It would, I believed, have done all that the 2-10-0 would do. It would have had a better boiler – one that was identical and interchangeable with the *Britannias*. The future surely lay with continuous brakes on all freight trains with emphasis on higher speeds and thus boiler capacity, rather than on starting tractive effort and adhesive weight. As events turned out, I might well have been wrong. There are still many thousands of wagons running about without power brakes – and it seems as though there will be for some years yet. The 2-10-0s, of which more were built than any of the other new standard classes, were perhaps the most successful of them all. They steamed well and were so free running as to be able easily to reach speeds in the nineties when working passenger trains. And they did their main job of working heavy freight trains exceedingly well.

I have devoted a good deal of space to the standard steam locomotives as it was from them that locomotive men derived the most intense technical interest during the first years of nationalisation. They were of course the subject of much controversy both within railway circles and in the technical press. But they were only one among a host of matters involved in the direction and management of a department with 100,000 men spending £100 million a year responsible for all the mechanical and electrical engineering activities of British Railways. Superimposed on all the normal day-to-day activities was the task of welding four large railways, proud of their history and traditions, into one organisation, all parts of which should be imbued with a common purpose. Service to the public was still then paramount, a principle which accorded well with the philosophy in which we had all been brought up and accepted without reservation.

CHAPTER TEN

Coming Events Cast their Shadows

Alternative forms of Motive Power and
the end of the Railway Executive

ALTHOUGH MY RESPONSIBILITIES for locomotive construction and maintenance were mainly concerned with steam, I was naturally involved jointly with Charles Cock, and later with Stanley Warder with the diesel and electric locomotives we already had in service.

The technical and economic aspects of the newer forms of motive power, electric and diesel traction, had been under more or less continuous review for main line services for at least twenty-five years prior to nationalisation.

On the Southern Region 720 miles of route, much of it extending well beyond the London suburban areas had been electrified on the third-rail 660 volt direct current system. Electric traction was also in operation on L.M.S. London suburban services operating from Euston to Watford. Intensive commuter services radiating from Liverpool to Southport and the Wirral peninsula, from Manchester to Bury and Altrincham, and from Newcastle-on-Tyne to the coast at North Shields were also electrified. Work was proceeding on the electrification of the suburban services from Liverpool Street to Shenfield.

The economics of main line electrification had been investigated on a number of occasions. The North Eastern Railway had electrified a short length of line carrying heavy mineral traffic between marshalling yards at Shildon and Newport in County Durham. They had, too, produced plans for electrifying the main line between York and Newcastle. They actually built a prototype electric locomotive – a 4-6-4 for high speed main line services. If Sir Vincent Raven had been appointed Chief Mechanical Engineer of the L.N.E.R. instead of Sir Nigel Gresley more would undoubtedly have been heard of this scheme. The Great Western had examined the possibilities of electrifying the West of England main line from Taunton to Penzance. And the Great Central, and later the L.N.E.R. prepared schemes for converting the Sheffield, Manchester and Wath routes over the Pennines through Woodhead tunnel, to electric traction.

Most important of all among the various investigations was the committee set up by the Ministry of Transport in 1929 with Lord Weir as chairman and Sir Ralph Wedgwood, Chief General Manager of the L.N.E.R. as one of its members. With all that has happened in the intervening years since 1931, when the Weir report was published, the remit to the committee makes interesting reading today. It was – 'In view of the progress which is being made towards widespread availability of high tension electrical energy, to examine into the economic and other aspects of the electrification of the railway systems in Great Britain with particular reference to main line working, and to report their conclusions'. Based on detailed plans and estimates of electrifying two main lines, the old Great Northern Railway between King's Cross, Doncaster and Leeds and lines in Lincolnshire, and the West Coast main line of the L.M.S. between Crewe and Carlisle, the Committee reported that to electrify the railways of Great Britain over a period of fifteen to twenty years would have cost the companies £261 million with a return on the investment of 7 per cent. Pointing out that over the previous ten years national expenditure on construction and maintenance of roads had cost the country something like £500 million, with no means of calculating profit or loss thereon, the committee further contended that the size of the sum involved in electrifying the railways should not, of itself, prevent most thorough consideration of the merits of electrification. But of course the times was not propitious. The basic industries of the country were in a state of depression. Road competition was increasing seriously.

The railway companies could neither find the sums required from their own resources, nor hope to raise the money from the public. Financial assistance from the Government would have been an essential prerequisite to any comprehensive scheme of main line electrification. It was not forthcoming at the time.

In 1936 the L.M.S. examined the case for converting the main line from Euston to Rugby to electric traction. It was far too small a project to have any hope of financial success. Alone among the various schemes considered, other than those of the Southern Railway, electrification of the Great Central lines between Sheffield, Manchester and Wath was authorised. The outstanding merits of electric traction could be exploited to the full over this very heavily graded route. Financial assistance from the Government, as part of the comprehensive measures to relieve unemployment, was provided. Works was commenced before the war, but had perforce to be suspended in 1940. By 1948 work was in full swing once more on the overhead power wiring, a new tunnel at Woodhead, and the new electric locomotives and multiple unit trains.

I have referred in a previous chapter to the growing challenge to steam from the rapid progress of diesel traction, particularly in the United States of America. Though diesel locomotives had already proved themselves technically and financially for shunting on our railways, this was far from being the case in general traffic. With only two 1600 h.p. diesel-electric locomotives in service and five more together with two gas-turbine locomotives under construction, trials on main line passenger and freight services were virtually only just beginning.

The two L.M.S. locomotives 10000 and 10001 were doing good work on the *Royal Scot* service between Euston and Glasgow Central. Valuable operating and maintenance experience was being gained with these two locomotives and with three others which the Southern had built. We continued to follow with close attention developments in diesel traction abroad, particularly in North America where it was already clear that steam locomotives would soon be wholly superceded. Conditions in America were obviously very different from our own particularly in regard to the cost and availability of diesel fuel and the scope, which the size of the country gave, for the attainment of very high average annual mileages over which to spread the higher capital costs of diesel locomotives compared with steam. However, it became clear from a letter to Sir Eustace Missenden received in April, 1948 that the Chairman of the British Transport Commission certainly did not accept that the conditions here were so different as to account for the small part which diesel traction had so far played in main line services on British Railways. Sir Cyril Hurcomb (as he then was) expressed the view that the future form of traction was probably the most important problem facing British Railways at that time. He was obviously not satisfied that the Railway Executive was exploiting on a sufficiently large scale the knowledge and experience which we had gained from twenty years study of diesel traction and from the visits which railway engineers had paid to the United States. He pointed out, correctly, that where our experience was really lacking was in regard to the true level of operating and maintenance costs of diesel traction under British conditions. Hurcomb assumed, rather optimistically perhaps in the light of later events, that we already knew the answers to all the purely technical questions relating to diesel and electric traction! Expressing disappointment that the Railway Executive had apparently decided not to go ahead with a L.N.E.R. scheme for converting the East Coast Anglo-Scottish services to diesel traction with twenty-five locomotives replacing thirty-two *Pacifics* and were intending to limit their tests with main line diesel locomotives to those already in hand on the London Midland Region, Hurcomb asked the Executive to set up a committee to report fully where the ultimate balance of advantage would lay for British Railways between steam, diesel, gas turbine and electric traction.

Thus was established in December 1948 the committee on Types of Motive Power under the chairmanship of Leslie Harrington. Before coming to R. E. Headquarters as a senior member of the Chairman's staff he had been with Missenden, Szlumper and Sir Herbert Walker at Waterloo. He had a wide general experience of railway affairs and had led a Southern Railway mission to America to study diesel traction. The other members of this committee were an operating man, a commercial man and an accountant. This certainly ensured that motive power would be looked at as a means to an end, not an end in itself! Though the committee had to come to us for a great deal of information, upon which to base their recommendations, I took a rather poor view of the fact that the department responsible for the design, provision and maintenance of every kind of motive power was not represented. It was however just as well, as Riddles would be entirely uncommitted and able to retain complete freedom of action on anything the committee might say.

Though it took rather a long time to complete – three years – the report was a competent and exhaustive review of all the factors affecting the choice of motive power for our railway system. The committee were impressed, as they could scarcely fail to be, by the success of diesel traction in the United States and of main line electrification and diesel rail cars in Europe. They concluded, rightly, that while further improvements could be expected in steam locomotives in the direction of increased mileage between repairs, reduction in repair costs and greater availability for traffic, there were no fundamental design changes by which the inherent limitations of steam traction could be overcome. And so, as in other countries, further substantial improvements in the standard of service on British Railways would involve increasing reliance on electric or diesel traction. True, in the longer term, if the level of service with which the committee was making its comparison was the high standard which was commonplace with steam traction in the years immediately before the war in 1939, when 12,000 miles per day were being run at booked speeds of sixty miles an hour and more. Most certainly not true, in the short term, if the comparison was with the lamentably low level to which our express services had been allowed to sink with only forty miles per day being run at a mile a minute at the time the committee were doing their work. The report had within it some signs of the pointless denigration of steam to which we became resigned and which did nothing to assist objective decisions on the many problems which were to arise during the next few years on the pace and timing of the replacement of steam traction. For example, in noting that, through the normal process of renewals, the average thermal efficiency of the steam locomotive fleet as a whole might be increased from about 6 per cent to 8 per cent it was not pointed out that such an increase was an improvement of $33\frac{1}{3}$ per cent. This, if realised on only half the coal consumption, would amount to 1·7 million tons annually and a saving of over £4 million a year – not altogether insignificant figures.

In addition to urging the extended use of diesel locomotives for shunting, the committee made three main recommendations as follows:

(i) that a scheme for the electrification of the Great Northern route from King's Cross to Grantham should be prepared and carried out;

(ii) that a comprehensive scheme should be drawn up for a large scale trial of diesel traction on main line services; and

(iii) that plans should be made for replacing steam hauled trains by diesel rail cars on a wide range of cross-country and other secondary services.

The extended use of diesel shunters was entirely non-controversial. They had fully proved themselves technically and financially. The Railway Executive were already engaged on a five-year plan for building diesel shunting locomotives. The third of the above recommendations was quickly accepted by the R.E. and we soon found ourselves much involved in the provision of new facilities at the Works and Motive Power Depots for the maintenance of diesel rail cars equipped with bus engines and control gear designed in accordance with road vehicle standards. The modifications which had to be made to the first batches of rail cars with underfloor engines and mechanical transmission to achieve anything like a reasonable standard of reliability in railway service, troublesome and expensive though they were, taught the suppliers and ourselves a good deal about the problems we were likely to encounter with any widespread introduction of diesel traction.

There was no dissent, either, from the thinking behind the proposals in regard to main line electrification. Whether the route from King's Cross to Grantham should be accorded first priority was no doubt arguable. It was in regard to the extension of diesel traction for main line passenger and freight services that the arguments arose.

Having regard to current experience at the time, Harrington's committee did not feel justified in proposing a change to diesel traction for a complete line or group of services. Their proposal for a large scale test of main line diesel traction was contingent upon a satisfactory outcome of trials with a 2000 h.p. single unit locomotive then being developed – pending which the limited experiments then in hand should be continued. If trials with the new 2,000 h.p. locomotive proved successful, then would be the time to embark on the large scale test with 100 of those locomotives supplemented by a number of smaller units for branch line and secondary duties.

The Railway Executive did not accept the recommendation for the large scale trial of diesel locomotives for main line duties. They saw no point in spending something over £7 million on 100 2,000 h.p. diesel locomotives when as shown by figures included in the committee's report, the 1,600 h.p. locomotives already in service, even when worked as single units were costing more to operate relatively high mileage rosters than steam *Pacifics*. Moreover, single unit 1600 h.p. locomotives were perfectly capable of working most of the traffic of British Railways. No more than 335 *Class 7* and *8* 4-6-2s comparable in capacity with 2,000 h.p. diesels were needed out of a total stock of 19,325 locomotives. A large number of 2,000 h.p. locomotives grouped together would be operating for most of their time well below their economic level. The locomotives already in service were quite sufficient to enable a reliable assessment to be made of the extent to which diesel traction would be financially justified under British conditions. There were still doubts, not perhaps wholly unreasonable, as to the wisdom of adopting as the principal form of traction, one which depended on imported fuel.

The Railway Executive saw the motive power pattern of the future as an increasing proportion of electric traction, as capital became available to convert routes with a traffic density sufficient to produce an adequate return on the investment, side by side with steam which, though diminishing in extent should be enabled to operate as efficiently as possible by exploiting the reduced maintenance and operating costs which modern design made possible, until it was finally displaced.

A report made to the Transport Commission by some of their own officers shortly after the Harrington Committee had reported, showed that they viewed the matters at issue rather differently from the Railway Executive so far as diesel traction was concerned. They were in favour of going ahead with the large scale trial of diesel traction. My own views on these controversial matters were set down in memoranda which I wrote in response to Riddles' requests for comments on the two reports. I expressed them later in public in my Presidential Address to the Institution of Locomotive Engineers in September 1953. Any reader who is sufficiently interested will find that they were consistent with the policy which the Railway Executive intended to follow. The passage of time, a new government and consequential changes in politics and people led to the formulation of a new policy, which as Chief Mechanical Engineer, I was required to implement after the abolition of the Railway Executive.

As a consequence of the monopoly of public transport which the railways had enjoyed between the eclipse of the canals and the emergence of motor road transport, they had always been subject to a considerable measure of Parliamentary control. It was not long after the election of a new government in 1951 that it became clear that conservative ideas on how a nationalised railway system should be organised were very different from those of their socialist opponents. A visit to Railway Executive headquarters by the new Minister of Transport, Alan Lennox-Boyd, before whom the senior officers were bidden to appear for cross-examination, left no doubt in my mind that we were in for a dose of political interference which would tend to hinder rather than help the work upon which we had been engaged for the past three years.

Decentralisation of management, with wide powers of independent action conferred upon the six railway regions, was clearly in prospect. Loosening of functional control from headquarters with the Regional departmental officers owing direct allegiance more to their Chief Regional Officer than to the Executive Member and his chief officers would clearly follow the change in managerial philosophy. The undoubted economics stemming from unification and rationalisation, difficult enough to achieve even with the direct authority which functional control had enabled us to exert, would require even more persistence and patience for their full realisation in the future.

New thoughts on organisation soon began to emerge. One of the first affecting us was a proposal to carve up the mechanical engineering departments in the Regions by removing maintenance of outdoor machinery and outside carriage and wagon activities from their jurisdiction. It was suggested that these, together with carriage cleaning, which was done by the Operating Department, should become the responsibility of a new maintenance department wholly under regional control. The idea behind this suggestion was presumably that everything to do with day-to-day running of the railway should be completely separated from the design and main Works activities of the department over which, in all common sense, central direction would have to continue. Riddles asked Ernest Pugson and me for our views. We pointed out that the proposed arrangement would differ little in principle from that which existed between the main locomotive Works and the Motive Power Department.

Clearly the arrangement could be made to work − but just as the regional motive power officers were required to conform to technical standards which we laid down, so also the people in charge of any new outdoor maintenance department would have to do likewise. So far as wagon repairs were concerned, we pointed out that since practically all freight wagons were pooled and that crippled wagons had often to be moved from one region to another to balance demand for repairs with available shop capacity, control from headquarters would still be needed. Nothing came of these proposals which, by fragmenting an organisation which should work as one, would have been harmful; but they showed the way the wind was blowing.

In spite of the fact that the urgent task of unification, which required for its fulfilment unchallenged direction from the centre, was by no means completed, and which could not possibly have been completed in so short a span as six years, the Railway Executive was abolished in October, 1953. In the light of all that has happened since, I am convinced that this purely political decision was wrong. Abolition of the Railway Executive was surely not an essential prerequisite to the decentralisation of management which was a principal objective of the 1953 Transport Act. The Area Boards which the Act required to be established were subservient to the British Transport Commission. They could equally well have been subservient to the Railway Executive. It is, indeed, an interesting speculation as to what would probably have happened had the Railway Executive been allowed to continue in office.

Once the initial period of nationalisation was over, the Railway Executive had itself gradually delegated additional responsibility for day-to-day management to the Regions. It is clear from what is stated in the explanatory statement contained in the White Paper* on the Railways Reorganisation Scheme presented to Parliament in July, 1954, that this process would have continued. In their new scheme of organisation the British Transport Commission took direct charge of certain specific matters 'such as the design, manufacture and standards of maintenance of locomotives, rolling stock, permanent way and signalling; labour relations of a major character; general level of charges; financial control in its broader aspects, higher appointments; the policies and principles to be adopted in railway operation; the inter-regional distribution of wagons; and commercial policy in general and national negotiations in connection therewith'. By thus retaining to themselves direct control of those activities from which the economies and increased efficiency of unification and rationalisation would mainly be derived, the need for this urgent work to continue to completion was acknowledged. The task could have continued under the Railway Executive without the loss of momentum that the upheaval inevitably entailed. There would have been a Modernisation Plan. One was prepared by the Railway Executive during Sir John Elliot's time as Chairman.

So far as the matters in which I was directly involved were concerned, a great deal of ground had been covered. Every important aspect of locomotive maintenance and construction had been, or was in the process of being critically examined. First and foremost, a uniform system for the organisation and control of repairs to locomotives had been introduced at all the Works and was producing good results. The number of engines under and awaiting repairs at Works had been reduced from 7 per cent to 5 per cent of the total stock. The time locomotives were out of service for repairs had been considerably reduced. This was one of the important factors which had enabled a reduction of nearly 10 per cent to be made in the total locomotive stock. Notwithstanding rises in wages and material costs which were taking place then as now, locomotive repair costs came down in Shops and Sheds together, by over a penny a mile from a shilling and a

* Railways Re-organisation Scheme, Cmd 9191, *H.M.S.O. London.*

halfpenny to just over eleven pence. On an engine mileage of approximately 500 millions a year, this was quite a lot of money.

Because it seemed to me important that the principles on which an efficient system for the maintenance of locomotives, whether steam, diesel or electric, must be based should be known and understood as widely as possible, I wrote a paper on the organisation and control of locomotive repairs for the Institution of Locomotive Engineers, which incidentally had done me the honour of inviting me to become their President for 1953–54.

Individual costing of repairs in Shops and Sheds had been applied to a representative selection of the locomotive stock, thus extending a practice from which the L.M.S. Railway had derived so much information on maintenance expenditure incurred by the various classes of locomotives, which helped to guide future locomotive policy.

There were wide differences in the organisation which the four group companies had adopted for the management of their Works. All were reviewed in detail and a standard pattern, based on sound production engineering principles, evolved for adoption at all the main Works as and when circumstances permitted. Though each of the Works necessarily continued mainly to look after the locomotives of the company to which it had belonged they were directed, particularly in the sphere of new construction, as component parts of one comprehensive production organisation, with work allocated and capacity utilised inter-regionally for the benefit of the railway as a whole. Production processes were submitted to detailed scrutiny and a standard system of manufacturing tolerances was initiated in place of the many incompatible systems hitherto in use to ensure an acceptable degree of interchangeability of manufactured components.

Arrangements for building new locomotives and boilers were reviewed by a committee, of which I was chairman, on which the Mechanical Engineer of each Region sat personally, together with the Works Accountant from Crewe. At various times before the 1923 amalgamations, new engines had been built at twenty-four railway works. The number of Works so engaged had been steadily reduced over the years until at nationalisation new locomotives and boilers were being built at ten only of the eighteen main Works. We were asked to recommend whether any changes should be made, with particular reference to economies which might accrue from concentrating new construction at a smaller number of Works – even at one Works only. Past experience had shown that the annual rate of renewal of locomotives had averaged 2·1 per cent of the stock – which at the time we were investigating the matter was equal to 400 new engines a year. Crewe and Swindon alone of all the Works had sufficient staff to encompass so large an output of new locomotives. But the distribution of men between the various craft grades is quite different in a Works engaged predominantly on repairs compared with one in which new building would provide the main work load. Any proposal to concentrate new building at one Works only would have brought insuperable staff difficulties in its train. Moreover, the number of new engines and boilers authorised to be built in any one year had fluctuated very widely and was likely to continue to do so. Thus the essential condition, namely a steady volume of work, for concentrating all new construction in one Works, even supposing this had been desirable from other points of view, would not exist. However, some further concentration of new building seemed sensible. We recommended that Horwich and Gorton, both of which were rather expensive compared with other Works, should cease new construction.

Much had been accomplished in standardising material specifications, and in rationalising the inspection of raw materials at manufacturers' Works. Five bronze and brass alloys successfully replaced thirty-seven different mixtures previously in use. Four white metal bearing alloys did the work for which thirteen alloys had hitherto been used. So, too, with steel and other raw materials. Standard specifications based where possible on B.S.I. standards were adopted in all Regions. The foregoing examples are just a small selection from among the multifarious subjects from which savings in working expenses accrued from standardisation of materials and methods.

Whatever views one may have held as to whether the abolition of the Railway Executive was right or wrong, the fact remains that the Railway Executive achieved a large measure of success in welding the four erstwhile railway companies into one coherent organisation. Savings in working expenses were running at something like £15 million a year towards the end of their six years in office. Riddles had every right to be well pleased with the contribution which his department both at headquarters and in all the Regions had made to the overall results.

Interspersed with all the hard work there were a number of most agreeable diversions, in which my wife was able to share, during these memorable years.

There were Garden Parties at Buckingham Palace, invitations to which came the way of Chief Officers at Railway Executive headquarters. I remember well the scorching hot day of our first Party when I drove Jean up to London from our home in Watford. She was wearing a new costume which she herself had made. I was in my shirt sleeves until on the outskirts of Marylebone I struggled into the same morning coat in which I had been married twenty years before! There was the inauguration of the new

Ocean Terminal at Southampton and lunch on board the *Queen Elizabeth* moored alongside. There was the opening by King George VI of the Festival of Britain on the South Bank, at which one of the *Britannia* locomotives, No. 70004 *William Shakespeare*, Southern diesel and electric locomotives, and an Indian State Railways engine, built by one of the private contractors, were exhibited. *William Shakespeare* was given a special exhibition finish at Crewe. She was hauled dead to Willesden whither Riddles and some of us with our wives went on a Sunday morning to make a final inspection before the engine completed her journey to the Exhibition site. She was indeed a magnificent sight, of which the men of Crewe could feel justifiably proud.

Not long afterwards there was the sad pageantry of the King's funeral, which we saw from seats in a stand at Paddington station, when the driver of *Windsor Castle*, which was not 'Windsor Castle' at all, but another engine to which the appropriate name-plates had been temporarily affixed, started the funeral train with such care and skill, that the familiar sharp bark of the *Castles* was wholly suppressed. There was the magnificent Coronation Naval Review at Spithead in 1953. As the official programme records, the British Transport Commission and the Railway Executive were honoured with an invitation from the Board of Admiralty to berth one of the Holyhead–Dublin ships, the *M.V. Cambria* in the lines. Those of us who were fortunate enough to be invited spent an unforgettable day and night aboard the *Cambria* — which included what looked to a mere railwayman uncommonly like a near collision with another railway ship approaching in the opposite direction as we steamed through the lines after the review by the Queen in the Royal Yacht of the assembled multitude of warships and merchant ships of every kind and description. And on leave, at least one journey each year on the night sleepers to Inverness and Fort William, and the furthest outposts of the railway in the Highlands of Scotland.

Membership of the Association of Railway Locomotive Engineers was a distinction one hoped to achieve in the old company days. So, too, one hoped in the fullness of time to be offered a commission in the Engineer and Railway Staff Corps and to be bidden as a delegate to an International Railway Congress. Both these agreeable perquisites, if such they may be called, highly esteemed among railway officers, came my way about this time.

The Engineer and Railway Staff Corps is, I suppose, unique among military formations. It consists of ten Colonels, twenty Lieutenant-colonels, thirty Majors and no other ranks. The history of the Corps may be found in 'All Rank and No File' written by Major G. E. C. Townsend. The rank in which railway officers are commissioned depends not at all upon previous military service, if any, but only on the appointment held in the railway service. The occasional arrival of letters addressed to Colonel R. C. Bond has often given rise to banter from the family. What sort of a unit, they ask, is one which has no uniform and is disbanded at the first hint of any hostilities? Fair comment perhaps; but let those who may be inclined to scoff read the foreword to Major Townsend's book written by Lord Robertson of Oakridge, then our Honorary Colonel. He said 'the Corps is a valuable link between the transport industry and the defence authorities' – and indeed it is. Moreover our annual dinner is one of the best which it is my privilege still to attend. It is a civilised occasion with the Royal Engineers band in attendance. Good food, good wine and good music are sufficient for good fellowship – there are no after-dinner speeches!

All the European Railways, and many in other countries further afield, were members of the International Railway Congress Association, which met every two years, usually in a foreign capital, to discuss reports and papers on many subjects of railway business prepared in the interval between meetings. I had seen something of the work involved in drafting questionnaires and gathering information from overseas railways during the time of my association with Roy Hart-Davies. He prepared Sir Nigel Gresley's report on Locomotive Testing to one of the pre-war Congress meetings – and very exacting work it was. The first Congress which I attended as a delegate was held in Rome. This was my first visit to the Italian capital where more than in any other modern city, one receives an irresistable impression that what one was taught at school of ancient history, did really happen. This congress, and two others in Stockholm and London proved to be about the best combination of business and pleasure within my experience. The journeys in special trains half way across Europe were fascinating in themselves.

The organisation was always superb. As delegates were allowed to be accompanied by their wife and one unmarried daughter, social activities were an important and enjoyable part of the proceedings.

An impressive opening ceremony usually performed by the Minister of Transport of the host country, which everyone was expected to attend, was followed by sectional meetings each morning at which reports on the various chosen subjects were discussed – and agreed conclusions reached for announcement at plenary sessions. It was a fairly safe bet that diametrically opposite views would be expressed by at least two of the delegations. Much time and ingenuity both in the meetings and behind the scenes was spent in trying to reach conclusions which everyone, or nearly everyone, could agree to without landing themselves in trouble with their managements when they returned home. Afternoons were devoted to visits to railway works, marshalling yards and so on, or to places of more general national and historic interest. In the evenings there were official receptions, dinners or a gala performance of some kind or other at the Opera House. There were alternative weekend visits in special trains of the very latest rolling stock to such places as Florence and Naples, with a trip across the bay to the beautiful island of Capri as an added attraction.

How much do these conferences really contribute to progress and greater efficiency in railway operation? To the continental countries with their land frontiers and international services, undoubtedly a great deal. They take these congresses very seriously. To us, and to other countries further away, inevitably rather less. A good deal of expenditure must have been incurred on these meetings by the participating countries over and above their subscription to the I.R.C.A. based, I believe, on track mileage. Because it is scarcely possible to identify any return on such expenditure, a tendency in some quarters in recent years to regard the Congresses as nothing more than a very enjoyable holiday, at the railway's expense, for those fortunate enough to be chosen to attend, is not altogether surprising. This is, of course, an altogether too parsimonious view of the matter. The value of these international gatherings cannot be measured in terms of £.s.d. alone.

The amalgamation of the International Congress Association with headquarters in Brussels, and the International Union of Railways based in Paris, both of which covered much the same ground, is no doubt entirely sensible in avoiding duplication and effecting substantial economies. But with the prospects of a Channel Tunnel and Great Britain's entry into the Common Market in mind, it would indeed be regrettable if British Railways did not continue to play a leading part in these international activities.

Riddles decided to retire from railway service on the day the Executive ceased to exist. We had hoped and indeed expected, that he would have been appointed as a member of the Commission. But this was not to be. Riddles' departure was genuinely regretted by all his staff at Marylebone. He had achieved a remarkable degree of harmony between the various sections of his department at headquarters. He enjoyed, and deserved complete loyalty and respect as a benevolent dictator, who knew exactly what he wanted. We did not necessarily all agree with all his decisions all the time. But we never sought a decision in vain, and knew exactly what was expected of us. Riddles gave his staff firm support in all that he asked them to do. He was an astute politician in railway affairs, and adept in retaining freedom of action in difficult situations. He had decided views, which he did not hesitate to express on the future development of motive power for our railways. As a general principle, to which of course there were exceptions, Riddles did not believe in an intermediate phase of main line diesel traction between steam and electrification. In this he was out of sympathy with the general trend of opinion at the time. For me, Riddles' retirement brought to a premature end a long association with him as a senior colleague and chief. I shall always remain indebted to him for many kindly acts along the way, for his confidence, and much wisdom freely imparted. I am glad that it fell to me to make the retiring presentation on behalf of the department at Marylebone.

CHAPTER ELEVEN

Chief Mechanical Engineer.

British Railways, Central Staff

1953-58

AS SOON AS IT BECAME KNOWN from a White Paper on Transport Policy, issued by the Conservative Government in May, 1952 that what our new political masters considered to be excessive centralisation was to be corrected by the drastic step of abolishing the Railway Executive, there was naturally a great deal of speculation, and some apprehension among us all at Marylebone as to what the future might hold in store. What was to happen to the Members of the Executive, and to the staff at headquarters? They would certainly not be welcomed back with open arms by the Regions whence they had come! Who, if any, among the Members might find themselves appointed to the Commission?

It was quite clear from the White Paper that the railways as a whole were to continue to be administered as a single entity under the control of the Transport Commission. This being the case, and however much autonomy in day-to-day management might be given to the Regions, there would obviously remain a number of important matters which commonsense would dictate should stay under the direct control of the central management body. There were substantial further economies still to be gained from pressing on with the unfinished work of standardising methods and equipment throughout the system – economies which most certainly would not be secured if the Regions were in future to be left entirely to themselves.

The B.T.C. were required by the 1953 Transport Act to prepare and submit for the approval of the Minister a scheme for the re-organisation of 'that part of their undertaking which consists in the operation of the railways'. But they were allowed twelve months, possibly more if the Minister felt so inclined, to do this. In the meantime, with a definite date, 1st October, 1953, already decided for the abolition of the Railway Executive, and indeed all the other Executives except London Transport, some form of organisation would have to be set up to fill the gaps – in particular so far as we were concerned, to enable the responsibilities discharged by the Railway Executive in managing the railways to continue without interruption. The Commission provided for the management of their Road Services, Docks and Inland Waterways by setting up subsidiary Boards not really very different from the abolished Executives they replaced.

In the case of the Railways however, the B.T.C. decided to take over the functions of the Executive and do the job itself, thereby probably sowing the seeds of its own destruction a few years later.

The underlying philosophy of the 1953 Transport Act was that the tight central control of the railways under which they had operated since 1948 should be eliminated. Responsibility for management was to be delegated to area authorities, such, for example, as the existing railway Regions. Though the Commission had decided to exercise themselves the powers of management hitherto delegated to the Railway Executive, and in so doing to retain direct control of certain matters – the reserved subjects – throughout British Railways, general effect was given to the intentions of the new Act in the Interim Organisation brought into operation on 1st October, 1953, by abandoning the functional system of supreme management. In this Members of the Executive, in addition to their collective responsibility for general management, each exercised through their officers at headquarters and in the Regions, direct authority from top to bottom of the departments for which they were responsible. Riddles was in fact, though not in name, Chief Mechanical and Electrical Engineer for the whole of British Railways. All the officers in charge of the mechanical and electrical engineering establishments in the Regions owed direct allegiance to him as their chief. They were just as much members of Riddles' team as we all were at Headquarters.

In place of these simple and straightforward arrangements, well suited to the initial task of welding four independent companies into one system – a task which I must repeat was by no means completed – the Interim organisation transferred departmental authority to the Regions. All the regional departmental officers hitherto responsible to a Member of the Executive – and to a very much lesser extent to his Chief Regional Officer – became responsible, at any rate in theory, only to the latter, re-named Chief Regional Manager. My Regional colleagues, mostly friends of long standing to whom for the last six years I had given instructions on behalf of Riddles, were not slow to make the most of the freedom they acquired in day-to-day management of their departments. But they were not free to do as they liked in the really important technical and professional matters which the Commission reserved to itself under the control of those who became their headquarters staff appointed for the purpose.

Thus the functions of the Railway Executive were divided between those which the Commission reserved to itself and those which they delegated to the Regions.

The broad pattern for the future having been decided, the Commission set about re-organising their own headquarters to correspond. As a first step they moved over from their offices in the London Transport building in Westminster and installed themselves in our own headquarters at 222, Marylebone Road – the old Great Central Railway Hotel opposite the station – already referred to throughout the railway service as the Kremlin. Railway Executive staff were merged with those of the Commission who had come over to join us. As the Commission had no engineering staff of their own, no problems arose as to who should be appointed to take charge of the engineering activities, which the Commission had reserved to themselves. I, and my colleagues in the same situation became Chief Officers of the B.T.C. instead of the Railway Executive. It was fortunately as simple as that. But the change was a good deal more than one of name only.

Only one member of the Railway Executive – J. C. L. Train (later, Sir Landale) – was to join the Commission of which he became the Engineering member. Before coming to the Railway Executive in charge of Civil and Signal Engineering, Train had held the all-line appointment of Chief Civil Engineer of the L.N.E.R. With his L.N.E.R. experience to guide him, Train should know how to reconcile and harmonise all-line responsibilities and interests with those of Divisional General Managers to whom his Divisional Engineers gave a service, when as no doubt sometimes happened, they appeared to be in conflict. This could be important in the future.

Organisation, and all that this word implies, did become increasingly important in its influence on our work from this time forward. Changes and developments in organisation there must be. But surely they should reflect changes and developments in the industry on which they are imposed. Inland transport in all its forms, and the relationships between them have changed profoundly during the forty-eight years of my working life, but not so suddenly or in such diametrically opposite directions as would seem to be implied from a consideration of the various re-organisations to which we were subjected.

With the abolition of the Railway Executive in 1953 we entered upon a period of internal conflict which, so far as I know, has not been resolved even yet – if indeed it ever can be to everyone's satisfaction in so complex an undertaking as a nationwide railway system. The arguments and battles were between two sets of forces which should not be, but often are, in opposition to each other. There was, first on the one hand, the general conflict between Headquarters and the Regions with one or other in the ascendant, depending upon the party in power, and the particular Transport Act by which we were governed at the time – a conflict with a political background quite unrelated to the needs of efficiency in the working of the railways. And, on the other hand, there was the battle which, stemming from the first, developed rather later between the engineers and the non-engineers. It was a conflict in which I was closely involved, and one on which I hold strong views based on some experience. I may perhaps be excused for setting them down in some detail.

Unless a qualified engineer deliberately chooses to devote his talents to invention or research in the secluded environment of academic life insulated from the compelling demands of engineering production, he will find himself sooner rather than later, required to direct and accept responsibility for the work of other people. Thus he will be much concerned that the arrangements made by his employers for the conduct of their business should be such as will enable him to carry the responsibilities placed upon him with confidence.

He will quite reasonably, expect the chain of command and the relationships established between himself and the other parts of the undertaking to ensure with certainty

(i) that the instructions he is empowered to give will be obeyed;
(ii) that he can satisfy himself as of right, and not by kind permission of someone else, that his instructions are in fact being carried out in the manner laid down; and
(iii) that if they are not, he can insist on effective remedial action.

The way in which a complex undertaking comprising a number of separate, though inter-dependent activities is organised must obviously be decided in the context of the enterprise as a whole. There are broadly two alternatives. In one, general management is concentrated at headquarters. There is a clear and unambiguous line of authority throughout each chief officer's department. In the other, the undertaking is divided more on a divisional or geographical basis, with a number of semi-autonomous bodies each containing within itself a share of the functions necessary for providing the service for which the undertaking exists. Functional control will be diluted, with the consequence that dual allegiance will become more prominent − it can never be wholly avoided − and human nature being what it is, more troublesome.

Even the most bigoted non-engineer must surely concede that, railways, by their very nature, depend on the science and practice of engineering more than on any other one thing for providing the transport services for which they exist. Engineers design, build and maintain the permanent way, signalling, motive power and rolling stock without which the traffic operators, the commercial gentlemen and all the rest can do nothing. This being so, it would seem sensible that the organisation should be designed to enable the engineering departments to carry out their work without any impediment to the attainment of optimum cost and efficiency. No less important, the chief engineers should enjoy, and be seen to enjoy, the confidence of those who appointed them.

During all the twenty-five years of my service with the L.M.S. and the Midland, this was certainly the case. I believe it was on the other three group companies too. It certainly was during the first six years of nationalisation.

Subsequently, however, with the passing of each new Transport Bill and the arrival of each new Chairman, the structure and organisation of the engineering departments were subjected to scrutiny and change sometimes in one direction, sometimes in another, but always at the cost of some disruption to the job in hand. So far as the mechanical and electrical engineering departments were concerned, in which I include the motive power department, some changes were of course required as a consequence of the displacement of steam locomotives by diesel and electric traction. But this of itself, did not require any upheaval in the well-proved relationship with other departments.

Over the years the general effect of the changes in organisation has been in fact, if not in theory, to make it more difficult for the engineers to secure compliance with the technical standards and maintenance procedures which they are required to lay down, upon which so much in terms of safety and reliability of operation depends. The responsibility remains, but authority to exercise it has been made less direct and has sometimes been challenged.

I remember an occasion when a Regional General Manager, himself an Engineer who should have known better, went so far as to countermand on his Region, an instruction limiting in the interests of safety throughout British Railways, the permissible wear in axleguards of wagons prone to derailment, issued by the C.M.E. of the B.R. Central Staff at the time. Compliance with this instruction necessarily involved some increase in expenditure on maintenance – but it was a standard of maintenance – a reserved subject. The C.M.E. prevailed, but only after he had threatened to resign, which he certainly would have done had his orders not been upheld by the Board. This was an isolated case; but that it could happen at all was symptomatic of an unhealthy situation.

Notwithstanding the difficulties arising from the loss of complete functional control, the chief engineers at headquarters were, until fairly recently, in the top level of management immediately below the Members of the Board, either directly or by representation through a member of their profession. In the 1953 Interim Organisation, the Chief Engineer reported direct to the Commission, one Member of which was a railway engineer of long experience. Coincident with the introduction in 1955 of the Statutory Re-organisation Scheme, the new Chairman, General Sir Brian Robertson interposed between the Commission and its Divisions, a body of senior officers at headquarters known as the General Staff. It was laid down in one of the documents on organisation issued at the time that, while holding the senior professional posts in their own field, the chief officers of the British Railways Central Staff, who, with the six Regions, constituted the Railway Division, were to be responsible to the Commission through the General Staff. Thus they now found themselves in the third, instead of the second level of management.

Although as a top-level body for doing jobs of a general character, which did not fall naturally to anyone else at headquarters, the General Staff served the Commission well, it was on the whole heartily disliked by the chief departmental officers as a needless encumbrance in the chain of command. Indeed, as Chief Mechanical Engineer, I disliked it myself. But the importance of engineering was recognised by the inclusion of a chief engineer in the General Staff with the title of Technical Adviser, an appointment to which I found myself promoted in due course! Thus the voice of the engineers was heard, and I think respected, by the highest levels of direction and management. Such also was the case when, with the dissolution of the General Staff soon after Dr. Beeching became Chairman of the Railway Board, the chief engineers once again reported direct. Today, unhappily, not one of the chief engineers at Railway Board headquarters is a member of the top-level railway management group. In the Report on Organisation presented to Parliament in pursuance of Section 45 of the 1968 Transport Act, the Engineering Departments and the chief engineers are not even mentioned.

Why has the present situation arisen — a situation in which the chief engineers at headquarters report to a gentleman with the odd title of Director of Systems and Operations and the Regional Engineers find themselves faced with removal from their own direct authority of the men in the divisions, districts and depots, who carry out the work for which they are ultimately held responsible? The reasons are, I believe, deep seated and derive from the politics of power within the railways long before nationalisation. I am inclined to think we are seeing a delayed reaction from non-engineers who in their earlier days resented the prestige and influence attaching to the heads of the railways' Engineering Departments. In his book 'The Railways and the Nation', Arthur Pearson, an ex-L.M.S. colleague of mine at Marylebone, contradicts a statement attributed to a well known writer 'that British Railways was run by engineers until Dr. Beeching came on the scene.' Pearson asserts that the railways have never been run by engineers. This is no doubt true in the sense that the engineers did not act in defiance of their General Managers or Directors Committees. But in saying, as he does, that 'Some of the best engineers in the country have assisted the management, but that is all,' Pearson does the engineers less than justice. Without them the managements would have nothing to manage. Some of the engineers in recent years have unwittingly contributed to the relative weakening of the authority of their successors. Some have made expensive mistakes, the reasons for which are never understood and seldom excused by those unversed in the science and practice of engineering. Engineers are no less prone to error than other people.

What is important, as it seems to me, to the future success and prosperity of British Railways is that the engineers should be accorded their rightful place on an equal footing with others in the highest level of executive management. At a time when the possibilities of higher speeds, with undiminished safety of operation are being exploited to the limit, primarily dependent upon engineers who alone are qualified to carry the responsibility involved, commonsense would seem to dictate no less.

Riddles' retirement, coinciding with the demise of the Railway Executive had two important consequences for those of us who remained. First, the combined department at headquarters was divided into three. Electrical and Road Motor Engineering were separated from the main body of mechanical engineering activities. Secondly, the transfer of more authority to the Regions had the effect of breaking down one all-line department into its Regional component parts. Thus, there emerged a Mechanical and Electrical Engineering Department, and a Carriage & Wagon Department in each Region, free to act with greater independence than at any time since 1947.

The changeover at headquarters was accomplished with the minimum of fuss and bother. One thing only caused some ripples on the surface. Custom and staff rules apparently decreed that private secretaries, once in a job, stayed in it and took on the newcomer. This did not suit me at all. I had no wish to offend the sitting tenant. But I was going to have quite enough on my plate without the added complications of a secretary who did not know my ways, nor I hers. I let it be known that I had no intention of abandoning the lady who had looked after me with efficiency and unfailing good humour for six years. Subtle questions of grade and salary were duly resolved. I retained my secretary, Lois McBay, to whom I owe so much, for a further five years.

The responsibilities which I inherited for the next few months until carriage and wagon activities were constituted as another separate department were notified to me in quite explicit terms. As Chief Officer (Mechanical Engineering), later to my great satisfaction redesignated Chief Mechanical Engineer, I became responsible to the Commission for the reserved subjects embracing:

1 The standards and codes of practice to be observed in the design, manufacture and maintenance of locomotives (excluding electrical components), carriages, wagons and mechanical engineering plant and equipment.

2 Preparation and submission, jointly with other Departments, of annual building programmes for locomotives and rolling stock.

3 Allocation and overall planning of the work to be done in the main railway workshops.

4 Examination of new works schemes for mechanical engineering submitted to the Commission for approval.

5 Examination of Regional budgets for maintenance and scrutiny of expenditure in relation to the budget.

6 Inspection of materials.

7 Allocation of materials to Regions in consultation with Chief Regional Managers and Headquarters Officers concerned.

8 Co-ordination of research and development affecting mechanical engineering.

9 Central negotiations with national bodies such as Government Departments, nationalised industries and professional Institutions.

10 Mechanical engineering staff questions – in a professional advisory capacity.

11 Planning the training of men for the higher posts.

Discharge of these responsibilities naturally required a continuous and unimpeded flow of information and reports from the Regions, which until the abolition of the Executive, had passed freely up and down the functional line. With the new organisation, everything of any consequence was supposed to be passed through the Regional General Manager on its way to the people who had the job to do, with irritation and delay as natural consequences. Riddles had always insisted that his people should render without reservation to the Chief Regional Officers the service they had every right to expect. Thus we had built up close and cordial relations with the Regional managements who, with mutual confidence well established had little wish to be bothered with technical matters. The Regional Engineers were more inclined to work to the letter of the law than those who had the right to insist on doing so.

By the time the new organisation came into effect the old company C.M.E.s had all retired and been replaced by their principal assistants who, but for nationalisation, could have expected, as I should have done, the same power and authority as their predecessors. They were, quite understandably, out to make the most of regional autonomy. Our job at headquarters was made more difficult than it need have been because the Commission apparently found it inexpedient to inform the Regions in detail of the duties they had allocated to their officers at the centre who 'will be responsible in conjunction with the Chief Regional Managers for ensuring that the various policies of the Commission are carried out from the point of view of British Railways as a whole'. It seemed as though the Commission was unwilling to let the left hand know what its right hand

had been told to do. Thus there was plenty of room for differing inter-
pretations by the Regional engineers, members of the Mechanical
Engineering Committee to the chairmanship of which I had been appointed, as to what constituted 'proper reference to and contact with the
Commission's specialist and technical officers'.

As a firm believer in strong central control in technical matters, I was
determined that all the resources of the C.M.E. Works and Drawing
Offices should continue to be utilised for the benefit of B.R. generally and
not solely in the interests of the Region in which they happened to be
located. But with design still undertaken in drawing offices now under
Regional control, it was not easy, unless people were prepared to abide by
the rules, to prevent Regions going off on their own, and starting things
which might not fit in with the wider interests of the railway as a whole.
With the Modernisation Plan bringing into service many hundreds of
millions of pounds worth of new equipment, firm control and co-
ordination of design was even more important than before. The benefits to
be derived from modernisation would certainly not be secured if the Commission allowed their intentions in reserving control of design to
themselves to go by default or be frustrated by Regional action. The submission, jointly by three Regions, of a proposal for new inter-city diesel
trains, about which we at Headquarters had not been consulted, finally
satisfied the Commission that the persistent complaints we had made of
Regions ignoring instructions were justified and that something needed to
be done. The Regional General Managers were reminded of their
obligations in regard to these matters.

Within a few months of getting down to business the Commission appointed a committee of chief officers, of whom I was one, to submit
proposals for the modernisation and re-equipment of the railways on the
assumption that our proposals would be capable of being started in five
years and completed within fifteen. We produced our plan after six months
intensive work – which of course, was necessarily superimposed on our
normal duties.

The aim of the Plan, to quote from the booklet published by the Commission in 1955 was 'to produce a thoroughly modern system able fully to
meet both current traffic requirements and those of the foreseeable future'
and 'to exploit the great natural advantages of railways as bulk
transporters of passengers and goods and to revolutionise the character of
the services provided for both – not only by the full utilisation of modern
equipment, but also by a purposeful concentration on those functions
which the railways can be made to perform more efficiently than other
forms of transport whether by road, air or water'.

The most important parts of the Plan so far as the Engineering
Departments were concerned were:

(i) The progressive replacement of steam locomotives by electric and diesel traction, with all that this involved in new facilities and equipment at the main Works, new motive power and rolling stock maintenance depots and massive programmes of staff training.

(ii) Widespread improvements to the track to eliminate speed restrictions and generally to permit higher speeds over the trunk routes.

(iii) Replacement of much of the existing mechanical signalling equipment by colour-light signals and power-operated signal boxes, the extension of automatic warning control to all main lines, and complete modernisation of the telecommunications network.

(iv) Replacement of many of the existing passenger coaches by multiple-unit trains and the introduction of new locomotive hauled vehicles with bogies of improved design to give a far higher standard of riding.

(v) Equipment of most of the freight wagons with continuous brakes, improved drawgear and buffers, together with the introduction of larger wagons and extensive modernisation of loading and unloading appliances, such as tipplers, to correspond.

(iv) Provision of new mechanised marshalling yards, involving heavy earthworks, extensive track laying and automatically controlled wagon retarders.

Presented as it was, with a good deal of publicity, as a comprehensive package to be completed within a definite term of years, with no reference to all that the Railway Executive had done during the previous six years towards restoring railway services to their traditionally high standards, anyone might have been excused for thinking that modernisation was something which only happened once in a while at irregular intervals.

The truth, of course, is quite the reverse. Modernisation is, or should be, a continuous process, with annual programmes for replacement of facilities and equipment, reflecting the best of contemporary technical development. This is what had happened before the 1939–45 war, though to a seriously inadequate extent. The railways, like all other heavy industries, had been hard hit by the economic depression of the thirties, and largely as a result of the great increase in road transport they were unable to raise sufficient new capital for large schemes of modernisation. During the war severely restricted resources of men and materials had necessarily to be devoted to essential maintenance to enable an unprecedented volume of traffic to be moved under all the difficulties and hazards of war. Virtually nothing could be renewed. Thus, the railways through no fault of their own, found themselves at the end of the war with much of their equipment out of date.

The Railway Executive had gone a long way in renewing locomotives, rolling stock and other equipment. Yet because governments had been forced to restrict investment in the railways because of other claims on the national resources judged to be more urgent, there was still much to be done as soon as funds could be made available. The Railway Executive had prepared a plan accordingly – but before it could be authorised the Executive was abolished.

The Commission's Plan, originally estimated to cost no less than £1200 million was accepted by the Government as courageous and imaginative. The Government concluded that as carriers of passengers over long distances and of suburban passengers in large numbers to and from work, and as carriers of bulk freight, the railways were essential and would continue to be so for as long as could be foreseen. The national interest required that the future of the railways should be assured.

Given reasonable stability in conditions external to an industry, fifteen years may not be too long a time over which to expect a comprehensive plan for a very large undertaking of national importance to be completed more or less unaltered. But at the time when the first instalments of the new equipment began to make their impact, it had become clear that important factors upon which the financial success of the Plan depended were not working out quite in accordance with the original assumptions. The Plan was therefore re-examined in 1956.* New assessments of costs made in 1957 increased the total estimated expenditure by 34 per cent, to £1600 million. As earnings in 1958 failed to reach the anticipated level, and working expenses had increased, a further review of the Plan was made.**

And so it has gone on over the years – events have falsified financial and economic assumptions. Reviews and re-appraisals in one form or another, including an examination at the request of the Chairman, Lord Robertson, by the Parliamentary Select Committee on Nationalised Industries before whom, with many others, I was called to answer questions, have been more or less continuous. Plans must be changed as circumstances dictate the need for change.

Whatever may have gone wrong with the commercial and financial estimates, due largely to causes outside the Commission's control, there was not much wrong with the engineering components of the Plan. That we had difficult problems to solve I do not deny. Trouble with the power equipment on trains for the 25,000 volt alternating current electrification, was so serious that some electric services had to be suspended for a time. Though for quite different reasons it was touch and go for some months as to whether the London Midland main line electrification from Euston to Liverpool and Manchester would be allowed to be completed. What a mistake it would have been to have stopped this magnificent project! The

* Proposals for the Railways, Cmd 9880, *H.M.S.O. London*, 1956.
**Re-appraisal of the Plan for the Modernisation and Re-equipment of British Railways, Cmd 813, *H.M.S.O. London*, 1959.

programme for fitting continuous brakes to mineral wagons ran into serious difficulties and had to be modified. The most important single feature of the Plan, the progressive replacement of steam locomotives by diesel and electric traction, was not exactly a painless operation – but it was successfully accomplished.

Some day I hope a full account of the Modernisation Plan, and its subsequent absorption into the Beeching Plan with its different approach to the dilemma of the railways being a public service as well as a commercial undertaking will be written. Such an account will be nothing less than a complete historical record of the development of our railway system during years which saw changes more fundamental in character and extent than ever before accomplished over so comparatively short a time. In spite of all that has happened during the intervening years who, looking at the whole inland transport problem from a wider, and as I think, more enlightened point of view than the purely commercial, will say that the confidence expressed by the British Transport Commission in 1954 in the continuing need of the country for an efficient railway system was misplaced?

The part of the Modernisation Plan which took up more of my time than anything else, both as Chief Mechanical Engineer, and later as Technical Adviser to the Commission, was the changeover from steam to other forms of motive power. When I joined the Midland Railway in 1920, steam traction was for all practical purposes the only form of motive power for all main line and most suburban services. Though the advantages of electric traction for the most intensive suburban services had been proved beyond any doubt, comparatively few lines had then been electrified. Nevertheless it was obvious that the future for suburban electrification was very promising. For main line services there were few routes over which the traffic density was high enough for electric traction to be a paying proposition. There appeared, at the time, no other form of motive power likely to present a serious challenge to the supremacy of the conventional, though thermally rather inefficient, steam locomotive. Moreover there appeared to be, and the course of events has proved that there was, very wide scope for further developments in power and efficiency of steam locomotives, within the allowable limits of space and weight, without any sacrifice of the cardinal virtues, in anything to do with railways, of simplicity and reliability.

One or two tentative experiments with diesel engined locomotives and rail cars had indeed been carried out. But they made no significant impact at the time. Nevertheless they were the small beginnings from which, little by little, over a period of thirty years, diesel engines and power transmissions, sufficiently reliable and robust to enable the inherent advantages of internal combustion to be applied to railway motive power were developed so successfully as to justify, on economic grounds, the almost total replacement of steam locomotives on the railways of the world.

The late nineteen-twenties can, I think, rightly be regarded as the beginning of the 'Years of Transition' – which I chose as the title of my Address to the Institution of Locomotive Engineers.* Those were the years during which the relative merits of steam and diesel traction became of real practical significance. The pros and cons were hotly contested in many papers and discussions before Engineering Institutions – not always with strict impartiality on either side. I suggested that the time had come to concentrate less upon argument and more upon making the most effective use of all the forms of traction which we had at our disposal.

I concluded my Presidential Address with these words – 'Let us finally remember that any form of motive power is only a means to an end – and what may be best at a particular time and place may not always and everywhere be the right solution. We have for many years now had more than one means to the common end. Let us use them all for so long as it is profitable to do so. And let us exercise our judgment upon them with strict impartiality having only in view the objective of the most efficient and economical transport service.'

The reasons which ultimately led to the replacement of steam locomotives as the principal form of motive power on our railways are too well known to require detailed repetition here. Suffice it to say that the economic and social conditions which had hitherto enabled steam traction to retain its supremacy were clearly changing. The fuel supply situation had changed from one of abundant good locomotive coal at a reasonable price, to one of declining quality and increasing price, particularly in relation to the cost of oil. It was becoming increasingly difficult to recruit staff for undertaking the heavy and rather dirty jobs inseparable from steam locomotive operation. Demands for reduction in air pollution and a higher standard of cleanliness generally had become much more insistent. The success which had attended the adoption of the newer forms of motive power in other countries, of which we were fully aware, lent strong support to the view that we ought to be able to obtain equally good results. We felt we knew the answers to most of the technical issues involved. But the question to which none of us really knew the answer was the extent to which diesel main line locomotives would be economically justified under our conditions. It was, I thought, likely to be strictly limited to long distance passenger services in which the locomotives would be able to run very high mileages per annum. In this I was wrong, as I soon came to realise.

* R. C. Bond Presidential Address, Journal, *Institution of Locomotive Engineers*, Vol. 43, No. 234, 1953.

Schemes for the replacement of steam locomotives by diesel units for complete areas, worked out in detail as part of our modernisation committee planning, showed that irrespective of the prospects for electrification, there would be few, if any, services on which the greater availability of diesel locomotives of the right type properly used, would not produce an increase in annual mileage per locomotive, compared with steam, sufficient to ensure an adequate return on capital expenditure with substantial savings in the overall costs of operation and maintenance. The ultimate elimination of steam traction on our railways thus virtually became a foregone conclusion.

Notwithstanding the intense interest I had derived from my personal involvement in the building of Ivatt's pioneer diesel locomotive, and should derive from the new diesels, for the general design of which I was now responsible, I did not look forward with pleasure to the end of steam traction. I would, surely, have been less than human had I welcomed without any reservations the part my duty required me to play in bringing about the eclipse of that most human of all mechanical engineering achievements – the steam locomotive – to which the whole of my working life had hitherto been mainly dedicated.

Some time before they were abolished, the Railway Executive had given approval to a number of schemes for using diesel multiple unit trains on secondary routes and branch lines. They were similar in all essentials to the trains on which I had often travelled during family visits to my wife's home in Northern Ireland. They were put into service most successfully during the time that Frank Pope, an old friend from L.M.S. days, and now a Member of the Commission, had been Chairman of the Ulster Transport Board. We and our contractors, with much help and advice from over the Irish Sea, were not long in finding out what had to be done to adapt road equipment to the more arduous conditions of railway operation.

But nothing had been done to follow-up the trials of our seven main line diesel locomotives, some of which had been in service for about five years. Their performance had not been uniformly satisfactory, but we had gained experience which was of great value to us in writing the specifications for the locomotives for the first really large-scale trial of main line diesel traction to which we should soon be committed. It was essential that the whole range of traffic working should be adequately covered. Provision was accordingly made for locomotives in three power groups (later increased to five) with engines ranging in output from 800 horsepower up to 2000 horsepower, the maximum then available in fully developed form. Individual axle loads were specified to be within the range of 16 to 20 tons with total weight, wheel spacing and overall dimensions designed to ensure that the new locomotives would impose no heavier loading on bridges and have as wide a route availability as the steam locomotives they were intended to replace. Maximum speed was specified as 75 and 90 miles per hour for the smaller and larger locomotives respectively.

Though the specifications allowed contractors considerable freedom in regard to detail design, there were some important matters in respect of which we felt it necessary for our requirements to be closely defined. Axle loads of 22·5 tons had been permitted with large diameter coupled wheels of steam locomotives, but there was a considerable volume of evidence from the United States that heavily loaded small diameter wheels of diesel locomotives imposed much higher stresses on the track than had hitherto been experienced. The ratio of axle-load to wheel diameter was considered to be important, and for the rail and tyre steels which we used a value of 4·5, with an absolute maximum axle-load of 20 tons, was imposed by the Chief Civil Engineer, with a view to avoiding rail fractures arising from excessive shear stress in the rail head. We were unable to comply strictly with this requirement in some of the locomotives we wished to order, but I was able to obtain the necessary dispensation from the Civil Engineers on the understanding that the design of any type of locomotive which we might decide to order in large numbers in the future would be modified to ensure strict compliance.

One other matter on which we specified our requirements closely was the design of bogies. Experience of the riding of the Manchester–Sheffield–Wath electric locomotives had shown that for speeds above seventy-five miles per hour the design of heavily loaded four-wheel bogies needed a good deal of further development. In contrast to this, the riding of the six and eight-wheeled bogies under our existing locomotives had been completely satisfactory and they were specified as the pattern for the immediate future. On the structural design of the main underframes and body we had no rigid views. My personal preference was for nose ends, after the American fashion, as affording some increased protection for the crew in the event of a collision, and generally enhancing the appearance of a locomotive. This was not a matter upon which to insist with outside contractors, but in the case of some 2000 h.p. locomotives allocated to Derby to design, I saw to it, that nose ends accommodating some of the auxiliary equipment were provided instead of an ugly flat ended body as first proposed.

Six of our first seven main line diesels had straightforward electric transmission. The seventh had an ingenious form of mechanical drive designed by Colonel L. F. R. Fell, a Rolls-Royce Engineer, by whom Ivatt had been persuaded to give his system a trial. The outcome was the L.M.S. 4-8-4 locomotive. It did good work for a time on the Midland main line, but spent a great deal of time out of service under repair. This locomotive had no less than six diesel engines. Two main engines, each of which was boosted by two diesel driven superchargers, added up to a total of sixty-four cylinders. There were almost as many gear wheels in the transmission system. I did not think much of the chances of this type of drive seriously competing with electric transmission. There did, however, seem to be distinct possibilities in hydraulic and hydro-mechanical transmissions adopted as standard by the German State Railways. The advantages claimed were lower first cost, lighter locomotives for a given power and reduced maintenance costs. We already had some diesel-hydraulic shunting locomotives in service, built by the North British Locomotive Co., which had given promising results. On their own initiative the firm had produced designs for 1,000 and 2,000 horse-power locomotives which would meet our general requirements. I had already seen what a medium powered locomotive built for Mauritius could do on test runs between Edinburgh and Glasgow, which we had arranged for the builders before the locomotives were sent abroad. A critical examination of the N.B. Locomotive Company's proposals, followed by visits to the German Railways and locomotive builders, convinced me that we should have some high powered diesel-hydraulic locomotives, though electric transmission with which we and our manufacturers had most experience, would predominate in our initial orders.

Invitations to tender to our specifications were sent out to all British locomotive building firms, to three in the United States, one in Canada and – why I do not now remember – one in Australia. The response was almost overwhelming. My hard-pressed staff wrestled with mountains of paper analysing and appraising more than 200 separate proposals. There were within the three engine power groups, quite surprising variations in performance characteristics, in power/weight and power/cost ratios, and in axle-loading and total weights. It was no easy matter to decide which among the various alternatives offered would best fill the bill.

The Modernisation Plan envisaged a total of something like 2,500 main line diesels being in service by 1970 – fifteen years ahead. It was from the very beginning our firm intention to standardise as soon as possible on the smallest number of designs and types of locomotives and power equipments which would meet operating needs efficiently. What we had learned from our visits to America and our own experience with shunting locomotives proved that the benefits to be derived from standardisation would be even more important with diesel traction than we knew them to be with steam. But sensible decisions on what to standardise from among the alternatives available required a wide range of experience and time in which to acquire it. Thus as a matter of deliberate policy, the first orders for 174 locomotives included seven makes of engine, eight variants of transmission, and mechanical parts from seven locomotive builders. Breadth of experience was thus assured. Adequate time in which to acquire it was to be secured by imposing a standstill on the placing of further orders for about three years – a proposal which was submitted to and accepted by the Commission. Unfortunately from the point of view of wise engineering decisions based on ascertained facts, the Commission changed their mind – but of this more later!

Quoted delivery periods for the new locomotives varied from fifteen months to two years – by no means too long for all that had to be done in preparation. Fuelling and maintenance facilities had to be installed at Motive Power Depots, for which we, jointly with others concerned, drew up standards for use in all Regions. Some additions to existing equipment were needed at main works, at which the diesels would receive heavy repairs. Footplate and maintenance staff had to be trained. In addition to our own training programmes, the manufacturers ran courses for our staff, which with the reputation and performance of their own products at stake, were as much in their interests as ours. Maintenance schedules had to be prepared and issued. They were necessarily based on recommendations contained in manufacturers' handbooks, which we had almost as much difficulty in getting out of the contractors as we had in extracting from the Regions the essential financial and other details for inclusion in the annual building programmes through which authority for the new locomotives was obtained.

Approval of building programmes in conformity with a timetable designed to allow continuity of production had always involved much persuasion and cajolery of the Regions, even when it was only a straight-forward question of new locomotives in replacement of those to be scrapped. Now, with detailed financial justification of the schemes for which the diesels were to be used rightly insisted upon by the Commission, it was even more difficult obtaining the data from which to compile the programmes on time. We did our best to make life easier for the Regions and ourselves, by issuing a standard code by which alone we at Headquarters could be reasonably certain that Regional schemes would be prepared on a uniform basis in regard to such matters as fuel and maintenance costs.

Other longer term aspects of the motive power revolution also demanded attention. We had to be looking ahead to the end of the three year trial period when further large orders for diesel locomotives would be placed. A small committee, of which I was chairman, was convened to obtain from the Regional General Managers their preliminary assessments of requirements for diesel locomotives, and to reconcile them with available manufacturing capacity in our own shops and contractors' works, bearing in mind other competing demands for diesel shunters and locomotives for the electrification schemes. Concurrently with this work, the Commission called for estimates of the number of new locomotives, steam or alternatively diesel, which the Regions thought they would need to maintain and improve their services during the interim period. As the Commission had already decided that no more steam locomotives for express passenger or suburban services were to be built, had indicated that they would look with extreme disfavour on any proposals to build steam freight locomotives, and had not, at the time the estimates were called for, abandoned the three-year standstill on placing further orders for main line diesels, it was all rather a pointless exercise.

On the technical front it was important that there should be a clear understanding of the factors upon which the future selection and standardisation of diesel locomotives would depend. Accordingly Stewart Cox, who I was indeed fortunate to have as my principal assistant, prepared a comprehensive report on the selection of diesel locomotive types, in which among other things, the traction characteristics of steam and diesel locomotives were compared, and the relative merits of single and multiple unit locomotive operation discussed.

There are three important ways in which the traction characteristics of diesel units differ from those of steam locomotives. A higher proportion of total locomotive weight is available for adhesion in most diesel locomotives, there is no limitation on output imposed by the physical endurance of a member of the crew, and the power available from the diesel engine is virtually independent of locomotive speed. Maximum drawbar pull at low speeds is limited in all locomotives by the weight available for adhesion. Whereas all the wheels of double bogie diesel locomotives can be, and usually are driving wheels, the requirements of safe operation and good riding preclude this for steam locomotives except those intended for relatively low speeds. Below a certain critical speed a steam locomotive cannot use as much steam as the boiler can supply. Thus the power available is limited until a speed is reached at which the cylinders can utilise effectively the full potential output from the boiler.

With the alternative forms of motive power, on the other hand, the full output of the source of power, limited only by adhesion or by the thermal capacity and control characteristics of the transmission equipment, is available throughout the whole speed range. Thus with locomotives of equal maximum sustained horsepower, the diesel has substantially more tractive effort available for acceleration, of which, full advantage can be taken in calculating point-to-point timings. What this means in everyday operation will be appreciated by comparing, for example, an L.M.S. *Class 8 Pacific* and an English Electric Deltic-engined diesel. Each is capable at full maximum output of hauling a 500 ton train at ninety miles per hour on the level. But whereas the steam locomotive would take about seventeen minutes from starting to reach 70 m.p.h. the Deltic can attain this speed in four minutes. And the time taken to run the first twenty miles on level track would be $20\frac{1}{4}$ and $15\frac{3}{4}$ minutes, representing average speeds of $59 \cdot 5$ and $76 \cdot 5$ miles per hour respectively – quite significant differences when it comes to compiling timetables.

Just as it was possible with steam locomotives to resort to double-heading when the power required was beyond the capacity of a single locomotive, so with diesel and electric traction the necessary power at the top end of the scale can be provided by coupling together two or more relatively small units, or by using one locomotive of adequate capacity. I had been brought up on a railway on which double-heading was by no means uncommon on express passenger trains, and on many of the heavier freight services was the normal method of operation.

In L.M.S. days it was some years before powerful locomotives in sufficient numbers were available to enable double heading to become the occasional exception to the obviously sound general rule of one engine per train. But with only one crew involved in either of the two alternative methods of providing the highest powers, the economics of using diesel units of moderate power in multiple would be quite different from those of double heading with steam locomotives. Units of moderate power used in multiple would have the advantage of almost universal route availability. Maximum utilisation would more easily be ensured because of the facility of operating units singly or in multiple as traffic conditions required. Fewer different types of locomotives would be needed with all that this can mean in reduced maintenance costs and less money tied up in spares. One of the Regions put in a report advocating 1200 horse power units only as the correct long term solution to the problem. But it was clear from the quotations we had received for the first batches of locomotives, and also from the ascertained costs of operating the two L.M.S. 1600 h.p. locomotives in tandem, that the overall cost of two or more units would be substantially more than that of one locomotive to produce the same output. For example, one *Type 4* 2300 h.p. locomotive was going to cost £100,000. Two *Type 2* locomotives to produce the same horsepower would cost £150,000. And whereas the weight of one *Type 4* locomotive is about 135 tons, two *Type 2s* would weigh anything between 150 and 200 tons. Operating and maintenance costs, as well as capital charges, become excessive if locomotive capacity is not well-matched to the work to be performed. Thus the reasons which had dictated the need for a number of power groups of steam locomotives were equally valid in the case of diesel traction. The heaviest duties did not in any event require more power than could be built into a single locomotive, and there is no doubt, as subsequent experience has proved, that the selection of a number of power ranges, rather than only one of medium capacity, was the best way of setting about the attainment of minimum costs combined with a high degree of operational flexibility.

A move towards standardisation was forced upon us much earlier than had been planned. Becoming concerned at their declining financial fortunes, and apparently believing that salvation lay in getting rid of steam traction as rapidly as possible the Commission abandoned their policy of a three-year trial period for the new diesel locomotives.

They let it be known that they were prepared to extend and accelerate the introduction of diesel locomotives, as rapidly as production capacity would allow, on the basis of schemes for concentrating diesel traction in areas from which steam would be completely eliminated. This change of policy carried with it two requirements – first, that the number of different designs of locomotive should be reduced to the absolute minimum, and second, that they should be thoroughly reliable and capable of doing the work for which they were intended. The whole purpose of the three year trial period was, of course, to enable these two most desirable objectives to be achieved. But by imposing these requirements and simultaneously denying us the time in which to gain experience on which sound decisions could be based, the Commission compelled themselves to rely on the judgment of their engineers to a geater extent than we ourselves felt altogether wise!

However, decisions had to be reached. Stanley Warder, Chief Electrical Engineer and I were asked to make recommendations on immediate limitation of variety, which, when approved by the Commission would form the basis for discussions with the locomotive and power equipment builders. The ideal arrangement would, of course, have been to have had a single series of mechanical parts, highly standardised as to renewable details, in which would be installed one basic design of power unit and transmission, the output of the engine being determined by the number of cylinders of one standard size. But as no one engine builder had sufficient capacity to produce power units for 500 locomotives, the number the Commission had in mind for inclusion in the 1957 building programme, this simple solution was not a practical proposition. However, we were able to limit our recommendations to two basic designs of engine and mechanical parts for locomotives with electric transmission, for all Regions except the Western, which until the later stages of dieselisation when inter-regional running with the L.M. Region became important, were allowed to confine themselves to two basic designs of diesel-hydraulic locomotives. The 3300 horse power Deltic locomotives for the East Coast main line came later, stemming from trials of a prototype loaned to us by the English Electric Company. The arrangements negotiated with the firm for the maintenance and running of these locomotives by which the company maintained the Deltic engines for an agreed cost per mile were quite novel, and worked very well on the whole, until Doncaster Works took over this work themselves.

I thought, and said at the time, that the British Transport Commission were wrong in abandoning the three-year trial period. Not long ago, when sitting next to my one-time Chairman, Lord Robertson, at a dinner to celebrate his induction as an Honorary Fellow of the Institution of Mechanical Engineers, I reminded him of the views which I had expressed, and which I still held. Lord Robertson remained equally convinced that the Commission were right in requiring us to press ahead as rapidly as they did. It is true, as subsequent events have proved, that the trial period would not have guaranteed us immunity from all the troubles by which we were subsequently beset. It is equally true that less haste in embarking on large scale production would have saved us a large part of the expenditure – well over £1 million – incurred in modifications to a substantial number of locomotives. There were no technical reasons whatever which made it necessary to build diesel locomotives at a rate which outstripped the ability of the Regions to look after them properly. The inevitable consequences were unreliable operation and general dissatisfaction all round, not to mention acrimonious arguments with contractors. A less rapid infusion of new diesel locomotives, though involving the retention in service rather longer than was actually the case, of some of the many hundreds of modern steam locomotives prematurely scrapped, would, in my opinion, have been a great deal better from the point of view of the standard of service to the travelling public. It might even have been better in terms of the overall financial results.

Looking back on it all, the remarkable thing is not that we had so many failures and delays in service, particularly during the winter months when unreliable steam heating boilers were a nightmare, but that this great motive power revolution was accomplished as well as it was. With a little more time it could have been done so much more efficiently!

At the time the decision was taken widely to extend the use of diesel and electric traction, there were nearly 18,000 steam locomotives in service. The new series of standard engines had already reached a total of 649, and 359 more steam locomotives were still to be built on authorised programmes. It was estimated, at the time, that something like 7,000 steam locomotives would still be in service in 1970, fifteen years ahead. There was every reason, therefore, to continue design and development work to ensure that, so long as they remained, steam locomotives would maintain the highest standards of which they were capable. Nothing would be gained, and much lost, by a policy of neglect.

Among the locomotives still to be built were fifty-three *Class 5* 4-6-0s and 181 *Class 9* 2-10-0 heavy freight engines. Good engines though the *Class 5s* were, they could, it seemed to me, be made even better by fitting poppet valve gear. Accordingly, I obtained authority for thirty of them to be so fitted. In spite of the advantages of separate inlet and exhaust valves and rotary operating mechanism, poppet valves had never in the past been able to establish themselves as a significant feature in British locomotive practice. During the last years of the L.M.S. Ivatt had equipped twenty-two *Class 5* 4-6-0s with Caprotti gear, the results from which were most encouraging, so much so that this type of valve gear was fitted to the one B.R. standard *Class 8* 4-6-2 71000 *Duke of Gloucester* built in replacement of the ill-fated *Princess Anne*. Tests with the *Duke of Gloucester* on the plant at Swindon, and out on the road, confirmed the results obtained from the L.M.S. *Class 5s* in which coal consumption was reduced by 5 per cent. Even more important than this saving in coal, experience had shown that the mileage between piston and valve examinations – 30-36,000 in the case of locomotives fitted with piston valves – could be doubled with pop-pet valves. Thus we could confidently expect them to run from one Works repair to the next without any intermediate attention at the sheds. All this was, in my judgment, more than enough to offset the additional cost of £1,750 per locomotive for the poppet valve gear. These thirty engines, one of which, No. 73154, was the last steam locomotive to be built at Derby, turned out very well. There is, I think, little doubt that had steam con-tinued longer, poppet valves would have supplanted piston valves, at any rate on the larger, high mileage locomotives.

Three other projects, one of which came to nothing, concerned the *Class 9* 2-10-0 freight locomotives. A Region to which a large number of these engines had been allocated, made representations that they would be more expensive to operate than their own 2-8-0s which they replaced. To be ready with an alternative in case the decision went that way, I had a scheme for a new standard 2-8-0 prepared. There might well have been a need for some locomotives of this type had steam continued for a few more years – but in the circumstances of the time it was right to continue with the ten-coupled engines already authorised. My 2-8-0 was, I suppose, the last to join the motley collection of 'locomotives that never were'.

I inherited from Riddles a project for equipping ten of the 2-10-0s with Franco-Crosti boilers, and I arranged myself for three others to be fitted with mechanical stokers. The Franco-Crosti boiler was quite conventional in itself except that instead of the hot gases passing out through a chimney in the normal position, they were turned 180° and passed back through a tubular heat exchanger before being ejected by a multiple jet blast-pipe and a chimney just in front of the fireman's side of the cab. The reduction in coal consumption was much less than had been predicted by the Crosti people; and as had so often happened with tubular feed water heaters in the past, the saving in fuel costs was swallowed up by increased maintenance charges. Added to this, and in contrast to the standard 2-10-0s, which were splendid engines to ride on, the Crostis were, as I found out for myself, extremely unpleasant due to smoke and steam from the chimney just outside the cab swirling round the footplate. The feed heater drums were ultimately removed, to the general benefit of the engines and their crews.

One of the most important items in the Modernisation Plan was the intention that all freight wagons should be equipped with power brakes. Great Britain was the only major industrial nation in which the bulk of the freight traffic was still conveyed in loose coupled hand-braked wagons. These had long been an anachronism standing in the way of radical improvement to the freight services as a whole. Express freight trains with all, or some of the vehicles, usually merchandise vans, fitted with vacuum brakes had, of course, been a normal feature of freight operation for many years. These trains ran regularly and safely at speeds up to sixty miles per hour. But virtually all the 600,000 coal and mineral wagons in service at nationalisation were fitted with hand brakes only. Thus the speed of heavy mineral trains was inevitably limited to an average of not much more than fifteen miles per hour.

The benefits which would accrue from having all wagons fitted with power brakes was certainly never in question. It was just one of those desirable projects which, due no doubt to the capital expenditure involved, the group companies had never felt able to authorise. However in 1950 the Railway Executive agreed that tests should be undertaken to determine the relative merits of the vacuum and air brakes for the operation of long and heavy mineral trains at speeds much higher than hitherto.

Two hundred 16 ton coal wagons were fitted with continuous brakes — half of them with the standard vacuum brake, and half with the Westinghouse air brake. Trials, totalling over 11,000 miles mainly between Toton and Brent on the Midland main line, were run with trains hauled by *Class 7 Britannia* 4-6-2s. One locomotive was sufficient for trains of seventy empty wagons, but two were needed to double-head trains of fifty and seventy loaded vehicles.

A committee, of which I was a member, with R. F. Harvey, Chief Operating and Motive Power Officer in the chair, was appointed to analyse the results and recommend which of the two brakes should be adopted as the future standard for British Railways. Attendance at some of the tests was an essential part of our work. Looking back from the footplate of the leading engine at seventy four-wheeled coal wagons snaking along at sixty miles an hour, wondering what sort of ride the guard was having in his van away in the distance, was something not easily forgotten. It soon became clear that the standard vacuum brake was inadequate for trains of seventy loaded mineral wagons. Moreover to achieve acceptable stopping distances with either type of brake it was found necessary to provide means whereby the braking force was increased when the wagons were loaded. Other modifications in design were essential. Screw couplings, improved buffers, and for the larger wagons, roller bearing axleboxes were necessary.

In brief, the tests showed that the air brake met all requirements. The vacuum brake had two serious short-comings – first, the time required to release the brakes was excessive, and second, due to the difference in time between the brake becoming effective at the front and rear of long trains, shocks between adjacent wagons, severe enough to cause broken couplings and sometimes even derailments were liable to occur. While the vacuum brake would be just about adequate for existing operating requirements, it would not do without further development for the longer and heavier trains of the future. For an indefinite time ahead, the load of mineral trains would have to be restricted to about 1200 tons equal to fifty 16 ton wagons. No such restriction would apply if the air brake was chosen. Since, in our opinion nothing should be done to inhibit the operation of much longer and heavier trains, we were unanimous in recommending the adoption of the air brake as the future standard for all rolling stock, passenger and freight, on British Railways.

Before deciding what to do, the Commission asked the Regional General Managers for their comments. All but one of them got cold feet. They were unwilling to face up to the operating problems that would arise during the transition period. These we had foreseen and discussed in our report. Nevertheless in spite of the fact that the chairman of our committee was the Chief Operating Manager himself, the Commission rejected our recommendation. Instead, they decided to continue with the vacuum brake for all locomotive-hauled trains and diesel multiple units. It was a perverse and costly decision, wholly lacking in foresight and imagination. It was, inevitably, reversed ten years later. But in the meantime British Railways were effectively condemned to two brakes instead of one, as all the many hundreds of electric multiple unit vehicles had the air brake anyway.

What, it may be asked, has all this to do with mechanical stokers? The brake tests had shown that if fifty or more loaded coal wagons were to be hauled at speeds up to sixty miles per hour by one locomotive, a combustion rate well beyond the capacity of hand firing would be needed. We already knew from trials with a mechanical stoker which Bulleid had carried out on one of the *Merchant Navy Pacifics*, that mechanical firing was an expensive luxury in terms of coal consumption per unit of work done. But that was not the point in the present context. It was solely to remove the physical limitation of hand firing, and thus to make continuously available the maximum evaporation of which the boiler was capable that we fitted three of the 2-10-0s with mechanical stokers. Tests on the plant at Rugby demonstrated that when the stoker was feeding coal at the maximum rate which the grate could burn, the efficiency of combustion was so much lower than normal that the evaporation was no higher than the maximum short-time rate with hand firing. But the stoker-fired locomotive could maintain this rate continuously, and thus had greater potential capacity. Unfortunately the traffic people were unable to find regular services on which the power of these locomotives could be fully exploited. By the time these engines might have been used on the kind of job for which they were intended the diesels had taken over.

It was not only the new standard locomotive which engaged our attention during these years. We kept the testing departments of Derby, Swindon and Rugby very busy on a programme of work directed to improving the performance of some well known classes of pre-nationalisation locomotives. This work, directed particularly to improving steaming and evaporative capacity, was most successful. Quite simple modifications to chimney and blast pipe proportions paid handsome dividends. Great Western *Kings, Castles* and *Halls*, good though they had always been, were much improved in steaming capacity. The L.M.S. *Jubilee* 4-6-0s, which by successive modifications over the years since they were first built, to boiler tube and front end dimensions, had become good, though never outstandingly good, steamers, had their maximum continuous evaporative capacity increased by 25 per cent to 25,000 lbs per hour. And so it was with other types, notably L.N.E.R. *V2 class* 2-6-2s and Ivatt's *Class 4* 2-6-0s, the steam rates of which were increased from 14,000 to 30,000 lbs and from 9,000 to 17,000 lbs per hour respectively. Locomotives modified in accordance with the test results became generally more reliable throughout their whole operating range, and better able to cope with adverse conditions arising from the general deterioration in the quality of locomotive coal which became increasingly tiresome during the last years of steam.

Important though this work was, it attracted a good deal less publicity than the rebuilding of Bulleid's *Merchant Navy* and *West Country Pacifics*. These remarkable locomotives won for themselves an assured place in the history of British locomotive engineering by their performance with the fastest and heaviest expresses on the Southern system. But they were expensive to operate and maintain. They acquired a reputation entirely consistent with that of their designer. Seldom content with the conventional, however well-proved in service, Bulleid introduced many novel features in these engines, intended to reduce the extent and cost of maintenance. But they had the opposite effect to that intended, and were moreover the direct cause of their coal and water — to say nothing of lubricating oil — consumption being significantly higher than that of other contemporary locomotives of comparable power. The notorious chain-driven valve gear, buried inaccessibly in its oil bath, was the main cause of the unreliability, failures in service and loss of availability from which these engines suffered. Steam distribution was very erratic, leading to low cylinder efficiency and coal and water consumption about 15 per cent higher than that of most other modern locomotives.

The so-called air-smoothed boiler casing was the cause of much trouble and expense in maintenance. It contributed directly to the unique propensity of these engines to catch fire! Oil vapour and leakage from the oil bath tended to saturate the boiler lagging; and it only required some hot cinders from the ashpan hopper doors to start a conflagration which sometimes required the attendance of the local fire brigade. Minor modifications had done little to eliminate the troublesome features of these engines. There was a clear case for major rebuilding, drawings for which were prepared at Brighton in close collaboration with my staff at Marylebone. The reliability of the rebuilt locomotives was improved as much as was their external appearance. Coal and water consumption in everyday service were reduced by about 10 per cent. A day out on the footplate of one of the rebuilt *Merchant Navys* working the Bournemouth Belle confirmed to my satisfaction that the rebuilding was a thoroughly sound job.

Another matter of vital importance – feed water treatment – continued to engage our attention as it had for many years past. Nothing caused more trouble and expense in boiler maintenance than the effects of unsuitable feed water. For as long as I can remember, the chemical treatment of locomotive water supplies was a continuing and tiresome problem, the solution to which seemed so elusive. Some of the railways tackled the matter more thoroughly than others, depending largely on the average quality of the natural water in the parts of the country they served. My first acquaintance with the vagaries of boiler feed water goes back to Midland days when I noticed that some water tanks and columns were painted yellow and others red. Drivers were enjoined to avoid, as far as possible, taking water from red painted supplies.

The L.M.S. first took the question of water treatment seriously in hand in the early nineteen thirties. It was estimated that if water supplies all over the system could be made to approximate in quality to the natural waters north of the Border, savings in boiler maintenance costs could amount to well over £100,000 per annum. Authority was therefore given to provide 158 water treatment plants in England and Wales and to fit 5,500 locomotives with continuous blowdown valves to maintain the concentration of soluble salts below the priming level. High hopes were entertained, but things did not work out quite as expected.

Over the next ten years a substantial improvement in boiler maintenance took place. Firebox condition was no longer the determining factor in bringing locomotives into the Shops. Mileage between heavy boiler repairs increased from 60,000 to over 100,000 miles. Boiler washout periods were extended. The consumption of boiler tubes was much reduced. But the effects of changes in boiler design and repair methods were making themselves felt at the same time. It proved impossible to identify any savings in repair costs as being directly attributable to water treatment. Indeed, taking into account the increased coal consumption and damage to the track formation from the continuous blowdown water, it was arguable that we should have been better off without it! But this could not possibly be right − experience in other countries, notably the United States, conclusively proved otherwise. There was a missing link somewhere.

We persevered, and sharpened up our methods, which had manifestly failed to secure consistently the conditions essential to success, namely

(i) that 100 per cent of the water intended to be treated must in fact be treated;

(ii) that the treatment and blow-down procedures must be fully comprehensive, eliminating scale and sludge and preventing priming and corrosion; and

(iii) that meticulous control over the whole operation must be exercised by daily chemical analysis of the water in the boilers.

An extended trial, under rigid supervision with fifty 2-8-0 standard freight engines and the softening plants between Toton and Brent was put in hand to point the way ahead. The work with which we had become so familiar in L.M.S. days was developed on an all-line basis after nationalisation. On the strength of experience, largely on the Southern Region, with a system of treatment in which chemical dosage of raw water on each individual locomotive was the essential feature, plans were prepared for adopting this system of treatment to all Regions. I am in no doubt that had steam traction continued, the painstaking work done over so many years by our water treatment people would have been crowned with complete success.

Though the greater measure of autonomy conferred on the Regions brought changes in the balance of power and removed from us direct responsibility for day-to-day activities we never allowed ourselves to become cut off from what was going on in the Works and Regional C.M.E. Headquarters. Our responsibilities for the reserved subjects made it no less necessary than in the past that we should get out and about into our own and contractors' Works. It would have been very easy, with the increased number of headquarters committee meetings, particularly as the Modernisation Plan gathered impetus, to have become completely office bound, and remote from the work of the department out in the Regions. Any serious risk of headquarters people becoming out of touch was, however, effectively safeguarded by the inter-regional departmental committee system which had operated efficiently for many years. This was continued unaltered by the Commission, who appointed their chief officers at Marylebone as chairmen of these committees. The remit to my committee was very wide. Anything and everything to do with the work of the department could be placed on the agenda for discussion.

The committees of members, through which the Railway Executive had conducted their affairs were also continued without much alteration. Two new bodies, a Technical Development and Research Committee, and a Research Advisory Council were, however, added. It was certainly very necessary for a clear policy for engineering and scientific research and development to be laid down and implemented, if only to ensure that the work undertaken by the Research Department and the engineering departments was properly co-ordinated and expenditure directed into the most productive channels. But there was, in my opinion, a serious weakness in the constitution of these two new bodies. The first consisted of three Commission Members together with Doctor den Hollander, head of the Netherlands Railways. The Research Advisory Council consisted of four university professors, one of whom was chairman, and three engineers, only one of whom, Sir William Stanier, had any practical railway experience. Neither the Chief Engineers nor the Director of Research were members of either of these two bodies. We – the chief officers – attended all their meetings. We submitted proposals for new projects, the expenditure for which, more often than not, would have to be approved by the Works and Equipment Committee.

We prepared reports on a wide variety of topics, either on our own initiative or at the request of the members. One such concerned the organisation and facilities required for development work, which had hitherto normally been done in design offices and production shops. Two new units, specifically devoted to development, were provided, one for carriage and wagon work at Faverdale and one for diesel locomotive performance at Derby.

The T.D. & R. Committee tended to involve itself with matters of detail which were far better left to the responsible chief engineers, and was vulnerable to approaches from people with particular technical axes to grind. The meetings occasionally provided us with some light entertainment. There was the day when we listened with astonishment to the opinion of one of the members that in no circumstances should the committee give a definite answer to a perfectly simple question as to whether the Ballater branch from Aberdeen should be operated by a diesel multiple unit or an electric battery rail car. One really good development – the liner train – was first suggested at a meeting of this committee by Mr. H. P. Barker, a part-time member of the Commission. To him should go the credit for the original thought from which the network of liner train services has developed.

The Research Advisory Council sometimes involved us in a good deal of unproductive work disposing politely of the more bizarre proposals put up for discussion. Neither the Advisory Council nor the Committee, was, in my view, as effective as they might have been. It would, I think, have been far better had there been one Research and Development Control Committee like that set up by Sir Harold Hartley on the L.M.S. Railway. This consisted of a few distinguished scientists and the chief engineering officers of the railway on whom fell the responsibility for putting into practice any new ideas and who could make their contribution on a basis of equality with the outside members.

The appointment of Dr. Francis den Hollander, head of the Netherlands Railways at the time, to a British Railways Committee was unprecedented. The initial reaction was one of mild resentment at a Dutchman being brought in to tell us how the run our railways. But this soon changed. Francis den Hollander is an engineer and administrator of great distinction. He played a prominent part over a wide field in the industrial and academic life of his country. He brought unrivalled knowledge and experience to bear upon our problems. He was most generous in extending invitations to us to visit Holland to see what had been done in restoring his railway from the devastation of war, and how they had tackled the problems of going over completely to electric and diesel traction. den Hollander had been instrumental in establishing at his headquarters in Utrecht an office of research and experiments (O.R.E.) a subsidiary body of the International Union of Railways, of which British Railways is a member. It was an education in itself to see den Hollander conduct a meeting of railway engineers from all over Europe, switching with the utmost ease and fluency from Dutch into French, German or English as the occasion demanded. Many were the times that I returned from O.R.E. meetings held in such agreeable places – Paris, Rome, Florence, Berne, Stockholm and Amsterdam – thoroughly ashamed of my inadequate French, and determined to do something about it! Alas for my good intentions, my French is as dim as ever!

It was somewhat ironic that on two of the most important matters upon which they had to advise the Commission, the T.D. & R. Committee saw fit to reject the advice den Hollander gave. He was firmly in favour of 1,500 volt direct current rather than 25,000 volt single phase alternative current as the standard system of electrification for our railways. He was equally firm in his advocacy of the air brake in preference to the vacuum brake. As to the first, he was probably wrong from the long term point of view, though 1500 volt direct current would have saved us a great deal of pain and grief with the lines which were first electrified under the Modernisation Plan. As to the second, den Hollander was unquestionably right as later events proved.

Another innovation was the Design Panel. This was a mixed body of

Commission, Railway and London Transport Officers, and outside experts under the chairmanship of a member of the Commission. It was set up to ensure, among other things in the sphere of industrial design, that the external appearance of our new equipment should conform to the best contemporary standards. A most desirable objective – but one which I feel we were quite capable of ensuring for ourselves without the elaborate, and no doubt very costly, artists' impressions commissioned from a number of industrial design consultants. We were meticulous in discussing the exterior appearance of our proposed new locomotives with the industrial design people as we were enjoined to do. But it was an irksome and time wasting business. We did not even achieve a recognisably standard external appearance for our locomotives, which was such an agreeable feature in the old company days. In a matter of this sort in which personal preference plays so large a part, who is to say what is good and what is not good, so long as functional requirements are met as efficiently as possible?

The external colours of coaching stock was another design matter about which our masters seemed unable to make up their minds with any degree of permanency. Having come by way of 'plum and spilt milk' and 'raspberries and cream' to the thoroughly practical maroon for locomotive-hauled main line stock – with two different shades of green for multiple units – they seemed unable to leave well alone. After passing through a phase in which Regions were allowed, if they wished, to paint vehicles for certain named trains in their old company colours – the Western Region painted some coaches in Great Western livery and the L.M. Region some *Duchess Pacifics* in Midland red – the present blue and pale grey colours were chosen for universal use despite the fact that a two-colour scheme of painting is likely to be more expensive in application. Moreover, anaemic colours, unless cleaned efficiently and often, soon look extremely shabby. I was told that maroon, which I favoured, was dull and redolent of the past! I heard one member of the Commission, well known for his down-to-earth commercial approach to all our problems, sum up the situation by saying that so far as he was concerned the outside of coaching stock could be painted black, provided the comfort and amenities for the customers inside the coaches were beyond reproach – a not unreasonable point of view!

With so many millions of pounds worth of new equipment, particularly locomotives and rolling stock to be built in our own Shops, or purchased from contractors over a period of ten years, it was in everybody's interest that the Commission's policy for the division of work between the two alternative sources of supply should be known to all concerned.

As a general rule it had for many years been the general policy of the railway companies to build new locomotives, carriages and wagons in their own Works for the very good reason that they could build them at less cost than they could buy them. Only when requirements were greater than the capacity of our own Shops, as for example during the years immediately following the two World Wars were orders place in any quantity with private firms.

Something over 3,300 locomotives were added to the stock between nationalisation and the time of which I am writing – 1954. Of these only 16 per cent were built by contractors, almost entirely on orders placed by the companies prior to nationalisation. The absence of a steady home market undoubtedly made life difficult for the private firms, dependent as they were on fluctuating overseas orders. I saw this for myself during my time with the Vulcan Foundry. From time to time, when prospects in the export market did not look very favourable, the private firms' trade association came in to the attack demanding a steady share, year by year, of our new locomotive building programme. The contractors argued, that our costs and theirs were not strictly comparable. They claimed that new building in railway shops was subsidised by the repairs which in the locomotive works absorbed about 90 per cent of the total men-hours employed. If, so the argument ran, new construction was charged with its proper share of all fixed and variable overhead expenses it would be found that so far from locomotives built in our own shops costing less than we could buy them for, they were in fact more expensive. Detailed investigations were made into this matter whenever it arose, but so far as any figures which I ever saw are concerned – and I believe I saw them all – the contractors' case did not stand up to examination. It was so obviously in our own interests that we should know precisely what our new building programmes were costing – and with the rigid control in the Works and the costings prepared by the Chief Accountant's Department wholly independent of the Works organisation, we certainly did know – that suggestions to the contrary though we took them seriously, were rather a forlorn hope.

Undoubtedly new building costs in our shops benefited from the fact that we had to have our main Works anyhow for repairs and maintenance. There would have been something seriously wrong if our costs had not been lower than contractors! We should have been rightly criticised if we failed to make full use of the advantages which possession of the Works bestowed upon us. I sometimes gained the impression during discussions with my contractor friends that they thought it almost morally wrong for us to make the most of our resources by combining new construction with the predominating maintenance activities. In pressing for a steady share of the home market the contractors were seeking for themselves what they seemed to object to so much in our case – a combined activity over which to spread their overhead expenses. That the companies, and British Railways after them, were right to manufacture the bulk of their rolling stock, including the mechanical parts of diesel and electric locomotives, in their own Shops, I am in no doubt whatever. It was equally right that we did not provide ourselves with facilities for the design and manufacture of diesel power units, transmissions and electrical equipment which were properly the province of existing contracting firms.

Although it was usual in railway organisations for raw materials and the myriad items of general and engineering stores to be purchased, and held in stock by a department quite independent of the users, all that went to the letting and management of contracts for rolling stock and general engineering plant was one of the functions of the responsible engineering department. This had always worked efficiently. But, as with so much else at the time, this seemed to make it almost certain that some sort of change would be imposed. A contracts officer was appointed in the Supplies organisation with responsibility for tender lists, conditions of contract and codes of practice for universal application. It relieved us of quite a lot of work, but divided between two departments work that could better be done by one. There was also appointed to the General Staff a Supplies and Production Adviser, who, coming from outside the service, must have found it difficult to avoid treading on the toes of the Technical Adviser. This appointment did not last long. It was abolished after about two years.

The ultimate elimination of steam traction would obviously involve radical changes in the plant, equipment and capacity at the main works. Equally radical changes would be involved in day-to-day maintenance of motive power and electric traction depots. While it did not necessarily follow that changes in departmental responsibilities would be needed, it could not be accepted without investigation that traditional arrangements should continue unaltered. Both matters were sufficiently important for the Mechanical Engineering Committee to take the initiative and report upon them before being asked to do so by the General Staff. We dealt with the problems of day-to-day maintenance first.

The existing organisation for running repairs, mileage examinations and servicing of steam and electric locomotives was quite straightforward. The work was the responsibility of the Motive Power Department and the C.M. and E.E. Department respectively. Diesel locomotives and multiple units were the joint responsibility of both departments. Electrical items on both were looked after by outdoor machinery electricians made available as required. With rapidly increasing numbers of diesels coming into service, this was an arrangement which might well be called in question.

As the Motive Power Department had no electricians of their own there were some members of my Committee who felt that it was desirable to keep all electrical maintenance firmly in C.M.E. hands. But in a note setting out the alternatives, I felt bound to point out that as men trained in our Works had always formed the backbone of the motive power technical staff, it would be difficult to argue convincingly against electricians trained in our Works being transferred to the Motive Power Department if, on grounds of general policy, this seemed the right course to recommend. We were however, overtaken by events.

Before my Committee was ready to report, I was required to submit my own views on this thorny question to the General Staff. It was quite clear to me that as steam declined in importance, some changes in departmental responsibilities would become essential. If existing arrangements continued unaltered, there would be the virtual certainty that, in areas to be partially electrified two parallel organisations for day-to-day maintenance would persist. New shops for electric multiple units might be proposed by the C.M. and E.E. Department in the same area as the Motive Power Department might be planning separate facilities for diesel locomotives and multiple units. A combined establishment under one department would almost certainly be a far more sensible solution. Everything pointed to the conclusion that responsibility for running maintenance of all forms of motive power should rest with one department, with all staff working in the depots under the direct control of the man in charge.

There were broadly three alternatives. The Motive Power Department could be absorbed either by the Chief Mechanical and Electrical Engineer's Department, or by the Traffic Operating Department. Or it could continue as a separate department in its own right. The first alternative would be entirely satisfactory from the maintenance point of view; the second less so. In the third alternative the Motive Power Department would be given responsibility for the day-to-day maintenance – mechanical and electrical – of all forms of motive power. As all other motive power functions, such as provision of power, rostering of staff and clearing the line after mishaps, had to continue as before, this – the third alternative – was the one which I recommended.

But other views prevailed. After consulting the Regional General Managers, the Commission decided that the Motive Power Department should lose its separate identity and be absorbed wholly by the Operating Department, the change taking place over an indeterminate time, depending on the spread of the new forms of traction. The men in charge at the depots would be held responsible for maintenance being done in accordance with the standards prescribed by the Chief Mechanical and Electrical Engineers who were acknowledged to have an overall responsibility for the serviceability of all locomotives, rolling stock and outdoor machinery. This was all right so far as it went, but it was a half-baked arrangement with dual responsibility, hitherto confined to the Regional Motive Power Superintendents themselves, permeating into every maintenance depot. The Commission decided at the same time that the

Carriage and Wagon Engineers should once more become an integral part of the Mechanical and Electrical Engineering Department – a thoroughly sensible step in the right direction. But what was given with one hand was taken away with the other, by a further decision to transfer control of out-door carriage and wagon maintenance from the C.M.E. to the Operating Department!

As to the main Works, we prepared a comprehensive report outlining the anticipated effect of the Modernisation Plan upon them. It had always been an important part – perhaps the most important part – of a Chief Mechanical Engineer's responsibilities to secure by every means available that his Main Workshops were as efficient as they could be in organisation, equipment and production methods.

It was no less important that their capacity should be properly related to the output likely to be needed within the foreseeable future. Any major change in the size or character of the railway of which the Workshops are a vital part, gives rise to the need for a critical review of workshop capacity. Such changes occurred at the amalgamations of 1923, and again at nationalisation. It is essential to ensure that when operated as component parts of one organisation, no longer as previously under separate ownership, that the Works will be suitably adapted to the new conditions. By rationalisation of activities, concentration of manufacture, retention of some Works at full capacity, and closure of others, substantial economies and greater efficiency were always obtainable.

Thus our report was just one more stage in a continuing process of investigation with which the members of my committee were thoroughly familiar. It was, however, rather more difficult than usual because of the radical changes in activities which would result from the progressive displacement of steam traction. We had, of course, to make a number of assumptions. The first was that the Plan would be completed, without substantial alteration within the specified period of fifteen years. This was perhaps a little optimistic! The second assumption – following from the first, was that the stock to be maintained on completion of the Plan in 1970, compared with that at the time we made our report, would be as tabulated opposite.

Present and Ultimate Stock Position

Rolling Stock	Existing 1955	New building	To be withdrawn	Ultimate 1970
Locomotives				
Steam	18,000	330	10,830	7,500
Electric	70	1,100	—	1,170
Diesel – Main Line	7	2,500	—	2,507
Diesel – Shunting	450	1,650	—	2,100
Total	18,527	5,580	10,830	13,277
Passenger Vehicles				
Locomotive hauled	37,200	13,700	27,770	23,200
Multiple unit, Electric	4,800	6,000	2,400	8,400
Multiple unit, Diesel	300	4,300	—	4,600
Total	42,300	24,000	30,100	36,200
Non passenger vehicles				
Bogie	4,500	2,400	1,900	5,000
Non-bogie	11,500	4,600	5,100	11,000
Total	16,000	7,000	7,000	16,000

Wagons	Existing 1955	New building	To be withdrawn	Ultimate 1974
Open Merchandise	309,700			200,000
Covered Merchandise	148,000			140,000
Mineral	606,900			351,000
Special	2,300	297,000	686,500	2,000
Cattle	12,600			9,000
Steel Carrying	47,100			40,000
Brake Vans	14,900			10,000
Total	1,141,500	297,000	686,500	752,000

It is specially interesting to notice that no less than 7,500 steam locomotives were expected to be still in service by 1970. They had all gone before the end of 1968!

There were at the time our report was written seventeen Locomotive and twenty-one Carriage and Wagon Main Works, employing 69,000 men. The broad conclusions which we reached were that while there would be little change in the activities and volume of output from the Carriage and Wagon Shops – indeed to cope with the fitting of continuous brakes to wagons additional staff would probably be required – there would be a substantial reduction in locomotive repairs making it possible to close four main and six subsidiary Works over a period of about seven years. The Works we recommended for closure were as set out on the next page.

Main Works

Ashford	}	Southern Region
Brighton		
Gorton	}	Eastern Region
Stratford		

Subsidiary Works

Barry	}	Western Region
Newton Abbott		
Bow	}	London Midland Region
Rugby		
Gateshead		North Eastern Region
Inverness		Scottish Region

Though it was acknowledged to be a comprehensive document covering fifteen years up to 1970, our report was not formally submitted to the Commission. Before this could be done, another report on diesel and electric traction and the passenger services of the future proposed, if my memory serves me right, by the Traffic Officers at Headquarters, attempted to look ahead as far as 1990 — 1990 no less — thirty-three years ahead! Not until then it was assumed, would steam be finally displaced. It was decided that any plan for the redeployment of workshops facilities would need to take account of this longer term traction policy. Another report was therefore compiled by a committee of the General Staff, which in fact looked only very tentatively beyond 1968! We had at least gone firmly to 1970! This report was in its turn completely superceded by the 1962 Workshops Plan. The crystal ball into which we were all gazing during these years was not very reliable!

Though the developments in diesel traction occupied most of our time, the claims of gas turbines as a promising alternative were not neglected. It was entirely in character with their long established tradition of being rather different from everybody else that, in their initial trials of alternative forms of motive power for heavy main line service, the Great Western should choose gas turbine propulsion in preference to the general trend towards diesel engines. This was fortunate, as we inherited thereby much valuable experience from two gas turbine locomotives with electric transmission. One was supplied by the Swiss firm of Brown-Boveri, and one by Metropolitan-Vickers. Neither was sufficiently successful to justify further locomotives being built. Nevertheless it was felt in some quarters that gas turbines should be able to compete with diesels in rail traction.

Thus, we became associated with a project, sponsored by the Ministry of Fuel and Power, for a gas-turbine locomotive to burn pulverised coal. The locomotive was to be built by the North British Locomotive Company, the power unit a gas turbine of 1,750 h.p. being supplied by Messrs. C. A. Parsons. Serious difficulties were encountered with some of the main components when undergoing tests in the works to such an extent that the locomotive was never completed. Equally discouraging was a design study, to which we contributed much of the basic data from the railway point of view, undertaken by a firm of consulting engineers for 1500 h.p. and 3000 h.p. oil-fired locomotives. A sufficiently good case could not be made to justify building any locomotives. Disappointing though this all was, our association with these projects, and the visits to contractors' works which this involved taught us a great deal.

A third project, undertaken by the English Electric Company was successful to the extent that a prototype locomotive was actually built and completed some thousands of miles of trial running over our main lines. This locomotive, known as *GT3*, was built by the Vulcan Foundry, which by then had become part of the English Electric empire. The engineer in charge of this farsighted project was John Hughes, expert in gas turbine design and very knowledgable on rail traction matters. He had, apparently, found my paper on Sir William Stanier's turbine locomotive No. 6202 of some interest in relation to his new design. As it was proposed to use mechanical transmission and a final drive similar to that on 6202, Hughes came to obtain our views on the general design of *GT3*. The alternatives were a double-bogie locomotive following contemporary diesel and electric practice, or one with a rigid coupled wheel base and main frames in accordance with conventional steam locomotive design.

The thinking behind this project was that, with a suitable turbine cycle and simple transmission, the advantages of gas turbines in terms of power/weight ratio, ability to burn low grade fuel, ease of maintenance and high availability could outweigh the disadvantage inherent in all gas turbines of high fuel consumption at less than full load. If this could be demonstrated in service gas turbine locomotives could become serious competitors to diesels. Thus it was important to avoid any complications in the general design irrelevant to the objective.

Of the two alternatives, it seemed to me preferable to have one final drive mounted direct on one coupled axle in a rigid wheelbase, rather than a duplex drive to each of two bogies, with the attendant complications of cardan shafts and bevel drives on a number of axles. I expressed my views accordingly. The locomotive as built was a handsome 4-6-0 with a separate corridor tender carrying fuel and a train heating boiler.

The main components of *GT3* were subjected to bench tests before assembly. After erection, but before the external casings were fitted, the locomotive underwent a comprehensive series of power and efficiency tests on the Locomotive Testing Plant at Rugby. Thereafter it ran several thousands of miles with special passenger trains at express timings over London Midland Region main lines, culminating in a series of runs between Crewe and Carlisle. I rode on the footplate and drove this splendid locomotive on one of these test trips. It rode very well but had characteristics all its own. There was a slightly disconcerting delay in response to movements of the regulator controlling the rate of fuel injection and thus the speed and output of the power turbine. This I believe, is typical of jet aero-engines but was quite unlike anything I had previously experienced on a locomotive.

Though *GT3* performed very well on the trial runs some further development was needed to ensure a sufficient degree of reliability for revenue earning service. Unfortunately the necessary funds were not forthcoming, and this locomotive went the way of so many imaginative projects in earlier years.

Following the admirable policy of the group companies of keeping themselves fully informed of contemporary practice on American railroads by visits of senior officers, the B.T.C. sent a party of twelve of us to the United States in the spring of 1957. I was able once again to indulge my love of the sea in all its moods, crossing the North Atlantic in the civilised luxury which only the Cunard 'Queens' could provide – out on the *Queen Mary* and home on the *Queen Elizabeth*.

This visit to America was for me, at the time, a much needed complete change of scene. My wife had died after a short illness, two months earlier. The bottom was knocked out of everything that made life worth living. No words of mine can pay adequate tribute to all that Jean had meant to me and our two children for close on twenty-five years. Four moves and seven houses, to say nothing of two periods in lodgings, during the first nine years of married life, is more than enough to test the devotion of any woman. But my wife never wavered in the unfailing support she gave me in everything, particularly in all that it takes to be a railwayman's wife.

The plans for the party, prepared before our arrival in New York by the Association of American Railroads, provided for separate tours covering each of four subjects on which information was required. They were:

 (i) Coaching stock design,
 (ii) Freight vehicles, containers and Road/Rail problems,
 (iii) Freight operation, and
 (iv) Diesel Motive Power.

My assignment was Diesel Motive Power, on which I was accompanied by R. C. S. Low. We knew each other well from Crewe days. He was at the time, diesel assistant at Derby, and, as always, a cheerful companion and most willing helper. In the course of four weeks of hard work, with scarcely a minute to ourselves, we visited the headquarters, locomotive works and motive power depots of eight railroads, two research establishments and the Le Grange Works of the Electro-motive division of General Motors near Chicago. We travelled nearly 9,000 miles by rail.

I did take one weekend off, travelling east to Boston and thence in a Budd railcar to Woods Hole en route to visit cousins living on Martha's Vineyard, an island of unspoilt beauty a few miles off the Massachusets coast. Deep sea fishing and sailing are the principal diversions for the fortunate residents of this delectable refuge from the turmoil of New York and Boston.

Three of the eight railroads we visited, the Union Pacific, the Western Pacific and the Milwaukee, had been selected for special study before our arrival. The choice could not have been better from my point of view. It gave me the opportunity, for the first time, of crossing the Rockies, through the Moffat tunnel 9,000 feet above sea level, and satisfying a long felt desire to visit California, particularly San Francisco, surely one of the most fascinating cities in the world.

Though rail passenger revenue was suffering severely from competition from air lines, motor coaches and private cars, many long distance prestige trains still enlivened the American railroad scene. With their vista-dome cars, superb catering and sleeping accommodation they provided a standard of amenity much superior to even the best of our trains at home – and they were very good. The two best in which we travelled were the California *Zephyr* between Omaha and Oakland and the Santa Fé *Super-Chief* from Los Angeles to Chicago. The first was operated jointly by three Companies – Chicago, Burlington & Quincy, Denver and Rio Grande, and the Western Pacific; the second by the Atchison, Topeka and Santa Fé alone. Going west, locomotives were changed at company boundaries – but on the eastbound journey, one four-unit 6000 h.p. locomotive hauled the fourteen-car train, weighing 925 tons, over 2,226 miles between Los Angeles and Chicago. The overall average speed including all stops – for fuelling, servicing, etc. – was 56·5 miles per hour.

On both these journeys I spent some time in the cab of the General Motors locomotives – with an adequate supply of cigars for the engineer and his mate. I rode a stretch between Winslow in Arizona and Gallup, New Mexico, 129 miles rising 1,860 feet at an average speed of seventy-two miles per hour, and a maximum of eighty-five. The locomotive performance was most impressive, and a demonstration of main line diesel traction at its best.

While in 1947 all the American and Canadian railway officers with whom I discussed the question agreed that the number of diesel locomotives in North America would grow at an increasing rate, none was prepared to forecast what the ultimate relationship between the alternative forms of motive power was likely to be. In both countries there were strongly held views that gas turbine locomotives would present a serious challenge. Indeed, as I record in an earlier chapter, both Canadian railroads hoped that the trend of development for main line services would be from steam direct to gas turbine propulsion. The situation over the intervening ten years had turned out very differently, as will be appreciated from the table overleaf.

	1947	1st January 1957
Number of diesel units in service	5,772	26,007
Percentage of traffic handled by diesel locomotives:		
Passenger	27·23%	91·02%
Freight	12·37%	88·49%
Shunting	31·75%	93·24%
Number of steam locomotives in service	35,108	3,690

Diesel traction had won the day. Nevertheless interest in possible alternatives had not entirely evaporated. There were twenty-five 4,500 h.p. oil-fired gas turbine locomotives on the Union Pacific, and work was still in progress at the Dunkirk laboratory of the Locomotive Development Committee of the Bituminous Coal Research organisation on a coal-fired gas turbine unit.

The Union Pacific locomotives mounted on four four-wheeled bogies and coupled to a 24,000 gallon tender were running 10,000 miles per month hauling 5,000 ton freight trains. We were able to inspect some of these monsters during our stay at Omaha. Their owners were sufficiently satisfied with their performance to order thirty more 8,500 h.p. locomotives.

The coal-fired project, which I had seen in its early stages in 1947, had 3,000 hours of running to its credit on test. On this occasion we saw the set start up on oil, switch over to coal and develop 2,500 horse power. Most of the early problems with combustion of the pulverised coal and separation of ash had been largely overcome. Unfortunately I fear no locomotive was ever built.

Summing up the results of our visit, we learnt much of immediate value in establishing diesel traction as a thoroughly reliable form of motive power. It was reassuring to find that the principles upon which we were working for operation and maintenance were entirely sound as judged by American experience. We certainly needed to revise the periods laid down for shop repairs. The United States railroads were obtaining much higher mileages between heavy repairs than we had then achieved. Much emphasis was laid on keeping locomotives constantly in service. To achieve minimum time in shops, full use was made of spare power units, bogies and traction motors, all of which were changed, when necessary, at classified repairs and locomotive units were in shops for only five to eight working days – sometimes less. There were no reasons why we should not do equally well.

and 53. An ingenious idea – which didn't work. An attempt to clear snow drifts on the High Peak line with jet aero-engines.

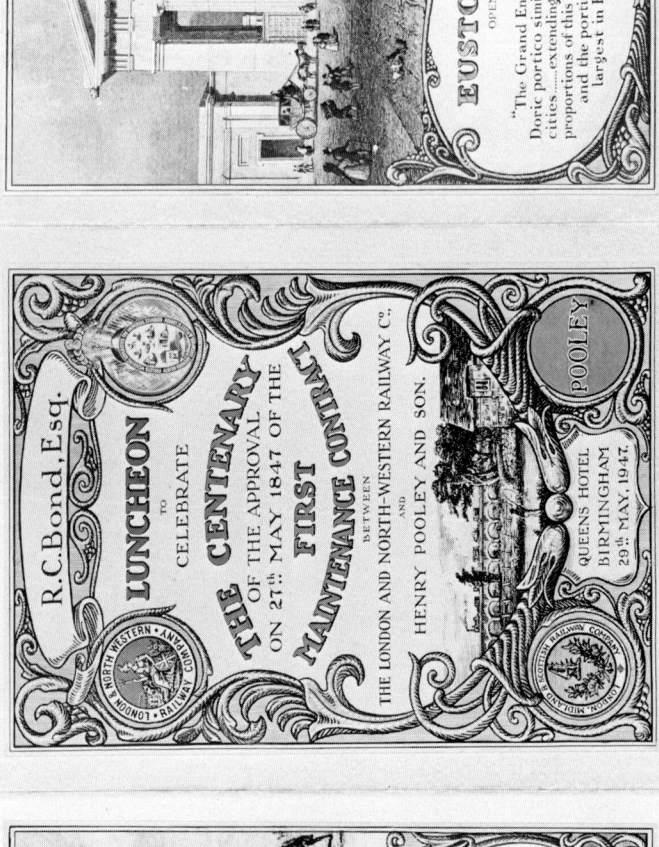

EUSTON STATION.
OPENED 20ᵗʰ JULY 1837.

"The Grand Entrance is formed of a majestic Doric portico similar to the Propylea of the Greek cities ......extending about 300 feet in width. ...The proportions of this splendid erection are gigantic, and the portico may be considered the largest in Europe if not in the world."

R.C.Bond, Esq.

LUNCHEON
TO
CELEBRATE

THE CENTENARY
OF THE APPROVAL
ON 27ᵗʰ MAY 1847 OF THE

FIRST
MAINTENANCE CONTRACT
BETWEEN
THE LONDON AND NORTH-WESTERN RAILWAY Cº.
AND
HENRY POOLEY AND SON.

POOLEY

QUEENS HOTEL
BIRMINGHAM
29ᵗʰ MAY 1947.

BIRMINGHAM STATION.
OPENED 9ᵗʰ APRIL 1838.

"The London and Birmingham Railway had a dignified terminus at each end. The station at Birmingham reflected the Euston portico in a minor key."

54. Souvenir of the Centenary of the first maintenance contract with Messrs. Henry Pooley and Son.

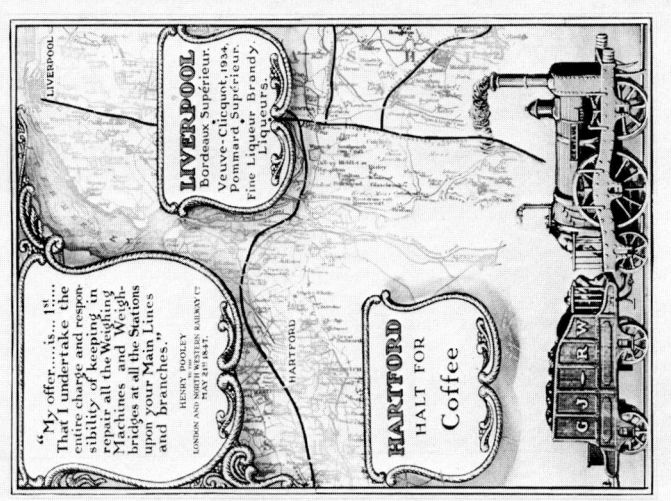

LIVERPOOL

Bordeaux Supérieur.
Veuve-Clicquot, 1934.
Pommard Supérieur.
Fine Liqueur Brandy
Liqueurs.

"My offer....is....!".... That I undertake the entire charge and responsibility of keeping in repair all the Weighing Machines and Weigh-bridges at all the Stations upon your Main Lines and branches."

HENRY POOLEY
to
LONDON AND NORTH WESTERN RAILWAY Co
MAY 21st 1847.

HARTFORD
HALT FOR
Coffee

A MAP OF THE
GRAND JUNCTION RAILWAY
PUBLISHED BY EC&W OSBORNE IN THE YEAR 1840.

STAFFORD
Grilled Salmon,
Sauce Remoulade,
New Peas,
New Potatoes.

CREWE
Fresh
Strawberry Melba
or
Wafers,
Cheese and Biscuits.

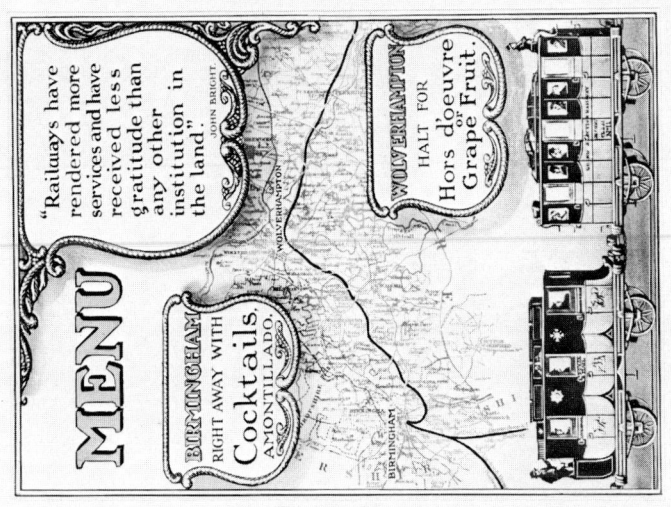

"Railways have rendered more services and have received less gratitude than any other institution in the land."
JOHN BRIGHT

MENU

BIRMINGHAM
RIGHT AWAY WITH
Cocktails.
AMONTILLADO.

WOLVERHAMPTON
HALT FOR
Hors d'oeuvre
or
Grape Fruit.

It was on the Great Eastern that the *Britannias* did some of their best work. No. 70030 *William Wordsworth* approaching Colchester on Norwich–Liverpool St. express.

An unusual view of a *Britannia* approaching Ipswich.

57. Robert Riddles.

One of the *Class 9* 2–10–0 fitted with Crosti Boiler.

59. The most important part of the Modernisation Plan – the replacement of steam by diesel and electric traction. Euston–Glasgow express approaching Penrith hauled by *Type 40* Diesel-Electric locomotive.

60. The West Coast Main Line – the final phase. Electric traction over Beattock Summit.

61. Diesels at Kyle of Lochalsh – the Gateway to Skye.

62. Motive Power Depot – New Style. Laira, Plymouth.

63 and 64. Crewe Erecting Shop – Yesterday and Today.

65. 2300 H.P. Diesel-Electric locomotive designed and built at Derby.

66. 2000 H.P. Diesel-Hydraulic locomotive built by N.B. Locomotive Co.

67. B.R. Standard *Class 5* 4–6–0 fitted with Caprotti valve gear.

68. Cab of B.R. Standard 2–10–0 fitted with mechanical stoker.   70.   25,000 volt flashover to a locomotive chim

69. Rebuilt *Merchant Navy* 4–6–2 No. 35003 *Royal Mail* on West of England express.

71. English-Electric Gas Turbine locomotive *GT3* under construction at the Vulcan Foundry. The designer, J.O.P. Hughes and the author on the locomotive.

72. *GT3* on special test train passing Shap Summit.

73. Refuelling Denver and Rio Grande triple unit diesel hauling the *California Zephyr* en route to Oakland, California.

74. Going East on the Santa Fe *Super-Chief* from Los Angeles to Chicago.

75 and 76. En route from Melbourne to Sydney. Steam and Diesel Motive
Power, New South Wales Government Railways.

77. The Duke of Edinbu:
watched by Sir Brian Rober
unveils the nameplate of *War*
class diesel hydraulic locom
Magpie.

78. Frances.

79. An off-duty social occasi
Frances and the author.

80. The President casts an an
glance at his notes. The Ar
Dinner of the Institutio
Mechanical Engineers 1963

81. The Royal visit to Wolve
Carriage Works.

82. Carriage and Wagon work at Crewe.

83. L.N.E.R. *A4 Pacific, Bittern* No. 60019 on which the author had his last trip on a steam locomotive in revenue earning service.

84. Large or small – the absorbing interest persists!

anything greater rather than less – but now they were shared between headquarters and the Regions; and the authority to discharge them was less readily accorded than before.

With the abolition of functional management from the top, the C.M.E. at headquarters was no longer directly responsible for the day-to-day work out in the Regions. But as chairman of the Mechanical Engineering Committee he was in fact much concerned with what went on in the Regions. And it was only in regard to day-to-day matters that responsibility was delegated down the line. The Commission took firmly to themselves through their chief officers at Marylebone, the same direct control of the important all-line matters – the reserved subjects – as the Railway Executive had done. Thus, compared with company days, the Regional C.M.E.s were shorn of that part of their predecessors' responsibility which made them known among the engineering profession – and indeed to a wider public – the design of the locomotives which ran on their railway. In regard to the reserved subjects the Regional C.M.E.s received their instructions from headquarters. It mattered not at all, in practice, that these were passed to them through their General Manager. They were effectively decided, on behalf of the Commission, by their professional colleague at Marylebone, whose appointment was senior to their own.

Although the chief officers of the B.R. Central Staff held the senior professional appointment in their own spheres of activity they worked under the general supervision of a General Staff adviser. All this added up to the fact that neither the Chief Mechanical Engineer at headquarters nor those in the Regions had the same unfettered freedom of decision in purely technical matters enjoyed by the great men of the past.

Nevertheless, in spite of these constraints, I had derived great satisfaction from my five years in charge of the department at headquarters. They were years of heavy responsibility during which far-reaching changes in railway engineering, which had been developing over a long time, established the pattern for many years ahead. Though, looking back on it all, the demands of the Modernisation Plan inevitably had a dominating influence on our work, yet the normal and familiar routine of departmental activity could not be pushed aside. Upon it depended everything that made up our contribution to the running of the railway. Locomotive repair programmes and expenditure budgets from the Regions had to be assembled, critically examined, and probably cut, before final approval was obtained. The important thing, for the avoidance of trouble in future years, was to ensure that output would always be sufficient for the miles made good by heavy repairs and condemnations to be at least equal to the miles run by the locomotives in any year. A close watch on output and expenditure in relation to budget had, as always, to be maintained. Meetings with Trade Union officials, many of whom I knew well from earlier days – indeed all that is now embraced by the term Industrial Relations, were no less demanding of time, tact and patience, often sorely tried, than before the launching of the Plan.

Year by year the Regional C.M.E.s strove with undiminished zeal to increase the miles run between consecutive heavy repairs, to maintain the percentage of locomotives under and awaiting repairs in the Works at no more than 5 per cent of the total stock, and by constant exhortation to reduce the days on Works to the lowest possible level. And without too much chivvying from my staff they did their best to produce the information we needed to compile the all-line locomotive building programmes in time to avoid any break in production from the Works. It was all intensely rewarding and I was sorry in many ways to relinquish my appointment as Chief Mechanical Engineer, and with it the chairmanship of the Mechanical Engineering Committee.

CHAPTER TWELVE

The Final Ten Years

1958–1968

Technical Adviser, British Transport Commission and General Manager, B.R. Workshops

THE GENERAL STAFF of the British Transport Commission, of which I now found myself a member, was something quite new in the sphere of railway organisation. The nearest equivalent of which I had any previous experience was, I think, the Executive Committee of the L.M.S. Railway. Before Sir Josiah Stamp, as he then was, became Chairman of the Board and President of the Executive in 1927, the L.M.S., like the other three group companies, had been run by a General Manager responsible to the Board of Directors. The chief officers reported direct to the General Manager, though major proposals involving expenditure above a certain limit, were submitted by the chief officers, after approval by the General Manager, to a committee of Directors, and by them to the Board.

Under Stamp's regime general management became the responsibility of an Executive Committee, over which he himself presided. He was assisted by three, sometimes four, vice-presidents and two or three other officers. The Commission Members, with non-functional responsibilities, may be regarded as the counterparts of the old directors; and the General Staff as very roughly equivalent to the L.M.S. Executive Committee, the vice-presidents of which, were interposed between the chief officers and the Board of Directors. The vice-presidents watched over and co-ordinated the activities of a number of related departments. They approved chief officers' submissions to their directors committees. The members of the General Staff, interposed between the Commission and the chief officers of the British Railways Central Staff, exercised a similar co-ordinating and supervisory function over the departments at Headquarters. Submissions from the B.R. Central Staff had to be accompanied by a General Staff paper of comment or approval.

The analogy between the General Staff of the British Transport Commission and the L.M.S. Executive Committee is admittedly fairly broad, but not, I think, too far-fetched. There were, of course, important differences between the two bodies. Chief among them was that Lord Stamp, and later Sir William Wood, who presided over the Executive, were themselves the chief executive of the L.M.S. Railway. The Secretary-General of the B.T.C., who took the chair at our meetings was certainly not the chief executive of British Railways. Sir Brian Robertson himself, was our chief executive. As its name implied, the Executive Committee of the L.M.S. was executive in the full sense of the term. The General Staff of the Commission was certainly not executive in quite the same way. We were given the title of Adviser, though in commenting on this, the Chairman himself acknowledged that we had executive duties as well as those of an advisory character. It was also explained that our duties extended over the whole of the Commission's undertaking – hence the choice of the title General Staff. We were the Transport – not only railway – staff of the Commission.

The work of the General Staff was regarded as a team effort. We met regularly every Monday morning and spent a good deal of time polishing up the papers for the next Commission meeting. Memoranda to the Commission came anonymously from the General Staff as a whole, whoever may have done the actual drafting. All were subjected to meticulous examination and much re-drafting. This was, I found, a tedious business which accomplished little else except saying the same thing is slightly different words! However, we got through a lot of business and worked together very harmoniously with our chairman, Major-General Wansbrough-Jones 'primus inter pares'. He was a friend of many years standing who, when I was serving my time at Derby, had come as a Royal Engineers subaltern to the Locomotive Works for a spell of railway training. He was a man of abounding energy and unfailing good humour in dealing with his sometimes headstrong colleagues.

The duties of the members of the General Staff were set out in precise detail in what was known throughout the service as the Grey Book. Mine were to co-ordinate technical opinion and advice tendered to the Commission, and to ensure that all technical matters which came before the Commission or their committees had received the consideration appropriate to their importance. I was required to guide technical development with the assistance of the chief technical and research officers of all activities, to co-ordinate technical practices, and to advise on the organisation of the technical and research departments. These were wide-ranging responsibilities, to which were added the duty of studying the minutes of the technical departmental committees, and advising the Commission Members concerning their approval or otherwise.

The four Chief Engineers at Headquarters worked under the general supervision of the Technical Adviser and reported to him. Thus I became directly concerned with the larger issues involved in all the engineering developments of the nationalised transport undertakings. If for no other reason, the size of British Railways in relation to the other constituents of the Commission, and the capital expenditure schemes of the Modernisation Plan made it inevitable that most of our time was taken up with railway matters. Obviously, it was in regard to railway problems that I could hope to make a more useful contribution than, say, to specialised aspects of road transport, docks, inland waterways or hotels. Nevertheless there were many interesting developments, notably in regard to London Transport and the manufacturing and maintenance facilities of the road services upon which one was required to give advice.

The adjustments involved in changing from running a department to influencing the heads of a number of departments as to the way in which they should go, were, at first, neither easy nor entirely welcome. It is one thing running a department with a first-rate staff, asking people to do things which, if necessary, one can instruct them to do. It is quite another matter having to gain points by argument and persuasion rather than by direct action. I prefer the latter; though in advising on mechanical engineering matters, for which I had previously been personally responsible, I had, sometimes, to remind myself that I was no longer in charge of the Chief Mechanical Engineer's Department at Headquarters!

There were, however, the compensations of a much wider sphere of influence. In all railway engineering projects of importance, civil, mechanical and electrical engineering are inevitably jointly concerned. Nevertheless there are many matters essentially the province of one department alone – such, for example, as flat-bottomed rails and continuous welded track; and the detailed design of modern signalling installations in which continuous track circuits and a few highly complex signal boxes with hundreds of relays and push-button panel control points and colour light signals over long stretches of main line routes.

As a railwayman, I was always intensely interested in these developments. But they had hitherto been outside my own departmental responsibilities. Now, however, I took a hand, with the chief engineer concerned, in advising the Commission as to decisions which should be taken.

With large civil engineering and signalling projects taking shape in many parts of the country, tours of inspection with the Works and Equipment Committee became a regular and most agreeable part of my duties. We travelled with, and enjoyed the hospitality of, the Regional General Managers in their private saloons hooked on to the rear of express trains to a convenient detaching point, and thence as a 'special' to the site of the new works. There is no better way of seeing the country and getting to know railway geography in all its ramifications. These journeys with the men actually in charge of the job, many of them old friends, were a welcome escape from the relative remoteness of headquarters, out on to the ground in close contact with all that goes on, day in and day out, in the running of a large railway system. Therein lies the true essence and fascination of a railwayman's life.

The electrification schemes were also making good progress to completion. Trial running on the London Midland, Eastern and Scottish Regions was building up mileage and experience with the new alternating current locomotives and multiple unit trains. Everything seemed to be going well. There were certainly no warnings of the troubles by which we were soon to be beset, arising from the choice of a dual voltage system of high tension alternating current as the power supply.

Except on the Southern Region where the obvious answer was to continue with third rail 660 volt direct current, the choice of power supply lay between direct current at 1,500 volts or high tension alternating current with overhead contact wires. Early electrification schemes in this country had used both direct and alternating current, though the former predominated. The Midland Railway electrified their line between Lancaster and Heysham in 1908 using alternating current at 6,600 volts and 25 cycles. One year later the London, Brighton and South Coast Railway converted the South London Line between London Bridge and Victoria to electric traction using alternating current. These two short routes were the only ones in this country on which practical experience of alternating current traction could be gained. Both were technically successful in themselves.

The Midland line reverted to steam traction some years later; and the South London line was converted to the direct current system which predominated on the Southern Railway suburban routes.

In other countries, however, both systems of power supply developed without either gaining a dominant position – some countries preferring direct current, others adopting alternating current as their standard. The advantages of electric traction on lines of high traffic density were well understood here at home. And if, as was hoped, a case could be made for main line electrification, it was important to decide which system of power supply should be chosen as the national standard. There were differences of opinion on this question. To resolve them, a committee under the chairmanship of Sir John Pringle, Chief Inspecting Officer of Railways, was set up in 1927, which recommended that future electrifications should use direct current, either at 1,500 volts with overhead wires, or at 650/750 volts with third rail current collection. An order accordingly was made by the Minister of Transport. The question was again considered soon after nationalisation. The Railway Executive and London Transport appointed a committee, with Charles Cock, our chief electrical engineer, as chairman, to report whether progress in electrical engineering technology had invalidated the conclusions of the Pringle Committee.

The principal recommendation of the committee was that future electrification should be on the 1,500 volt direct current overhead wire system.

Pringle's conclusions were thus confirmed. The committee, however, drew attention to the possibilities of single phase 50 cycle alternating current and suggested that an experimental installation on this system should be considered.

Not long before the publication of our Modernisation Plan, the French Railways notwithstanding the success of their 1500 volt d.c. electrification from Paris to the Mediterranean coast, had electrified their main lines carrying very heavy traffic in the north eastern industrial area, using single phase 50-cycle alternating current at 25000 volts. They had done this on the strength of experience gained on 55 route miles of line between Aix-les-Bains and La Roche sur Foron equipped experimentally with this system of power supply. A demonstration of the system, for the benefit of foreign railway engineers and electrical contractors, to which the Railway Executive was invited to send representatives, was staged at Annecy in 1951. Robert Riddles, who went to France with Stanley Warder, was much impressed by what he saw, and obtained authority for electric operation to be restored between Lancaster, Morecambe and Heysham using single phase alternating current at industrial frequency, with D.C. traction motors and mercury arc rectifiers. Very promising results were obtained. As a consequence, in spite of the short time since we had decided on direct current as the future standard system, the B.T.C. called for comparative estimates of costs for electrifying and operating the London Midland main line from Euston to Liverpool and Manchester, using 1,500 volt direct current and single phase alternating current at industrial frequency and 25,000 volts. On a capital expenditure around £120 million, the a.c. system was estimated to cost nearly £6 million less than d.c. with annual costs less by about £1 million. The cost of the power supply equipment was less because with high voltage alternating current the overhead wires and supporting structures are lighter and thus cheaper to erect and maintain. A large part of the economy of a.c. traction derives from bringing the high tension current direct to the train – the locomotives and motor coaches themselves acting as the substations necessary with direct current systems. Experience in France had demonstrated that, ton for ton, alternating current locomotives were capable of higher performance than their d.c. counterparts – and were as reliable. Current consumption was also less.

Everything seemed to point to the conclusion that the a.c. system offered substantial economies, had greater potential for technical development, and should be adopted as the future standard on British Railways. Acting on the advice of Stanley Warder, the Commission so decided.

This was undoubtedly a bold decision and as later events have proved, the right one. At the time, however, there were some who, remembering den Hollander's advice, thought it was wrong. It would have been much easier both for ourselves and the contractors supplying the electrical equipment, to have continued with the well tried d.c. system. One of the penalties of very high voltage is the need to provide substantially more clearance between live parts of the overhead system and adjacent structures. With 1,500 volts 4″ clearance is quite adequate. Between live wires at 25,000 volts and earth, 11″ was considered to be necessary. Warder and his people were certainly working with a good safety margin, as was proved by a demonstration one very cold winter's night at Colchester, staged for the benefit of trade union officials. There had already been one or two nasty accidents due to men taking insufficient care when climbing on to tenders of locomotives standing under live wires. A locomotive making plenty of smoke was placed under a length of wire energised at 25,000 volts. The wire was slowly lowered as we waited tensely for the bang. Only when the wire as within 2″ of the chimney top and a dummy man sitting astride the boiler did the flashover occur. The sufficiency of 11″ clearance and the need to obey the rules were both convincingly demonstrated.

It was not going to be too difficult or expensive to provide 11″ clearance out in the country. But in congested urban areas with many overbridges and tunnels it was quite a different matter. Thus it was decided to use a lower voltage, 6,250 volts, permitting a smaller clearance, over such sections with automatic switching from one voltage to the other by means of track magnets at the changeover points. The locomotives and multiple unit trains had to be able to operate over their full speed/power range at either voltage. The designers of their electrical equipment were certainly faced with difficult, and perhaps unpredictable problems. This indeed proved to be the case. Within five weeks of the inauguration of the Glasgow suburban electrification, and notwithstanding 80,000 miles of trial running, we were confronted with serious trouble which led to the suspension of the service and an enforced return to steam working. The immediate cause of this was a serious failure to the transformer on one of the multiple units. This was not the first case in which transformers had been in trouble. There had been four previous failures all showing the same signs of severe overheating of the secondary windings. This had led to vapourisation of the cooling oil, a build up of pressure, and, in two cases, to an explosion, the most serious of which had shattered the equipment compartment in one of the coaches, injuring three people.

From the moment the cause of the first failure had been diagnosed – incorrectly as it turned out – as a breakdown of cooling oil circulation, modifications were put in hand, and went on day and night. I was, of course, aware of the troubles and of the steps being taken to cure them. On the evidence then available, they seemed likely to be effective. But failures occurred later on modified sets. Clearly, the real cause of the transformers overheating had not been found.

At 3.00 a.m. on Sunday morning 18th December, 1960, I was wakened by a telephone call from Stanley Warder. He told me a further failure had occurred the previous afternoon. The cover of a transformer tank had burst open and come down perilously near the track. It had been decided, after consultation with the Chief Inspecting Officer, that in the interests of public safety to suspend the electric services forthwith. Arrangements were already in hand to restore steam traction. There was to be a meeting at Marylebone at 9 o'clock, and would I please be there!

This was a grievous set-back to our electrification schemes, from which so much was expected. The suspension of the Glasgow services had caused much public concern. The Ministry of Transport ordered an enquiry into the whole affair.* It was conducted with extreme thoroughness by Brigadier Langley, the Chief Inspecting Officer. From one point of view, things might have been very much worse. Had the failures occured some months – even weeks – later than they did, when steam locomotives might no longer have been available on the spot, the provision of an alternative service would have presented very serious problems. As things were, steam operation was back within one weekend. The transformer failures in Scotland also served to direct the searchlight of Langley's penetrating mind on to the cause of breakdowns of motors, rectifiers and battery charges on trains working over the 6·25kV sections of the London suburban lines of the Eastern Region. They had been sufficiently numerous to force some reduction in services.

The Sunday morning meeting, with John Ratter in the chair, marked the beginning of one of the most fascinating pieces of engineering detective work with which I have been concerned. My earlier experience of electric traction in India served me well. But the problems then were mainly mechanical.

Now I was to be given a liberal education in some of the more abstruse aspects of electro-technology. I was able to contribute nothing to the solution of the problems – but I learnt a great deal from visits with Langley and Warder to contractors's works to examine damaged transformers and traction motors. Little by little, the pieces of the jig-saw fell into place. All the troubles in Scotland were found to be caused by severe voltage surges imposing heavy electro-magnetic forces which the transformer windings as orginally designed could not withstand. Similar surges due to the opening of the main circuit breaker when changing from one voltage to the other, or from loss of contact between the overhead wires and the pantograph broke down the insulation of the traction motors on the Eastern Region.

* Failures of Multiple Unit Electric Trains on British Railways, Final Report, Ministry of Transport, *H.M.S.O. London*, 1962.

It was fortunate that these troubles came to a head after, and not before, an International Conference held in London, organised jointly by the B.T.C. and the two trade associations representing the electrical and locomotive industries. Its purpose was to show delegates from forty overseas countries something of the progress of our electrification projects. Electric services, already operating between Crewe and Manchester, were soon to be extended over a further 600 route miles, including the conversion of the existing direct current system between Liverpool Street and Southend to 6·25kV alternating current. There was much of interest to show our overseas visitors.

Conferences were much in fashion at this time. There had, in the past, been few important technical developments on the railways which had not been the subject of papers to one or other of the Engineering Institutions. It was entirely in accordance with tradition, therefore, that the first comprehensive account of the technical features of the Modernisation Plan as a whole should be presented at a conference organised jointly by the three Institutions – the Civils, Mechanicals and Electricals – in May, 1961. I was asked to present a paper* – one of five – on the Engineering Aspects of the Plan – and was both surprised and pleased to receive the Watt gold medal of the Institution of Civil Engineers. The papers gave rise to excellent discussions. One contribution from Mr. E. L. E. Wheatcroft, a partner of Merz and McLellan, the eminent electrical consulting engineers deserves to be particularly remembered. In commenting on Warder's paper** on electric traction he said that 'the publicity given to the troubles had exaggerated them out of all proportion to the engineering achievements. It was nonsense to say that they reflected on the competence of British engineers and British manufacturers. The troubles would be overcome with no more difficulty than the teething troubles of all new engineering all over the world, – and they were.

Though the last steam locomotive to be built for British Railways, a standard *Class 9* 2-10-0 No. 92220 *Evening Star* was turned out from Swindon in March, 1960, and it had been abundantly clear for a considerable time that we were irrevocably committed to diesel and electric traction, with as rapid an elimination of steam as it was possible to contrive, there still remained a good deal of sensitivity to analyses of facts or expressions of opinion from outside the service which might tend to cast doubts on the wisdom of our motive power policy. Toward the end of 1960 a paper† entitled 'Economic results of diesel-electric motive power on the

* R. C. Bond 'The Engineering Aspects of the Modernisation Plan for British Railways' Proceedings, *Insitution of Civil Engineers*, Vol. 18, 1961.
** S. B. Warder 'Electric Traction in the British Railways Modernisation Plan' *Institution of Civil Engineers*, Vol. 18, 1961.
† H. F. Brown 'Economic Results of Diesel Electric Motive Power on the Railways of the United States of America' Proceedings, *Institution of Mechanical Engineers*, Vol. 175, No. 5, 1961.

railways of the United States of America' by H. F. Brown a well known New York consulting engineer was planned to be read at the Institution of Mechanical Engineers. Its theme, in a single sentence, was that so far from producing a 30 per cent return on the investment as had so often been claimed, diesel locomotives in main line service were costing the U.S. railroads more in total than equivalent steam power of modern design.

Brown's paper was certainly controversial. It contained official statistics of unimpeachable reliability in support of his contentions. These, it was thought, might prove to be rather embarrassing. There was, I was told, some suggestion that, as a member of Council and Vice-President having some influence in Institution circles, I might contrive to have the paper deleted from the programme! The paper was, of course, read as planned at a meeting at which I took the Chair. It attracted a large attendance, and provoked a lively discussion which did nobody any harm.

Some four years later, however, statistics from the paper were used in support of a case, already put to us more than once, that we should stop scrapping our steam locomotives and convert those that remained to oil firing, at the same time fitting them with an unusual design of blast-pipe and superheater. This was a long and tiresome story. When I was Chief Mechanical Engineer I had declined to try the special design of blast-pipe. With steam on the way out, expenditure thereon could not be justified, in my opinion, by any economy which might accrue for a short time only, on our modern locomotives. Pressure was, however, later applied by the back door. Instructions were received that a trial had to be undertaken. The results of tests carried out at Rugby on standard 2-10-0 locomotives were entirely as we had predicted, but it took some time and much patience finally to shake off our pursuers.

I have already referred briefly to the examination of the organisation and policies of the British Transport Commission by the Parliamentary Select Committee on Nationalised Industries. At about the same time as the Committee was conducting its enquiry, the Minister of Transport appointed a special advisory group, under the chairmanship of Sir Ivan Stedeford to cover much the same ground. Dr. Richard Beeching was a member of this group. The Modernisation Plan, in particular the electrification from Euston came in for critical examination, as I well remember from a meeting of the group at Euston. We assembled in the shareholders Meeting Room at the top of the marble staircase in the Great Hall – now alas, with the Doric Arch symbolic of so much railway history, swept away. The London Midland officers put up a most impressive performance in presenting the scheme to the inquisitors.

Though the findings of the Stedeford Committee remained shrouded in secrecy, signs were not wanting that another upheaval was on the way. This finally erupted in the Transport Act, 1962. Two years earlier the

Prime Minister, Mr. Harold Macmillan had announced in Parliament that there would have to be changes in the nationalised transport industry, particularly the railways, and in the structure of the B.T.C. itself. The Transport Act, 1962 imposed the same drastic treatment on the Commission as the 1953 Act had imposed on the Railway Executive. The Commission was to be abolished, and separate Boards established for each of the main components of the Commission's empire. We were back more or less where we had started fourteen years earlier!

Sir Brian Robertson, who had led us with such distinction through a period of high hopes and mounting financial problems, retired in June, 1961. Until one came to know him well, our Chairman, tall and very dignified, gave the impression of being an austere, aloof man – and sometimes not a little frightening. Many a time I have seen chief officers, saying their piece at Commission meetings, wilt under the Chairman's stare. He would listen intently to what was being said, and without a word of commendation or otherwise, pass on to the next victim. It could be very disconcerting. One of our number, a large and imposing man held in affectionate regard by us all, was not infrequently to be seen perspiring freely before the ordeal was over. Sir Brian was, in fact, a most kindly and considerate man to all who worked for him. He won respect and loyalty throughout all ranks of the railway service. We were sorry to see him go with much of the Plan for which he will always be remembered still to be completed.

Our new Chairman, Dr. Beeching, had rather different ideas on headquarters organisation from those of his predecessors. The members of the Railway Board were given functional responsibilities, very similar to those exercised by the members of the Railway Executive. One level of management was removed by the General Staff ceasing to act as a coordinating body in the overall chain of command. The Railway Sub-Commission, whose function was to deal with railway matters requiring co-ordination between the Regions when the General Staff were unable to settle them, was also quietly discarded. A British Railways Management Committee was constituted, the members of which were the Chairman, the full time Members of the Board, the Regional General Managers, and when the Workshops became a separate Division, the General Manager of the Workshops. Whatever may have been the merits of this new, and undoubtedly, simpler organisation, co-ordination between the departments at headquarters and the Regions was much weakened.

With the dissolution of the General Staff and the four chief engineers now reporting direct to the Board Member, a large part of my job seemed for a time to have virtually disappeared. Nevertheless, there were many technical matters constantly arising concerning more than one department which still had to be given attention. Although the General Staff had been disbanded, I retained my appointment as Technical Adviser and continued to be involved in the questions of the day, among which I particularly remember the discussions at the Technical Committee on the long-term policy for heating of diesel-hauled passenger trains. Was steam or electricity the correct answer? The economics of the matter were all in favour of steam. Serious consideration was once more being given to the adoption of air brakes as the one and only standard for the future. There were, in addition, special assignments of great interest – plans for liner train services, the organisation of materials inspection, the perennial arguments on the responsibilities of the Regional C.M.E.s *vis-a-vis* the Traffic departments for maintenance of locomotives and rolling stock, and a visit to Australia.

Among the international bodies in whose work we participated, was the Railway Sub-Committee of the Economic Commission for Asia and the Far East. This is a United Nations organisation for promoting international collaboration in giving aid to developing countries in that part of the world. Conferences were held every two years. Conducted very much on the lines of the International Railway Congress meetings, they had the added spice of European delegations vying with each other in offering help – all of course, with the objective of obtaining orders for railway equipment for their own industries. I inherited from John Ratter the leadership of the United Kingdom delegation to two of these – in Melbourne and Sydney in 1962 and Bangkok in 1964. The principal item on the agenda on both occasions was the operation and traffic capacity of single line railways. An ample supply of literature on the subject, and the other main items for discussion – diesel traction and scientific research – prepared by the United Kingdom Railway Advisory Service, a body set up jointly by the Ministry of Transport and ourselves to provide a consultancy service for foreign railways, had been distributed before our arrival in Melbourne. Our papers were well received. We were asked, and on behalf of the U.K., I undertook to have a comprehensive text book on single-line working prepared in time for the Bangkok meeting two years later, whither I was accompanied, among others, by O. S. Nock, a signal engineer and author of international repute.

He had been mainly responsible for the production of the book. The official sessions of these conferences were, as usual, supplemented by a full, and in the sweltering humid heat, exhausting, programme of visits and excursions. The highlights of the Australian tour were visits to Canberra and the Blue Mountains. In Bangkok we were given a grandstand view from the Dombari station with spotlessly clean wood-burning steam locomotives in the background, of a procession of Royal barges conveying the King of Thailand down the river on a ceremonial visit to the Temple of Dawn – a unique spectacle. There were evening parties and receptions to which all and sundry were invited. At the Soviet Embassy cocktail party in Bangkok there was at least one uninvited guest – my architect daughter, who had arrived quite unexpectedly with twenty-four hours on her hands due to a defect in the aeroplane taking her on holiday to Japan.

Most of the delegates departed homewards from Thailand in a luxurious diesel-hauled special train to Singapore, with all the attendant Thai Railway officers in military uniform, as is their invariable custom when going out on the line. I bade them farewell, and returned direct by air to spend a few days with my son working for a British firm of consulting engineers in Teheran.

These E.C.A.F.E. meetings gave me a wonderful opportunity of seeing the railways of countries to which British railway officers could not normally hope to be sent. They gave me too, my first taste of long distance journeys by air. I find them very much to my liking. Travelling westwards via the United States, Honolulu and Fiji, the first sight of Australia coming in over Sydney Heads with the magnificent harbour and bridge below is something worth seeing, not once but many times. The homeward flight via Darwin, Singapore, India and Iran completed my first circuit of the world – on time over every sector. No other form of transport, not excluding railways, seems to me to bring together all the physical sciences and engineering disciplines in the attainment of a single objective to quite the same extent as international airline operation.

One of the first things which was done, after Dr. Beeching became Chairman, was to place the main workshops once more under central management by removing them entirely from Regional control and forming them into a separate Headquarters Division under the functional direction of a Commission Member. For the first five years of nationalisation all the main mechanical engineering workshops had been centrally controlled from Railway Executive headquarters as integral parts of the mechanical and electrical engineering departments. This was a simple straightforward organisation, which everyone understood. It worked well, gave good service to the Regions, and was productive of substantial economies in construction and maintenance costs and rationalisation of capacity. As a consequence of the 1953 Transport Act, the management of the Workshops passed into the hands of six separate Regional departments. It then became difficult to co-ordinate the activities of individual Works. Though new building programmes were allocated by the mechanical engineering committee, and other technical matters requiring an agreed course of action in all Regions were dealt with in the same way, the Regional Engineers were able to do more or less as they liked in running the Works in their territory. The B.T.C. were not unmindful of the advantages of central direction of the main Workshops, as is evident from a paragraph in the Explanatory Statement to the Railway Re-organisation Scheme 1954, stating that 'it might be that some activities now controlled regionally could with advantage be separated and formed into central services, e.g. the work in the main mechanical engineering workshops'.

At the same time as the Workshops were removed from Regional control it was decided also to transfer responsibility for the Drawing Offices, in which new designs as well as routine work was undertaken, from the Regional Engineers direct to the Chief Mechanical Engineer at Board headquarters. New design was of course, a reserved subject.

These were thoroughly sound moves. But central control of the Workshops did not of necessity require the formation of a separate Division. It would have been perfectly possible to have transferred control of the Works, as well as the Drawing Offices, to the C.M.E. at Board headquarters. He would have required additional staff – but they could have been found from the Regional C.M.E.'s offices – whence, in fact, many were transferred to the new Workshops Division.

Alternatively the whole of the six Regional Departments, not only the Works and Drawing offices, could have been removed from regional control and integrated as one all-line department under the control of the C.M.E. at Marylebone, and acting as a contractor to the Regions. This could certainly have been made to work very well – but it would have been incompatible with the philosophy of management current at the time. Moreover it must be conceded, having regard to the powers delegated to them that the Regions could reasonably insist on retaining jurisdiction over:

(i) the size and composition of the fleet of locomotives and rolling stock allocated to them;
(ii) the C.M.E.'s shopping bureaux, which in consultation with the appropriate Works decided whether, and if so when, locomotives and rolling stock should be sent in for repairs;
(iii) the repair classification and amount of work to be done on individual units; and
(iv) the annual maintenance budget.

A basic principle of sound railway mechanical engineering is that ultimate responsibility for design, construction, maintenance, and the technical aspects of operation of locomotives and other rolling stock should rest with one man – the Chief Mechanical Engineer. It nearly always was so in the old company days. It had been so in Railway Executive days. With the devolution of much authority to the Regions, the application of this principle was seriously weakened. The formation of a separate Workshops Division would weaken it still further. Responsibility

would become vested in three, and sometimes four, authorities, namely:
  (i) the C.M.E. at Board Headquarters;
  (ii) the Main Workshops Division;
  (iii) Regional C.M. and E. Engineers;
  (iv) Divisional Maintenance engineers, on the staff of non-technical Divisional Managers through whom instructions on technical matters would have to be passed.

Responsibility would have been less divided had the Workshops been placed under the Chief Mechanical Engineer at Marylebone. And difficulties which later arose from staff, enticed by salaries fixed unilaterally out of line with agreed scales, moving to other work, would have been less tiresome.

However, a scheme for forming a Workshops Division was prepared upon which I was asked to comment. In due course the decision was taken. And who am I to cavill? Had the Workshops Division not been formed, I should not have held one of the most rewarding and responsible appointments of my whole career some four years later — that of General Manager of the Division.

Here I depart from a generally chronological account to complete this story. The formation of the Workshops Division required yet another reorganisation of the Mechanical and Electrical Engineering Departments. Proposals were drawn up accordingly, which were to apply to all Regions. As before, the chief engineers of the Central Staff remained responsible for the reserved subjects. The arrangements laid down five years earlier for control of maintenance done outside Main Works had never satisfied the C.M.E.s, on whom responsibility for the serviceability of all locomotives, rolling stock and outdoor machinery had been placed. Some change of emphasis was written into the new proposals. Though depot maintenance was to remain under the control of an engineer on the local manager's staff, it was categorically stated that C.M. & E.E.s would assume responsibility for the Running and Maintenance organisation at all levels. These two proposals were perhaps, scarcely entirely consistent with each other! They gave rise to the familiar futile argument as to who was the Maintenance Engineer's boss. As John Ratter, with much patience, did his best to point out that so long as these men remained on the staff of the local manager they inevitably had two bosses — their relations with whom were, however, quite different. In the end the Board accepted both propositions, which really was not very helpful! The Board could not, apparently, bring themselves to accept the one thing that would have enabled the C.M.E.s to discharge their responsibilites for maintenance properly — namely that the men who did the work should be responsible to them and nobody else. However, everybody did their best. Much depended on the freedom accorded by Regional General Managers to their C.M.E. in talking direct to the Maintenance Engineers.

Only on the Southern Region where, in apparent defiance of the Board ruling, the C.M. and E.E. retained unchallenged control of the work done in outside depots, did peace reign.

The situation was further confused about twelve months later, when a directive on management structure left the Regions free to decide for themselves whether to place responsibility for maintenance on the Chief Mechanical Engineer or on Divisional Managers. At about the same time, unreliability in traffic of some of the new diesel locomotives was causing serious concern to the Board. In a report outlining what needed to be done to put matters right, it was stated to be quite essential for the C.M.E.s to be given unequivocal responsibility for locomotive maintenance and for the men who carry it out. This surely should have settled the matter, but it did not. The arguments came up again in 1964, and yet again in 1965. By this time Sir Stanley Raymond was Chairman of the Board. He asked one of his part-time colleagues, to give his opinion on what could be done to resolve the conflict. To the best of my recollection, the views expressed can be summed up as follows:

   (i) a cardinal error was made when, in 1957, the B.T.C. decided that the Motive Power Department should be absorbed by the Operating Department;
  (ii) much of the trouble had been caused by the fallacy that all devolution is good, and all centralisation is bad;
 (iii) it is a fact that, in railway engineering, it is the most vertical organisations that work with least friction;
  (iv) the C.M.E.s should be made completely responsible for maintenance of locomotives and rolling stock, and that the men engaged in the work should be wholly responsible to the C.M.E.

To me, this seemed no more than plain common sense.

But it is one of those arguments in which the protagonists on either side are unlikely ever to be wholly reconciled.

The case for placing the Workshops under central management was made by Sir Steuart Mitchell, whom Dr. Beeching had brought in as a member of the Commission and Railway Board. Sir Steuart came to us from the Royal Ordnance Factories, of which he had been Director-General. He was already well versed in the problems of adjusting capacity of a large production organisation to accord with changing requirements. He argued in support of his case that the Workshops should be run for the benefit of British Railways as a whole – not just for the Region in which they happened to be situated. It was common ground that the effects of the Modernisation Plan would make it necessary to reduce Workshop capacity. This could best be done by closing some Works completely and reducing the size of others, over a period of five to ten years. But the optimum choice of which to close and which to continue, would require the maximum degree of rationalisation and distribution of work-load without regard to Regional boundaries. And this could be done more effectively by one central management than by six regional managements. The establishment of central management was thus regarded as an essential preliminary to the revision of the earlier Workshop Plans, which had been made in the context of Regional control.

Three years had elapsed since the last comprehensive report on the Works, to which I briefly referred in a previous chapter, had been compiled. The recommendations it contained were being carried out, particularly in regard to closing subsidiary Works. But the increasing rate of displacement of steam locomotives by diesel and electric traction, and the changes in traffic volume during the intervening period, made it necessary for this earlier plan to be revised in the light of changing conditions.

Whatever he may have thought privately, Sir Steuart Mitchell did not make the mistake, which some of those brought in from outside made, of giving the impression that he held other than a high opinion of the competence and ability of the life-time railway officers on whom he would perforce have to rely for help and advice. Those of us whom Sir Steuart consulted while he was working on his plan – and he consulted all who could help him – knew far more about the Works and their contribution to running the railway, those which were good and those not so good, and the men in charge of them, than Sir Steuart could possibly hope to know. It was a pleasure to give him whatever help he sought. At the Chairman's request, I had assembled a large dossier of general and statistical information on all the Works for Sir Steuart's use. I was summoned from time to time to discuss the proposals he intended to make. Sir Steuart probed deeply into possible alternative courses of action. Together with Harrison, we visited many of the Works. It was during these visits that Mitchell formed his opinion that the good Works were very good indeed, comparing well with the best in private industry. There were some others of which he did not think so highly!

Sir Steuart Mitchell's Plan was a masterpiece of closely reasoned argument in support of the recommendations made. It was based on the principle that the greatest economy is to be obtained by having the smallest possible number of Works compatible with operating needs, the shops to be retained being those shown, by their output and costs, to be the most efficient, located in the right geographical locations. It was based, also, as all such plans should be, on the predominant activity of railway shops – heavy repairs – with new construction added within the pattern dictated by the heavy repair requirements. The importance from the point of view of minimum production costs of the retained Works operating, wherever possible, well above the level of a single shift was emphasised. But where two alternative courses of action were possible, one dictated by narrow considerations of production costs, the other by wider considerations of service to the Regions, the latter prevailed. A case in point was the recommendation to include Temple Mills, Stratford, among the wagon works to be retained and developed.

The Temple Mills capacity of 4,000 heavy repairs per annum could have been more economically provided at Ashford. But this would have entailed haulage of repairs arising on the London Midland and Eastern Regions over heavily loaded routes crossing the Thames to the Southern Region – a course to which all three Regions objected. As a further example, it would have been possible for the assumed output in 1972 of locomotive repairs and new construction to have been produced by two Works only, the choice of which by reason of their size and low costs, would have been Crewe and Derby. But this solution would not have been satisfactory from the traffic operating point of view.

Flexibility was built into the plan to cater for unforeseen changes in demand without the load on any Works falling below a full single shift, or, on the other hand, having to re-instate capacity once abandoned. Productivity, however that elusive criterion may be defined, was considered to be generally too low. A basic assumption in the manpower calculations was that, over five years, an improvement of from 15 per cent to 25 per cent could be obtained. Many of us who had been fighting for years to gain acceptance of realistic, though fair, methods of work measurement and to stop the constant upward drift in piecework balances, were inclined to be sceptical about achieving so large an improvement. However, we could but try!

Sir Steuart unfolded his plan to the Trade Unions in the old Railway Executive Board Room at Marylebone on 19th September, 1962. It was a grim meeting. As was to be expected, the proposals to close sixteen of the thirty-two main Works, involving over 20,000 men becoming redundant, met with a very hostile reception, culminating in a one-day strike at all the Works. What the Unions hoped to gain from this particularly futile protest, it is difficult to imagine.

The 1962 plan differed from the earlier ones in two important respects. First, new, and much more generous, financial provisions than hitherto were to be made for the staff declared redundant. Second, the plan (of which an excellent account is given in a paper by[*] R. C. S. Low to the Institution of Locomotive Engineers) was concerned not only with shutting Works.

It dealt also, in a very positive way, with bringing those to be retained thoroughly up-to-date in regard to machine tools and other production

[*] R. C. S. Low 'The Re-organisation of British Railways Workshops' Journal, *Institution of Locomotive Engineers*, 1967.

equipment. The shop buildings, heating, lighting and staff amenities were to be modernised to the best contemporary standards. Individual schemes for re-equipping each of the continuing Works were prepared, costing in total £17 million spread over three years, from which savings in operating £3·8 million per annum were expected, together with savings of £3·3 million, on non-variable overheads at the Works to be closed. It fell to my lot, in due course, to endeavour to establish that these savings had in fact been achieved.

It should not be inferred that capital expenditure on this scale implied neglect of the Works during the ten years they had been under Regional control. Considerable sums were spent each year on new machine tools, and other equipment. But the average level of expenditure had been inadequate and there were substantial arrears of maintenance to be overtaken. Without central control it is, I think, unlikely that any plan for re-organisation of the Works would have measured up fully to the needs of the situation. More than that, I have always thought that, in the then existing financial situation, no-one except a Board Member, brought in from outside the service, would have had the temerity to seek, let alone obtain, authority for capital expenditure on the Workshops on such a scale.

My duties no longer involved me in direct responsibility for the work of others, nor were they as demanding of time and daily attention as those to which I had been accustomed for many years. But if as a result of the headquarters re-organisation these changes had to come, they could not have come at a more convenient time. I had been invited to accept nomination as President of the Institution of Mechanical Engineers for 1963–64. This was an invitation which I was naturally most anxious to accept. But I knew from experience as a member of Council of the Institution, that the Presidency was very nearly a full-time job, the obligations of which, for one year, would often have to take precedence over my railway duties. Acceptance thus entirely depended upon the Chairman's permission. This, Dr. Beeching cordially gave. Shortly afterwards, I set out for Melbourne and Sydney with ample time during the long air journeys to think about the Presidential Address I should have to deliver within twelve months.

From the earliest days of my apprenticeship at Derby one of my objectives was to become qualified as soon as possible for student membership of the appropriate engineering Institutions. We were strongly encouraged to do so by Sir Henry Fowler. The theoretical training at Derby Technical College was, so far as I was concerned, directed entirely to preparing myself for the examinations of the Institutions of Civil and Mechanical Engineers.

Membership of one of the Institutions is the hall-mark of any professional engineer. It is up to the Institutions themselves, and the leaders of the engineering industry to see that it always remains so. A University degree in one of the engineering disciplines, desirable though it may be today, is not of itself enough. Corporate membership of one of the chartered Institutions and, as a corollary, the right to the title of Chartered Engineer bestowed by the Council of Engineering Institutions, is alone the guarantee of the requisite standards of practical and theoretical training, experience and responsibility.

The Institution of Mechanical Engineers is naturally the appropriate Institution to which a mechanical engineer should seek to be elected. But membership of the Institution of Civil Engineers was no less appropriate, and conferred a certain distinction. Contrary to popular belief, the sphere of influence of the 'Civils' extended far beyond the bounds of harbours, tunnels, dams, the permanent way and bridges commonly regarded as the province of civil engineers. The Institution was established and given its Charter 'For the general advancement of *Mechanical* Science, and more particularly for promoting the acquisition of that species of knowledge which constitutes the profession of a Civil Engineer, being the art of directing the Great Sources of Power in Nature for the use and convenience of man. . . .' When the Institution was founded in 1818 there were broadly only two engineering disciplines – civil engineering and military engineering. That was the distinction. Most of the Chief Mechanical Engineers of the railway companies were members of the Institution of Civil Engineers. They were, of course, members of I.Mech.E. also after it was founded. They would, as likely as not, present important papers on locomotive subjects to the Institution of Civil Engineers, with the enhanced prestige which that attracted. Clearly, corporate membership of the 'Civils' was a distinction to be won.

With the ever widening span of engineering technology, one Institution alone could not cater for the needs of the whole profession. Specialisation was inevitable. The time had come, in 1847, for eminent mechanical engineers to wish to have an Institution of their own, which soon took, and has ever since retained, the lead in the mechanical engineering branch of the profession.

Many, in fact, I suppose, most – engineers join a professional body only to acquire the qualification which this bestows, without which they might be ineligible for the higher engineering posts in their employers' organisation. It was, I believe still is, and I hope it always will be, a requirement for candidates for the more senior appointments in the railways engineering departments to be Chartered Engineers. But those who take no active part in Institution affairs lose a great deal they might otherwise gain. That however, is a matter for them. I have always derived great pleasure from my participation, over a period of fifty years, in Institution activities. One naturally tended to concentrate upon the 'Mechanicals' and of course, the erstwhile Institution of Locomotive Engineers, which celebrated its Golden Jubilee in 1961. This was a splendid occasion, marked by a visit from the Duke of Edinburgh to an exhibition of locomotives and rolling stock staged by the British Transport Commission at Marylebone, in honour of the Institution. Prince Philip named one of the *Warship* class diesel-hydraulic locomotives *Magpie* after the frigate which he had commanded. I was standing close by – Sir Brian Robertson handed me the Union Jack which had covered the name plate before its unveiling. It remains one of my treasured possessions.

Without being unduly conceited, one could reasonably hope, in the fullness of time, to become President of the Institution of Locomotive Engineers. But to become President of the Institution of Mechanical Engineers was an honour to which one could scarcely hope to aspire. However, election as a member of Council, and later as a Vice-President, at least made the Presidency a possibility, but by no means a foregone conclusion.

Thus, it was a matter of great satisfaction when I was told by the President that he intended to nominate me to succeed him in the Presidential chair. I went through the nerve-racking ordeal of being asked to wait outside the room while my colleagues on the Council discussed the President's nomination. Apparently all went well. The nomination was accepted and the members of the Institution elected me as their President for 1963–64.

Though I had served a liberal apprenticeship of twelve years as a member of Council and was familiar with the procedure to be followed, taking the chair for the first time at Council meeting as President, with everyone wondering, as I well knew, how the new incumbent would perform is no easy matter. The Secretary, Kenneth Platt, as always a tower of strength, had briefed me well. The meeting passed off smoothly.

The established routine of Institution life varies little from year to year. It is an inseparable combination of business and social activities. As to the former, there is a virtually full-time programme of engagements for which the President must be available at the secretary's behest. As to the latter, there is a never-ending stream of luncheons and dinners, many of them involving a speech. Whatever other attributes a President possesses, he must have a cast-iron digestion and a reasonably strong head. I am fortunate in never having had to worry about my weight!

The principal functions of the year, in the order in which they take place are the Summer Meeting, the Presidential Address delivered in London and at the local branches, and the Annual Dinner. If one's term of office coincides with the year in which it is the turn of the 'Mechanicals' to pay a presidential visit to overseas branches on behalf of the three major Institutions – that is an additional duty.

There are many social functions at which the President would be sadly at a loss without a wife by his side. I had the great good fortune to have married Frances Heriz-Smith, with whom Jean and I had enjoyed close friendship for many years. The lonely years were behind me.

The Summer Meetings are organised by one of the local branches of the Institution. During my year it was the turn of the East Midlands centred on Nottingham. This was a happy coincidence, bringing Works at Derby within the area to be covered by technical visits. I was glad to have had some previous experience of leading a Summer Meeting. In 1954 the Institution of Locomotive Engineers spent two days based on Chester, visiting our Works at Crewe, and Shotton Steel Works, whose Chairman, Sir Richard Summers, a director of the L.M.S. and later a member of the London Midland Area Board, was a good friend to all locomotive men. The Nottingham meeting, extending over five days, was a much more strenuous assignment. Indeed, I think we drove our members rather too hard and sent them home exhausted. Technical sessions at the University were supplemented by full day visits to Works in Derby and Grimsby, and to places of historic interest. The Duke of Rutland, who entertained us at Belvoir Castle was chairman of the local reception committee and principal guest at the dinner which traditionally brings these meetings to a close.

The day in Derby was taken up by visits to the Locomotive Works, the Railway Research Laboratories and Rolls-Royce, where I fear we arrived very late. We had, of course, over-run our time at the Locomotive Works. In accordance with tradition – one which I always encouraged – the Shops had been swept and polished to perfection. Many nostalgic memories passed through my mind as Frances and I arrived in a Rolls-Royce to be welcomed at the Works which I had first entered on foot and in overalls, forty-four years before.

Of all the duties confronting the President, the most daunting was, for me, the speech at the Annual Dinner. Held at the Dorchester in November, between six and seven hundred members and their guests habitually attend. How do the wizards of the kitchen contrive a repast for such numbers with temperature and timing so perfectly co-ordinated? Surely they must have much in common with production engineers!

The Institution's list of official guests contain the names of men distinguished in many walks of life – Ministers of the Crown, Ambassadors and High Commissioners, heads of the armed forces and leaders of industry and academic life. To address such an assembly larger in number than the House of Commons with every member in his place, is a formidable undertaking. Compared with this the Presidential Address is easy.

It is a fair assumption that those who come to the Address do so to hear what the President has to say. It would be unwise to assume the same about those who attend the Annual Dinner. When delivering his Address, the President speaks on a subject of his own choice – one on which he is probably an acknowledged authority.* At the Dinner he replies to the Toast of the Institution and proposes one to the guests. He must give some account of what the Institution has been doing; and say something about the political and industrial questions of the day affecting the engineering profession. All this may, or perhaps may not, provide material for a scintillating discourse.

I am most envious of accomplished after-dinner speakers. They are, in my experience, not very numerous. As for the rest of us, a golden rule is to err on the side of brevity. The patience of one's audience must not be strained beyond endurance. Nothing is more disconcerting than to hear an animated conversation going on in far corners of the room by some who may be bored but lack the manners to keep silent while the victims are on their feet. There is one thing more. Never fail to have in your pocket the whole thing written out in full in case your memory deserts you!

The toast of the Institution, proposed on this occasion by the President of the Board of Trade, the Rt. Hon. Frederick Errol, having been duly honoured, the moment of truth arrives. The toastmaster, resplendant in his red tail-coat, enquires deferentially whether I am ready. What a fatuous question! I have been ready and anxious to get the job done for days past. Stretching away to the horizon in every direction, a vast sea of faces above the white ties. Can I command their attention for just ten minutes? I shall soon know. Yes, it seems I can! I nearly came unstuck, but nobody else knew. Resuming my seat with a sigh of relief and a large of glass of brandy, I sat back and enjoyed my Chairman, Dr. Beeching's, response on behalf of the guests.

Late evening functions, of which there were many, often involved staying in London for the night. In this, as in all other matters, the Institution looks after its Presidents very well. Until Frances complained of its shortcomings from a woman's point of view, a flat on the third floor of No. 6 Old Queen Street, immediately behind the Institution building had for many years been provided for the President and his wife. I had used it alone on a number of occasions. It seemed to me both comfortable and convenient. Not so my wife! It was only when she stayed there with me for the first time that I was given to understand that, unless something was done, it would be the last time. It had not occurred to me before that there was no dressing table, no long mirror, no this and that, so necessary to a woman of fastidious taste. In vain I gently pointed out that wives of better men than I had stayed there without complaint – at any rate, they had

* 'A Commentary on the change from Steam Traction on British Railways and some thoughts on the future', R. C. Bond, *Institution of Mechanical Engineers*, Nov. 1963.

stayed there. All to no avail. Frances made her views plainly known to Ken Platt, from whom she had a most sympathetic hearing. A Council Minute of 24th July, 1963 records that the President's flat was quite unsuitable for the purpose for which it was being used. The President and Secretary were authorised, when necessary, to spend the night at hotels or clubs in future. We took this as applying to our wives also!

It was during my time on the Council that serious concern about the status and long-term future of the engineering profession began to be expressed. There was a widespread feeling that the contribution made by engineers to society, upon which the very existence of modern industrial nations depend, was taken for granted and received scant recognition outside the profession. The existence of so many chartered Institutions was confusing to the public, and prevented Engineers being regarded as members of a single profession. Their influence on the trend of current affairs was largely unco-ordinated, and thus limited in its impact. The status of the profession suffered accordingly. Young men of the highest quality were not being attracted to engineering in sufficient numbers to safeguard the future and maintain our position in the technological race. Too many of them were choosing pure science as a career.

There were some signs that we were all becoming a little too concerned with status to the exclusion of achievement, from which enhanced status would automatically follow. Nevertheless the absence of any central organisation representative of the profession as a whole, able to act with authority, and speak with one voice on the problems of the day, was a serious handicap to engineers. They did not enjoy public esteem commensurate with the importance of their contribution to society.

The Presidents of the three senior Institutions who, for many years past, had met regularly to discuss matters of common interest, saw the need for an authoritative body representative of all the Chartered Institutions, and took the initiative in negotiations which led to the formation in 1962 of the Engineering Institutions Joint Council, 'to promote and co-ordinate in the public interest, the development of the science, art and practice of engineering'. This quotation is taken from the programme handed to those of us who were fortunate enough to be present at a Reception held at The Science Museum in November 1965 in the presence of Her Majesty the Queen to Celebrate the granting of a Royal Charter to the Council of Engineering Institutions (the new title of E.I.J.C.) of which Prince Philip consented to become the Founder President.

The Council of Engineering Institutions is a federation of fifteen Chartered Engineering Institutions with a total membership of over 300 thousand. It is empowered to grant the title of Chartered Engineer to corporate members of the constituent bodies. C.E.I. is much concerned with, and sets the standards to be observed in regard to education, training, competence and conduct of professional engineers. It co-operates with, and is consulted by, Government Departments, The Royal Society, Universities and national and international industrial and academic bodies in all matters affecting the engineering profession. It has gained recognition at home and abroad as the body representing the British engineering profession as a whole.

During the early formative years Ken Platt acted as honorary secretary of E.I.J.C. To him should go much of the credit for the successful outcome of the long and complex negotiations by which fifteen Institutions, all proud possessors of their own Charters, and jealous of their traditions and sovereignty, were persuaded to work together for the common good.

As President, I became one of three representatives of the Institution of Mechanical Engineers on the Joint Council. And more recently, as chairman of the Overseas Relations Committee of C.E.I. and ex officio, a member of the Board, I have seen at first hand the working of C.E.I. as at present organised. It is building up its strength and reputation. But if it is fully to justify the hopes and aspirations of its founders, some changes are, in my opinion, necessary. Something will have to be done to prevent the tail wagging the dog. Some system of proportional representation reflecting more accurately the membership strength of the constituent Institutions will surely have to be devised and accepted, in the general interest by the smaller and less influential constituents.

The formation of E.I.J.C. caused anxiety to some Institutions which, not being chartered, were ineligible for membership of the new body. Where the learned society activities in which they specialised were covered, albeit in a more general way, by one or more of the Chartered Institutions, they were concerned lest their own membership and influence should suffer. The Institution of Locomotive Engineers was one of those. It had been in existence for over fifty years and had gained for itself a very special position in railway mechanical engineering circles. Though not a qualifying body, it was strict in requiring candidates for membership to have reached a standard of academic and practical training and experience roughly equivalent to that of the senior Institutions. The papers presented to the Institution were of a very high standard. Most of them would have been accepted for the railway group or division of the Institutions of Mechanical or Electrical Engineers. It was justly proud of its contribution to railway engineering, and was held in high regard and supported by railway companies all over the free world.

But membership of the Institution of Locomotive Engineers alone was insufficient for those aspiring to senior positions on British Railways, and many overseas railways for whose officers British qualifications were required. Membership of one of the Chartered Institutions was essential. The young men entering the profession, upon whom the future prosperity of any Institution ultimately depends, unwilling or unable to afford more than one subscription, tended increasingly, and quite rightly, to join one of the Chartered Institutions as a first priority. Thus the longer term future of the Institution of Locomotive Engineers was seen to be very uncertain. The Council of the Institution, of which as a Past President I was a life member, gave earnest consideration to the question of petitioning for a Royal Charter, thus opening the door to membership of E.I.J.C. and a position of equality in the engineering heirarchy. It had to be borne in mind, however, that railway engineering interests were already well covered by the Chartered Institutions. In these circumstances it was doubtful, to say the least, that a petition for a charter would have been successful. The decision not to proceed, but as an alternative, to open negotiations with the 'Mechanicals' with a view to amalgamation was, in my opinion, absolutely right.

A joint working party, was set up to work out the details and present a scheme to the two Councils. It is a matter of great satisfaction to me that the amalgamation and the consequent formation of the Railway Division of the Institution of Mechanical Engineers have been so successfully concluded. This example of farsighted statesmanship could well be followed by others. Further amalgamations of this character will, I hope, take place in the future and pave the way ultimately to the formation of one British Institution of Chartered Engineers, comprising a central body and subordinate divisions dealing with grouped learned society activities, as a successor to the Council of Engineering Institutions and the present chartered bodies. Such an organisation could well best serve the public interest and the needs of the engineering profession as a whole.

Just as the needs of Institution members living and working away from London are met by the formation of Local Branches, so for those working in foreign countries the Institutions established similar branches or local groups to enable their members to enjoy a full programme of technical and social activities – and also to provide means whereby the influence of the British Institutions can be exerted for the benefit of the overseas countries, particularly in regard to the technical education and training of their own engineers. The three senior Institutions have always worked together in this important activity. Members overseas are inevitably isolated from the main stream of Institution life. As some compensation it is the custom for one of the three Presidents each year to visit the members in a number of foreign countries. It happened to be the turn of the I.Mech.E. during my year of office.

Accompanied by our wives, Ken Platt and I set out during my last month as President, to meet our members resident in the Middle East. We were away for three weeks visiting Kuwait, Iran and Israel in that order, with a few days in Malta on our way home. Ever since my journey to and from India thirty years earlier, I had a wish, hitherto unfulfilled, to see something of the countries bordering the Eastern Mediterranean, the Red Sea and the Persian Gulf, with their long history of civilisation stretching back to ancient times, and the immense power for good or mischief which their oil reserves, exploited and developed largely by British and American engineers and scientists, enable them to wield today.

My previous acquaintance with this turbulent part of the world, with evidence of past and present conflict there for all to see — burnt out armoured cars on the road south from Tel Aviv, and armed sentries behind barbed wire overlooking Jersualem — had been limited to an hour or so at airports on other journeys further afield. The need for a special passport for Israel only, and the route followed by our El Al aircraft from Tehran to Tel Aviv carefully avoiding flight over Syrian territory bore witness to the underlying tension. The choice of the Middle East for my visit to overseas members was thus most welcome, especially under the V.I.P. conditions which are always most generously arranged for Presidential tours.

The abiding impression which remains in my mind is one of vivid contrast between ancient and modern, still inextricably mixed up together, Kuwait, a city of opulent modern buildings, dripping with money, and on the outskirts, the desert, tents, and nomadic tribesmen in a cavalcade of motor cars with pennants flying returning from Mecca. Vast ocean-going tankers tied up at the Kuwait Oil Company's jetties at Ahmadi, contrasted strongly with ancient dhows sailing slowly out on the Persian Gulf. And in Iran, the magnificent Karadj Dam and generating station up in the mountains not far from Teheran are in strange contrast to houses down in the city with plumbing and toilet arrangements of the most rudimentary kind. The Persian crown jewels of unimaginable value protected by the most sophisticated devices which modern science can contrive are stored in a city where there was, and so far as I know still is, the possibility of witnessing the execution in public of a convicted criminal. In Israel too, the ancient cities of Nazareth and Jersualem, with all that they mean to Christian civilisation, live alongside scientific and engineering projects of outstanding merit resulting from the boundless energy and dedication of the modern Israeli state.

Planning an extensive tour of foreign countries involves much hard work by Institution staff and those for whose benefit it is arranged. Certainly nothing was left undone which could contribute to the success and enjoyment of our mission. Time, and the distances involved — 9,650 miles in all — made travel by air essential. Indeed, to my regret, all that I was able to see of the railways was the workshops and motive power depot of the Iranian Railway in Teheran. Our flights were uneventful, all strictly punctual and, with one exception, most comfortable. The exception was the flight out from Beirut to Kuwait in a Middle East Airlines Caravelle.

Arriving in the dark something seemed to go wrong with the pressurisation as we were held circling the airport for a considerable time. We were warmly welcomed by a deputation of senior officials and wives from the Kuwait Oil Company, at whose guest house at Ahmadi, surrounded by all the paraphenalia of an oil field and refinery, we were staying. To our acute embarrassment, we were stone deaf, and took time to recover!

Every day from early morning to late at night, a full programme of meetings, visits to Works and Universities, and evening receptions had been arranged. Approval of the plans was taken for granted. Only once did I rebel, when in the sticky heat of Tel Aviv, I insisted on being given time for a bath before addressing a meeting of the Association of Engineers and Architects in Israel. It was hard work, though most rewarding as everyone seemed pleased to see us.

To learn at first hand something about the major engineering problems, and of the ways in which our Institutions could help in their solution, appointments were made for us to meet the Ministers involved, and our Ambassadors in Kuwait and Teheran. The first of these meetings was with the Kuwaiti Minister of Electricity and Water. While waiting to be summoned we were plied with very strong black coffee, and watched, fascinated, a constant stream of Arabian gentlemen, in flowing robes of black or brown, who seemed to have the right of entry to the Minister's private room unannounced. All very different from the ways to which we are accustomed when meeting the high and mighty. Difficult though it may be to identify positive results, we were left in no doubt as to the value of these discussions in building up friendly relations with those able to influence engineering developments in foreign countries.

Malta was, of course, in a different category. By no stretch of the imagination could the George Cross Island then be described as a foreign country. It was all so very British, dominated by the Royal Navy, the Dockyard and the Phoenicia Hotel. We left, after all too short a visit, with cordial expressions of goodwill, and a special request from the Governor, Sir Maurice Dorman. He had given us a splendid lunch in his very English home at San Anton Palace, and asked that regular visits – if possible annual visits – should be made at Presidential level, to ensure proper liaison between our Institutions and engineers in Malta.

And so home to report to Council, and to the conclusion of my year of office. This ended, as it began, at the Annual General Meeting, when members can come along and express their approval or otherwise of the conduct of affairs. There are always a few, the same every time, who could be relied on to call us to account for our shortcomings! Vice-Admiral Sir Frank Mason, one time Engineer-in-Chief of the Fleet, was my successor. Frank and I had been at school together in Ipswich fifty years before – he a senior prefect, I, an insignificant member of the lowest form!

Despite the heavy demands on my time of Institution affairs over the past twelve months, I had been able to keep fully abreast of my railway duties. Thinking about this, there was only one conclusion to be drawn. Unless the scope of my duties was to be widened – and with the new organisation firmly established, this seemed unlikely – I was going to be less fully occupied than I would wish.

Apart from my own affairs, this was, on the whole, a rather depressing time. The Reshaping Report – the so-called Beeching Plan – in attracting too much attention to the massive reduction of route mileage which it foreshadowed and too little to the positive constructive proposals, did nothing to boost morale or encourage confidence in the future as the Modernisation Plan had done. There was, however, a silver lining to the cloud of uncertainty. All of us, to whom the future of the railway meant so much, knew that what was being done to ensure the technical and operational success of the Modernisation Plan was not in vain. It was beyond doubt that the trunk routes to remain and be developed, and the services over them, would be very good indeed.

The work on which I had been engaged was certainly not lacking in interest or variety. I was much concerned with career planning and management selection of staff in the Mechanical and Electrical Engineering Departments and the Workshops. The Supplies Manager and I were asked to investigate the possibilities of further standardisation of general engineering spares. We consulted other nationalised industries, particularly the Central Electricity Generating Board, whose chairman, Lord Hinton of Bankside, trained in the Locomotive Works at Swindon, took a personal interest in our problems. I was concerned, too, with our commercial and operating people in discussions with the C.E.G.B. and the National Coal Board on the delivery of coal to power stations by the Merry-go-Round trains of permanently coupled 32 ton hopper wagons. Bunkers at collieries to speed up the loading of these trains were agreed to be desirable by all concerned, but nobody seemed anxious to pay for them.

The forthcoming opening by the Duke of Edinburgh of our new Research Laboratories at Derby, happily named after Sir Harold Hartley, provided the occasion for me to express my views on the planning and conduct of research, and on the relationships which should exist between the Research and Engineering Departments in making the most effective use of the new facilities.

Interest and variety in abundance, but no direct executive responsibility. This was not to my liking. So, with my Presidential year behind me, and after much thought, I told John Ratter that unless I could look forward to another appointment commensurate with my standing as a chief officer and with no less responsibility than had been mine as Chief Mechanical Engineer, and as Technical Adviser before the General Staff was disbanded, I proposed to retire at the end of the year. Being then over 60, I was free to make my own decision. I certainly had no wish to go before reaching the full retiring age of 65.

In the event, however, this personal problem was settled to my complete satisfaction. I was invited by Owen Houchen, the General Manager of the Workshops, to join his headquarters staff, and was appointed by the Board to a newly created post of Technical Adviser to the Workshops Division.

Houchen had been brought into the railway service by Sir Steuart Mitchell. When the latter retired in 1964, Houchen was given a seat on the Board, retaining his appointment as General Manager. My work in connection with career planning and management selection for the Workshops – in the role, as Sir Steuart put it, of an 'elder statesman' – had brought me into close contact with the new Board Member. We had built up a very cordial relationship.

The separation of the Workshops from the Regions had not met with universal approval. Thus, it was important to the management of the new Division that they should establish themselves firmly and justify their independence. In doing this they had tended to isolate the Workshops from the day-to-day running of the railway. They did not, in my opinion, bear sufficiently in mind that the Works existed, as they always had done, only as an integral part of the railway, primarily to provide an essential service of repairs and maintenance. New construction was, of course, important, but far less so than repairs. And the small amount of manufacturing permitted to be done for other people was, relatively, of no importance whatever. The Workshops were intent on building up their own internal productive efficiency, sometimes, it seemed, to the exclusion of the interests of their customers – the railway Regions, themselves part of the same undertaking.

Dissatisfaction with the service the Regions were receiving had begun to make itself felt. Admittedly, the Workshops had been working under severe difficulties. Sixteen of the Works were to be closed. Those that were to remain were in the throes of re-organisation. But the Regions neither knew in detail, nor cared very much about all these difficulties, which so far as they were concerned were of the Workshops' own making.

The Regions were not interested in jam tomorrow. They wanted bread today in the form of locomotives, carriages and wagons out of the Shops and back in traffic as promptly as before. There was clearly some lack of understanding between the two sides of each others' problems. Houchen was much concerned to put this right.

The importance of Regional General Managers knowing what the Workshops were doing, and being able to make their own views known effectively, was recognised in the letter to the Regions announcing my appointment. My role in regard to this matter was clearly stated. In addition, it was made clear that I had authority to act for the General Manager, not only in regard to liaison with the Regions, but also over the whole field of Workshops interest. I was well content that I should once more be fully occupied. There was no longer any question of early retirement.

When I took up my new appointment on 1st January, 1965, work had already started on the re-organisation schemes, estimated to cost nearly £18 million. Each Works prepared its own plan within general principles laid down from the Workshops new headquarters at Castlefields, Derby. Overall control and co-ordination of the re-organisation and re-equipment plans was in the hands of R. C. S. Low. An outdoor type much addicted to climbing mountains, he had the happy knack of getting along well with everybody. The work for which he and his team were responsible was making excellent progress.

Staff administration was the responsibility of Edgar Larkin, than whom no-one was better qualified to undertake this always difficult, and, in the circumstances, thankless task. The number of men employed in the Works had fallen by close on 20,000 in two years. The redundancies posed problems which Larkin, in collaboration with the Ministry of Labour and Local Authorities handled with great skill and understanding. Edgar Larkin knew all the Works inside out. Houchen had no anxieties for the matters for which Edgar was responsible.

It was in the Production Section of the Division where the trouble lay. It was there that responsibility resided not only for overall control of output in conformity with programmes and budgets agreed with the Regions, but also for the daily contacts with the Regions in settling all the many problems which arise in repair and maintenance work – and which must be given immediate priority attention. Unfortunately the organisation had failed to gain the confidence either of the Works Managers or the customers. Two of the senior assistants, both good men who had worked under my direction in earlier years did not combine well together. Their functions tended to overlap. It was not a happy set up. Changes were clearly necessary. In the meantime, it was by devoting most of my time to the Production section of his organisation that I could help Owen Houchen most.

It did not take long to break down the arms-length relationships between the Workshops and the Regions, and to restore the confidence of the General Managers in the ability and determination of the Works to meet all their obligations at their budgetted costs. It took a little longer for a few of the Workshops people themselves to accept, without demur, that pre-occupation with re-organisation schemes, and such like distractions, would not be accepted either as a reason or excuse for any falling off in performance and efficiency, measured by the good old-fashioned, but permanently valid, criteria of days-out-of-traffic, number and percentage of

Board he seemed firmly settled for some long time. But where politics are concerned, nothing can be relied on. His replacement, after only $2\frac{1}{2}$ years in office, by H. C. Johnson (later Sir Henry) from Euston surprised us all. Though he may not have endeared himself to everyone, Raymond had striven might and main for the interests of the railway as he saw them.

In telling me what he wanted done, the Chairman said this – 'An important part of your new job will be to work yourself out of the job' – to see to it, in other words, that I had someone ready to take over when the time came for me to go. I knew already who I wanted as my Deputy General Manager (Production). If I could get him, this part of my remit would be easy. As to the rest, ten months as Technical Adviser had given me plenty of opportunities to discover the weak spots.

None of the usual minor irritations were involved in taking over from Houchen. I did not even have to move to another room. What was much more important, I retained my excellent secretary, Margaret Gunn, who had looked after me and my affairs with such care and efficiency for seven years. The administrative arrangements continued unaltered. I remained directly responsible to Houchen, and reported monthly to the Workshops Committee of the Board, of which Houchen had been chairman since Sir Steuart Mitchell's departure.

Graduated levels of authority for sanctioning expenditure on new Works Schemes followed the usual pattern. My limit was £25,000 on any one scheme, a sum which, ten years ago, gave one reasonable freedom in getting on with the job. Twice a year I was required to give an account of my stewardship to the Board. As General Manager of the Workshops I became a member of the British Railways Management Committee of all the full-time Board Members and the Regional General Managers. It was there that policy was formulated for acceptance by the Board, and important decisions taken. I was soon to learn that it was at that Committee, more than at any of the others I attended, that I was liable to be shot at by my customers, and long standing friends, the Regional General Managers, for any alleged shortcomings in Workshops performance.

The headquarters of the Workshops was divided between London and Derby. The General Manager and his principal assistants concerned with overall policy and direction affecting all the Works, were located at Marylebone. We were thus in close and constant touch with all the other headquarters' departments of the railway. Derby was an excellent choice for the operational centre. It is within easy reach of London. Two of the larger Works are there. It is a convenient place from which to visit most of the other Works either by rail or road. We held our weekly management meetings there, as well as the monthly meetings attended by all the Works Managers. Our offices at Derby were first at Castlefields House, and later at the Railway Technical Centre opened in 1967. Castlefields House, a combined office block and shopping centre was, I always thought, an unfortunate choice. Its situation in the town, quite a long way from either of the two Works or the other railway offices clustered round the Midland Station, accentuated the feeling of isolation from the rest of the railway — which was bad. It offended against all my ideas of what a railway headquarters establishment ought to be — no doubt old-fashioned prejudice! By contrast, the Railway Technical Centre is very good indeed. It is well situated between the Locomotive Works on one side, the Carriage Works on the other, and with the Research Department and Design Offices and Development Workshop of the Chief Mechanical and Electrical Engineer housed in the same complex of buildings, everyone who should work together can do so with ease and convenience.

By the end of my first year in the hot seat, 85 per cent of the reorganisation schemes had been completed. A very fair summary of the situation at this time is contained in the Railway Board's Annual Report for 1966. Two paragraphs from the section dealing with the Workshops are, I think, worth quoting: Paragraph 248 – 'Drastic changes in industry cannot be made effortlessly, and the continued development during 1966 of the plan to streamline and modernise the Railway Workshops was, as in previous years, both demanding and difficult. But with completion of plans drawing nearer, the outline of a slimmed and rejuvenated organisation, well set to manufacture and repair for a railway system which itself is changing swiftly, began to emerge'. This was perhaps a slight understatement: 'had emerged' was really nearer the mark! But amends are made in Paragraph 252 – 'The standard of service available from the Workshops was further enhanced by changes in organisation made early in the year to achieve greater co-ordination throughout the activities of design, manufacture, overhaul and repair of locomotives, rolling stock and mechanical engineering equipment generally. Closer collaboration was thus established between Workshops, all departments at headquarters and regional managements'.

Some idea of the scale of our activities, and how the money was being spent can be gained from the statistics of output and expenditure for 1966, tabulated opposite.

The figures (right) give only the bare bones of the story. Contributing to the expenditure under each statistical head were heavy programmes of conversions and modifications to vehicles in traffic. Two types of diesel locomotives, 170 in all, were being re-engined after a relatively short time in service; and 700 engines of another type were having to be re-balanced to eliminate harmful vibrations. Ten electric locomotives from the Southern Region were under conversion to electro-diesel power for the Bournemouth electrification. Over 100 coaches were being altered from steam to electric heating for the same scheme; and 150 Travelling Postal

British Railways Workshops Division

Output & Expenditure 1966

Output

	Repairs	New Building
Locomotives	3,757	62
Carriages	14,853	400
Wagons	137,467	1,552
Containers	21,541	332
Multiple Unit Engines	2,814	—

Expenditure and Allocation

Expenditure:	Staff Costs	£43·7 million
	Materials	33·5 million
	Other Expenses	4·1 million
	Total	£81·3 million
Work Done:	Repairs:	
	Locomotives	£16·9 million
	Carriages	6·0 million
	Multiple Units	8·4 million
	Freight Vehicles and Containers	10·4 million
	Other Work and Materials for Regions	16·5 million
	New Locomotives and Rolling Stock	21·9 million
	Other work	1·2 million
		£81·3 million
Staff employed:	Salaried Staff	6,141
	Wages Grades	35,785
	Total	41,926

vehicles were being urgently modified to give greater security after the Great Train Robbery. Several thousand 16 and 21 ton mineral wagons were being fitted with vacuum brakes. These were just a few of the jobs that the Works had to fit into their normal repair and building programmes.

As will be seen from the tabulation above, the largest single item of maintenance expenditure was for repairs to locomotives – mostly diesels. On this we still had much to learn. The amount and cost of work to be done at each repair was increasing. The fleet of diesel main line locomotives as a whole had not reached the average age at which costs per mile level out, become independent of age and proportional only to the mileage run or engine hours since the last shop repair. The number of unscheduled repairs arising from casualties and failures of equipment in-traffic, though decreasing, was still much too high.

During 1964 the Workshops had turned out less than half the classified repairs called for by the budgets agreed with the Regions. This could mean only one of two things – either

(i) that we were failing to liquidate by repairs the mileage being run, and thus heading for serious trouble; or, if not,

(ii) that the basis for calculating the number of classified repairs was unrealistic, and that many unscheduled repairs must have been contributing to making good mileage run.

Although the C.M.E.'s people at Marylebone had issued complete schedules for the work to be done at each classified repair, the Regions appeared to be interpreting them differently when proposing locomotives for shops. Some of the Works, too, were paying scant attention to them. They had apparently forgotten the guiding principle that a classified repair must restore the locomotive as a whole to fit condition to run the prescribed period before coming in for repairs again. This had arisen from the people at Castlefields attempting, wrongly, to treat diesel locomotives as an assembly of main components – body, bogies, power unit and train heating boiler – and compiling repair programmes on the basis of components, repairs to which tended to get out of phase. The inevitable result was that many locomotives had to come into shops before running the prescribed minimum periods or mileages between classified repairs.

Steam locomotives were just as much an assemblage of components as diesel and electric locomotives. There was no difficulty in so organising their repairs as to keep everything in phase. The same would have to be done with diesel locomotives. One of the main components – obviously the body – would have to be regarded as the 'locomotive' for the purpose of planning programmes of repairs, adequate in numbers and of the right classification fully to liquidate the mileage being run in the most economical way. The efficiency of repairs to the main line diesels steadily improved. The figures tabulated opposite, taken from contemporary reports speak for themselves.

One of the factors which contributed to the improved repair performance, and to the higher standard of service to the Regions was a substantial improvement in the availability of spares, most of which were manufactured in our own shops. Unless we were short of raw material or finished items from contractors, as was not infrequently the case, the remedy for any shortages of spares lay entirely in our own hands. Here I was fighting a battle on two fronts. I was under constant pressure from the Workshops Committee to reduce the value of spares in stock – pressure which our improving overall results enabled me successfully to resist. The Works Managers were under constant pressure from me to treat stores stock orders as No. 1 priority, reduce the number outstanding and get

Repairs to Main Line Diesel Locomotives

Year	Percentage of Stock under and awaiting repair at Works	Average Days out of traffic. Classified Repairs	Ratio of Unclassified to Classified Repairs
1965	8·2	38	4 : 1
1966	7·5	34	2·1 : 1
1967	6·6	27	1·27 : 1
1968	5·3	26·6	1·20 : 1

material into the stores.

The amount of money tied up in stores stock was something like £47 million – a large sum indeed, but small in relation to the capital value of the locomotives and rolling stock for which the spares were required. While the value of stock held for steam locomotives was declining rapidly, that for the new locomotives and coaching stock was increasing far more. Replacement parts for diesel and electric locomotives are both numerous and expensive – but we had to have them, whatever the Committee might say. They would have had a great deal more to say, and with good reason, if our repair performance had gone the wrong way, instead of improving. It is far cheaper to have money tied up in stock than in locomotives and rolling stock standing out of service waiting material. I was well content that the delivery period for stores stock orders was reduced by one-third, and that 90 per cent of the requisitions for material received from regional depots were met on demand – the remaining 10 per cent, often for items sent into the Works for repair, within seven days.

As one of the principal reasons for bringing the Works under central control was to ensure that they would be operated as one comprehensive organisation serving impartially all the Regions, the arrangements for ensuring co-ordination between the Works – geographically widely dispersed from Inverurie in the north of Scotland to Eastleigh in the south of England – and securing that all were working to a common end assumed considerable importance. In Railway Executive days, Riddles had established the custom of holding a conference of his senior officers, from headquarters and the Regions, at one of the Works, or sometimes amid the beautiful surroundings of Gleneagles Hotel, where business, and pleasure on the golf courses harmonised most agreeably together. Houchen had instituted similar arrangements, which I continued unaltered.

Twice a year the Works Managers and my senior headquarters staff assembled for a two-day conference at New Lodge, Windsor, a country house acquired by the B.T.C., which combined the functions of a training college for staff in the Hotels and a residential centre for meetings of departmental officers on whom the talents of the embryo chefs were tested.

The accommodation was most comfortable and the catering beyond reproach. These conferences were run on much the same lines as the much larger ones held by the B.T.C., and the Board for their senior officers at Felixstowe, Balliol College or the Station Hotel at York, venues which seemed accurately to reflect the personal characteristics of the Chairman of the time. At Oxford we did at least have the option of staying at the Randolph, an option I had no hesitation in exercising the second year. The rooms in college were a trifle spartan!

One or more of the Works Managers and Headquarters staff were detailed to read papers on subjects chosen for them. Chief Officers of other departments were invited to come and tell us where we were falling short of their expectations. Current performance was reviewed, future objectives and policies announced, and controversial issues discussed with no holds barred. The two days were very well spent not only letting everyone know what was expected of them, but even more so as a means of building up and consolidating a team spirit and enthusiasm among those on whom the success of the Division finally depended.

Most valuable as these gatherings were, it was, in my experience, no less important for the General Manager to visit regularly all his Works. Only by so doing will the full potential of Works Managers and their men be turned to good account. I regarded it as fair criticism of myself if, at one of our Windsor meetings, a Works Manager was able to charge me with not having spent a day with him going round his Works, meeting his staff and Works Committee within a reasonable period of months. Difficult though it often was to get away from all the paper and out to where the work was being done, I endeavoured to visit at least one Works every week. Ashford and Temple Mills, both within easy reach of half-day visits were liable to receive more than their fair share of attention, providing excellent reasons for getting out of the office to avoid unwelcome visitors.

Conducting visitors round his domain is a normal part of any Works Manager's duties, enjoyed or otherwise depending on the understanding and appreciation shown.

There is an old story of a Bishop of Chester who, at the end of a visit to Crewe, said to the Works Manager – 'And what exactly do you say you do in these Works, Mr. Lemon?' Such lack of understanding is unusual! How very different it was when in April 1966, Her Majesty the Queen and H.R.H. Prince Philip paid a visit to Wolverton Carriage Works, the home of the Royal train.

Sad though it is, but perhaps inevitable, the loyalty which the railway companies inspired in those who worked for them – and which contributed so much to their success and quality of service – is today less stong than it was. There was a family feeling among the staff employed by the Midland Railway – as there was among those who worked for the other companies. The old loyalties were transferred to the new group companies. Over the years they grew in strength and influence. I doubt whether the same can be said today. Nevertheless, though British Railways may not mean very much to them, there yet persists strong feelings of pride in their own Works among the men and women in the railway workshops. This always comes to the surface when special visitors are to be shown round, and special efforts are called for to put on a good show.

Until a few years ago it was a perquisite of the Works Manager at Wolverton to travel with the train on Royal journeys to be on hand in the unlikely event of any mechanical trouble arising. He was thus not unfamiliar with Royal occasions. Preparations for the Royal visit had been in hand at Marylebone and Wolverton for many weeks. Owen Houchen and I went over the route in detail more than once. Nothing was left to chance. We need not have worried. Wolverton put on a splendid show.

There was no mistaking the enthusiasm of the men and women in the Works. Our visitors' genuine interest in all they were shown was plain to see. Prince Philip's questions were penetrating and much to the point. One or two I could not answer without reference to the shop foreman concerned. Prince Philip said laughingly to me when leaving – 'Well Bond, you know more about these Works now than you did an hour ago!' The fourth of April, 1966 was indeed a red-letter day for Wolverton and the Workshops Division.

Notwithstanding the continual preoccupation with day-to-day matters – output, expenditure, industrial relations and re-organisation plans, I had to keep in mind the Chairman's injunction about working myself out of the job within about two years. There were, as it seemed to me, three major matters which demanded attention. First, I had to have someone on my staff to whom I could hand over with complete confidence. Next, there were some changes which would need to be made in the headquarters organisation at Derby. Thirdly, it was essential to have prepared a definite plan of succession to the senior posts in all the Works, which would meet our foreseeable needs for at least five years ahead.

The first of these problems was solved to my complete satisfaction by the appointment of Eric Robson as my Deputy General Manager (Production). He was at the time Chief Mechanical and Electrical Engineer at Euston. He was a Workshops man to his fingertips, with wide experience both of carriage and wagon, and locomotive work as a chief officer at headquarters and in two Regions. A strict disciplinarian, he would stand no nonsense from anyone, and was just the man I needed to help me sort out the production set-up at Castlefields. Though he could have taken over from me at any time, we could reasonably expect to have two years together, unless anything untoward happened. And, of course, it did!

Harrison decided to retire early. Robson was an obvious candidate for the post, to which he was appointed. I was very sorry he had to go, but, naturally, I could do no more than make a token protest. However, as Chief Engineer (Traction & Rolling Stock) he became a member of my Workshops Committee, and thus retained a direct interest in all that we were doing. This was most helpful to me, and as events unfolded, to him also. Eric Robson did in fact succeed me as General Manager. The Board could not have made a better choice when the time came for me to go.

An important section of our headquarters organisation had been wholly concerned with supervision of the re-equipment plans. Completion of this major re-organisation would not mean that finality had been reached. On the contrary, further adjustments to capacity and equipment to keep abreast of technical developments and changing needs would be a continuing part of our activities. The general tendency would undoubtedly be towards further contraction particularly in regard to wagon repairing capacity. On the other hand, the rapidly expanding use of freightliner containers then being built at Derby, Horwich and Glasgow had already made it necessary to provide additional facilities for construction and repair. After reviewing possible sites at six Works, two adjoining Shops at Derby Carriage and Wagon Works, originally intended for wagon repairs, were converted into a production unit to build 4,000 containers per annum. I was under some pressure to find a greenfield site, on the theory that wages costs in a new shop outside any existing railway boundary might well be lower than would otherwise be the case. This was a quite untenable proposition. The new shop would be staffed by men already in the service anyway!

Such changes as might be needed over the next few years would be unlikely to involve the same high levels of expenditure and supervision which had hitherto been required. The time had come to reduce headquarters staff and eliminate some anomalies in staff arrangements.

One such involved our Industrial Engineer. An expert in work study, seconded to us from the Civil Engineer's department, he was engaged in the difficult task of introducing new forms of payment by results into our Works. This was work of great importance; and it was essential that the Industrial Engineer should be permanently transferred to us.

Work study had become an important aspect of management philosophy on British Railways. Greater productivity and efficiency from a smaller number of staff, with higher wages, were the objectives in view. As Director of Work Study, Edgar Larkin was in charge of the whole operation.

The Grove, at Watford, the L.M.S. wartime headquarters had been converted into a training centre at which large numbers of staff were indoctrinated in the new techniques. In many fields of railway operation substantial benefits accrued from the work study incentive schemes. In regard to the Workshops I am not so sure what the final balance sheet will show.

In the Annual Report of the British Transport Commission for 1961, it was acknowledged that the Workshops presented a special problem in that they were traditionally piecework establishments and the staff had hitherto opposed any change. This was scarcely surprising. Straight piecework was far too soft an option to be willingly abandoned. The agreements with the trade unions which, over the years, had governed the application of piecework in all our Shops were drafted in a way which made effective control very difficult. An average man working normally was supposed to be able to earn a balance of not less than 33 per cent of his basic rate. In theory, and sometimes in practice the sky was the limit in an upward direction. A piecework price depends upon the time a job takes to complete. The only accurate basis for deciding this is continuous timing on the job. To this, in most Works, the men had always had a rooted objection. Negotiation of piecework prices thus boiled down to a battle of wits and hard bargaining between the foreman and man concerned. The average balances earned varied widely between the Works. In some, with a long tradition of strict control, piecework balances were maintained at a reasonable level. In others, this was not always the case. In all Works new prices tended to be set in relation to the average earnings at the time. Inevitably there was a constant upward drift in bonus payments which became more and more difficult to contain.

The first of our Works in which a full scale work-study scheme was introduced was Inverurie. It was most beneficial to management and men alike. Progress had been made at some other Works where the attitude towards accurate measurement and payment directly related to work done showed signs of becoming less rigid. But general acceptance of work study was going to take a considerable time.

When the Workshops H.Q. was first set up in Derby two senior men were appointed, one in charge of production, the other responsible for productivity. This had proved unsatisfactory and needed to be changed. It was suggested to me that the matter could be resolved by making one man responsible for both functions in the locomotive Works, the other taking the Carriage and Wagon Works under his wing. But this would have undermined the policy we had been following successfully for a number of years in integrating all our Workshops activities. Crewe for example, was no longer a locomotive Works only. In addition to building carriage bogies, they were doing a very good job on programmes of modification to coaches and all-steel hopper ballast wagons. The Works Managers often complained that they already had too many headquarters people breathing down their necks. A solution on the lines suggested would have done nothing to remove that source of irritation. We amalgamated the two sections of our headquarters production organisation under one senior man.

The 1962 Plan was virtually complete. The financial results of each separate scheme were being back-checked against the original estimates on which authority had been obtained. This was no easy task in view of the changes in wage rates, material costs and work load which had occurred over the past three years. It was essential to know whether the promised economies from the schemes had been realised – as indeed they had. The time had come for another look ahead; and for long-term planning to become a permanent full-time feature of the Workshops organisation.

There was at this time a particular need to strengthen our planning organisation. In the Queen's Speech at the opening of Parliament it was announced that legislation would be introduced to remove the restrictions placed on the manufacturing powers of the nationalised industries.

The powers under which we operated were defined in Section 13 of the 1962 Transport Act. By them we were permitted to manufacture and repair anything we needed for our own use, or for any of the other Boards previously part of the British Transport Commission. We were not allowed to do work for other people. It was not uncommon for us to be asked to undertake general engineering jobs which, had it been permissible, we could have tackled without detriment to our railway commitments.

Ever since this matter was first raised I had been involved in discussions regarding the additional powers we would like to have, and the manner of their use. It was generally accepted that we should welcome freedom to undertake outside work to fill capacity at periods of slack internal demand in machine shops, foundries and similar manufacturing facilities, though without any obligation to enter the industrial field on a wider scale, or to provide facilities in manpower or equipment over and above that needed for our own purposes. This was entirely consistent with the policy of the Workshops plan, a principal objective of which had been to eliminate excess capacity.

But the matter appeared to be developing along rather different lines. The proposal to extend our powers was controversial, and had important political implications. The Confederation of British Industry considered that it was not in the national interest, and that, in any case, nationalised manufacture should be undertaken by companies operating under the Companies Acts, or when only a part of a nationalised industry competed with private enterprise it should trade as a separate entity. Presumably to meet these views, the pros and cons of constituting the Workshops as a separate company were discussed. And in strengthening the 'commercial' side of our headquarters establishment to meet the new conditions I was enjoined to ensure that steps were taken to promote orders from outside industry.

Although any changes which might be made by the 1968 Transport Act would not become effective until after I had retired, I was unhappy at the trend of events. I felt we were in danger of getting our priorities wrong, and made my views known. I had serious misgivings about the Workshops being formed into a company separated from the rest of the railway.

It was in no small measure due to the philosophy of separation being encouraged, rather than otherwise, when the Workshops Division was formed that our reputation suffered and the Regions had to put up with a service not so good as it should have been. I had been striving for the past two years, I think with some success, to make my people understand that they were very much part of the whole railway organisation. Nor, except in regard to containers would it have been wise, at the time, to promote orders from outside if our railway commitments were to remain first priority, as they always should.

I was probably unduly apprehensive. It is a matter of history that a new company, British Rail Engineering Limited came into existence on 1st January, 1970, in place of the Workshops Division. As stated in the Railway Board's Annual Report for that year – 'Its establishment followed the grant to the Board in the 1968 Transport Act of powers to use the main works spare capacity to manufacture for outside industry. The company's object is to exploit the new opportunities to the full, while continuing to regard as its primary duty the provision of a construction and repair service to the railways'. It is the last phrase in that quotation which matters. As the company is controlled by a subsidiary Board answerable only to the Railway Board, the railway position will, no doubt, be fully safeguarded. Indeed, as a side effect it may even be strengthened. The freedom which British Rail Engineering has to fill capacity which the railway does not use may stimulate the commercial and operating gentlemen to make up their minds on new building programmes without the chronic delays which we had to learn to live with in the past. The company will not be able to afford to slow down to avoid expensive breaks in production. Nor, I imagine, will they hold capacity unfilled indefinitely. This may have a most salutary effect on their principal customer!

Though my sixty-fifth birthday was now only two months away, the facts of imminent retirement made little impact on my mind and none at all on my day-to-day activities. Full of interest as always, they went on without perceptible change. I was, however, concerned to know who was to follow me as General Manager. The future well-being of the Workshops required that an announcement should soon be made.

For reasons which I can only surmise, there was to be some delay in making the appointment; and I was asked to postpone my departure by a couple of months to allow the Board time to reach their decision. This I was very willing to do. Apart from anything else, I should have more time in which to make a final round of visits to all the Works.

I set out first to the north of Scotland – to Inverurie Works which, with St. Rollox, Glasgow, re-organised and in full production, we wished soon to close. This was a serious matter for the town, and gave rise to a Government Enquiry – but in due course the inevitable had to happen. One of my previous visits to our most northerly main Works will live long in my memory. I had arranged to travel south from Aberdeen over the L.M.S. route to Glasgow on the footplate of whatever locomotive was booked to work the afternoon express. I had expected a Type 4 diesel – but I was wrong. Nothing could have pleased me more than to see an *A4 Pacific* backing down to work the train. The engine was No. 60019 *Bittern*, one of the locomotives of this famous class preserved in private ownership. This trip on an L.N.E.R. locomotive over an L.M.S. route – most appropriate for one who had once been a joint officer of the two companies – was my last footplate ride on a steam locomotive in revenue earning service. And what a splendid ride it was. *Bittern* had been cleaned to perfection. She had a tender full of good coal and steamed so well that it was not easy to keep her from blowing off. We gained time with ease on the heavy train. I could have wished for nothing better – except perhaps a *Duchess*!

It was, I think, only when having presented my usual six-monthly report to the Board, the chairman, Sir Henry Johnson, concluded his comments, generous and complimentary as they were, by saying 'As this is the last time Mr. Bond will present the Workshops report etc. etc.' that it really began to sink in that my lifetime with locomotives – in any official capacity – had not much longer to run. I was not looking forward to retirement; nor was I fearful of it. A devoted wife and family, and many friends spread widely over the country, because of the many moves throughout my railway service, were a guarantee of a continuing purpose in life. With my restless nature, and a gold pass in my pocket, I would never need to wonder what to do next!

Inevitably, I should miss the personal relationships, and the insistent demands of a full and busy life. But I was determined that once out I would keep out, and not haunt the office, as some are inclined to do for a time, trying the patience and good nature of old friends who still have a job to do. I was to receive most generous presentations from my staff in London, Derby and all the Works, and from my colleagues at Marylebone. To all of them I owe so much. It was indeed a kind thought of my staff, and Works Managers to entertain me at dinner in the Midland Hotel at Derby, where so many years ago I had spent the night before I first crossed the bridge over the station to the Locomotive Works.

Retirement would certainly not extinguish my absorbing interest in locomotives and railway engineering. I could look forward to many opportunities at Institution meetings and elsewhere, to revive memories with old friends of the great days of steam to which we all made some contribution, to hear with approval – or maybe, otherwise – what those who now bear the responsibility are doing, and to speculate with them on the future of the great service in which we spent our working lives.

L.M.S. News Bulletin No. 2

TRAIN & STEAMER SERVICES
Wednesday, 12th May, 1926

FROM EUSTON
Main Line
  7.30 a.m. (Restaurant Train) to GLASGOW, serving principal places en route.
  8.30 a.m. (Restaurant Train) to HOLYHEAD calling at Willesden, Rugby & Crewe with connection to Chester.
  9.30 a.m. (Restaurant Train) to LIVERPOOL calling at Northampton, Rugby, Tamworth, Stafford and Crewe with connection to Chester.
  10.00 a.m. to Watford, Bletchley, Rugby, Stafford, Crewe and MANCHESTER.
  10.30 a.m. to Northampton and Shrewsbury, calling at principal stations.
  11.00 a.m. (Restaurant Train) to Bletchley, Northampton, Rugby, Coventry and BIRMINGHAM.
  3.00 p.m. to Rugby, Coventry and BIRMINGHAM.
  4.50 p.m. Principal Stations to RUGBY.
  6.00 p.m. Northampton, RUGBY and intermediate Stations.
  N.B.: Corresponding Main Line Services are being maintained into EUSTON from Holyhead, Liverpool, Glasgow, Manchester, Birmingham, etc.

LOCAL
  7.15 a.m., 11.30 a.m., 2.00 p.m., 3.50 p.m., 5.20 p.m., 6.00 p.m. to Watford and Stations to Bletchley. (6.00 p.m. goes on to Northampton and Rugby.)

LOCAL ELECTRIC
EUSTON & WATFORD – 15 minutes service 7.00 a.m. to 8.15 p.m. in each direction.
WILLESDEN & BROAD STREET – 20 minutes service 7.00 a.m. to 6.30 p.m. in each direction.

FROM ST. PANCRAS
MAIN LINE
  6.00 a.m. to DERBY, calling at principal stations. Connections to Nottingham, Sheffield, Leeds, Buxton & Manchester.
  9.45 a.m. Restaurant Train to MANCHESTER & LEEDS. Connections for Chesterfield & Sheffield.
  1.10 p.m. to DERBY (Restaurant Train) calling at principal stations.
  2.30 p.m. (Restaurant Train) to NOTTINGHAM via Melton, calling at principal stations.
  N.B.: Corresponding Main Line Services are being maintained into ST. PANCRAS from stations before mentioned.

LOCAL

St. Pancras to St. Albans and most intermediate stations 7.00 a.m., 9.00 a.m. 11.00 a.m., 12 noon, 3.00 p.m., 4.00 p.m., 5.00 p.m. St. Pancras to St. Albans, Luton and Bedford and most intermediate stations 10.00 a.m., 1.30 p.m., 3.30 p.m. (to Luton), 5.15 p.m., 5.45 p.m. (to Luton).

Restaurant Car Facilities

Restaurant Cars on the 7.15 a.m. Derby to Gloucester, 1.10 p.m. Gloucester to Derby in addition to other parts of the Main Line.

STEAMSHIP SERVICES

HOLYHEAD & KINGSTOWN

Sailing, from Holyhead to Kingstown Mon., Wed. and Fri. in connection with Irish Mail leaving Euston at 8.30 a.m.; and in opposite direction Tues. Thur. and Sat. in connection with Irish Mail leaving Holyhead at 10.00 a.m. for Euston. Both trains will serve important points en route.

FLEETWOOD & BELFAST

A Steamer Service will be given in both directions on Mon., Wed. and Fri.

LARNE & STRANRAER

A regular service on Tues., Thurs. and Sat. is maintained from Tues. May 11th in each direction.

THE CLYDE

From Mon. May 10th a regular service 3 days a week between Wemyss Bay & Arran calling at Millport.

PRINTED TIME TABLES

Printed time-sheets shewing the temporary services throughout the system, are now posted at the stations. Supplementary trains will be added as and when required.

TRAIN SERVICES DAY BY DAY

	Date	No. of Trains
Wed.	May 5th	446
Thurs.	May 6th	672
Fri.	May 7th	814
Sat.	May 8th	916
Mon.	May 10th	1,227

Very few parts of the L.M.S. from Thurso in the extreme north to Shoeburyness in the south and Bristol and Swansea in the west are without a train service, new branch lines being opened every day.

SCOTTISH SERVICES IMPROVING

Scottish services continue to improve. The train service now cover Glasgow, Inverness, Aberdeen, Perth, Edinburgh, Dundee, Stranraer, Dumfries, Ayr, Stirling, Wick and other places.

A service is now running between Inverness and the Kyle of Lochalsh, also between Glasgow and Oban.

Fifteen additional trains were run yesterday.

MILEAGE RUN

Since Tuesday morning 4th inst., 100,000 train miles have been run.

Train mileage yesterday amounted to 29,042 miles compared with 23,205 miles the previous day.

MEN AT WORK

The steady movement back to work continues. There are now 45,231 men working against 44,451 yesterday. Twenty more engine drivers reported for duty yesterday and fifty-four signalmen.

GOODS TRAIN SERVICES

Over 100 trains were run over all parts of the system (an increase of about 80 per cent over the previous day) conveying principally foodstuffs, perishables and petrol.

Thousands of tons of goods were cleared from stations yesterday and deliveries effected in London, Manchester, Birmingham and other centres. Foodstuffs and other traffic were also collected.

Trains of cattle, potatoes and meat continue to move to the industrial centres.

A heavy trainload of meat was worked through from Aberdeen to London yesterday.

Trains of petrol are running from the ports to inland places.

FISH TRAFFIC

Two hundred tons of fish were unloaded at and despatched from Fleetwood. Twenty trawlers are expected today.

MILK TRAFFIC

Since Wednesday the 5th May 23,553 churns of milk have been worked into London (Euston & St. Pancras) by the L.M.S.

SIGNAL BOXES OPEN

Additional signal boxes are being opened every day and the total runs into several hundreds.

BANANAS

Two trains of bananas left Avonmouth, one for Birmingham and Carlisle, and one for Leeds and Sheffield.

VOLUNTEERS

The number at present enrolled who are not regular employees is over 12,000. Many regular employees of the Company have volunteered to do special work other than their own duty.

TRAINING SIGNALMEN

Schools of instruction have been organised at various centres for training volunteers in the duties of signalmen, drivers, firemen etc.

GREAT CREDIT IS DUE TO THE LOYAL STAFF
AND TO THE VOLUNTEERS FOR THE SPLENDID
EFFORTS THEY HAVE MADE AND THE
EXCELLENT RESULTS ACHIEVED.

When you have read this, please pass it on.

(Published by the London Midland and Scottish Railway Company, Euston Station, London).

London Midland and Scottish Railway Company

NOTICE TO DRIVERS, GUARDS, SIGNALMEN AND OTHERS CONCERNED RESPECTING THE WORKING OF SIGNALS AND THE EXHIBITION OF A RED FLAG AT SIGNAL BOXES ON THE SECTIONS OF LINE WHERE TRAINS ARE TELEPHONED FROM POINT TO POINT

Commencing on Friday, May 14th:

In order that the attention of Drivers may be called to Signal Boxes which are Telephone Posts on sections of the line where the signalling of trains by telephone from point to point is in operation, a red flag must be exhibited from such Signal Boxes, and the fixed signals kept normally at Danger.

On the approach of a train for which the section in advance is clear, the fixed signals must be lowered and the red flag withdrawn unless a train is approaching in another direction for which the section in advance is not clear, in which case the fixed signals must remain at Danger for both trains and the red flag remain exhibited, and when the train for which the section is clear is near to the home signal, the signals for that train may be lowered and the Driver instructed to proceed.

On sections of the line where trains are telephoned from point to point, the signals at Signal Boxes which are not Telephone Posts or Level Crossings must be kept normally in the 'All Right' position, unless it is necessary for them to be placed at Danger for the protection of an obstruction.

CHIEF GENERAL SUPERINTENDENT.

Derby, May 12th, 1926.

APPENDIX C

GENERAL MANAGER'S OFFICE,
EUSTON STATION,
LONDON, N.W.1.
May 20th, 1926.

Dear Sir,

When the Trades Union Council announced their intention to call a General Strike of Workers in all Industries, with the object of compelling compliance with the demands of the Miners, the whole nation, for a moment, was staggered. So soon, however, as the first shock passed, the Government and people set themselves to combat this grave menace, which was recognised by them as a deadly blow aimed at democratic constitutional Government.

With characteristic British courage, the Government and the people sought to carry on the business of the Country, and so far as the London Midland and Scottish Railway are concerned, the huge task which confronted us was successfully surmounted. This was only possible because of the enthusiasm and determination with which you, and all other members of the staff who remained at their posts, carried on. In many cases long hours were worked, and difficult and unusual tasks were performed; these were carried out with great efficiency, and with the utmost cheerfulness. It was only through this splendid spirit that the Railway was enabled to continue limited but excellent services, and so make its invaluable contribution to the complete defeat of the scheme to hold up the life of the community.

I wish to convey to you the thanks of the Chairman, Directors, and myself, for the great help you gave the Company in meeting the emergency by your loyal services, and to inform you that, as a small recognition of the part you have played, a grant of nine days' standard pay will be made to you.

The occasion is one of great importance in the history of constitutional Government of this country, and I will shortly send to you a suitable Certificate placing on permanent record your services in the hour of the Nation's need.

Yours faithfully,
H. G. Burgess

Mr. R. C. Bond,
Clock No. 5973
Premium Office.

Bibliography

Page

Symes S. J. Contribution to the discussion of paper *The Reorganisation of Crewe Locomotive Works*
Beames H. P. M. Proc. I. Mech. E. 1928   38
Bond R. C. *The Walschaert Locomotive Valve Gear* Proc. I. Mech. E. 1923   39
Nock O. S. *The Midland Compounds* David & Charles Dawlish 1964   44
Cox E. S. *Locomotive Panorama Volume 1* Ian Allan London 1965   50
Government of India, Delhi *Pacific Locomotive Committee Report* 1939   77
O'Brien H. E. *The Management of a Locomotive Repair Shop* Journal I. Loco. E. Vol. X No. 45   90
Herbert T. M. *Locomotive Firebox Conditions Gas Compositions & Temperatures Close to Copper Plates*
Proc. I. Mech. E. 1928   93
Smith S. A. S. *The British Railways Mechanised Iron Foundry-Horwich* Journal I. Loco. E. 1955   99
Churchward G. J. *Large Locomotive Boilers* Proc. I. Mech. E. 1906   103
Bond R. C. *Ten Years Experience with the L.M.S. Non-condensing Turbine Locomotive 6202* Journal I.
Loco. E. No. 91   109, 261
Nock O. S. *William Stanier—An Engineering Biography* Ian Allan London 1964   110
Gresley H. N. *Locomotive Experimental Stations* Proc. I. Mech. E. 1931   114
Ell S. O. *Developments in Locomotive Testing* Journal I. Loco. E. Vol. 43 1953   116
Holcroft H. *Locomotive Adventure Vol. 2* Ian Allan London 1965   136
Bulleid O. V. S. *Presidential Address to Institution of Mechanical Engineers* Proc. I. Mech. E. 1947   191
Cox E. S. *British Railways Standard Steam Locomotives* Ian Allan London 1966   201
Cox E. S. *British Standard Locomotives* Journal I. Loco. E. 1951   201
Cox E. S. *Experience with British Railways Standard Locomotives* Journal I. Loco. E. 1954   201
Bond R. C. *Organisation & Control of Locomotive Repairs on British Railways* Journal 232 I. Loco. E.
1953   219
Government White Paper *Transport Policy* (Cmd 8538) H.M.S.O. London   225
Pearson A. J. *The Railways and the Nation* Allen & Unwin, London   230
Modernisation and Re-equipment of British Railways B.T.C. London 1955   233
Government White Paper *Proposals for the Railways* (Cmd 9880) H.M.S.O. London 1956   235
Government White Paper *Re-appraisal of the Plan for the Modernisation and Re-equipment of British
Railways* (Cmd 813) H.M.S.O. London 1959   235
Bond R. C. *Presidential Address to The Institution of Locomotive Engineers: Years of Transition* Journal I.
Loco. E. Vol. 43 No. 234 1953   237
Hughes J. O. P. *The Design Development of a Gas Turbine Locomotive* Journal I. Loco. E. 1962   261
Ministry of Transport *Failures of Multiple Unit Electric Trains on British Railways* Final Report
H.M.S.O. London 1962   275
Bond R. C. *The Engineering Aspects of the Modernisation Plan for British Railways* Proc. I.C.E. Vol. 18
1961   276
Warder S. B. *Electric Traction in the British Modernisation Plan* Proc. I.C.E. Vol. 18 1961   276
Brown H. F. *Economic Results of Diesel Electric Motive Power on the Railways of the United States of
America* Proc. I. Mech. E. Vol. 175 1961   276

Government White Paper *Railways Reorganisation Scheme* (Cmd 9191) H.M.S.O. London 1954   281
Low R. C. S. *The Reorganisation of British Railways Workshops* Journal I. Loco. E. 1967   285
Bond R. C. *Presidential Address to the Institution of Mechanical Engineers: A Commentary on the change
   from Steam Traction on British Railways and some thoughts on the future* Proc. I. Mech. E. 1963   290
British Railways Board Annual Report & Accounts 1966 H.M.S.O. London   302

Index

Locomotive Types and Classes

BRITISH RAILWAYS

4-6-0 Class 5 Mixed Traffic *202. 246*
4-6-2 Clan Class *202*
4-6-2 *Britannia* Class *203, 208*
4-6-2 *Duke of Gloucester* 71000 *202, 246*
2-10-0 Class 9 Freight *201, 208, 246*

WAR DEPARTMENT

2-8-0 *Austerity 200*
2-10-0 *Austerity 200*

DIESEL, GAS TURBINE & ELECTRIC LOCOMOTIVES

BRITISH RAILWAYS

Diesel

B-B Type 2 1250 H.P. Diesel-electric *243*
B-B N.B. Loco. Co. 1000 H.P. Diesel-hydraulic *240*
C-C Type 4 2300 H.P. Diesel-electric *239, 243*
C-C N.B. Loco. Co. 2000 H.P. Diesel-hydraulic *240*
C-C *Deltic* 3300 H.P. Diesel-electric *242*
C-C L.M.S. 1600 H.P. Diesel-electric 10000/1001 *164, 213*
4-8-4 2000 H.P. Fell Diesel-mechanical *239*

Gas Turbine

4-6-0 English Electric G.T.3 *261*

Electric

B-B 1500 volt D.C. Manchester–Sheffield–Wath *239*
4-6-4 North Eastern Railway—Prototype *211*

OVERSEAS RAILWAYS—ALL TYPES

EUROPE

France

Steam 4-6-0 P.L.M. 4 cylinder compound with Velox boiler *123*
Steam 4-6-2 Est. 4 cylinder compound 231-029 *123*
Steam 4-8-2 Est. 4 cylinder compound 241-032 *123*

Germany

Steam 4-6-0 Super High Pressure—Schmidt Henschell Boiler *82*
Diesel 4-6-4 1300 H.P. with compressed air transmission *80*

Sweden

Diesel 2-6-2 1000 H.P. with mechanical transmission *265*

India

Electric 0-6-6-0 Great Indian Peninsular Freight *67*
Electric 4-6-2 Great Indian Peninsular Express Passenger *75*
Steam 4-6-2 Indian Standard XA Class *77*
Steam 4-6-2 Indian Standard XB Class *77*
Steam 4-6-2 Indian Standard XC Class *77*
Steam 2-10-0 G.I.P. 4 cylinder heavy freight *76*

UNITED STATES OF AMERICA

Steam 4-6-4 New York Central R.R. Class J.3 *173*
Steam 4-8-4 Delaware & Hudson R.R. *173*
Steam 4-8-4-8-4 Chesapeake & Ohio R.R. Steam-turbo-electric *171*
Steam 6-8-6 Pennsylvania R.R. Turbine *171*
Diesel C-C Pennsylvania R.R. 6000 H.P. Triple Unit *174*
Gas Turbine 4-4-4-4 Union-Pacific Oil Fired *264*
Electric 4-6-6-4 Pennsylvania R.R. *174*

TYPES PROPOSED BUT NOT BUILT

L.M.S. RAILWAY

4-6-0 3 CYLINDER Compound Derby 1923 *50*
4-6-2 3 & 4 cylinder simple. Horwich 1923–24 *50*
4-6-2 4 cylinder Compound Derby 1925 *50*
4-6-2 Modified *Duchess* Class 1945 *160*
4-6-4 Enlarged *Duchess* Class 1945 *160*
2-8-2 3 & 4 cylinder simple Horwich 1923–24 *50*
2-8-2 4 cylinder Compound Derby 1926 *50*

BRITISH RAILWAYS

4-6-2 Class 5 Mixed Traffic *202*
2-8-0 Class 8 Heavy Freight *246*

General Index
Appointments are, in general, those held at time of reference in the text.